Data Science, Machine Intelligence, and Law

Volume 7

Data-driven technologies, such as AI systems and robotics, have the potential to improve our lives, our society and our economy. At the same time, the development and use of these technologies raise unresolved legal and ethical issues. Our new peer reviewed book series brings together works from different legal fields, dealing with the legal, social and economic impact of these technologies, exploring on the one hand the opportunities for law and legal practice, and on the other hand, the ethical and legal frameworks they require. The series especially welcomes book proposals dealing with the legal and/or ethical aspects of data science and the emerging discipline of machine intelligence, which encompasses perception (sensing), AI (planning) and robotics (acting). In this way, our book series aims to contribute to an informed dialogue across the various disciplines about the chances and risks of data-driven systems.

Federica Casarosa • Francesca Gennari •
Arianna Rossi
Editors

Enabling and Safeguarding Personalized Medicine

Springer

Editors
Federica Casarosa
LIDER-Lab, DIRPOLIS
Sant'Anna School of Advanced Studies
Pisa, Italy

Francesca Gennari
LIDER-Lab, DIRPOLIS
Sant'Anna School of Advanced Studies
Pisa, Italy

Arianna Rossi
LIDER-Lab, DIRPOLIS
Sant'Anna School of Advanced Studies
Pisa, Italy

ISSN 2730-5899 ISSN 2730-5902 (electronic)
Data Science, Machine Intelligence, and Law
ISBN 978-3-031-99708-2 ISBN 978-3-031-99709-9 (eBook)
https://doi.org/10.1007/978-3-031-99709-9

This work was supported by Sant'Anna School of Advanced Studies.

This Springer imprint is published by the registered company Springer Nature Switzerland AG
The registered company address is: Gewerbestrasse 11, 6330 Cham, Switzerland

This book is dedicated to:
FC: A Dianora, che mi ha riportato a Pisa
FG: To my blood and soul family for the never-ending support and joy as well as laughter. PS: You know who you are
AR: I dedicate this book to my mentors, to whom I owe my gratitude for inspiring me to strive for ethical research and free thinking. A special thanks goes to Gabriele Lenzini

Acknowledgment

The drafting of this edited volume and its publication in open access are financially supported by the projects "Biorobotics Research and Innovation Engineering Facilities" "IR0000036"—CUP J13C22000400007 (BRIEF) and "SoBigData.it: Strengthening the Italian RI for Social Mining and Big Data Analytics" "IR0000013"—CUPB53C22001760006. All the chapters that do not report a different acknowledgement must be considered as an outcome of the BRIEF project.

This edited volume would not have been possible without the continuous support of Professor Giovanni Comandé. A special thanks goes to Eleftheria Ntanou, Sara Battaglia, and all the other staff members of the Sant'Anna School of Advanced Studies who contributed to this publication with their valuable work. We would also like to acknowledge the fruitful discussions with our colleagues on the two projects and the LiderLab (Laboratorio Interdisciplinare Diritti e Regole).

Contents

Contributors

Irene Giovanna Aprile IRCCS Fondazione Don Carlo Gnocchi ONLUS, Florence, Italy

Andrea Blatti LIDER-Lab, DIRPOLIS, Sant'Anna School of Advanced Studies, Pisa, Italy

Federica Casarosa LIDER-Lab, DIRPOLIS, Sant'Anna School of Advanced Studies, Pisa, Italy

Georgios Christou Sant'Anna School of Advanced Studies, Pisa, Italy

Giovanna Elisa Calabrò Department of Human Sciences, Society and Health, University of Cassino and Southern Lazio, Cassino, Italy

VIHTALI (Value in Health Technology and Academy for Leadership & Innovation), Spin-Off of Università Cattolica del Sacro Cuore, Rome, Italy

Simona Crea The BioRobotics Institute, Sant'Anna School of Advanced Studies, Pontedera, Pisa, Italy

Department of Excellence in Robotics and AI, Sant'Anna School of Advanced Studies, Pisa, Italy

Floriana d'Ambrosio Section of Hygiene, University Department of Life Sciences and Public Health, Università Cattolica del Sacro Cuore, Rome, Italy

Michele Emdin Health Science Interdisciplinary Center, Sant'Anna School of Advanced Studies, Pisa, Italy

Fondazione Toscana Gabriele Monasterio, Pisa, Italy

Ilaria Fagioli The BioRobotics Institute, Sant'Anna School of Advanced Studies, Pontedera, Pisa, Italy

Department of Excellence in Robotics and AI, Sant'Anna School of Advanced Studies, Pisa, Italy

Alessio Fasano IRCCS Fondazione Don Carlo Gnocchi ONLUS, Florence, Italy

Chiara Gallese University of Turin, Turin, Italy

Renza Barbon Galluppi Associazione Rete Malattie Rare, Venice, Italy

Francesca Gennari LIDER-Lab, DIRPOLIS, Sant'Anna School of Advanced Studies, Pisa, Italy

Marco Germanotta IRCCS Fondazione Don Carlo Gnocchi ONLUS, Florence, Italy

Sabrina Grigolo Patient Expert EUPATI, Rome, Italy

Maria Cristina Mauro IRCCS Fondazione Don Carlo Gnocchi ONLUS, Florence, Italy

Alessandro Mazzarini The BioRobotics Institute, Sant'Anna School of Advanced Studies, Pontedera, Pisa, Italy

Department of Excellence in Robotics and AI, Sant'Anna School of Advanced Studies, Pisa, Italy

Ciro Pappalardo Section of Hygiene, University Department of Life Sciences and Public Health, Università Cattolica del Sacro Cuore, Rome, Italy

Andrea Parziale LIDER-Lab, DIRPOLIS, Sant'Anna School of Advanced Studies, Pisa, Italy

Health Science Interdisciplinary Center, Sant'Anna School of Advanced Studies, Pisa, Italy

Ludovica Paseri Law Department, University of Turin, Torino, Italy

Claudio Passino Health Science Interdisciplinary Center, Scuola Superiore Sant'Anna, Pisa, Italy

Fondazione Toscana Gabriele Monasterio, Pisa, Italy

Arianna Rossi LIDER-Lab, DIRPOLIS, Sant'Anna School of Advanced Studies, Pisa, Italy

Milena Sirtori Patient Expert EUPATI, Rome, Italy

Daniela Spajic KU Leuven, Centre for IT & IP Law, Leuven, Belgium

Stefano Tramacere LIDER-Lab, DIRPOLIS, Sant'Anna School of Advanced Studies, Pisa, Italy

Department of Computer Science, University of Pisa, Pisa, Italy

Leopoldo Trieste Institute of Management, Sant'Anna School of Advanced Studies, Pisa, Italy

Giuseppe Turchetti Institute of Management, Sant'Anna School of Advanced Studies, Pisa, Italy

Introduction

Federica Casarosa, Francesca Gennari, and Arianna Rossi

Abstract The transformative vision of a European Health Union, driven by digital innovation and personalized medicine, is based on the idea that health data, when shared responsibly, can enhance individual care and public welfare. This collected volume is situated within the EU's evolving legal and policy landscape and introduces key themes such as data altruism, cybersecurity, and AI governance in healthcare. The volume's structure is presented through three thematic sections: enabling personalized medicine, mapping stakeholder challenges, and addressing liability concerns. Each contribution offers interdisciplinary actionable insights for policymakers, researchers, and industry actors. Given the tension between visionary policy and practical implementation, there is a pressing need for sustainable, inclusive, and patient-centered healthcare systems. This volume calls for continued research to navigate the complexities of personalized medicine as a timely response to Europe's digital health transformation.

Europe has a vision: a society where our medical histories are easily accessible at the tip of a finger no matter where we are. Electronic health records and other data related to our health flow freely but in keeping with respect for European values such as the privacy of our most sensitive information. In this new world, advancements in e-health and telemedicine mean medical personnel can engage with us holistically, devising the most appropriate therapy for our specific needs and personal characteristics. Patients become the decision-makers, developing a partnership with practitioners[1] that transforms the traditional methods of delivering healthcare into a patient-centered process. The benefits are widespread, spilling over into human, social, economic, and planetary well-being.[2] And what we find at

[1] Edgman-Levitan and Schoenbaum (2021).

[2] World Health Organization European Region (2024).

F. Casarosa · F. Gennari · A. Rossi (✉)
LIDER-Lab, DIRPOLIS, Sant'Anna School of Advanced Studies, Pisa, Italy
e-mail: Francesca.Gennari@santannapisa.it; Arianna.Rossi@santannapisa.it

F. Casarosa et al. (eds.), *Enabling and Safeguarding Personalized Medicine*, Data Science, Machine Intelligence, and Law 7,
https://doi.org/10.1007/978-3-031-99709-9_1

the end of this spectrum is that when data are not only used for the welfare of one individual but, rather, are safely shared with an "as open as possible, as closed as necessary" approach, the wealth of information shared can strongly support advancements in research, innovation and policymaking, such as developing new drugs and medical devices, optimizing how healthcare is provided, enhancing public policies, and boosting European competitiveness globally.[3]

This is a novel vision of society that counts on the progress of technologies as an accelerator of individual and public welfare. It is also steeped in the firm belief that sharing information is a crucial element for advancing science—one that emerges from the ashes of the global COVID pandemic in the early 2020s. Accelerated by this outbreak and the immeasurable harm it caused, the European Union has looked to strengthen many of the policies that previously underpinned fragility in the continent's numerous national health systems. Today, a new set of policies strategically addresses existing weaknesses, while driving modernization and innovation towards a more resilient Europe. This political priority, called the European Health Union is charged with a set of manifold actions, the expected benefits of which are not confined to broader equity in access to healthcare but also seek to improve the health status of European citizens at large. As such, the European Health Union is expected to have a wide impact on the complete functioning of Europe's societies and economies.[4]

One of the founding elements of the European Health Union is the security of medical supplies. Accordingly, the new policy framework includes updated legislation to govern the development and sale of medical devices. To this end, both the Medical Devices Regulation (MDR)[5] and the In Vitro Diagnostics Regulation (IVDR)[6] were drafted to better protect public health and address safety concerns. For instance, the new regulations increase transparency over the lifecycle of medical products and ensure better monitoring when they are put on the market.[7] Another key pillar of the legislation concerns creating more resilient, accessible, and inclusive health systems. Mindful of the extraordinary benefits that an open science approach brought to the fight against the pandemic (e.g., rapid vaccine development[8]), the EU has placed strong emphasis on digitalizing instruments and services across the healthcare sector as well as on e-health so as to enable broader access to

[3] Machado and Polónia (2022).

[4] European Commission (2024), p. 3.

[5] Regulation (EU) 2017/745 of the European Parliament and of the Council of 5 April 2017 on medical devices, amending Directive 2001/83/EC, Regulation (EC) No 178/2002 and Regulation (EC) No 1223/2009 and repealing Council Directives 90/385/EEC and 93/42/EEC.

[6] Regulation (EU) 2022/112 of the European Parliament and of the Council of 25 January 2022 amending Regulation (EU) 2017/746 as regards transitional provisions for certain in vitro diagnostic medical devices and the deferred application of conditions for in-house devices.

[7] European Commission (2024), p. 9.

[8] Watson (2022).

healthcare. In these ways, the new policies reflect evidence-based policy-making to future-proof Europe.[9]

Notably, distinct actions support this goal. For example, the European Parliament has passed financial and legislative instruments designed to boost research and innovation in both the public and private sectors. A European health data space has been created as part of a broader EU data strategy.[10] Based on the idea that "data should be available to all – whether public or private, big or small, start-up or giant",[11] the strategy envisions the free flow of personal and non-personal data across organizations, sectors and Member States. This principle is destined to promote competitive innovation, advance scientific research, and provide the necessary evidence for better decision-making. Another principle underpinning the policy framework is an "as open as possible, as closed as necessary" mindset. This brings sharing data into line with European values through a strong legal framework that is based on data protection, consumer protection, safety, cybersecurity, competition, and fundamental rights.[12] This is why the existing digital acquis is strengthened by regulations that strive to establish: diverse, trustworthy data governance mechanisms (via the Digital Governance Act);[13] the safe design and commercialization of artificial intelligence systems (with the AI Act);[14] and a harmonized level of cybersecurity for digital products (with the Cyber Resilience Act).[15]

Among the many objectives arising from this complex and visionary policy architecture, a key goal concerns realizing the full potential of personalized medicine, which is widely understood as a medical model based on the phenotypes and genotypes of individuals sourced from data like molecular profiles, medical imaging, and lifestyle information. It is felt that, with these data, practitioners should be able to: determine a person's predisposition toward a disease; deliver timely and targeted prevention; and/or tailor the right therapeutic strategy for the right person at the right time. Moreover, all these objectives should be achievable within a healthcare system that is "patient-centred" i.e., a system that is better geared to respond to the needs of patients than the status quo.[16] Recognizing the uniqueness

---

[9] See e.g., the EU4Health Program, European Commission (n.d.).

[10] Regulation (EU) 2025/327.

[11] European Commission (2020), p. 1.

[12] European Commission (2020), pp. 1 and 5.

[13] Regulation (EU) 2022/868 of the European Parliament and of The Council of 30 May 2022 on European data governance and amending Regulation (EU) 2018/1724 (Data Governance Act).

[14] Regulation (EU) 2024/1689 of the European Parliament and of The Council of 13 June 2024 laying down harmonized rules on artificial intelligence and amending Regulations (EC) No 300/2008, (EU) No 167/2013, (EU) No 168/2013, (EU) 2018/858, (EU) 2018/1139 and (EU) 2019/2144 and Directives 2014/90/EU, (EU) 2016/797 and (EU) 2020/1828 (Artificial Intelligence Act).

[15] Regulation (EU) 2024/2847 of the European Parliament and of The Council of 23 October 2024 on horizontal cybersecurity requirements for products with digital elements and amending Regulations (EU) No 168/2013 and (EU) 2019/1020 and Directive (EU) 2020/1828 (Cyber Resilience Act) (Text with EEA relevance).

[16] European Council (2015), p. 3.

of each human condition and the many factors that influence it, data-driven treatments and digital robotic devices are increasingly being developed to help patients and medical personnel benefit from accurate, personalized diagnoses and therapies. Further, the results are having a double-edged effect—at once improving the quality and safety of care for individuals while also bolstering the sustainability of entire healthcare systems.[17]

However, customizing healthcare requires there be synergies between healthcare systems, medical personnel, and patients, as well as cooperation with other branches of research and practice. Proactively including more patients in the system is one route to enhancing the efficacy of personalized medical interventions, but this is also an approach that must be evaluated for its sustainability. Further, the framework for developing new medical devices must account for the complex interplay of norms concerning personal and non-personal data, AI governance, cybersecurity, health law, and liability regimes without raising barriers to technological innovation, development and commercialization.

In the ever-evolving domain of medicine, where some of these new regulations have only recently been adopted, many stakeholders are facing challenges in navigating the new legal landscape. There appears to be a divide between the vision described and the reality of practice. For instance, access to health data for secondary uses is still limited, while legal provisions that protect certain kinds of data (such as personal data or information protected by intellectual property rights) are felt to be obstacles. The many questions that arise call for guidance so as to enable medical products and services that are "safe-by-design". Here, the most innovative research is taking an interdisciplinary approach that deliberately involves a range of different stakeholders from the healthcare economy. Many such collaborations are now being established at the very beginning of the research project and so reflect the concept of responsible data science, where ethical values are steering the reliable use of health data, particularly when the end product or service involves AI.

As an output of the "Biorobotics Research and Innovation Engineering Facilities"[18] and "SoBigData.it: Strengthening the Italian RI for Social Mining and Big Data Analytics"[19] PNRR projects, this volume represents a collection of theoretical, empirical, and case study-based contributions that span disciplinary boundaries to identify and critically dissect the most pressing issues arising from Europe's new policy architecture. Accordingly, most of the chapters suggest some course of action for particular stakeholders of the digital economy, including legislators, policymakers, and scientists. The contributions are organized into three thematic sections.

The first part ("Facilitating and protecting personalized medicine") provides an overview of some of the most pressing legal, ethical and practical challenges that need to be solved to enable health data sharing for commercial purposes or for the

---

[17] European Council (2015), p. 4.

[18] https://biorob-hub.eu/.

[19] https://www.sobigdata.it/.

public good. Research has been regulated in the digital strategy because various regulatory mechanisms can foster scientific advancements for tailored treatments. In this light, it is paramount to determine to what extent research endeavors are free from constraint when experimenting with new technological paradigms. In doing so, it becomes necessary to understand whether the research exemptions in recent law share similar meanings and scopes. This is a mission that Paseri undertakes by identifying different conceptualizations of the notion. Paseri also provides several criteria for action and governance mechanisms based on open science that could have a positive impact on realizing the full potential of personalized medicine. Notably, new legislative interventions also introduce concepts that put the individual at the center of transformative practices, essentially assigning them a new proactive role in contributing to science. The notion of data altruism introduced in the Data Governance Act (DGA) is key in this respect, where the greater availability of health data is meant to foster better diagnoses and treatments. Two authors examine this concept. First, Rossi explores the role of consent in the reuse of personal data for altruistic purposes, highlighting legal and technical challenges to its user-friendly implementation. In response to them, she provides practical recommendations, with a focus on personalizing the consent experience in a way that offers dynamic interoperable data controls. Complementary to this perspective, Spajic seeks to disentangle the overlaps and conflicts between the DGA as a cross-sectoral piece of legislation, the European Health Data Space (EHDS) Regulation as sector-specific legislation, and the General Data Protection Regulation (GDPR). She shows that existing misalignments, for example in terms of purpose limitation, can cause uncertainty and become practical hurdles to data altruism.

The EHDS Regulation sets forth stringent requirements that are meant to enable trustworthy and secure data sharing, with an important note that the data concerned are not just personal and non-personal health data but also socioeconomic and demographic data as well. In this context, health-related data are seen as a valuable asset and even a currency, and therefore access is tempting to both cybercriminals and data brokers alike. Today, anonymization is a key technique for ensuring the confidentiality of data but it is not foolproof. As a consequence, anonymized datasets may yet reveal personal information while not being tied to the stringent requirements that govern personal data. Gallese argues that we should overcome the blurred distinction between personal and non-personal data. Rather, our aim should be to increase protection over all kinds of data, and the very notion of anonymization should be redefined. Offering a complementary perspective on cyberthreats to health data, Casarosa focuses on wellness devices that have a medical-like function but are not medical devices, yet whose data may be used and/or reused for biomedical progress. She addresses the regulatory challenges and obligations that manufacturers face when security is compromised under the Cyber Resilience Act, the GDPR, the AI Act and the EHDS Regulation. As such, this chapter highlights the practical difficulties that arise from a piecemeal legal framework.

The second part ("Scoping challenges through the players of the personalized medicine ecosystem") broadens this horizon, by seeking to recompose the views of the actors involved in the digital innovation of patient-centered care. After retracing the history of personalized medicine, Emdin and Passino focus on empathy as the foundation between physician and patient, as it constitutes the necessary impetus for searching for the most appropriate therapy. While laying down the benefits of this welcome turn in healthcare, they also warn against several hurdles to the success of personalized medicine, such as sustainability risks, the poor representativity of data, the research efforts still required, the socioeconomic disadvantages that certain countries suffer from, and the ethical, legal, and social concerns that arise from targeted treatments. The chapter by Pappalardo, d'Ambrosio, and Calabrò underscores the robust contribution of Health Technology Assessment for ensuring that digital health technologies are developed and implemented in a cost-effective, equitable, and responsible manner throughout their whole lifecycle. While this assessment framework may work well with static medical diagnosis, it struggles when faced with the dynamic nature of emerging technologies. This is why the authors call for revisions to the methodology. Among other suggestions, they recommend that real-world data and real-world evidence, such as patient-reported outcomes, be embedded in the methodology to more reliably gauge the actual benefits and risks of the technologies being assessed. In this way, health technology assessments might ensure more patient-centered care.

Health Technology Assessments are also at the core of the article by Trieste and Turchetti, who add an economic dimension to the evaluation process. Additionally, they lay down other challenges posed by personalized approaches to traditional evaluation methods. These authors also address the complexity and heterogeneity introduced by patient-tailored healthcare in terms of sustainability, recommending that evaluations also include the organizational and economic impacts of personalized medicine. This chapter offers concrete KPIs for a range of stakeholders, together with other tangible outcomes derived from performing Health Technology Assessments.

A stakeholder category that is too often ignored in the personalization processes, unless it is the subject of care, is that of patients. Grigolo, Barbon Galluppi, and Sirtori explore the progressive evolution of the role of expert patients as an indispensable agent within each phase of planning and executing personalized care. The proactive role they take on within the emerging medical framework completely replaces the traditional view of patients as passive receivers of care. Similarly, Christou assumes the role of an entrepreneur in the face of these newly introduced regulations, such as the Medical Device Regulation, to illustrate how medical device companies might struggle to comply with the host of new product safety requirements set in the legislation. He attributes many of these problems to traditional business models, a lack of resources, and a lack of capacity and knowledge.

Another empirical contribution is provided by Fagioli, Mazzarini, Gennari, and Crea, who delve into the cutting-edge bioengineering techniques that are adopted in the personalized control of active bio-robotic protheses. They argue that an integrated approach to responsible biomedical R&D requires ex-ante regulatory evaluation. As an example, they explore the applicability of the new AI Act's requirements and obligations as they pertain to robotic protheses. This section concludes with a multifaceted overview of the barriers to integrating robotics into rehabilitation, drafted by Aprile, Germanotta, Mauro, and Fasano. The authors maintain that, to overcome these obstacles, it is imperative that we not only devise novel organizational models of treatment but that we also ensure they are evaluated for sustainability. Additionally, effectively training the medical personnel who administer these technologies is key, alongside robust regulatory frameworks that streamline reimbursement policies and ensure equitable access for all.

The third and last part ("The challenges of personalized medicine to liability") focuses on the ex-post issues posed by the adoption of highly specialized medical technology. Despite the effectiveness of medical devices and therapies, patients may suffer harm, which can be as personalized as the technology causing it. But how do the liability rules respond to such challenges in these cases? Parziale asks whether the newly introduced norms of the Product Liability Directive and the proposed AI Liability Directive may simply prompt medical device manufacturers to adopt countermeasures to address the new risks. They also suggest that the new rules do not offer sufficient guarantees to the "first victims" of unknown risks. Blatti and Tramacere illustrate another liability challenge posed by tomorrow's medicine by arguing that the medical predictions made by AI-based devices may be unrealistic and inappropriate when implemented in real-world conditions. Within such devices, design choices become paramount and should address transparency and accountability of various stakeholders, if the AI Act is to reduce all the likely risks to a patient's health. The chapter concludes with observations on a new standard of care that could emerge—one that may or may not draw from the obscurity of machine learning approaches in a similar way to the evidence-based frameworks already used in healthcare today. Lastly, Gennari analyzes ex-post liability under the new policy architecture as it applies to the software embedded in AI-based prosthetics. She highlights that the prescribed liabilities could positively influence market updates to these highly technical devices.

Thanks to these contributions that include both members of the BRIEF Law and Policy Hub (LaPoH) and fruitful collaborations with different institutions, this volume presents a suite of uniquely original analyses as well as a set of recommendations to be considered when assessing the EU's emerging digital strategy. The three sections of this book integrate pioneering theoretical and empirical knowledge about the cutting-edge technologies used in personalized medicine. The perspectives taken combine the various domains of law, medicine, computer science, bioengineering, and economics. In this ever-evolving area of knowledge, these observations and findings, which were first presented at the BRIEF conference held in Pisa on 14 October 2024 and now appear in these pages, only aim to provide preliminary answers to the many questions that the world of personalized medicine opens up. Further research is necessary to design a more equitable healthcare system where individual differences are valued.

Acknowledgements This research was financially supported by the "Biorobotics Research and Innovation Engineering Facilities" "IR0000036" – CUP J13C22000400007 (BRIEF) project.

References

Edgman-Levitan S, Schoenbaum SC (2021) Patient-centered care: achieving higher quality by designing care through the patient's eyes. Isr J Health Policy Res 10:21. https://doi.org/10.1186/s13584-021-00459-9

European Commission (2020) Communication from The Commission to the European Parliament, The Council, The European Economic and Social Committee and The Committee of the Regions – A European Strategy for Data

European Commission (2024) Communication from The Commission to the European Parliament, The Council, The European Economic and Social Committee and The Committee of the Regions. The European Health Union: acting together for people's health

European Commission (n.d.) EU4Health programme 2021-2027 – a vision for a healthier European Union. https://health.ec.europa.eu/funding/eu4health-programme-2021-2027-vision-healthier-european-union_en

European Council (2015) Council conclusions on personalised medicine for patients OJ C 421, 17.12.2015, pp 2–5

Machado AC, Polónia DF (2022) Legal and technological aspects for the creation of a European Health Data Space. In: 2022 17th Iberian Conference on Information Systems and Technologies (CISTI), pp 1–6

Watson C (2022) Rise of the preprint: how rapid data sharing during COVID-19 has changed science forever. Nat Med 28:2–5. https://doi.org/10.1038/s41591-021-01654-6

World Health Organization European Region (2024) Health as a driver and beneficiary of well-being economies - Briefing note

Facilitating and Protecting Personalized Medicine

Defining Scientific Research Within the EU's Politics of Data: The Impact on Personalized Smart Medicine

Ludovica Paseri

Abstract Personalized smart medicine is currently a major strand of research in the health sector that promises to profoundly innovate clinical practice and patient care through massive amounts of data processing. However, within the current and proposed EU legal frameworks on data governance, there are multiple definitions of "scientific research" or "research purposes", and none of them are consistent nor harmonized. This is particularly relevant since European lawmakers frequently impose special rules over scientific research activities. Hence, this chapter aims to investigate whether and to what extent the EU legal framework influences health research for personalized smart medicine. Here, focus is placed on the notions of scientific research according to different legal provisions and what consequences this has for studies in the field of personalized smart medicine. A normative analysis reveals three interpretations of what constitutes scientific research: narrow, broad, and undefined. With these three definitions in hand, the study outlines several different criteria for action and governance that must be taken into account in any framework designed to guide research into personalized smart medicine. The action criteria include FAIRness, accountability, and proactivity, while the governance criteria encompass participation rules, data stewardship, and horizontal coordination.

1 Introduction

The emergence of personalized smart medicine is prompting a profound transformation in healthcare. Most notably, the ability to adapt treatments to the genetic make-up, environmental conditions, and lifestyles of individual patients is fostering

---

L. Paseri (✉)
Law Department, University of Turin, Torino, Italy
e-mail: ludovica.paseri@unito.it

F. Casarosa et al. (eds.), *Enabling and Safeguarding Personalized Medicine*, Data Science, Machine Intelligence, and Law 7,
https://doi.org/10.1007/978-3-031-99709-9_2

a "patient-centric healthcare system".[1] A good proportion of this revolution involves processing large amounts of data—both personal and non-personal—in situations where it is often difficult to distinguish between the two. Personal data might include genetic information, medical records, and other sensitive details about a patient. Yet, analyzing and aggregating such data may lead to patterns or models from which no personal data emerge. This blurs the boundaries between personal and non-personal data, challenging existing regulatory frameworks and requiring a nuanced approach to data governance.[2]

Given its promise of profoundly innovating clinical practice and patient care through massive amounts of data processing, personalized smart medicine is currently a major strand of research in the health sector. In the EU's legal framework on data governance, the so-called "EU politics of data"[3] "scientific research" and "research purposes" are defined multiple times in multiple different ways and none are consistent nor harmonized.[4] This is particularly relevant since European lawmakers frequently impose special rules to regulate scientific research activities. Hence, this chapter aims to investigate whether and to what extent the EU's legal frameworks influence health research into personalized smart medicine. The focus of this investigation is on the definition of scientific research according to different legal provisions and what consequences this has for studies in the field of personalized medicine.

Defining the notion of scientific research is relevant since the field of personalized smart medicine is increasingly becoming characterized by the interplay between the public and private sectors. That is, the healthcare sector and publicly funded research is more and more often partnering with private companies involved in the scientific process, especially when it comes to distributing data monitoring and processing devices.[5] The fact that personalized smart medicine frequently involves a collaboration between the public and private spheres is not problematic

[1] Spruit and Lytras (2018), p. 645.

[2] Graef et al. (2018).

[3] The formula "politics of data" adopted in this chapter refers to Pagallo (2022) where it is used to indicate the European legal framework over data. This notion considers "the novelty of current human data-driven societies in accordance with a basic tenet of Aristotle's 'politics', or 'practical sciences'". Here, Pagallo wonders: "How shall the law strike the balance among multiple regulatory systems that compete in society, such as ethics and social mores, the forces of the market, and generally, what Aristotle dubs as "economics" in the eighth book of the Nicomachean Ethics (Aristotle, 2000)?" Pagallo (2022), p. 2. This formula has been adopted in different contexts. For instance, Alaimo and Kallinikos (2024), pp. 29–33, where is relate the politics of data to an "epistemic shift" that promotes "a vision of society governed by regularities and statistical law" Alaimo and Kallinikos (2024), p. 33, where data shifts "from being a cultural artifact serving a function to something that was believed to exist independent of the reality of conventions of which is part" Alaimo and Kallinikos (2024), p. 30. According to Micheli et al. (2020), p. 3 "The notion of data politics emphasises the 'performative power of data'. It understands data not only for its representational capacities, but also as a force 'generative of new forms of power relations'".

[4] Meiring et al. (2023).

[5] Schneider (2019).

per se. Nevertheless it is important to bear in mind that, while public actors generally have a mandate to advance the scientific knowledge associated with public health, private sector players are typically motivated by the pursuit of profit and competitive positioning.[6] That said, both can contribute in complementary ways to innovation and progress. The priority when developing personalized medical solutions is to balance these diverging interests in such a way as to ensure ethical conduct within the scientific process as well as a fair distribution of the benefits. This is a scenario that requires governance mechanisms[7] in the field of health research for personalized smart medicine that can guarantee that the research sector without restricting scientific advancements.

Thus, the analysis of this chapter, which is outlined in Sect. 2, begins with framing personalized smart medicine as sitting somewhere between clinical practice and scientific research. The aim here is to focus on the role of data in this context. The next step, in Sect. 3 is to examine the various definitions of scientific research as outlined in the European legal framework for data governance. Three different notions of scientific research are identified in this analysis: narrow, broad, and undefined. Each of these definitions is discussed in its own subsection. Then, given this framework for understanding what constitutes scientific research within the context of the EU politics of data, Sect. 4 explores the implications of this polysemy in the field of personalized smart medicine. These implications include a proposed set of criteria for action and governance mechanisms that are relevant to the design for a framework guiding research into personalized smart medicine. Lastly, Sect. 5 concludes the chapter by discussing some future perspectives for the ethical and regulatory challenges facing research in the field of personalized smart medicine.

2 Personalized Smart Medicine Between Clinical Practice and Scientific Research

Not all patients react in the prescribed and hoped-for manner when given the same treatment or medication. Consider epilepsy patients: around 30% of patients are resistant to existing treatments.[8] Personalized medicine aims to bypass this obstacle by proposing a tailor-made approach to the patient[9] that is based on several factors, most of which are related to genomic information.[10] Technological developments play a fundamental role in this dynamic, as computer models are needed to identify personalized therapies. Additionally, the "availability of wearable smart sensors, wireless connectivity, artificial intelligence, and the Internet of Medical Things is

[6] Mirowski (2023).

[7] Durante (2015).

[8] Henning et al. (2019).

[9] Chadwick (2014).

[10] Cordeiro (2014).

changing the personalized/precision medicine research and implementation landscape".[11] Further, the amount of data from different sources that needs to be processed to achieve personalization is overwhelming: "The data flowing [...] will come from genetic databases, medical records, tissue banks, and other clinical sources of 'big data'".[12]

Currently, however, medicine is mainly based on the treatment of manifest diseases, while personalized medicine appears to be more of a goal to be achieved rather than a reality.[13] For this reason, cutting-edge health research is placing significant emphasis on personalized smart medicine. At the experimental level of research, there has been some momentum with the application of AI systems to personalized medicine. For example, there have been several efforts to use personalized medicine as a means to detect cancer in the early stages of the disease.[14] As a result, the development, and also the success, of personalized smart medicine is closely related to advances in science, particularly in the research fields of genomics and biology, but also in bioinformatics and data science. This is not surprising since effective personalized medicine techniques can only be implemented as a result of a deep intertwining of these fields. According to some scholars, personalized medicine is now in experimental phase ("research phase"[15]) and it "needs to be carefully transferred to the clinic in order to evaluate the impacts of providing information about health risks on patients' attitudes and behaviours, as well as on their anxiety".[16] At the moment, such proclamations are making the research side of personalized smart medicine even more relevant than the clinical side.

Yet one of the consequences of these advances is that developments in the field of personalized smart medicine become closely entangled with issues of research ethics. Research ethics particularly impact personalized smart medicine in terms of social acceptability[17] and also in relation to the issue of under-representing certain segments of the population.[18]

From the angle of social acceptability, "ethics is used to render the promise forged by personalized medicine promoters credible and acceptable among the different groups of actors concerned, namely researchers, clinicians, and public health decision-makers",[19] but also patients. In other words: "Over time, traditional research ethics principles aimed at protecting individual participants have become supplemented with social obligations related to the interests of society and the

[11] Lin and Shengjun (2022), p. 1.

[12] Ho et al. (2020), p. 1.

[13] Goetz and Schork (2018).

[14] Ullah et al. (2020).

[15] Barazzetti et al. (2021), p. 825.

[16] Ibid.

[17] Barazzetti et al. (2021).

[18] Walker et al. (2022).

[19] Barazzetti et al. (2021), p. 819.

research enterprise at large".[20] This shows the nature of genomic and personalized medicine as a "social endeavour".[21] Barazzetti et al. show that, when considering the benefits of personalized medicine for public health, critical aspects of the matter become socially acceptable.[22] As an illustration, consider one of the most critical aspects of personalized smart medicine such as the high costs it imposes on the healthcare systems. Proposing personalized medicine as "the result of an ethical boundary work"[23] and committing to "render promises ethical"[24] by involving the local population, communicating transparently, and adopting a "public health approach"[25] means society should accept this downside of high costs.

On the other hand, consider that one of the bottlenecks in personalized smart medicine is the risk that certain segments of the population will be under-represented, "since identifying [the] patient populations most likely to benefit from a treatment could in practice restrict access to treatment for those judged less likely to benefit".[26] This problem raises issues of equity,[27] which unfortunately are not new. In fact, under-representing certain populations has been widely investigated in connection with data-driven research.[28] The problem of under-representation in personalized smart medicine is aptly described by Shannon Vallor who point out that data and algorithms tend to mirror the past, reflecting the same errors, limitations, and biases we are striving to distance ourselves from.[29]

In this context, research ethics may have an impact in shaping personalized smart medicine and promoting the principle of solidarity as the basis of a healthcare system.[30] This can occur when orienting the actions and one's research activities to the principle of justice,[31] which, according to John Rawls, is represented by the idea that all major social goods should be distributed equally, and that there can only be equal distribution if it benefits the most disadvantaged.[32] On this point, it has been argued that: "The principle of solidarity is of major importance in the discussion of health and genetics due to the emphasis laid upon the protection of weaker groups in society and commitment to the fair distribution of healthcare services".[33]

---

20 Vos et al. (2017), p. 1.

21 Vos et al. (2017), p. 9.

22 Barazzetti et al. (2021).

23 Barazzetti et al. (2021), p. 819.

24 Barazzetti et al. (2021), p. 826.

25 Ibid.

26 Walker et al. (2022), p. 9.

27 Chadwick (2014).

28 See e.g., Staunton and De Vries (2020); Tan et al. (2018); McCartney et al. (2024).

29 Vallor (2024).

30 Árnason (2012).

31 Ibid.

32 Rawls (1971).

33 Árnason (2012), p. 112.

Keeping this ethical framework in mind, it must be emphasized that, from a regulatory perspective, the set of these "emerging, high-throughput, data-intensive biomedical assays, such as DNA sequencing, proteomics, imaging protocols, and wireless monitoring devices"[34] and their role in personalized medicine is subject to multiple regulatory data regimes, with further specificities if the processing is framed in the context of scientific research.

3 Interpretations of Scientific Research in the EU's Politics of Data

In the EU legal framework on data governance, the terms "research activity" and "scientific research purposes" are frequently referred to in different contexts and with reference to different objectives. However, there are considerable variations in each definition. As highlighted by Meiring et al., "there is no harmonised EU definition of scientific research; its meaning and possibly scope varies by legislative instrument".[35]

Given that European lawmakers frequently provides for a promotional legislation over scientific research endeavors, defining an activity as "scientific research" can have major advantages. In addition, the many and varied references to scientific research have "not produced a consolidated and coordinated legislative instrument of reference for the research sector".[36]

This problem of definition is all the more urgent in the field of research on personalized smart medicine, which involves different actors, both public and private, and has significant implications for the health of individuals.[37]

Exploring the framework of the EU politics of data, three different connotations emerge concerning the notion of scientific research: (i) in some circumstances, the definitions focus on publicly-funded scientific research; (ii) in other instances, the definitions take a broad interpretation of the notion of scientific research, and usually one that involves the activities of both public and private actors; and (iii) in still other cases, reference is made to scientific research without providing any definition and without referring to any other legal text containing a definition.

[34] Goetz and Schork (2018).

[35] Meiring et al. (2023), p. 3.

[36] European Commission (2024), p. 51.

[37] Pagallo (2022b).

3.1 A Narrow Notion of Scientific Research

In recent years, European lawmakers have set out several regulatory provisions that specifically refer to the data processing associated with scientific research activities conducted by publicly funded research organizations. This is the case of the Open Data Directive (ODD)[38] and Directive (EU) 2019/790, namely the "Copyright and related rights in the Digital Single Market" Directive.[39]

First consider the ODD, which regulates the re-use of information assets held by the public sector, i.e., open data. This piece of legislation defines scientific research extremely narrowly in that it only addresses the processing of data for research purposes by public research organizations or publicly-funded research entities. Notably, this is the first time "research data" have fallen within the scope of the European legal framework on open data.[40] In the Directive, research data, is defined as "documents in a digital form, other than scientific publications, which are collected or produced in the course of scientific research activities and are used as evidence in the research process, or are commonly accepted in the research community as necessary to validate research findings and results".[41] Article 10 of the ODD mandates member states to adopt national strategies that aim to make "publicly funded research data openly available ('open access policies'), following the principle of 'open by default' and compatible with the FAIR principles". However, the openness promoted is not indiscriminate. On the contrary, European lawmakers specifically provide grounds for closure that have to be taken into account when deciding whether to make research data open and re-usable—namely "intellectual property rights, personal data protection and confidentiality, security and legitimate commercial interests".[42]

At first glance, these grounds for closure might lead one to think that scientific research on personalized medicine, even if carried out by publicly funded research organizations, should be taken out of the scope of the legislation due to the large amount of personal data involved or that private actors are usually collaborators. However, this is not the case. These two elements, i.e., the processing of personal data and the co-participation of public and private actors only become factors that have to be taken into account on a case-by-case basis for each individual research project.[43]

---

[38] Directive (EU) 2019/1024 of the European Parliament and of the Council of 20 June 2019 on open data and the re-use of public sector information (recast), ELI: http://data.europa.eu/eli/dir/2019/1024/oj.

[39] Directive (EU) 2019/790 of the European Parliament and of the Council of 17 April 2019 on copyright and related rights in the Digital Single Market and amending Directives 96/9/EC and 2001/29/EC, ELI: http://data.europa.eu/eli/dir/2019/790/oj.

[40] Guarda (2021).

[41] Article 2(9) ODD.

[42] Article 10 ODD.

[43] Paseri (2024).

Further, if, at the end of this balancing process, the reasons for closing off the research data involved in the project should prevail, it would still be beneficial—if not necessary—to ensure the datasets are compatible with the FAIR principles. The FAIR data principles, developed by the scientific community,[44] are a set of guidelines that aim to provide a common basis for ensuring good management of research data from a technical point of view. FAIR is an acronym that stands for findability, accessibility, interoperability and reusability, features that are further specified to assure that data are supported by metadata, that they are correctly described, have the most suitable licenses, and are equipped with unique identifiers that ensure their long-term preservation, among other stipulations.

According to Article 4(3) of the Treaty on the Functioning of the European Union (TFEU): "In the areas of research, technological development and space, the Union shall have competence to carry out activities, in particular to define and implement programmes; however, the exercise of that competence shall not result in Member States being prevented from exercising theirs".[45] For this reason, the national dimension of this legal framework is crucial, and can vary considerably from one Member state to another.[46] Thus, defining scientific research becomes even more complex, entailing risks of fragmentation of the legislation.

In terms of publicly-funded research, the stance taken by European institutions in Directive (EU) 2019/790, which deals with the Copyright and related rights in the Digital Single Market Directive, is also an integral part of the jigsaw.[47] Articles 3 and 4 of Directive (EU) 2019/790 provide for exemptions in case of the application of text and data mining techniques for the purposes of scientific research. For example, Recital 10 holds that "As research is increasingly carried out with the assistance of digital technology, there is a risk that the Union's competitive position as a research area will suffer, unless steps are taken to address the legal uncertainty concerning text and data mining". However, despite this caveat, some have pointed out limitations to the current legal framework, especially concerning the exceptions made for research and education under the Directive. One of these limitations is the lack of harmonisation at the European level.[48]

Additionally, Directive (EU) 2019/790 dwells on the notion of scientific research in recital 12, emphasizing the need to have a "common understanding",[49] of what scientific research is. The legislation identifies as research organizations any "uni-

[44] Wilkinson et al. (2016).

[45] Consolidated version of the Treaty on the Functioning of the European Union (2012).

[46] Paseri (2024).

[47] Meiring et al. (2023).

[48] Caso (2020).

[49] Research organisations across the Union encompass a wide variety of entities the primary goal of which is to conduct scientific research or to do so together with the provision of educational services. The term 'scientific research' within the meaning of this Directive should be understood to cover both the natural sciences and the human sciences. Due to the diversity of such entities, it is important to have a common understanding of research organisations", Recital 12, Directive (EU) 790/2019.

versities or other higher education institutions and their libraries, also entities such as research institutes and hospitals … carry out", thus directly encompasses health research.

In this regard, Article 2 of Directive (EU) 2019/790 defines a "research organization" as a university, including its libraries, a research institute or any other entity, the primary goal of which is to conduct scientific research or to carry out educational activities involving also the conduct of scientific research: (a) on a not-for-profit basis or by reinvesting all the profits in its scientific research; or (b) pursuant to a public interest mission recognized by a Member State; in such a way that the access to the results generated by such scientific research cannot be enjoyed on a preferential basis by an undertaking that exercises a decisive influence upon such organisation.

About this last aspect, Recital 8 premises that:

> Organisations upon which commercial undertakings have a decisive influence allowing such undertakings to exercise control because of structural situations, such as through their quality of shareholder or member, which could result in preferential access to the results of the research, should not be considered research organisations for the purposes of this Directive.[50]

Hence, European lawmakers seemingly intend to exclude private researchers from the benefits of regulatory exceptions. This makes it rather complex to determine whether definitions and regulatory controls apply in situations of public-private intertwining for research such as, generally, the field of personalized smart medicine research. In addition, the ODD states that "Member States should be free to decide, at national level and after discussions with relevant stakeholders", while Recital 15 of Directive (EU) 2019/790 refers to exceptions when performing text and data mining for research purposes, as already mentioned.

The definition of scientific research activities proposed in Directive (EU) 2019/790 is also particularly relevant because it has been adopted in the Data Services Act (DSA).[51] Recital 97 of the DSA provides information on the access to platform data pursuant Article 40 of the DSA, stating that the intention is to provide:

> a framework for compelling access to data from very large online platforms and very large online search engines to vetted researchers affiliated to a research organisation within the meaning of Article 2 of Directive (EU) 2019/790, which may include, for the purpose of this Regulation, civil society organisations that are conducting scientific research with the primary goal of supporting their public interest mission.

[50] "Despite different legal forms and structures, research organisations in the Member States generally have in common that they act either on a not-for-profit basis or in the context of a public-interest mission recognised by the State. Such a public-interest mission could, for example, be reflected through public funding or through provisions in national laws or public contracts", Recital 12, Directive (EU) 2019/790.

[51] Regulation (EU) 2022/2065 of the European Parliament and of the Council of 19 Octo-ber 2022 on a Single Market For Digital Services and amending Directive 2000/31/EC (Digital Services Act), ELI: http://data.europa.eu/eli/reg/2022/2065/oj.

3.2 A Broad Notion of Scientific Research

While some regulatory frameworks set out a very narrow definition of scientific research (i.e., scientific activities conducted by public actors, publicly funded, or pursuing public interests), in others prescribe a very broad definition. These include the General Data Protection Regulation (GDPR)[52] and the Regulation on the European Health Data Space (EHDS).[53]

The GDPR, in providing a legal framework for the processing of personal data at European level, necessarily also involves the research sector. In this regard, Recital 159 states that "the processing of personal data for scientific research purposes should be interpreted in a broad manner including, for example, technological development and demonstration, fundamental research, applied research and privately funded research". It goes on to specify, with relevance to personalized medicine research, that "Scientific research purposes should also include studies conducted in the public interest in the area of public health".[54] The rationale behind adopting this extended definition of scientific research to also involve private research is understandably to ensure maximum flexibility for the research sector, while at the same time ensuring protection for the widest range of data subjects. As Sjöberg states, "it truly is an advantage, legally speaking, to have certain personal data processing formally labelled as scientific research".[55] However, the European Data Protection Supervisor (EDPS) in a relevant opinion in 2020 stated definitively that: "In this context, where trust plays such a crucial role, performing an activity deemed to be research cannot be a carte blanche to take irresponsible risks".[56]

That said, the GDPR envisages several exceptions to its mandates when it comes to scientific research.[57] Article 89 GDPR regarding "Safeguards and derogations relating to processing for archiving purposes in the public interest, scientific or historical research purposes or statistical purposes", states that the processing of personal data "for archiving purposes in the public interest, scientific or historical research purposes or statistical purposes, shall be subject to appropriate safeguards [...] for the rights and freedoms of the data subject", i.e., identified, or identifiable natural person. Under the GDPR, these "appropriate" safeguards are established by identifying the most suitable organizational and technical measures. In identifying such measures to guarantee the rights and freedoms of the individual, it is crucially

[52] Regulation (EU) 2016/679 of the European Parliament and of the Council of 27 April 2016 on the protection of natural persons with regard to the processing of personal data and on the free movement of such data, and repealing Directive 95/46/EC (General Data Protection Regulation), ELI: http://data.europa.eu/eli/reg/2016/679/oj.

[53] Regulation (EU) 2025/327 of the European Parliament and of the Council of 11 February 2025 on the European Health Data Space and amending Directive 2011/24/EU and Regulation (EU) 2024/2847, ELI: http://data.europa.eu/eli/reg/2025/327/oj.

[54] Paseri et al. (2021).

[55] Magnusson Sjöberg (2017).

[56] EDPS (2020), p. 9.

[57] Ducato (2020).

important to consider the principles of data minimization, according to which the personal data processed must be "adequate, relevant and limited to what is necessary in relation to the purposes for which they are processed", as enshrined in Article 5(1)c of the GDPR.

In addition, the GDPR itself provides several exemptions to processing personal data for research purposes, one of which involves allowing each member states to establish their own exemptions for research activity.[58]

The EHDS also adopts an extended definition of scientific research. Here, the legislation specifically highlights the secondary use of data, allowing secondary use of health data acquires central relevance as a means that "should enable public, private and not-for-profit entities, as well as individual researchers, to have access to health data for research, innovation, policymaking, educational activities, patient safety, regulatory activities or personalised medicine".[59] The EHDS does not elaborate extensively on the notion of scientific research but does clarify in Recital 61 that:

> The provision of the data should also support activities related to scientific research. The notion of scientific research purposes should be interpreted in a broad manner, including technological development and demonstration, fundamental research, applied research and privately funded research. Activities related to scientific research include innovation activities such as training of AI algorithms that could be used in healthcare or the care of natural persons, as well as the evaluation and further development of existing algorithms and products for such purposes.[60]

Importantly, Article 2(1)a of the EHDS states that the definitions of the GDPR also apply to the scope of the EHDS Regulation. As mentioned, the GDPR specifies which activities can be regarded as scientific research in Recital 159, assuming "a broad conception of research, including technological development, fundamental and applied research and privately funded research and studies conducted in the public interest in the area of public health".[61]

However, extending the definition of research purposes under the EHDS has raised criticism given that "the aim of stimulating the European economy by granting free access to citizens' health data can backfire and have detrimental effects on public trust in and support for medical research".[62] In particular, two major limitations have been outlined. The first issue pertains to a matter of ethics; it concerns the risk that the requirement of individual consent to re-use data may "limit the

[58] Reference goes to Articles 5(1)b, 5(1)e, 9(2)j, 14(5)b, 17(3)d, 21(6) of the GDPR for the exemptions directly provided for in the Regulation; and to Articles 15, 16, 18, 21, 19 of the GDPR for the instances in which member states have leeway, see Paseri (2024), p. 163.

[59] Recital 61, EHDS.

[60] Consider the wording of the EHDS Proposal, where the recital stated: "The provision of the data should also support activities related to scientific research (including private research), development and innovation, producing goods and services for the health or care sectors, such as innovation activities or training of AI algorithms that could protect the health or care of natural persons".

[61] EDPS (2020), p. 11.

[62] Marelli et al. (2023), p. 2.

representativeness of datasets".[63] This could even be seen an increased risk in the context of research on personalized medicine. The second critique relates to the fact that an extended definition of scientific research "can have detrimental effects on public sectors, such as involvement of tech corporations in research agenda setting and growing dependencies on privately owned computational infrastructures for the provision of public goods, such as health".[64] These forms of technological dependence may be the outcome of unbalanced public-private partnerships, which only begin with research projects into personalized medicine but may also extend to the clinical and patient care sphere. Think about, for instance, the restricted availability of proprietary instruments or lock-in mechanisms.

After examining these broad and narrow notions of scientific research adopted by the European lawmaker in the field of data governance, there are also several cases where hard-law texts mention scientific research without defining the concept. These cases are discussed next.

3.3 An Undefined Notion of Scientific Research

In some cases, EU lawmakers have regulated the field of scientific research without either providing a definition of what constitutes scientific research or pointing to another piece of legislation containing a definition. Consider the Data Governance Act (DGA)[65] and the EU Regulation on Artificial Intelligence, i.e., the Artificial Intelligence Act (AI Act).[66]

The scientific research sector is particularly touched by the DGA, especially with regard to the mechanism of data altruism, both in its ethical and legal implications.[67] Conspicuously, however, the DGA lacks a definition of scientific research.[68] In

[63] Ibid.

[64] Marelli et al. (2023), p. 3; Tamar (2021).

[65] Regulation (EU) 2022/868 of the European Parliament and of the Council of 30 May 2022 on European data governance and amending Regulation (EU) 2018/1724 (Data Governance Act), PE/85/2021/REV/1, OJ L 152, 3.6.2022, pp. 1–44, ELI: http://data.europa.eu/eli/reg/2022/868/oj.

[66] Regulation (EU) 2024/1689 of the European Parliament and of the Council of 13 June 2024 laying down harmonised rules on artificial intelligence and amending Regulations (EC) No 300/2008, (EU) No 167/2013, (EU) No 168/2013, (EU) 2018/858, (EU) 2018/1139 and (EU) 2019/2144 and Directives 2014/90/EU, (EU) 2016/797 and (EU) 2020/1828 (Artificial Intelligence Act), ELI: http://data.europa.eu/eli/reg/2024/1689/oj.

[67] Paseri (2024b).

[68] It should be specified that recital 12 DGA mentions "the exchange of data between re-searchers for non-commercial scientific research purposes" only to clarify the scope of the regulatory text, not to provide a definition of the notion adopted in the Regulation with reference to the application of the data altruism mechanism. It also states that "The re-use regime provided for in this Regulation should apply to data the supply of which forms part of the public tasks of the public sector bodies concerned under law or other binding rules in the Member States", the Regulation specifies that in the case of "Re-search-performing organisations and research-funding organisations could also be

Recital 16 of the DGA the intention to promote the use of data for scientific research in pursuit of public interest purposes is spelt out. Then, Article 2(16) of the DGA, by defining the data altruism mechanism, emphasizes the need for compliance with the condition of re-use for public interest purposes such as "scientific research purposes in the general interest". However, although this explicit reference to the public interest in Recital 16 necessarily includes public actors, it does not exclude the involvement of private actors as one can easily argue that private research organizations and hybrids are also governed under the spirit of pursuing "data altruism" and "the general interest". The notion of public interest and the so-called "cognate concepts such as the public or common good or the general interest"[69] can not necessarily be considered synonyms, since they do not precisely correspond. As Boot explains:

> Appeal to the public interest plays such a crucial role—often providing, in effect, a justification for an exception to the application of a rule—legal scholars have repeatedly lamented the absence of a clear definition of the public interest, arguing that it has led to ad hoc applications of the concept ... and 'judicial idiosyncrasy'. ... Indeed, what exactly is meant by 'the public interest' all too often remains a mystery.[70]

In the DGA, and in particular for data altruism, it is not possible to completely exclude forms of public-private research or research conducted entirely by private-sector actors. *A fortiori*, consider that Recital 25 of the DGA holds that the fees imposed by the public sector for re-using data be reduced in cases where the data are to be re-used for non-commercial or scientific research purposes (among other circumstances). Also consider that the DGA, in the context of setting fees, points out that even if "scientific research purposes should be understood to include any type of research-related purpose regardless of the organisational or financial structure of the research institution in question", there is an "exception of research that is being conducted by an undertaking with the aim of developing, enhancing or optimising products or services".

Another key piece of legislation lacking a definition of scientific research is the AI Act. From the very beginning, the 2021 proposal[71] and all its subsequent versions have not included an exemption framework for scientific research.[72] However, the current version of the AI Act explicitly states in Recital 25 that "it is necessary to ensure that this Regulation does not otherwise affect scientific research and development activity on AI systems or models prior to being placed on the market or put

---

or-ganised as public sector bodies or bodies governed by public law", then "This Regula-tion should apply to such hybrid organisations only in their capacity as research-performing organisations".

[69] Boot (2022), p. 2.

[70] Ibid.

[71] Proposal for a Regulation of the European Parliament and of the Council laying down harmonised rules on Artificial Intelligence (Artificial Intelligence Act) and amending certain Union legislative acts, COM/2021/206 final, ELI: https://eur-lex.europa.eu/legal-content/EN/TXT/?uri=celex\%3A52021PC0206.

[72] Ebers et al. (2021); Smuha et al. (2021).

Table 1 The notion of scientific research in the EU politics of data

Narrow notion	Scientific research that is publicly funded or conducted by public entities	– Open Data Directive (ODD) – Copyright and related rights in the Digital Single Market Directive
Broad notion	An extended interpretation of scientific research involving activities resulting from both public and private actors.	– General Data Protection Regulation (GDPR) – European Health Data Space Regulation (EHDS)
Undefined notion	Refers to scientific research without providing a definition for it or referring to another legal text containing a definition.	– Data Governance Act (DGA) – AI Act

into service". Additionally, Article 2(6) of the AI Act establishes that: "This Regulation does not apply to AI systems or AI models, including their output, specifically developed and put into service for the sole purpose of scientific research and development". Currently, despite the inclusion of an exemption regime for research activities in the field of AI, even taking into account the recitals, the definition of research activities under the AI Act is still missing.

Considering the fact that activities carried out for research purposes are excluded from the application of the regulatory text, the definition of what constitutes a research activity becomes crucial. Partially clarifying this ambiguity, the recital 25 specifies that "That exclusion is without prejudice to the obligation to comply with this Regulation where an AI system falling into the scope of this Regulation is placed on the market or put into service as a result of such research and development activity and to the application of provisions on regulatory sandboxes and testing in real world conditions". Yet, any further considerations on this matter will have to wait for the AI Act to come into force. For the time being, the unclear notion of scientific research in the EU politics of data can be ascribed to three different interpretations, as summarized in Table 1. But what are the implications of this complex and complicated European regulatory framework on the health research strand of personalized smart medicine? These are discussed next.

4 The Impact of the EU Legal Framework on Personalized Smart Medicine

Thomas Bingham, in exploring the notion of the rule of law, illustrates that, in some instances, omitting a strict definition in a legal text may be reasonable in order to "leave it to the judges to rule on what the term means if and when the question arises for decision".[73] In some senses, this ensures that a definition is "forged not in the abstract but with reference to particular cases and it would be possible for the

[73] Bingham (2011), p. 7.

concept to evolve over time in response to new views and situations".[74] While acknowledging this need, the research sector has many specificities and many facets, each of which are linked to different domains of knowledge and scientific investigation. Thus, attention needs to be paid to the specific definitions of scientific research and its implications at a general level. One of the challenges with defining the concept of scientific research in the various different EU regulatory texts is that such definitions run the risk of turning opportunities into losses, to limiting scientific progress, and to constraining technological advancement. In our case, an ambiguous regulatory framework that does not clearly define what scientific research is may mean health research in the field of personalized smart medicine simply does not get done. This would be unfortunate since the field currently needs a major effort to bring research into clinical practice so as to benefit large segments of the population.

Against this backdrop, the goal with this examination is to identify some criteria that can guide the actions of public researchers in the field of personalized smart medicine (Sect. 4.1) and then, broadening the outlook, to develop some consideration for appropriate governance mechanisms (Sect. 4.2).

4.1 Defining Scientific Research Legal Framework for Personalized Smart Medicine

In the experimental phase of personalized smart medicine, public actors tend to play a central role[75] the scientific research process. However, they face a very fragmented set of legal frameworks, and they are also challenged with major hurdles, such as their dependency on technology, as discussed in Sect. 3.2. From the investigation of the notion of scientific research in the EU politics of data, three criteria relevant for the public actors involved in personalized smart medicine research are identified: FAIRness; accountability; and proactivity.

FAIRness emerges from the narrowest notion of scientific research, which only involves research activity carried out by public or publicly-funded institutions. As studies in the field of personalized smart medicine typically involve collaboration between the public and private actors, most research projects require a case-by-case assessment of whether they fall under the ODD's Article 10 research data sharing regime. However, one criterion that can orient the action of public actors is to adopt common guidelines for an accurate management of research data such as, for example, the FAIR data principles.[76] In this manner, operating at the level of self-

[74] Ibid.

[75] On the role of the public sphere in the definition of personalized medicine policies see Groth Jensen et al. (2023).

[76] For instance, guidelines published by the national authority "Agenzia per l'Italia Digitale" (AgID) have suggested the application of FAIR principles also in the management of public sector data in general AgId (2023).

regulation,[77] a common but flexible approach is drawn up to the specific needs that arise on a case-by-case basis. Hence, in numerous cases, public policies developed at the local level—i.e., at the level of the research center or university involved in the research project—have outlined common rules concerning how data are curated and managed, equipping those data with persistent identifiers, rich metadata, provenance information, and more.

Second, with regard to the broad notion of scientific research, the legal framework provided by the GDPR is also a benchmark for processing personal data for the purposes of personalized smart medicine research. When data processing involves personal data and non-personal data, making it difficult to identify a clear distinction, a useful criterion for directing action is that provided by the principle of accountability under Article 5(2) of the GDPR, which prompts consideration on data management and enables reasoned justification of the choices made. This principle is not only aimed at compliance with the European data protection framework, but also becomes a useful guiding criterion for action in addressing ethical challenges, such as those of social acceptability discussed above. In this regard, consider that "In biomedical research the improvements in diagnostic testing and the promise of personalized medicine have heightened public demands and expectations for transparency and accountability in health care".[78] Therefore, making the accountability principle of the GDPR a general principle of research data stewardship may be a means to fulfil these expectations of transparency.

Third, concerning regulatory texts that do not provide a clear definition of scientific research, not having a clear understanding of what falls under the scope of a specific regulation and what is instead excluded, the criterion of the proactive action may be fruitful, turning attention to the advantages provided by regulatory instruments that do not define the field of research. With proactive participation, the public actors involved in this dynamic may be able to guide the development of the research, making themselves leading actors, setting targets, and steering choices. For instance, in relation to data altruism, research institutes exploring personalized smart medicine could frame themselves as "data users" according to Article 2(9) of the DGA.[79] This would afford access to data certified by a data altruism organization without having to assume undue security responsibilities. Alternatively, foundations connected to medical research centers or universities could be designated as data altruism organizations according to Chapter IV of the DGA. In such cases, the use

[77] In Rajam (2020) the regulatory challenges of personalised medicine are discussed, focusing on the role of self-regulation and co-regulatory measures. Specifically, in relation to the FAIR principles, it is stated that "These principles provide guidance for public research for a scientific data management and stewardship and are relevant to all stakeholders in the digital economy and has also been adopted by the EU commission under its 2020 program [...]. Although the FAIR principles have been criticized for not understanding the research processvery well yet it provides a sense of public accountability for data oriented research in general [...]", see Rajam (2020), p. 382.

[78] Rajam (2020), p. 381.

[79] "a natural or legal person who has lawful access to certain personal or non-personal data and has the right, including under Regulation (EU) 2016/679 in the case of personal data, to use that data for commercial or non- commercial purposes", Article 2(9), DGA.

of data can be fruitful for scientific research by minimizing the costs that would be generated by engaging private actors. In addition, another benefit of being proactive in compliance is to be ready for commercialization by default, which is especially essential if AI systems, with the associated AI Act implementation obligations, are involved when bringing products developed in the research sector to market.

These general criteria for guiding public actors in personalized smart medicine become relevant when overarching governance mechanisms are established, ensuring alignment among the actions of various stakeholders.

4.2 *Governance Mechanisms*

The governance of personalized smart medicine is a topic that has recently been the subject of considerable examination.[80] However, the scientific research phase of personalized medicine has not been investigated as thoroughly as the clinical phase. Further, in light of the EU politics of data, three observations are developed regarding the governance mechanisms of the research and experimental phase of personalized smart medicine, concerning the rules of participation; the relevance of data stewardship; and the need for horizontal coordination.

In a research context heavily characterized by public-private interplay, such as that of personalized smart medicine, it becomes essential for public actors to outline clear rules of participation, as a means to promote transparency, control and an ethical management of data.[81] For example, by establishing the rules of participation, public entities can require that data not only be analyzed in a systematic way, but also by taking into account how treatment varies for individuals with different socio-economic backgrounds. As a matter of fact, normally, to maximize the beneficial effects of a therapy or treatment, focus would be placed on approaches that perform for the largest proportion of those affected or those who will access that treatment, limiting attention to heterogeneity. Yet, considering that "wealthier and more highly educated individuals often have preferential access to new technologies and treatments",[82] different groups with non-privileged socio-economic conditions risk being cut off from access to the treatment. So, when identifying the rules of participation, public actors can choose to prioritize the approaches that take greater account of heterogeneity and minorities with the aim of promoting equity in health.[83]

A further factor worth considering is the need for responsible data stewardship.[84] Data stewardship can be defined as the "process and attitude that makes one deal responsibly with one's own and other people's data throughout and after the initial

[80] *Ex multis* Dove (2013); Tarkkala et al. (2019); Özdemir (2024).

[81] Paseri (2024).

[82] Ward (2012), p. 868.

[83] Ward (2012), p. 869.

[84] Wilkinson et al. (2016); Mons (2018).

scientific creation and discovery cycle".[85] Data stewardship is a very complex process, which requires the involvement of different competencies. First of all, it calls for a deep knowledge of the research field in which one operates. Second, it requires technical competence in data curation. Third, it demands respect for the ethical principles of good research conduct, but it also asks for some basic legal knowledge, related to the legal regime of data. The complexity of this process implies major investments at the local level, i.e., by universities and research centers, in order to train *ad hoc* individuals to deal with these crucial issues and to design a process that is able to harmonize all these different needs. Data stewardship is central to any field of scientific research, but it may be even more sensitive in the field of personalized smart medicine,[86] which aims to "process hundreds of parameters from multiple sites, be adaptable while remaining in sync at multiple locations, real-time syncing to analytics and be compliant with international privacy legislation".[87] Investment in data stewardship would be beneficial from many points of view, but especially in scenarios with regulatory uncertainty or an interplay between public and private entities.

Another aspect to be emphasized is the need for horizontal coordination. Analyzing these regulatory frameworks reveals that the EU's member states are integral to governing data use in the scientific research sector. However, given the current uncertainty of legislation at the member state level, a governance mechanism that might compensate for this shortcoming could be horizontal coordination between the various research entities in the field. National legislation could also be beneficial to the social acceptability of personalized smart medicine.[88] In this context, think about the role that research consortia or shared research infrastructures can play. These forms of collaboration could represent national interfaces that foster coordinated participation in research projects in the field of personalized smart medicine at the European level. Existing examples include the European Partnership for Personalised Medicine[89] and the International Consortium for Personalised Medicine. Notably, both these organizations adhere to different national regulatory frameworks by providing guidelines, discussing common approaches, and outlining codes of conduct for those involved in researching personalized smart medicine.

---

[85] Mons (2018), p. 36.

[86] Rodriguez and Ghanaim (2023).

[87] Jacobs et al. (2024).

[88] Barazzetti et al. (2021).

[89] Consider that the European Partnership for Personalised Medicine (EP PerMed) is co-funded by the European Commission under the 'Horizon Europe' Framework Programme for Research and Innovation, see: http://www.ricercainternazionale.mur.gov.it/era/european-partnership-2021-27/ep-permed.aspx.

5 Conclusion

The aim of the chapter was to investigate the impact that the multiple definitions of scientific research within European legislation might have on data governance over research sector in the field of personalized smart medicine. The analysis reveals a set of fragmented and often unclear regulatory frameworks that challenge compliance by the health research sector and may risk hindering its progress.

The investigation also reveals forms of technological underuse prompted by legal factors.[90] The uncertainty in these regulatory frameworks risks losing opportunities in the field of personalized medicine research, while also presenting obstacles to scientific progress. Unfortunately, it is the quality of healthcare to patients that bears the brunt of these consequences.

The outlined criteria for action and governance—i.e., FAIRness, accountability, proactivity coupled with participation rules, data stewardship, and horizontal coordination—are intended to support public actors as part of the governance of scientific research. Personalized smart medicine, which promises to hold great potential for improving the healthcare of individuals, at the moment mainly concerns the research phase rather than the clinical one. Given the high stakes, the choices currently made in research governance have the potential to improve—or damage—the quality of future healthcare.

Acknowledgements This research was financially supported by the "Biorobotics Research and Innovation Engineering Facilities" "IR0000036" – CUP J13C22000400007 (BRIEF) project.

References

AgID (2023) Determinazione n. 183/2023, Linee Guida recanti regole tecniche per l'apertura dei dati e il riutilizzo dell'informazione del settore pubblico

Alaimo C, Kallinikos J (2024) Data rules: reinventing the market economy. MIT Press, Cambridge

Árnason V (2012) The personal is political: ethics and personalized medicine. Ethical Perspect 19(1):103–122

Barazzetti G, Bühler N, Audétat M et al (2021) Making personalized medicine ethical: a critical examination of the new promises of 'personalized health' in Switzerland. Sci Public Policy 48(6):818–828

Bingham T (2011) The rule of law. Penguin Uk, London

Boot ER (2022) Public interest, Oxford research encyclopedia of politics

Caso R (2020) Il conflitto tra diritto d'autore e ricerca scientifica nella disciplina del text and data mining della direttiva sul mercato unico digitale. Trento Law and Technology Research Group Research Paper, 38

Chadwick R (2014) The ethics of personalized medicine: a philosopher's perspective. Pers Med 11(1):5–6

Consolidated version of the Treaty on the Functioning of the European Union (2012), OJ C 326, 26.10.2012, pp 47–390, ELI: http://data.europa.eu/eli/treaty/tfeu_2012/oj

---

[90] Pagallo (2022b).

Cordeiro JV (2014) Ethical and legal challenges of personalized medicine: paradigmatic examples of research, prevention, diagnosis and treatment. Revista Portuguesa de Saúde Pública 32(2):164–180

Dove ES (2013) Questioning the governance of pharmacogenomics and personalized medicine for global health. Curr Pharmacogenomics Person Med. Formerly Current Pharmacogenomics 11(4):253–256

Ducato R (2020) Data protection, scientific research, and the role of information. Comput Law Secur Rev 37(105412):1–16

Durante M (2015) The democratic governance of information societies. A critique to the theory of stakeholders. Philos Technol 28:11–13

Ebers M, Hoch V, Rosenkranz F, Ruschemeier H, Steinrötter B (2021) The European Commission's proposal for an Artificial Intelligence Act—a critical assessment by members of the Robotics and AI Law Society (RAILS). J 4(4):589–603

European Commission (2024) Directorate-General for Research and Innovation: Improving access to and reuse of research results, publications and data for scientific purposes – Study to evaluate the effects of the EU copyright framework on research and the effects of potential interventions and to identify and present relevant provisions for research in EU data and digital legislation, with a focus on rights and obligations, Publications Office of the European Union: Luxembourg, https://data.europa.eu/doi/10.2777/633395

European Data Protection Supervisor (EDPS) (2020), A Preliminary Opinion on data protection and scientific research

Goetz LH, Schork NJ (2018) Personalized medicine: motivation, challenges, and progress. Fertil Steril 109(6):952–963

Graef I, Gellert R, Husovec M (2018) Towards a holistic regulatory approach for the European data economy: why the illusive notion of non-personal data is counter- productive to data innovation. TILEC Discussion Paper, 1–17

Groth Jensen L, Svendsen MN, Snell K (2023) Strategies on personalized medicine and the power of the imagined public. New Genet Soc 42(1):e2260939

Guarda P (2021) Il regime giuridico dei dati della ricerca scientifica. Università degli Studi di Trento, Trento, p 33

Henning O, Lossius M, Lima M, Mevåg M, Villagran A, Nakken K, Johannessen Landmark C (2019) Refractory epilepsy and nonadherence to drug treatment. Epilepsia Open 4(4):618–623

Ho D, Quake SR, McCabe ER et al (2020) Enabling technologies for personalized and precision medicine. Trends Biotechnol 38:497–518

Jacobs JJL et al (2024) A data management system for precision medicine. MedRxiv:1–44

Lin B, Shengjun W (2022) Digital transformation in personalized medicine with artificial intelligence and the internet of medical things. Omics: J Integr Biol 26(2):77–81

Magnusson Sjöberg C (2017) Scientific research and academic e-learning in light of the EU's legal framework for data protection. New Technol Big Data Law:43–63

Marelli L et al (2023) The European health data space: too big to succeed? Health Policy 135:1–4

McCartney AM, Scholz AH, Groussin M, Staunton C (2024) Benefit-sharing by design: a call to action for human genomics research. Annu Rev Genomics Hum Genet 25:369–395. https://doi.org/10.1146/annurev-genom-021623-104241

Meiring A, Yakovleva S, Irion K, van Hoboken J et al (2023) Information law and the digital transformation of the university. Part I. Digital sovereignty. Institute for Information Law, 1–101. https://www.ivir.nl/part-i-digital-sovereignty/

Micheli M, Ponti M, Craglia M et al (2020) Emerging models of data governance in the age of datafication. Big Data Soc 7(2):1–15

Mirowski P (2023) The evolution of platform science. Soc Res: Int Q 90(4):725–755

Mons B (2018) Data stewardship for open science: implementing FAIR principles. Chapman and Hall/CRC
Özdemir V (2024) Global governance for personalized medicine, politics of uncertainty, and Pierre Bourdieu. OMICS: J Integr Biol 28(5):211–212
Pagallo U (2022) The politics of data in EU law: will it succeed? Digit Soc 1(3):1–20
Pagallo U (2022b) Il dovere alla salute: Sul rischio di sottoutilizzo dell'intelligenza artificiale in ambito sanitario. Mimesis, Milano-Udine
Paseri L (2024) Scienza aperta. Politiche europee per un nuovo paradigma della ricerca. Mimesis, Milano-Udine
Paseri L (2024b) The ethical and legal challenges of data altruism for the scientific research sector. In: Arias-Oliva M, Pelegrin-Borondo J, Murata K, Souto Romero M (eds) The leading role of smart ethics in the digital world. Universidad de La Rioja, Logroño, pp 189–200
Paseri L, Varrette S, Bouvry P (2021) Protection of personal data in high performance computing platform for scientific research purposes. In: Gruschka N, Antunes LFC, Rannenberg K, Drogkaris P (eds) Privacy Technologies and Policy. APF 2021. Springer, Cham, pp 123–142
Rajam N (2020) Policy strategies for personalising medicine "in the data moment". Health Policy Technol 9(3):379–383
Rawls J (1971) A theory of justice. Oxford University Press, Oxford
Rodriguez LL, Ghanaim E (2023) From public resources to improving health: how genomic data sharing empowers science and medicine. Genomic Data Sharing:9–29
Schneider G (2019) Disentangling health data networks: a critical analysis of Articles 9(2) and 89 GDPR. Int Data Priv Law 9(4):253–271
Smuha NA, Ahmed-Rengers E, Harkens A et al (2021) How the EU can achieve legally trustworthy AI: a response to the European Commission's Proposal for an Artificial Intelligence Act. Available at SSRN 3899991
Spruit M, Lytras M (2018) Applied data science in patient-centric healthcare: adaptive analytic systems for empowering physicians and patients. Telemat Inform 35(4):643–653
Staunton C, De Vries J (2020) The governance of genomic biobank research in Africa: reframing the regulatory tilt. J Law Biosci 7(1):1–20
Tamar S (2021) Blind-sided by privacy? Digital contact tracing, the Apple/Google API and big tech's newfound role as global health policy makers. Ethics Inf Technol 23(Suppl 1):45–57
Tan S-H, Petrovics G, Srivastava S (2018) Prostate cancer genomics: recent advances and the prevailing underrepresentation from racial and ethnic minorities. Int J Mol Sci 19(4):1255, 1–31
Tarkkala H, Ilpo H, Snell K (2019) From health to wealth: the future of personalized medicine in the making. Futures 109:142–152
Ullah M, Akbar A, Yannarelli GG (2020) Applications of artificial intelligence in early detection of cancer, clinical diagnosis and personalized medicine. Artif Intell Cancer. https://www.wjgnet.com/2644-3228/full/v1/i2/39.htm
Vallor S (2024) The AI Mirror: how to reclaim our humanity in an age of machine thinking. Oxford University Press, Oxford
Vos S, van Delden JJ, van Diest PJ, Bredenoord AL (2017) Moral duties of genomics researchers: why personalized medicine requires a collective approach. Trends Genet 33:118–128
Walker MJ et al (2022) Induced pluripotent stem cell-based systems for personalizing epilepsy treatment: research ethics challenges and new insights for the ethics of personalised medicine. AJOB Neurosci 13(2):120–131
Ward MM (2012) Personalized therapeutics: a potential threat to health equity. J Gen Intern Med 27:868–870
Wilkinson MD, Dumontier M, Aalbersberg IJJ et al (2016) The FAIR Guiding Principles for scientific data management and stewardship. Sci Data 3:1–9

Data Altruism Consent: A Move Forward Towards the Creation of a European Health Data Space?

Daniela Spajić

Abstract The social potential associated with using and reusing personal data is immense. Although the General Data Protection Regulation seeks to allow personal data, such as healthcare data, to be re-used for the public interest, the full potential of this regulation has not yet been realized. In fact, maximizing the common good that can be extracted from such information required new and additional legal frameworks. The Data Governance Act was the first piece of EU legislation established to support data sharing across sectors. An important cornerstone of this regulation is that it supports data sharing for altruistic purposes through a "data altruism consent form". This instrument aims to foster data sharing by improving trust in individuals and businesses to voluntarily share their data. The Data Governance Act, and in particular this data altruism consent, is also playing a pivotal role in creating a European health data space—a space that should serve as a rich data resource for improving healthcare. This chapter therefore investigates the concept of data altruism consent from a legislative perspective—the goal being to outline the legal challenges associated with providing consent. The chapter begins by explaining how this new concept has been established under the Data Governance Act, after which I discuss its application in the European health data space and how the consent interrelates with the newly established European health data space regulation.

1 Introduction

In 2020, the European Commission put forward the proposal for a regulation on European data governance. Seeking to impose a common data governance structure across numerous different sectors, this horizontal regulation, colloquially called the

D. Spajić (✉)
KU Leuven, Centre for IT & IP Law, Leuven, Belgium
e-mail: daniela.spajic@kuleuven.be

F. Casarosa et al. (eds.), *Enabling and Safeguarding Personalized Medicine*, Data Science, Machine Intelligence, and Law 7,
https://doi.org/10.1007/978-3-031-99709-9_3

Data Governance Act (DGA),[1] came into force in 2022 and has been applicable since September 2023. While the DGA pursues multiple aims, an important one to the healthcare sector is to foster data sharing for altruistic purposes based on two facilitators. First, individuals give permission for their data to be shared by providing their consent through a form, known as the "data altruism consent form". Second, registered data intermediaries, called "data altruism organisations", connect individuals and data holders with those who wish to use the data. A data holder is defined as "any legal person, including public sector bodies or international organizations, or a natural person who is not a data subject with respect to the specific data in question, which, in accordance with applicable Union or national law, has the right to grant access to or share certain personal or non-personal data".[2] Meanwhile, a data user is "a natural or legal person who has lawful access to certain personal and non-personal data and has the right, including under Regulation (EU) 2016/679 in the case of personal data, to use that data for commercial or non-commercial purposes".[3]

Data altruism consent is one of the cornerstones in the creation of the European health data space. The goal is to create a platform where individuals can authorize the use of their electronic health data for primary or secondary purposes. According to the European Health Data Space regulation (EHDS),[4] electronic health data includes both non-personal and personal data for instance from electronic health records, genetic data, and health data from biobanks.[5] The DGA lays out the ground rules for the creation of various data spaces, which subsequently support the creation of the EHDS as a sector-specific framework for re-using patient data to support healthcare. However, the DGA does raise some questions over consent in terms of how that consent relates to the General Data Protection Regulation (GDPR),[6] which is Europe's leading data protection framework. Additionally, since the DGA lays the foundation for establishing various data spaces in Europe, it not only carries the issue of ambiguity between the DGA and the GDPR (e.g., in relation to the definition of consent that appears to contradict each other in both legislations) into the forthcoming regulations over a European health data space but also creates additional issues given the overlaps between all three pieces of legislation—the DGA, the GDPR, and the EHDS.

---

[1] Regulation (EU) 2022/868 of the European Parliament and of the Council of 30 May 2022 on European data governance and amending Regulation (EU) 2018/1724 (Data Governance Act) PE/85/2021/REV/1, OJ L 152, 3.6.2022, pp. 1–44.

[2] DGA Article 2(8).

[3] DGA Article 2(9).

[4] Regulation (EU) 2025/327 of the European Parliament and of the Council of 11 February 2025 on the European Health Data Space and amending Directive 2011/24/EU and Regulation (EU) 2024/2847, PE/76/2024/REV/1, OJ L, 2025/327, 5.3.2025.

[5] EHDS Articles 2(2)(a–c), 51.

[6] Regulation (EU) 2016/679 of the European Parliament and of the Council of 27 April 2016 on the protection of natural persons with regard to the processing of personal data and on the free movement of such data, and repealing Directive 95/46/EC, OJ L 119, 4.5.2016, pp. 1–88.

With the aim of exploring if and to what extent data altruism consent might contribute to a successful European health data space, this chapter discusses the legal intricacies at play between the DGA, the GDPR, and the EHDS. In the next section (Sect. 2), I outline the key elements in the DGA that underpin this issue while focusing on data altruism consent as a mediator for improving the quality of healthcare, research, and overall public health. Next, I explore the legal challenges associated with data altruism consent given the existing consent requirements in the GDPR (Sect. 3). Since the GDPR constitutes the guiding law over data protection, these challenges can also be linked to the EHDS legislation, which builds upon the GDPR even though it creates a self-standing legal basis for accessing electronic health data for secondary purposes.[7] Finally, I examine the potential challenges arising from data altruism consent in the specific context of the EHDS (Sect. 4).

2 The Definition of Data Altruism

Europe's push to create a common data altruism consent form is an exercise in increasing trust with the individuals who have data to share. The idea underpinning these various data spaces is that people should contribute their data freely, voluntarily and without reward so as to achieve loftier objectives associated with the general public interest and to benefit human kind.[8] Thus, these spaces provide data holders with transparent information about how and who is accessing their data as a means of building trust. They also make any data not directly stored by the citizen more easily accessible by the data users.[9] Notably, although the DGA outlines a universal consent form, this form is meant to be adapted to suit each desired sector.[10]

2.1 Data Altruism as Outlined in the DGA

The original proposal[11] for the DGA before it was enacted defined data altruism as "consent by data subjects", which gave the impression that this new piece of legislation was trying to introduce a new, much broader concept of consent than that established under the GDPR. However, the definition established in the final text in Article 2(16) of DGA specifies data altruism as the voluntary sharing of data on the basis of consent. Importantly, the DGA suggests consent as an adequate legal basis for not just data processing in general but also for processing data for scientific

[7] EHDS Recital 52, Article 53.

[8] European Commission (2024).

[9] European Commission (2020).

[10] DGA Recital 52.

[11] European Commission (2020).

research based on data altruism.[12] The wording of the final DGA illustrates more clearly the reference to consent as established in Article 4(11) of the GDPR in conjunction with Article 2(5) of the DGA. Although, that said, there are still some legal ambiguities with this definition, as I will show later in the chapter.

According to Article 2(16) of DGA, data altruism means:

> The voluntary sharing of data on the basis of the consent of data subjects to process personal data pertaining to them, or permissions of data holders to allow the use of their non-personal data without seeking or receiving a reward that goes beyond compensation related to the costs that they incur where they make their data available for objectives of general interest as provided for in national law, where applicable, such as healthcare, combating climate change, improving mobility, facilitating the development, production and dissemination of official statistics, improving the provision of public services, public policy making or scientific research purposes in the general interest.

Data altruism is per se not an entirely new concept to Europe's existing data protection frameworks. The GDPR considers reasons for data processing that serve the general idea of the common good, including scientific research and the public interest in public health.[13] More importantly, data controllers processing personal data for altruistic purposes have to comply with the GDPR, particularly because the DGA does not establish a new legal basis for consent, and therefore its altruistic consent does not constitute a self-standing legal basis for processing personal data.[14] In fact, Article 1(3) of the DGA confirms that it operates without prejudice to the GDPR and that, in the event of a conflict between both legislations, the GDPR prevails. In spite of this, the subordination of the DGA vis-à-vis the GDPR has still implications on the consent.[15,16]

2.2 *General Interest: An Extensive Concept*

The notion of "general interest" is a broad notion. Hence, it should not come as a surprise that it is used in many different legal domains. The concept, often used in civil law and consumer protection, has also been used to refer to matters of public health and healthcare.[17] At the EU level, services of general interest are divided into three groups, i.e., economic, non-economic, and social interests (which can be both

---

[12] DGA Recital 50, which suggests relying on GDPR Articles 6(1)(a) and 9(2)(a) and in compliance with GDPR Articles 7 and 8 for the processing of personal data and special categories of personal data respectively.

[13] Spajić (2023).

[14] DGA Article 1(3).

[15] GDPR Articles 6–7 and 9.

[16] Chassang and Feriol (2024).

[17] Directive 2006/123/EC of the European Parliament and of the Council of 12 December 2006 on services in the internal market, OJ L 376, 27.12.2006, pp. 36–68, Recital 7; European Commission (2017).

economic and non-economic in nature).[18] Services of general interest, no matter their nature, are defined as those addressing the vital needs of citizens in their everyday lives.[19]

The notion of "general interest" manifests itself as an overarching notion that encompasses more than the public interest. The concept of general interest partially overlaps with the concept of public interest, but not all matters of general interest are in the public interest, since general interest can cover both commercial and noncommercial interests. The term public interest typically refers to matters that are in the interest of the many, meaning the interest of the public, versus that of one or a few individuals.[20] European jurisprudence as enacted by the Court of Justice of the European Union also recognizes the notion of public interest as a multifaced concept, encompassing public policy, public health, and more.[21]

However, the notion of general interest as referred to in Article 2(16) of the DGA seems closer to the notion of the public interest at least in terms of its listed objectives of general interest. The provision mentions several different overarching purposes to serve the community, including improving healthcare, combating climate change, and improving public services. Moreover, the Article also appears to narrow the scope of application for scientific research by referring to "scientific research in the general interest" as one of the potential altruistic objectives that Member States could pursue. That said, for the processing of personal data for scientific research under the GDPR, Recital 159 clarified that the notion of "scientific research" should be interpreted broadly covering both publicly and privately funded research. Regardless, the concept of scientific research has been subject to debate,[22] which has sometimes been considered an impediment to research. What types of research one can hold up and definitely claim as being scientific research in the general interest are yet to be determined.

Notably, in the initial proposal for the DGA,[23] the terms "common good", "data altruism", and "general interest" were used interchangeably. However, without providing further explanation, the term common good was eventually removed from the final text. Chapter IV of the DGA outlines several requirements when processing personal data based on data altruism, but it does not include a clear legal definition for the term general interest. Rather, it simply provides a few examples of areas for national legislators to determine which areas could be considered to fall into the general interest—of which healthcare is one. It is therefore up to each Member State

[18] Ibid.

[19] Lenaerts (2012).

[20] Weber (2022).

[21] See, for instance, European Court of Justice (2017) Case of Peter Puškár v. Finančné riaditeľstvo Slovenskej republiky, Kriminálny úrad finančnej správy, C-73/16, ECLI:EU:C:2017:725, Judgement. 2017.

[22] See, for instance, European Data Protection Supervisor (2020), p. 23; Slokenberga (2021).

[23] European Commission (2020).

how to fill the notion of "objective of general interest".[24] Different Member States may each develop different interpretations, which could have a significant impact on cross-border data sharing.[25] Thus, it will ultimately fall to the data altruism organizations to ensure any research activity for which data are shared meets the requirements outlined in Articles 18 and 22 of the DGA. In addition, these organizations will, all on their own, need to engender "trust that the data made available for altruistic purposes is serving an objective of general interest".[26] Complying with requirements, specifically that data altruism organizations are both not-for-profit and fully transparent, should help to foster some amount of trust.[27] But still, intermediaries that operate altruistically but which may not be officially registered as data altruism organizations could populate the landscape, muddying the waters.[28]

Fortunately, the idea of data altruism is also found in the GDPR, which constitutes the guiding data protection legislation at the European Union level. This is because the GDPR integrates purposes that serve the overarching objective of the general interest since it enables data processing for scientific research or for public interest in public health. At the national level, some Member States have adopted legislation that allows personal and health data to be reused for the common good. For instance, Germany has enacted the Patient Data Protection Act,[29] which is an amending law enabling patients to consent to the donation of their health data from their electronic medical records for research purposes. Similarly, the German Corona data-donation app[30] developed by the German public health authority, the Robert-Koch Institute, is an example of altruistic data sharing, encompassing the transmission of information about one's heart rate and sleeping behavior through a fitness wristband or smartwatch.[31]

As per Article 16 of the DGA, Member States can establish national policies for data altruism designed to help individuals that, first, makes any of their personal data held by a public body voluntarily available for altruistic data sharing and, second, notifies individuals about how their data are being re-used in the general interest.

[24] See DGA Article 18(b).

[25] European Commission (2024).

[26] DGA Recital 46.

[27] Ibid.

[28] Ibid.

[29] Patient Data Protection Act (2020) (Gesetz zum Schutz elektronischer Patientendaten in der Telematikinfrastructure (Patientendaten-Schutz-Gesetz-PDSG)), 19.10.2020, BGBl. 2020 I Nr. 46, p. 2115) (Germany). Available at: https://www.bundesgesundheitsministerium.de/patientendaten-schutz-gesetz.html?advnr=5307999&cHash=65c6a31e0fd1723a01ec1b1cc03224d5.

[30] Brockmann (2024).

[31] Spajić (2021); data.europa.eu (2022).

3 Ambiguities in the Concept of Data Altruism Consent Arising from the Relation Between the DGA and the GDPR

Consent has legal significance in Europe's data protection frameworks as they pertain to medicine, constituting an act of enforcement of a person's free will.[32] Under the GDPR, consent to the processing of personal data is composed of four essential requirements: consent must be freely given, specific, informed and unambiguous.[33] Many have debated the demands on consent as a concept and the technical transposition of its requirements.[34] Moreover, there have been pleas to adopt more flexible approaches to the requirements of specific and informed consent, such as dynamic consent[35] and broad consent.[36] In particular, broad consent has been put forward as an approach that could be supported by the GDPR, and more specifically by Recital 33, which appears to provide some flexibility in terms of the "specificity" requirement. The Recital considers that it may not always be possible to determine the purpose of all data processing operations at the time the data are collected. The objective of broad consent is therefore to enable the future, yet not foreseeable, processing and sharing without having to re-request consent from individuals over and over again.[37]

The specificity requirement is closely related to the purpose limitation principle. Therefore, even broad consent would necessitate some degree of specificity as to the general area of a research project or, at the least, a high-level description of it in order to be able to rely on broad consent.[38] The European Data Protection Supervisor stresses that Recital 33 does not rule out the consent requirements laid out in Articles 4(11), 6(1)(a), 7 and 9(2)(a) of the GDPR. Hence, suppose it is not possible to specify the purposes of the research. In such cases, the data controller would be obliged to "carefully evaluate the rights of the data subject, the sensitivity of the data, the nature and purpose of the research and the relevant ethical standards". They would also need "to ensure the essence of the data subject's right to valid consent" through transparency and other safeguards.[39] By contrast, data altruism consent under the DGA applies to any objective of general interest that is provided for in national law, including, amongst other things, healthcare.[40] Notably, Recital 52 DGA stipulates that the European data altruism consent form should contribute

[32] Mantovani and Quinn (2014).

[33] GDPR Article 4(11), 6(a).

[34] Lähteenoja et al. (2024).

[35] Budin-Ljøsne et al. (2017); European Data Protection Board (2020).

[36] Hallinan (2020).

[37] Mikkelsen et al. (2019).

[38] European Data Protection Board (2021).

[39] European Data Protection Supervisor (2020).

[40] DGA Article 2(16).

to additional transparency for data subjects, and enable the granting and withdrawal of consent to streamline data altruism. Notably, this type of consent is different from broad consent in that it suggests escaping the need to determine the concrete project for which the data can be used at the time of the data collection. In the context of the European health data space, it may even be up to the health data access bodies to decide which projects get access to the data and for which altruistic reasons.[41]

Yet, Article 2(5) DGA refers its definition of consent to Article 4(11) GDPR and Recital 50 DGA stipulates that data altruism consent will rely on the meaning of consent founded under the GDPR as per Article 6(1)(a) and Article 9(2)(a), respectively for the processing of personal data and special categories of personal data. Thus, data altruism consent creates challenges in terms of the specificity requirement and ultimately the purpose limitation principle as per Article 5(1)(b) GDPR which requires that the data is collected for specified, explicit and legitimate purposes. This leads to a collision between the requirements established under the DGA and the consent requirements of the GDPR.

Further, data altruism consent can create challenges with regard to data minimization and data quality.[42] Article 5(1)(c) of the GDPR requires that only personal data that is adequate, relevant, and limited to what is necessary to achieve the purposes at hand should be processed. When giving altruistic consent, the specific processing activities for which the data will be used are generally not fully clarified at the time of the data collection. Individuals therefore may provide consent for a variety of altruistic purposes without knowing the envisaged transactions for which their data will be used. If no specificity of purpose is given at the time of collection, it is difficult to assess whether the data collected are actually "adequate and necessary" for processing under altruistic consent. One possibility for addressing these issues with data minimization could be to process the data in anonymized form.[43] Also, where data anonymization may reduce data quality and data accuracy, applying pseudonymization techniques like encryption could mitigate some of the privacy risks associated with processing personal data.[44]

Another point of contention between the two pieces of legislation is data accuracy. Depending on where the data is stored, the principle of data accuracy laid down in Article 5(1)(d) GDPR may be challenged. This will depend particularly on the role of the intermediary, namely whether a data altruism organization stores the data or whether the data remains in the premises of the data provider like a hospital storing patients' medical files so that the intermediary constitutes rather a connecting service between the data provider and the data user. While data providers will regularly have to comply with the GDPR and thus the data accuracy principle, the principle may be difficult to uphold if the data is transferred to and stored at the premises of the data altruism organization or another data space. A patient's health

[41] EHDS Article 57(1)(a).

[42] Chassang and Feriol (2024).

[43] EDPB-EDPS (2022).

[44] Zerdick (2021).

condition can change over time and if the shared data is not kept up-to-date, this may lead to incomplete datasets.

4 Altruistic Consent and Its Relation to the Secondary Use of Health Data Under the EHDS Regulation

The EHDS regulation supports the primary and secondary use of electronic health record data. Thus, it should not come as a surprise that this legislation also considers the data altruism consent established under the DGA. Data altruism aims to improve healthcare by sharing electronic health data, both personal and non-personal,[45] for "secondary" use, where secondary use refers to using data for any purpose set out in Chapter IV of the EHDS, other than for the initial purpose the data were collected or produced for.[46] However, the exact role of data altruism organizations as laid out within the EHDS appears somewhat elusive. Some provisions explain the role of data altruism organizations and how they foster data sharing. Specifically, Article 73(4) of the EHDS indicates that recognized data altruism organizations may process electronic health data using a secure processing environment, whereas Article 89(4) of the EHDS stipulates that a data altruism organization can provide international governments access to non-personal electronic health data. Further, Recital 78 of the EHDS lays out that health data access bodies should cooperate with competent authorities as per the DGA to supervise the activities of data altruism organizations in the healthcare sector. According to the EHDS, personal electronic health data includes electronic health and genetic data as defined in Articles 4(13) and (15) of the GDPR.[47] Non-personal electronic health data means data other than personal electronic health data, encompassing both data that has been anonymized so that it no longer relates to an identified or identifiable person and data that has never been related to a data subject.[48] Secondary use is defined as the processing of electronic health data for purposes set out in Chapter IV of the EHDS regulation, other than the initial purpose for which they were collected or produced.[49]

To this end, electronic health data for the purposes set out in Chapter IV of the EHDS will be collected by default. Meanwhile, individuals will generally maintain the right to opt-out of their data being used for the secondary use of their data. Article 51 of the EHDS lists the minimum categories of electronic health data that ought to be collected, including, for instance, data from electronic health records (e.g., patient summaries or electronic prescriptions),[50] data on factors impacting on

[45] EHDS Article 2(2)(c).

[46] EHDS Article 2(2)(e).

[47] EHDS Article 2(2)(a).

[48] EHDS Article 2(2)(b).

[49] EHDS Article 2(2)(e).

[50] EHDS Annex I.

health, and human genetic, epigenomic, or genomic data. Therefore, re-using these types of data for a range of purposes should be possible. Chapter IV of the EHDS lists multiple reasons justifying the secondary use of electronic health data for purposes in the public interest and, particularly, in the areas of public and occupational health and scientific research related to the health and care sectors. In this way, the European health data space promises to create a space for electronic health data that can be shared between health data holders and the potential users of those. A health data holder can be a natural or legal person, public authority or other body in the healthcare or the care sector who has either the right or obligation to process personal electronic health data for the certain purposes such as the provision of healthcare or public health in its capacity as a (joint) controller, or who has the ability to make available non-personal electronic health data through control of the technical design of a product or related service.[51] A health data user, on the other hand, is defined as a natural or legal person which has been granted lawful access to electronic health data for secondary use pursuant to a data permit, data request or an access approval by an authorized participant in Health Data @EU.[52] How the health data space is going to technically operate at a national level, however, is not entirely clear.

Additionally, Chapter IV of the EHDS regulates that data altruism organizations can provide access to the health data they store based on the data altruism consent provided by individuals.[53] For instance, a health data access body or a data altruism organization may provide international governments access to the minimum permissible amount of non-personal electronic health data.[54] However, the definition established for secondary use, meaning data processing for a purpose other than for which it was initially collected or produced, appears to be at odds with the data altruism consent. If consent was given while the purpose of use was unclear, then consent evaporates. Moreover, if the consent specifically aims to contribute to the European health data space, then sharing or using the data does not constitute secondary use as altruistic consent lays the foundation for sharing the data. By doing so, data altruism consent frames the boundaries within which the data included in the EHDS can be used for secondary (altruistic) purposes.

Article 40 of the original EHDS draft[55] put forward by the European Commission incorporated a provision dedicated to data altruism in healthcare. The provision foresaw that data altruism organizations processing personal electronic health data should comply with the rules set out in Chapter IV of the DGA,[56] leaving room for interpretation concerning the interplay between Article 40 of the EHDS proposal

[51] EHDS Article 2(2)(t)(i-ii).

[52] EHDS Article 2(2)(u).

[53] DGA Article 2(16).

[54] EHDS Article 89(4).

[55] European Commission (2022).

[56] European Commission (2022), EHDS proposal Article 40(1).

and the DGA.[57] Interestingly, the provision of Article 40 dedicated to data altruism in health is missing in the text of the corrigendum[58] and the final text, but the text still accounts for it.[59] Health data access bodies, which are bodies holding a supervising and guiding role in transposing the vision of a European health data space under this framework,[60] shall cooperate with data altruism national competent bodies[61] and supervise the activities of data altruism organizations in the health or care sector.[62] Recognized data altruism organizations processing electronic health data must comply with the necessary security measures using a secure processing environment.[63] Furthermore, and most importantly, the regulation clarifies that the DGA sets out the general rules for managing data altruism, while additional criteria need to be established for applying data altruism to healthcare given that the data collected is so sensitive.[64] Such additional criteria, which have yet to be determined, will be established through the rulebook foreseen in Article 22 of the DGA and may require further investigation in terms of the interrelationship between the DGA and the EHDS framework.

In this context, the sensitive nature of electronic health data that is shared within the European health data space must be accounted for. Even though the DGA sets out the general requirements for data altruism consent, these requirements may not be aligned with the purpose that the EHDS seeks to achieve. Data altruism consent, as discussed above, includes various purposes of general interest that cannot be identified exhaustively in the legislation. Hence, any data shared could possibly be accessed by private or public stakeholders. The purpose of Europe's health data space is to improve healthcare—this being a sensitive sector that collects delicate patient information. This type of information is typically subject to strict access requirements. Still, in the context of the EHDS, private actors could make a request for data.[65] By indulging stakeholders who do not necessarily have to demonstrate a professional link to the healthcare sector, the wide definition of data altruism might intensify the issue and challenge a patient's right to medical confidentiality, which is a pivotal cornerstone for guaranteeing trust in medicine.[66]

Despite the concept of data altruism appearing to be broader than the purposes covered under the EHDS, the DGA also neglects that the GDPR does not require relying on consent as a legal basis for all altruistic reasons. The (re-)use of special categories of personal data, such as health data, is exempt from the general

[57] EDPB-EDPS (2022), para. 97.

[58] European Parliament (2024) Corrigendum.

[59] E.g., EHDS Article 2(1)(c); DGA Article 2(16), Article 57(2)(c); EHDS Article 73(4).

[60] EHDS Article 57.

[61] EHDS Article 57(2)(c).

[62] EHDS Recital 78.

[63] EHDS Article 73(4), (1)(a-f).

[64] EHDS Recital 78.

[65] Terzis (2022), p. 354; Spajić (2025).

[66] Spajić (2025).

processing prohibition according to Article 9(1) of the GDPR, for instance, if data processing is necessary for reasons of public interest in the area of public health[67] or scientific research.[68] Recital 53 of the GDPR stresses that special categories of personal data should be processed for health-related purposes only where necessary to achieve those purposes for the benefit of natural persons and society as a whole. Also, the text of the EHDS takes this into account in that it covers limitations to opting-out of secondary data use. More specifically, Member States may integrate exceptions to an opt-out consent at the national level for reasons referred to in Article 53(1)(a-c) of the EHDS. These reasons include public interests in the area of public and occupational health, policy making and regulatory activities, statistics related to the health or care sectors, and for scientific research done for important reasons of public interest by public sector bodies.[69] Leaving aside the potential fragmentation arising from integrating opt-out mechanisms at a national level, an opt-out approach subject to certain limitations may be preferable in consideration of some ethical streams.[70]

Overall, it is currently unclear how any data collected under the premise of data altruism consent could be used for secondary purposes based on the compatibility clause applicable to the further processing of personal data. This question occurs because of Recital 50 of the DGA, which refers to the compatibility clause of Article 5(1)(b) GDPR without further clarification. According to the compatibility presumption, further processing for scientific research purposes should not be deemed incompatible with the initial purposes for which the data were originally collected. The presumption applies only if adequate safeguards as per Article 89(1) GDPR are respected when processing personal data further for scientific research.[71] Nonetheless, if national legislation permits healthcare providers to process data concerning health so as to provide care, the provider would still need to identify an exemption as per Article 9(2) of the GDPR in order to process health data for scientific research.[72]

5 Conclusion: Does Altruistic Consent Constitute a Move Towards Creating a European Health Data Space?

This analysis of this chapter illustrates that the data altruism consent established under the DGA may not yet be fully equipped to help create a trustworthy European health data space. The notion of general interest is broad and unclear and, therefore,

[67] GDPR Article 9(2)(i).

[68] GDPR Article 9(2)(j).

[69] EHDS Article 71(4).

[70] Vedder and Spajić (2023).

[71] European Data Protection Board (2021).

[72] European Data Protection Board (2021).

requires further specification. Additionally, the specification of the notion of general interest at the national level are likely to lead to fragmented approaches across the EU countries. It remains to be seen how this ambiguity will affect cross-border data sharing if one EU country justifies collecting data for a reason not covered by another state's general interest.

In terms of altruistic consent, the EHDS refers to the DGA which, in turn, refers to the GDPR to outline the requirements of consent. This legislative chain indicates that the GDPR sets out the main consent requirements and that the DGA does not create a separate legal basis but that it specifies the (altruistic) reasons for which data can be collected.[73] However, as presented in this chapter, the concept of data altruism creates multiple legal challenges. Just two examples include data minimization and the purpose limitation principle, which are carried into the EHDS regulation. Thus, creating adequate consent mechanisms[74] that mitigate these issues is key.

Additionally, there is a misalignment of interests concerning the application of data altruism consent in the healthcare context through the same legislative triangle. Specifically, the broad definition of data altruism established under the DGA could possibly open the door to the use of electronic health data for commercial players which may sit in contrast with the use of sensitive patient data. In the context of healthcare, the concept of data altruism needs to be re-aligned so as to meet the motivating values of the European health data space. Eventually, this leads to subsequent questions of fairness, namely whether altruistic data sharing, as envisaged under the DGA, is truly altruistic if stakeholders can leverage financial revenues from data that others have donated for free. One could argue that the value does not stem from the data itself but the way it is processed and analyzed. At the same time, however, innovation is not possible without data. Rather, both data and innovation are inextricably linked as one is not possible without the other, raising questions of reciprocity.

Acknowledgement The research for this article was, in part, undertaken as part of a project that received funding from the European Union's Horizon 2020 research and innovation program under the Marie Skłodowska-Curie Grant Agreement No 814177 and the European Union's Horizon Europe research and innovation program under Grant Agreement No 101095717. This research was also financially supported by the "Biorobotics Research and Innovation Engineering Facilities" "IR0000036" – CUP J13C22000400007 (BRIEF) project. The views and opinions expressed are those of the author(s) only and do not necessarily reflect those of the European Union or the Health and Digital Executive Agency. Neither the European Union nor the granting authority can be held responsible for them.

[73] EDPB-EDPS (2021).

[74] Lähteenoja et al. (2024).

References

Brockmann D (2024) Corona Data Donation Project | News & Analyses. [cited 2024 Jul 4]. Corona Data Donation Project | News & Analyses. Available at: https://corona-datenspende.github.io/en/

Budin-Ljøsne I, Teare HJA, Kaye J et al (2017) Dynamic consent: a potential solution to some of the challenges of modern biomedical research. BMC Med Ethics 18(1):4

Chassang G, Feriol L (2024) Data altruism, personal health data and the consent challenge in scientific research. Eur Data Prot Law Rev 10(1):57–68

data.europa.eu (2022) Data portals and the Data Governance Act [cited 2024 Jul 4]. Available at: https://data.europa.eu/en/publications/datastories/data-portals-and-data-governance-act

EDPB-EDPS (2021) EDPB-EDPS Joint Opinion 03/2021 on the Proposal for a regulation of the European Parliament and of the Council on European data governance (Data Governance Act). Version 1.1. Available at: https://www.edpb.europa.eu/system/files/2021-03/edpb-edps_joint_opinion_dga_en.pdf

EDPB-EDPS (2022) EDPB-EDPS Joint Opinion 03/2022 on the Proposal for a Regulation on the European Health Data Space. Available at: https://www.edpb.europa.eu/our-work-tools/our-documents/edpbedps-joint-opinion/edpb-edps-joint-opinion-032022-proposal_en

European Commission (2017) Services of general interest - Find out what services of general interest are and what the EU does to ensure citizens have access to them. Available at: https://commission.europa.eu/topics/single-market/services-general-interest_en

European Commission (2020) Proposal for a Regulation of the European Parliament and of the Council on European data governance (Data Governance Act (DGA) proposal) COM/2020/767 final

European Commission (2022) Proposal for a Regulation of the European Parliament and of the Council on the European Health Data Space (EHDS proposal). Available at: https://eur-lex.europa.eu/legal-content/EN/TXT/?uri=CELEX%3A52022PC0197

European Commission (2024) New practical guide to the Data Governance Act | Shaping Europe's digital future. Available at: https://digital-strategy.ec.europa.eu/en/library/new-practical-guide-data-governance-act

European Data Protection Board (2020) Guidelines 05/2020 on consent under Regulation 2016/679. Version 1.1. Adopted 4 May 2020. Available at: https://www.edpb.europa.eu/our-work-tools/our-documents/guidelines/guidelines-052020-consent-under-regulation-2016679_en

European Data Protection Board (2021) EDPB Document on response to the request from the European Commission for clarifications on the consistent application of the GDPR, focusing on health research. Adopted on 2 February 2021. Available at: https://www.edpb.europa.eu/sites/default/files/files/file1/edpb_replyec_questionnaireresearch_final.pdf

European Data Protection Supervisor (2020) A Preliminary Opinion on data protection and scientific research. Available at: https://www.edps.europa.eu/sites/default/files/publication/20-01-06_opinion_research_en.pdf

European Parliament (2024) CORRIGENDUM to the position of the European Parliament adopted at first reading on 24 April 2024 with a view to the adoption of Regulation (EU) 2024/... of the European Parliament and of the Council on the European Health Data Space P9_TA(2024)0331 (COM(2022)0197 – C9-0167/2022 – 2022/0140(COD))COR01_EN. Available at: https://www.europarl.europa.eu/meetdocs/2024_2029/plmrep/COMMITTEES/ENVI/DV/2024/12-04/2022_0140COR01_EN.pdf

Hallinan D (2020) Broad consent under the GDPR: an optimistic perspective on a bright future. Life Sci Soc Policy 16(1):1

Lähteenoja V, Himanen J, Turpeinen M et al (2024) JRC Publications Repository The landscape of consent management tools – a data altruism perspective. Available at: https://publications.jrc.ec.europa.eu/repository/handle/JRC137572

Lenaerts K (2012) Defining the concept of 'services of general interest' in light of the 'checks and balances' set out in the EU treaties. Jurisprudence 19(4):1247–1267

Mantovani E, Quinn P (2014) mHealth and data protection – the letter and the spirit of consent legal requirements. Int Rev Law Comput Technol 28(2):222–236

Mikkelsen RB, Gjerris M, Waldemar G et al (2019) Broad consent for biobanks is best – provided it is also deep. BMC Med Ethics 20(1):71

Slokenberga S (2021) Setting the foundations: individual rights, public interest, scientific research and biobanking. In: Slokenberga S, Tzortzatou O, Reichel J (eds) GDPR and Biobanking. Law, Governance and Technology Series, vol 43. Springer, Cham. https://doi.org/10.1007/978-3-030-49388-2_2

Spajić D (2021) CiTiP blog. The German corona-data-donation-app as an example of the concept of data donation. Available at: https://www.law.kuleuven.be/citip/blog/the-german-corona-data-donation-app-as-an-example-of-the-concept-of-data-donation/

Spajić D (2023) Patient data sharing for the improvement of healthcare and medical research: towards a moral duty of patients to share health-related data?, PhD dissertation, defended on 18 April 2023, KU Leuven

Spajić D (2025) Transforming the secondary use of patient data in the European health data space: a challenge for the patient's right to medical confidentiality? In: Slokenberga S, Ó Cathaoir K, Shabani M (eds) The European health data space: examining a new ear in data protection. Routledge. https://doi.org/10.4324/9781003544111-7

Terzis P (2022) Compromises and asymmetries in the European health data space. Eur J Health Law 30(3):345–363

Vedder A, Spajić D (2023) Moral autonomy of patients and legal barriers to a possible duty of health related data sharing. Ethics Inf Technol 25(1):23

Weber K (2022) Öffentliches Interesse. In: Weber, Rechtswörterbuch, 28th Edition 2022. C. H. Beck Verlag, München

Zerdick T (2021) Pseudonymous data: processing personal data while mitigating risks | European Data Protection Supervisor. Available at: https://www.edps.europa.eu/press-publications/press-news/blog/pseudonymous-data-processing-personal-data-while-mitigating

One Form to Rule Them All: Towards a Personalized, But Standardized, European Data Altruism Consent Form

Arianna Rossi

Abstract Data altruism is a novel concept established by the Data Governance Act that aims to increase the availability of data for purposes that meet the general interests of society. However, realizing this future relies on the data subjects giving their consent to use the data collected. As of this time, little is known about how a European data altruism consent form might allow a transparent, user-friendly, and lawful process for granting and withdrawing consent to the re-using one's personal information. This article therefore explores some of the most pressing legal, design, and technical challenges that need to be addressed to enable a trustworthy exchange of data and consent permissions. Given that decisions about whether one's data can be used mostly depend on personal and contextual factors, I argue for the implementation of dynamic consent with standardized, interoperable semantic specifications used as viable means to personalizing consent. This would be the most lawful and efficient way to support individual autonomy.

1 The Value of Data Sharing for Altruistic Purposes

In an era where data silos and data monopolies are deprecated due to the concentration of the knowledge and power they engender, the European Union is seeking to counter this tendency by encouraging its citizens to share their data in an effort to boost innovation, optimize public services, and improve public policies. The underlying reasoning is simple, yet powerful: if organizations, especially public organizations, are spending resources to gather data in the wake of digitalization, why shouldn't this data be made available and re-used to create actionable knowledge? Among the various legislative initiatives that seek to break down the barriers to data exchange, the concept of sharing data for purposes of general interest has received

A. Rossi (✉)
LIDER-Lab, DIRPOLIS, Sant'Anna School of Advanced Studies, Pisa, Italy
e-mail: Arianna.Rossi@santannapisa.it

F. Casarosa et al. (eds.), *Enabling and Safeguarding Personalized Medicine*, Data Science, Machine Intelligence, and Law 7,
https://doi.org/10.1007/978-3-031-99709-9_4

renewed attention. To this end, the Data Governance Act (DGA)[1] has established the concept of data altruism, defined as "the voluntary sharing of data on the basis of the consent of data subjects to process personal data pertaining to them … without seeking or receiving a reward that goes beyond compensation related to the costs that they incur where they make their data available for objective of general interest as provided for in national law, where applicable, such as healthcare, [...] improving the provision of public services, public policy making or scientific research purposes in the general interest".[2] Note that, because this article only focuses on the consent to share personal data for altruistic purposes in the context of healthcare, I have omitted irrelevant parts of the definition. For example, I will not touch on the conditions for processing and reusing non-personal data because it is outside of the scope of this contribution, even though non-personal data may include personal data that has been anonymized.

In particular, healthcare and health research are domains where more data could have a great impact on societal welfare. Yet, in practice, progress is hampered by a multitude of different legal, technical, data management, and trust issues.[3] The Corona Data Donation project[4] typifies the groundbreaking potential of data altruism. This project, launched by researchers during the early phases of the COVID-19 outbreak, took the form of a mobile application which collected the data of over half a million German residents for 2.5 years through their wearable devices. The data captured included the users' resting heart rates, daily step counts, and sleep duration under normal conditions. These data were then used as a baseline for comparison against algorithmically identified systematic deviations. Thus, the researchers were able to infer indicators of the virus's onset, such drops in a subject's daily step count coupled with a simultaneous rise in their resting pulse. Interestingly, those data have since been used to compute the effectiveness of vaccinations over both the short and long terms.[5] Hence, from data that were scarce or even non-existent at the time, scientists were able to derive incredibly useful information, including real-time patterns of the pandemic's spread, evidence of the efficacy of self-administered tests, and, together with some survey data, newfound insights on the social factors that influence protective behavior.[6] Such information can be transformed into actionable knowledge, like advancing scientific research; producing, developing, and disseminating statistics; promoting evidence-based policymaking; and improving public healthcare services.

All of the laudable activities have been enabled by the voluntary sharing of sensor data and coincide with the "purposes of general interest" as mentioned in the

[1] Regulation (EU) 2022/868 of the European Parliament and of the Council of 30 May 2022 on European data governance and amending Regulation (EU) 2018/1724 (Data Governance Act) PE/85/2021/REV/1, OJ L 152, 3.6.2022, pp. 1–44.

[2] DGA, Article 2(16).

[3] Abboud et al. (2022).

[4] Robert Koch Institute (2025).

[5] Wiedermann et al. (2023).

[6] Corona Datenspende (2025).

definition of data altruism under the DGA. This chapter narrows the scope of data altruism to the benefits that health-related datasets gathered via scientific research studies can bring to personalized medicine, which is more broadly understood as an approach that gears medical treatment to the individual characteristics of human beings.[7] To support the free flow of information, individuals should be able to knowingly determine the permissible reuse of their data for altruistic objectives, i.e., they should be able to give consent to their data's use, while the permissions granted by that consent should be promptly shared and unambiguously interpreted across organizations. Under the legislation, data altruism organizations act as data intermediaries that obviate legal and technical barriers, address the trust issues that hamper data sharing by organizations and individuals, and lower the transaction costs associated with such activities.[8]

Such organizations may in particular support autonomy: the people's ability to help determine the use of information about them represents a fundamental concept in the functioning of modern democratic societies. However, this autonomy is threatened by a rapidly unfolding digital transformation that has, to date, been characterized by uncertain outcomes and secretive goals of exploitation. Today, corporations and nations worldwide are competing for monopolistic data appropriation and far-from-inclusive achievements, while longstanding issues of data misuse by private and public organizations alike persist. The notion of control over one's own data has been chiefly impersonated by consent as a tool for self-determination, which the DGA compounds with a wide array of instruments that supposedly restrain existing imbalances of power. By fostering more horizontal relationships between data subjects, data holders, and data users, and by cultivating more opportunities and means to access and control information, the DGA contributes to more inclusive data governance.[9] Personalizing information and the ability to make choices that respond to idiosyncratic needs may also then support mindful decision-making in line with one's own values.

From the standpoint of promoting voluntary data exchange, the DGA stipulates that the European Commission should develop a European data altruism consent form to allow uniform consent management across its Member States. However, the Commission also needs to lay down the requirements for information transparency towards data subjects prior to their decision to offer consent and for tools for managing a subject's permissions for using their data in a rulebook.[10] Both the consent form and the rulebook should be drafted in consultation with relevant stakeholders.

Within this context, this chapter makes the following contributions to the literature:

---

[7] National Research Council (2011), p. 12.

[8] European Commission (2020).

[9] Micheli et al. (2023), p. 18.

[10] See Article 22 of the DGA.

1) It delineates the scenarios where research organizations and individuals may want to resort to health data altruism as a supplement to the legal obligations established by the European Health Data Space (EHDS) Regulation;[11]
2) It illustrates the complex interplay of consent requirements deriving from the General Data Protection Regulation (GDPR)[12] and the DGA concerning health data collected in research settings that has been shared for altruistic purposes;
3) It identifies and critically discusses some of the challenges that arise from the regulatory framework, as well as the existing hurdles to a user-friendly and lawful implementation of consent; and
4) It examines personalized dynamic consent and semantic web technologies as potential solutions to challenges related to usability, legality, and interoperability.

2 Research Scenario

2.1 The Rise of Data Intermediation and Data Altruism

Even though the benefits of data sharing are evident, many obstacles stand in the way of us realizing a thriving society based on free-flowing information. Barriers to data sharing across organizations include fears that data may be misused, limited technical and cultural know-how, and legal concerns including privacy breaches.[13] Such concerns are particularly understandable when the data include health information. This is why an ecosystem of data intermediaries has flourished, many of which promise to empower individuals and organizations to regain control over the use of their data and direct it towards goals they endorse, instead of hopelessly relinquishing such control to other parties.

One of the concerns of the DGA is to help organize and regulate the conditions under which data intermediaries provide digital services, i.e. the organizations that facilitate data flows between data holders and data users.[14] Currently, data intermediaries offer a broad range of functionalities that inspire the trust necessary for exchanging data. As Schweihoff et al.[15] reports, these functions include:

[11] Regulation (EU) 2025/327 of the European Parliament and of the Council of 11 February 2025 on the European Health Data Space and amending Directive 2011/24/EU and Regulation (EU) 2024/2847 (Text with EEA relevance) PE/76/2024/REV/1 OJ L, 2025/327, 5.3.2025.

[12] Regulation (EU) 2016/679 of the European Parliament and of the Council of 27 April 2016 on the protection of natural persons with regard to the processing of personal data and on the free movement of such data, and repealing Directive 95/46/EC (General Data Protection Regulation) OJ L 119, 4.5.2016, pp. 1–88.

[13] Schweihoff et al. (2024), p. 3.

[14] Schweihoff et al. (2024), p. 4.

[15] Schweihoff et al. (2024).

1) enhancing or ensuring the confidentiality of data; offering a way to encrypt and/or anonymize data; and providing support for legal agreements;
2) enabling data control and regulating access management;
3) providing the necessary infrastructure for exchanging data and standards (like marketplaces, APIs, and connectors);
4) compiling data catalogs that store data securely and make them available;
5) facilitating data governance through security mechanisms and making data processing including data aggregation easier, as well as helping individuals to manage their own data, including via consent management tools;
6) enabling identity management;
7) supporting transactions by connecting actors in the data economy; and
8) establishing data sharing processes with a view to their compliance, customizations, data quality, and data usage policies.

Within the broad landscape of data intermediaries, the DGA envisages two categories of actors: data intermediation services (DISs) and data altruism organizations (DAOs). Data intermediation services are defined as services that aim "to establish commercial relationships for the purposes of data sharing between an undetermined number of data subjects/data holders and data users through technical, legal, or other means, including for the purpose of exercising the rights of data subjects in relation to personal data".[16] Even though the purposes of affording technical, legal or other enablers of data exchange are shared, DISs establish relationships of a commercial nature between data users and data holders, whereas DAOs act for non-for-profit reasons.[17] Although the DGA covers both personal and non-personal data reuse, my focus in this article is on personal information that might be processed conditional to the consents made available by data altruism organizations for altruistic reasons. Noably, DAOs may collect data directly from data subjects, but they can also reuse data collected by others for either their own purposes or those of third parties.[18] In this way, they can assume the role of either data controllers or data processors. With this in mind, one way to support data altruism is to offer the means to easily manage consent permissions that allow certain entities to use these data for specific purposes, as detailed in Sect. 4.

2.2 Applicable Scenarios Where Consent to Health Data Altruism Is Pertinent

It is beyond the scope of this chapter to examine the interplay between the DGA and the recently approved EHDS Regulation. Yet, it is impossible to advance any further in this analysis of consent to health data altruism without delineating the scope of the EHDS and the conditions under which data altruism is meaningful for the reuse

[16] DGA, Article 2(11).

[17] DGA, Article 18(c).

[18] DGA, Recital 50.

of health data. Whereas the DGA delineates a common data governance model that transcends sectorial boundaries, the EHDS Regulation complements such requirements with rules that govern the sharing of health information for primary and secondary purposes. In terms of these secondary purposes, the EHDS Regulation mandates that health data holders with the right or obligation to process electronic health data for the purposes described at Article 1(2)(t)(i), including research and innovation, should make available the data they hold, so that it can be reused for other purposes.[19] Access to such data is subject to the authorization of health data access bodies[20] who may grant it only when the reuse is necessary for a closed list of purposes, including scientific research related to health or care sectors.[21] In other words, any organization dedicated to research and innovation, regardless of whether it is governed by private or public law, may act either as a data holder when it collects electronic health data via its research and innovation activities, or as a data user when it requests authorization to reuse health-related data for scientific research purposes.[22]

Since the availability of health data for reuse is obligatory under these circumstances, the success of the EHDS relies on a legal obligation as the legal basis for data sharing, rather than on consent by the data subjects. If people wish not to have their data processed for secondary purposes, they have the right to opt out.[23] Hence, if all the health-related data collected as part of research studies were made available for further use due to a legal obligation by default, my first analysis would conclude that consent to voluntary data sharing is irrelevant.

However, I can foresee a few scenarios in which consent to health data altruism may still be pertinent:

(i) Until the EHDS Regulation becomes applicable (or more particularly, until the provisions for secondary data use become applicable in 2029 and 2031 depending on the category of data), research organizations may want to resort to data altruism to maximize the accessibility to the data they collect. For instance, these organizations may wish to use the data to bolster open science and meet national policy objectives,[24] respect their funding entities' conditions or participate in self-regulatory activities;[25]

(ii) Similarly, before the 2029–31 horizon, the so-called "health-information altruists"[26] may want to make their data available to contribute to the common welfare, for instance through personal data spaces;

---

[19] EHDS, Article 51.

[20] EHDS, Article 57(1)(a).

[21] See the exact definition of admissible scientific research uses at Article 53(1)(e), EHDS.

[22] Defined very broadly, see Article 51, EHDS.

[23] EHDS, Article 71.

[24] See e.g., the Italian Piano Nazionale per la Scienza Aperta (PNSA), Rossi et al. (2022).

[25] See e.g., the Coalition for Advancing Research Assessment (CoARA), available at: https://coara.eu/.

[26] Kohane and Altman (2005), p. 2075.

(iii) Data subjects may have exercised their right to opt-out granted under the EHDS Regulation, but might still want to make their data available selectively, retaining more granular control, for example by selecting particular organizations that have access;
(iv) As foreseen by Article 16 of the DGA, national policies that put technical or organizational arrangements in place may support the willingness of individual citizens to grant access to their data voluntarily;
(v) Even when the EHDS Regulation becomes applicable, public bodies like research organizations may find it convenient to request or demonstrate consent for data access using DAOs. This would be a convenient way to circumvent the resource issues associated with complying with the DGA. For example, in Italy,[27] the DGA has been aligned to national legislation with a financial invariance clause that does not assign any additional resources for implementing the Act.

3 Consent to Health Data Altruism: Requirements and Challenges

The present analysis predominantly concerns a scenario where a research institution gathers health-related data from research participants who consent to the reuse of data for altruistic purposes. Necessarily, this entails that the research institution passes on the data to a DAO that provides access to data users, as illustrated in Fig. 1. In this scenario, consent needs to abide by several legal requirements deriving from the GDPR and the DGA, which are explained below. Further, this section explains that certain data flows are based on different types of consent with more or less specified purposes. Yet, despite the complexity of these data flows, the data altruism organization must support self-determination in the consent giver through a number of obligations intended to enhance trust. That said, these obligations create several legal, technical, and design challenges which are discussed in greater detail towards the end of this section.

3.1 GDPR Requirements for Consent to Scientific Research

3.1.1 Consent Requirements

Consent should involve an actual choice for the individual, i.e., it should be freely given, and should be tied to a specific purpose. Moreover, consent should be preceded by transparent information that enables informed decision-making and should

[27] Decreto Legislativo (2024).

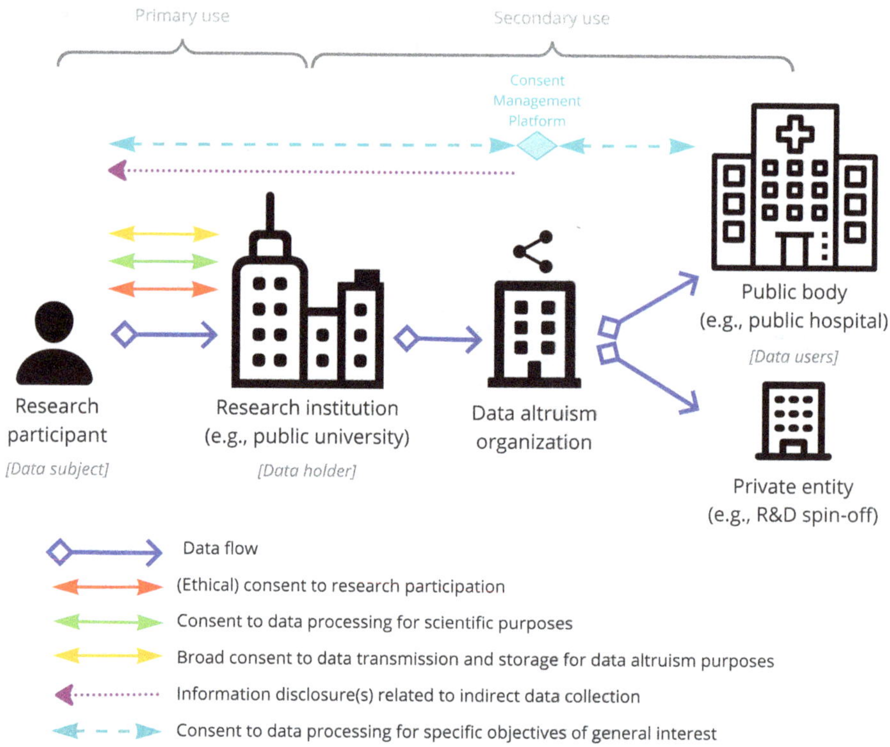

Fig. 1 This figure illustrates the data flows between the various actors, the related consent authorizations that are asked for and the information disclosures that are required when data collection is indirect

be signaled with an affirmative action, i.e., "an unambiguous indication of the data subject's wishes".[28] Further, consent should be implemented "in a manner which is clearly distinguishable from the other matters, in an intelligible and easily accessible form, using clear and plain language".[29] As an essential element for valid consent, the information disclosures should be transparent and should incorporate the substantial requirements listed in Articles 13–14 of the GDPR. These requirements mandate that certain information items be provided, such as the purpose of processing and the recipients of the data. This is coupled with the formal requirements provided in Article 12 of the GDPR, which mandate the quality, accessibility, and comprehensibility of the information. Dedicated guidelines specify that transparency should be user-centric,[30] meaning that information should be tailored to the information needs and abilities of the intended audience, while visual means of communication are explicitly encouraged,[31] especially when they help to inform

[28] GDPR, Article 4(11).

[29] GDPR, Article 7(2).

[30] Article 29 Working Party (2018), p. 5.

[31] Article 29 Working Party (2018), pp. 11–12.

individuals. Moreover, the data subject is entitled the "right to withdraw his or her consent at any time" which should be "as easy [...] as to give consent".[32] Further, when special categories of data are at stake, the explicit consent of the data subject is one of the few legitimate grounds that constitutes an exception to the general prohibition of processing such data.[33]

3.1.2 Broad and Specific Consent to Scientific Research

All that said, the specificity of consent clashes with the open and undetermined nature of scientific research. The granularity of the consent given is intrinsically linked to the purpose specification principle, according to which the processing purpose needs to be limited in scope and rigorously defined.[34] However, Recital 33 does provide for some flexibility when it is not possible to fully identify the purpose for which the data will be used at the time they are collected. Recital 33 states that, as long as the purpose is described upfront in general terms and further specified as the research study progresses, individuals can consent to specific stages of the research as they become better defined. Still, even when not further specifiable, the European Data Protection Board recommends that the research areas be narrowed down—that is it be made clear how the purpose relates to the context where the data is gathered, and that any reasonable expectations on the part of the research participants are respected.[35] On this point, the Italian Data Protection Authority issued an opinion clarifying the conditions under which such an exceptional broad consent combined with a *consenso a fasi progressive* is admissible.[36] They state that lawful consent must be tied to specific research projects rather than mere research areas, which should conform to the methodological and deontological rules and the best practices that are specific to disciplinary domains.[37]

3.1.3 Research on Health Data and Transparency

Owing to the sensitivity of health information, the European Data Protection Board recommends applying "a stricter interpretation" to this flexible approach along with a "high degree of scrutiny".[38] To complement the breadth of the approach while upholding high standards of protection, "appropriate safeguards [...] for the rights and freedoms of data subjects" should be put in place, such as data minimization,

[32] GDPR, Article 7(3).

[33] GDPR, Article 9(2)(a).

[34] European Data Protection Board (2020), p. 30.

[35] European Data Protection Board (2021), pp. 8–9.

[36] Garante per la Protezione dei Dati Personali (2022).

[37] European Data Protection Board (2020), p. 28.

[38] European Data Protection Board (2020), p. 31.

pseudonymization and anonymization[39] "to ensure the essence of the data subject's rights to valid consent are served".[40] Transparency complements such measures in the form of progressive disclosures that update the data subjects about advancements in the research project and ensure that "over time, the consent will be as specific as possible".[41]

All parties involved in the processing activities should, in addition, respect the provisions on information disclosures laid down in Article 13 when they gather data directly from data subjects. Moreover, parties need to respect Article 14 when data collection is indirect, such as is the case with data reuse by DAOs and data users. A substantial overlap between the information items required in these two conditions can be observed, with the difference that, when data collection is indirect, the source of data should also be disclosed[42] and the timing of the information provision can vary. Article 14(3) provides for a maximum of a 1-month delay after obtaining the data. If the personal data are used to communicate with the data subjects, they should be informed on such occasion, while, if the data are made available to other recipients (i.e., the data users), the disclosure should occur the first time that they are passed on. Notably, Article 14(5)(b) puts forward an exception to the information obligation in the case of scientific research and other general interest purposes when providing information proves impossible, it would require a disproportionate effort, or it would render impossible or seriously impair achieving the processing objectives. In such cases other safeguards apply, such as "making the information publicly available" (e.g., in a newspaper or on the research project's website), even though the European Data Protection Board recommends "the implementation of more dynamic ways of informing data subjects".[43]

3.2 *Data Altruism Organizations' Consent Requirements in the DGA*

Article 2(16) reporting the definition of data altruism leaves little doubt on the legal ground on which data altruism is based, i.e., consent as defined in article 4(1) of the GDPR.[44] However, recital 50 introduces regulatory ambiguity[45] when it states that "[t]ypically, data altruism would rely on consent of data subjects", thereby implying that a different legal basis may be admissible. This may be the case when data are further processed for scientific research purposes that should "not be considered to be incompatible with the initial purpose", in accordance with the GDPR's provision on purpose compatibility.[46] When it comes to managing multiple general interest

---

39 GDPR, Article 89(1).

40 European Data Protection Board (2021), p. 8.

41 European Data Protection Board (2020), p. 31.

42 GDPR, Article 14 (2)(f).

43 European Data Protection Board (2021), p. 10.

44 DGA, Article 2(5).

45 Chassang and Feriol (2024), p. 68.

46 Lalova-Spinks et al. (2023), p. 6.

purposes that entail more severe risks, though, consent may be an appropriate legal ground.[47] In line with the flexible approach delineated above, Recital 50 of the DGA recognizes that individuals may consent to using their data for certain areas of scientific research (provided that the relevant scientific research ethics standards are upheld); or only to certain areas of research; or only to parts of a research project.

In line with article 14(3) GDPR, the DAO must clearly inform data subjects "prior to any processing" of the objectives of general interest and, whenever possible, the specified, explicit and legitimate purposes for which it permits the processing by a data user.[48] Further, the DAO must also provide tools for consent management that enable data subjects to easily withdraw their consent,[49] for example when they do not agree with the processing operation they are informed of. In addition, the DGA lays down requirements for a data altruism consent form that enables data sharing operations with "additional legal certainty and user-friendliness". These clauses particularly apply when it comes to scientific research.[50] First, the form should gather consent across Member States in a uniform format as opposed to the current piecemeal approach.[51] Second, the form should be implemented a "modular approach allowing customization for specific sectors and specific purposes".[52] In other words, it should be standardized across nations and sectors, whilst still being able to accommodate any specific contextual needs that may arise, for instance, from the variety of data categories that can be donated and the related data protection rules.[53] Third, the conditions for granting and withdrawing consent should be in line with the legal requirements established by the GDPR, for instance for what concerns the granularity of the controls over "specific data processing operation[s]".[54] Lastly, the form should be printable on paper and to rendered into an electronic machine-readable format.[55]

3.3 *Illustrating Research Data Flows Via Consent(s)*

The data flows between the entities involved in data altruism are governed by consent permissions for the use, transmission, storage, and re-use of the data, as depicted in Fig. 1. Within the scenario introduced at the beginning of this section, the research institution asks for several consent permissions upfront, namely:

[47] Chassang and Feriol (2024), p. 65.

[48] DGA, Article 21(1).

[49] DGA, Article 21(3).

[50] DGA, Recital 52.

[51] DGA, Article 25(1).

[52] DGA, Article 25(2).

[53] DGA, Recital 52.

[54] DGA, Article 25(3).

[55] DGA, Article 25(4).

(ethical) consent to participate in scientific research and explicit consent to process their health data for a specific research project, unless another legal ground applies. Note that I have intentionally left aside the complexity that would be added by asking for informed consent for a clinical investigation, as required by Article 63 of the Medical Devices Regulation,[56] or for participating in a clinical trial as described in Article 29 of the Clinical Trials Regulation.[57]

The university as the data controller and data holder also asks for consent to transfer and store the data it has gathered with the DAO for data altruistic purposes, unless the compatibility assessment for further processing required by article 6(4) GDPR is positive. The assessment must be conducted on a case-by-case basis and, thus, it is difficult, if not impossible, to establish general conditions of compatibility between the original and the new purpose. When these are not met, the purpose must be re-specified and "a specific separate consent for the new processing" may be necessary.[58] I posit that data altruism consent would be quite broad at this stage and would require specification by the actual data users that request access to the data: only if specifically informed about the intended purposes of data use, data subjects can provide a valid consent and remain in control of their data.[59] If this is agreed, the DAO should then recontact the individuals to inform them that they store and make available the data for altruistic purposes, in accordance with Article 14(3)(a) GDPR. In addition, the organization should reach out to them "prior to any processing" to inform them of the objectives of general interest (and whenever possible of the specific purposes) pursued by the data users that it allows to access the data[60] and to disclose mandatory information about the data processing.[61] Even though current scholarly debate suggests that other legal bases for data altruism and for the further processing by data users[62] may be admissible, as exemplified earlier, these transparency obligations, coupled with those concerning the provision of tools for easy consent withdrawal[63] and the requirement for the form to enable consent withdrawal from specific data processing operations[64] suggest that the legislators envisioned a granular management of personal data based on individuals' consent.

[56] Regulation (EU) 2017/745 of the European Parliament and of the Council of 5 April 2017 on medical devices, amending Directive 2001/83/EC, Regulation (EC) No 178/2002 and Regulation (EC) No 1223/2009 and repealing Council Directives 90/385/EEC and 93/42/EEC. OJ L 117, 5.5.2017, pp. 1–175.

[57] Regulation (EU) No 536/2014 of the European Parliament and of the Council of 16 April 2014 on clinical trials on medicinal products for human use, and repealing Directive 2001/20/EC.OJ L 158, 27.5.2014, pp. 1–76.

[58] Article 29 Working Party (2013), pp. 26–27.

[59] European Data Protection Board (2020), p. 13.

[60] DGA, Article 21(1).

[61] GDPR, Article 14(3)(c).

[62] Lalova-Spinks et al. (2023), p. 7. The authors also suggest that data altruism consent could encompass the processing by data users, which would thus constitute primary use, rather than further processing, because the intention to enhance the availability of data motivated the data collection in the first place.

[63] DGA, Article 21(3).

[64] DGA, Article 25(3).

This interpretation may provide the specificity that is needed for the broad consent to data altruism to be further specified, as DAOs' intermediation service (e.g., in the form of a consent management platform) would enable data users to swiftly inform data subjects about data reuses once these are identified and negotiate granular permissions over time. Under this light, DAOs would fulfill an important role as enabler of research and would facilitate compliance with the transparency and consent obligations imposed by the GDPR. It remains to be understood, though, if they will help data users to additionally obtain other kinds of consent, such as research ethics consent to participation in non-interventional retrospective medical research studies.[65]

3.4 *Additional Safeguards Around Data Altruism Consent*

It goes without saying that making more health and other personal data available, especially those data associated with social stigmas, such as mental illnesses or sexually transmitted diseases, carries severe risks. Indeed, the EU Data Strategy strives to strike a balance between boosting the economic capacity of the continent and protecting its values and interests, under the motto "as open as possible, as closed as necessary".[66] As underscored earlier, providing consent for the vaguely defined objectives of "the general interest" appears to be at odds with the specificity requirement of the current legislative framework. Hence, additional safeguards become necessary—akin to consents for medical treatment and to participating in scientific research. Here, the autonomy of the people seems to be upheld by a "framework of supporting assurances [that] undergird and warrant consent agreements",[67] such as ethical and professional standards, institutional best practices, and codes of conduct. In this scenario, the research protocols that scientists submit to the competent ethics review boards will reasonably include the intention to share data for altruistic purposes. Moreover, data holders may formalize service agreements with trusted DAOs, constituting an additional insurance against malpractice.

In the new data governance framework designed by the DGA, the intention to establish trust mechanisms that draw a safety net around the self-determination of data subjects is well visible. For example, DAOs may want to resort to ethics councils or boards, which may include representatives from civil society, to ensure that the high standards of scientific ethics are maintained and fundamental rights are protected.[68] Further, data altruism organizations are subject to the following requirements that, I argue, strengthen the institution of consent:

[65] Lalova-Spinks et al. (2023), p. 6.

[66] European Commission (2020).

[67] Nissenbaum (2011), p. 36.

[68] DGA, Recital 46.

a. Official public registration:[69] Recognized DAOs should be included in a public register[70] maintained by a competent national authority (e.g., the AgID in Italy) and at the Union level by the European Commission. At the time of writing (May 2025), only one organization from Spain had been enrolled in such a registry;
b. Official trust seals:[71] Registered DAOs may publicly display the label "data altruism organization recognized in the Union" and a common logo[72] meant to convey a sense of safety to the public and guaranteed by a trustworthy third party, i.e., the EU;
c. EU jurisdiction: This refers to the place of establishment[73] or the legal representative[74] of the DAO , which must be a legal person pursuant to national law[75] and must be located a Member State to facilitate compliance and potential redress within the same jurisdiction;
d. Objectives of general interest: The DAO must promote objectives of general interest established in national law where applicable[76] and process data only for the purposes authorized by data subjects;[77]
e. Not-for-profit nature and neutrality: The DAO must not act for reasons of profit. They must be legally independent from any other organization that operates to make profit[78] and must perform data altruism activities via a structure with functions that are separate from its other activities;[79]
f. Transparency obligations:

    i) to ensure traceability: The DAO has obligations to keep "a full and accurate record"[80] of all data users, their processing purposes, the fees paid (if any) and the duration of processing;
    ii) to support oversight: The DAO must draft an annual activity report[81] addressed to a national competent authority with information encompassing the activities, the pursued purposes of general interest, a list of data users (including the techniques used to preserve privacy), the results of the processing, and any sources of revenue plus expenses.
    iii) to ensure informed decision-making: the DAO must also clearly and comprehensibly communicate to the data subject the objectives of general interest that it promotes, and the specific, explicit, legitimate purpose of the processing

[69] DGA, Articles 19, 17(1) and (2).

[70] European Commission (2024b).

[71] DGA, Article 17(2).

[72] European Commission (2023).

[73] DGA, Article 19(1),(2).

[74] DGA, Article 19(3).

[75] DGA, Article 18(a).

[76] DGA, Article 18(a).

[77] DGA, Article 21(2).

[78] DGA, Article 18(c).

[79] DGA, Article 18(d).

[80] DGA, Article 20(1).

[81] DGA, Article 20(2).

where applicable, "prior to any processing" (i.e., every time a data user requires access to data).[82] DAOs should find ways to keep individuals informed of the use of their data.[83] National arrangements may further specify the information that needs to be provided to data subjects.[84] The rulebook that the EC will need to draft[85] (see point i below) will further clarify how to inform data subjects of "sufficiently detailed, clear and transparent information" about use of data, about the measures against its misuse, and about the consent management tools.

g. Ease of consent management. To enable data subjects to easily give and withdraw consent,[86] DAOs must provide "easily usable" tools, that should constitute "effective and clearly communicated technical means to withdraw and modify consent at any moment".[87] The European Commission rulebook should further specify the requirements for ensuring the security of the tools;
h. Prohibitions to misleading marketing practices (fairness).[88] DAOs must avoid using misleading practices that entice data subjects to provide their data, for example by providing false information or somehow unduly influencing their decision-making, thereby recalling the Unfair Commercial Practices Directive's prohibition on misleading practices[89] (it goes without saying that data altruism organizations cannot be assimilated to traders as defined in the Directive and their relation with data subjects is not of a commercial nature);
i. Compliance with the EC rulebook.[90] The European Commission, through delegated acts, will develop a rulebook to guide DAOs in four crucial respects:[91] (1) laying down information requirements that enhance user-facing transparency on the use of data (see point f(iii)) above), on the tools for consent management, and on the measures adopted to avoid any data misuse. This is complemented by (2) "communication roadmaps" to raise awareness among data subjects on data altruism; (3) necessary technical and security requirements for reaching an appropriate level of security of the data storage and processing and of the consent tools; and (4) recommendations on the interoperability standards that will facilitate data exchange.

All these measures come together to form a novel governance framework that aims to strengthen the accountability and trustworthiness of data processing for altruistic

[82] DGA, Article 21(1).

[83] DGA, Recital 46.

[84] DGA, Article 16.

[85] DGA, Article 22(a).

[86] DGA, Article 21(3).

[87] DGA, Recital 46.

[88] DGA, Article 21(2).

[89] Directive 2005/29/EC of the European Parliament and of the Council of 11 May 2005 concerning unfair business-to-consumer commercial practices in the in-ternal market and amending Council Directive 84/450/EEC, Directives 97/7/EC, 98/27/EC and 2002/65/EC of the European Parliament and of the Council and Regulation (EC) No 2006/2004 of the European Parliament and of the Council ('Unfair Commercial Practices Directive') OJ L 149, 11.6.2005, pp. 22–39.

[90] DGA, Article 18(d).

[91] DGA, Article 22.

reasons. Evidently, these factors need to be complemented with the measures foreseen in the GDPR on responsible data management by data controllers and data processors (depending on which role the data altruism organization takes on). This includes the adoption of a data protection by design and by default approach,[92] the likely appointment of a Data Protection Officer (e.g., if sensitive data are processed at scale)[93] and the evaluation and mitigation of risk with appropriate means,[94] including by conducting Data Protection Impact Assessments when necessary.[95] National provisions often supplement such measures, notably regarding the processing of health data.[96]

3.5 *Challenges of Health Data Altruism Consent*

A number of challenges arise from this analysis so far that are briefly summarized as follows. First, what exactly constitutes scientific research is not defined in the DGA,[97] which does not only bring indeterminacy to the application of the norm but also collides with the definitions provided in other legislations such as the GDPR, while the notion of public interest is equally blurred.[98] It is therefore left to DAOs to determine if the purposes pursued by data users are in line with public interest, and hence if the requested data can be accessed. Compliance by data altruism organizations is monitored by the competent authorities that register the organizations, but these are ex post assessments that may, at their worst, simply mean DAOs are delisted from the national register when a violation is found as per Article 24(5). Obviously, the data protection authorities can tangentially investigate infringements related to personal data.

Second, the validity of consent is also challenged by the idiosyncratic nature of data altruism consent. The tension between the openness of scientific research and the specificity of consent may, in principle, be solved with an initial broad consent that is more narrowly specified as and when the purposes are better determined (admitting that this is possible). Notably, the same exception would not apply to other purposes of general interest, which may be equally undetermined when one asks for a consent to data altruism. If this consent is not asked at the moment of data collection by a data holder, it may be very cumbersome for DAOs to get hold of a large variety of data donated voluntarily, because the alternative would be that individuals directly donate their data to the DAOs—a scenario that, despite being

[92] GDPR, Article 25.

[93] GDPR, Article 37.

[94] GDPR, Article 24.

[95] GDPR, Article 35.

[96] GDPR, Article 9(4).

[97] See in this volume Paseri, "Defining Scientific Research under the EU Politics of Data: The Impact on Personalized Smart Medicine", sec. 1.3.

[98] See in this volume Spajic, "Data altruism consent: A move forward towards the creation of a European health data space?", sec. 2.2.

desirable, may be limited by practical obstacles, such as the lack of real incentives for data subjects who cannot be compensated due to the very nature of data altruism. In addition, at the time of collection, the categories of recipients (i.e., the data users) are generally unknown. Yet, according to the GDPR's transparency requirements, they must be spelled out for consent to be informed. In other words, data altruism consent risks not being sufficiently specific and informed, and it is not clear if these flaws can be redressed with an initial broad consent that is specified later.

Third, there is great uncertainty in terms of how consent experiences will be designed in practice. This is despite the obligations placed on DAOs to offer tools for consent management that are easy to use and to inform concerned individuals before a new processing operation starts so that they can adjust their consent preferences. For example, if we imagine these tools as mobile apps, it would be very confusing for an individual to be recontacted by various DAOs through different channels. However, to date, there is no standard digital solution for consent management—neither one specifically geared towards the needs of data altruism nor a general-purpose one.[99] That said, the data ecosystem is ripe with consent management tools that variously, but not simultaneously: i) identify and authenticate users; ii) manage consent permissions; and iii) enable the portability of data.[100] What is clear, though, is that the form envisioned by the legislators does not resemble the traditional consent document that most are familiar with.

4 Designing and Personalizing Dynamic Consent Experiences

There are many possible scenarios of data exchange. As such, data altruism organizations are subject to a highly complex set of obligations. This suggests a need for innovative and user-friendly solutions that allow data subjects to make informed, real-time decisions about who can use their data and for what purpose. Even though many voices raise criticism to consent as an instrument of self-determination,[101] consent is here to stay and we should thus design better, more dynamic ways of managing consent. By better, I mean these solutions should avoid the weaknesses of the current contemporary approaches to digital consent—approaches that deprive people of their autonomy through deceptive designs,[102] instead of bolstering it. Tomorrow's tools should inform data subjects at an appropriate time and with increasing specificity when needed. Importantly, the experience should also be user-friendly as usability is a precondition of accountability in data management practices. This is because it underpins respect for the policies governing the use of data

[99] European Commission JRC (2024a), p. 3.

[100] European Commission JRC (2024a), p. 10.

[101] See for instance Carolan (2016).

[102] See e.g., Gunawan et al. (2022) and Bielova et al. (2024b).

that are embedded in the front-end and back-end of data management tools. The access to data that consent permissions authorize needs to be accurately documented for transparency and accountability reasons. Additionally, establishing empirical guidelines for those designing the data altruism consent form is paramount to fostering trust in data sharing. However, this is beyond the scope of the limited space in this chapter. Nevertheless, my aim is to introduce existing technologies that address two elements: a user interface that incorporates both the requirements of transparency and of consent by displaying the information notice and offering controls over consent management; and technologies that enable machine-readability by expressing data permissions and by automating and documenting how one's data is used.

4.1 Beyond Consent Forms and Towards Dynamic User Experiences

4.1.1 Personalized Dynamic Consent

Traditionally, consent has been provided at a single point in time.[103] However, today, with data being constantly reused, consent must be given or withdrawn at many different points in time. As such, two-way communication is needed[104] before, during, and after consent.[105] Otherwise, how can data subjects revoke their consent in real time and at will?[106]

Given the consent requirements of personalized medical research, dynamic consent is, arguably, the most suitable solution. This is because dynamic consent can accommodate the various nuances of data altruism, such as providing numerous specific consents to data use that specify the initial broad consent. Dynamic consent is currently being experimented with in the field of biobanking research. It is formulated as a "personalized consent and communication platform"[107] that "allows participants to review and change consent choices over time via a personalized digital interface".[108] This model of consent gives rise to a continuous deliberative process that aligns with the evolution of people's preferences. Thus, it can be updated to reflect new processing opportunities that arise, such as a new organization asking for access to data or a new research project starting. Bespoke solutions are supported, both in terms of tailoring the options on data usage and in terms of methods of communication.[109] In one of the few existing longitudinal studies, communica-

[103] Rossi and Haapio (2021), pp. 118–119.

[104] Lee et al. (2023), p. 8.

[105] Mascalzoni et al. (2022), p. 1395.

[106] Dankar et al. (2020), p. 916.

[107] Dankar et al. (2020), p. 916.

[108] Lay et al. (2025), p. 181.

[109] Lee et al. (2023), p. 8.

tion was personalized in terms of the language and the frequency of communication.[110] The authors also used a multimedia approach that could cater to either those with digital skills or those who preferred paper-based or vocal communication.

Even though empirical evidence of how this concept works in practice is still limited, dynamic consent promises to uphold the autonomy of individuals via greater transparency, control, and engagement. It also promises to support research by enabling the researcher to obtain consent for further uses, affording withdrawal options and reducing the time, burden, and administrative costs associated with reconsenting. Additionally, such platforms should help to improve compliance with ever-changing legal requirements.[111] Increased direct communication with the individuals also brings a particularly appealing benefit in the context of data altruism—namely, the possibility of receiving further information after the data processing has been completed, such as the latest developments in research, the dissemination of findings, and other outcomes generated thanks to the donated data.[112] This can be thought of as non-pecuniary compensation.

However, the sheer number of consent decisions required may be overwhelming, which would act against autonomy rather than in its favor. If information overload were to occur, individuals might withdraw their consent.[113] To date, studies have not shown that this happens, but it is still a possibility.[114] Here, tiered layered consent discussed in genetic testing contexts constitutes an interesting solution, as it provides information in layers, e.g., from general default information to specific information. Consent is given in certain categories, such as purposes, the actionability of results, or the expected level of emotional impact.[115] In this way, such approaches promote granularity without overwhelming the person. Rather, each individual gets to decide the level of detail they prefer.

Similar to consent fatigue, information fatigue represents a major concern that is only destined to grow as the amount of data exchange and consent requests increase. Providing relevant yet concise information is a recognized issue, i.e., the so-called transparency paradox.[116] Academia, business,[117] and even the data protection authorities[118] themselves have all proposed innovative solutions, such as layering information to respond to various users' profiles and needs. Transparency, though, does not necessarily need to be one-size-fits-all solution. Rather, as recommended by the European Data Protection Board in the dedicated guidelines, it should be user-

[110] Mascalzoni et al. (2022), pp. 1395–1396.

[111] Lay et al. (2025), p. 182 and pp. 195–196.

[112] Lee et al. (2023), p. 8.

[113] Dankar et al. (2020), pp. 916–917.

[114] Mascalzoni et al. (2022), p. 1396.

[115] Bunnik et al. (2013).

[116] Nissenbaum (2011).

[117] Rossi et al. (2019).

[118] Article 29 Data Protection Working Party (2018); Commission Nationale de l'Informatique et des Libertés (n.d.); Creative Commons Italy & Garante per la Protezione dei Dati Personali (2025).

centric.[119] This opens up the possibility of tailoring requests for data use to the preferences of the data subjects. For instance, some people may prefer graphics, comics, or videos, to text. Others may prefer simple vocabulary, while others still might appreciate expert-level jargon.[120] As such, these tailored requests may be more effective at informing specific individuals about what their data will be used for than traditional methods.

Of course, it needs to be determined as to whether dynamic consent can uphold comprehension and autonomy in practice in the different scenarios that data altruism enables, since it is an under-researched topic in the biomedical domain. Mostly, dynamic consent has been applied to genomic research.[121] For example, the fact that the categories to which people may consent are defined by default has been pointed out as a limitation to self-determination.[122] A lack of sufficient literacy on the part of users (be it health literacy, digital literacy, data literacy, AI literacy, risk literacy) is also another critical issue pertaining to consent models. Additionally, users need time and a certain level of motivation to be able to confidently navigate the permissions and control policies offered to them. Dynamic consent requires them to continuously express decisions that are in line with their preferred values while also understanding the implications of their choices. Without addressing these challenges, dynamic consent users risk disengagement and marginalization.[123]

Moreover, preferences are also highly personal and highly contextual. So, although one might apply some general rules to streamline how users convey their preferences, like tiered consent, this approach may still be too coarse-grained. However, there is at least one emerging technology that seeks to tackle this issue: personalized privacy assistants. These are intelligent agents that provide personalized privacy notices, explanations and recommendations, but can also automate decision-making by learning the privacy preferences of their users over time, configuring settings semi-automatically, and making privacy decisions on their behalf.[124] Currently, personalized privacy assistants are still experimental, but they have been patented.[125] Notably, though, several questions about their legal and ethical legitimacy still need to be answered.

4.1.2 Influencing Decision-Making Through Design

The way information and options are designed and presented to individuals is an extremely powerful mechanism and can either encourage or discourage their intention to share data. There is an abundant body of literature that demonstrates how the behaviors, perceptions, and trust of human beings can be influenced by the way a

[119] Article 29 Working Party (2018), p. 5.

[120] Doan et al. (2024).

[121] Dankar et al. (2020), p. 919.

[122] Wiertz and Boldt (2022), p. 275.

[123] Lee et al. (2023), p. 8.

[124] See e.g., Chang and Barber (2023).

[125] See the Personalized Privacy Assistant Project (2025).

user interface is designed—this is why design considerations for the data altruism consent form are of the utmost importance. Unfortunately, consent fatigue is presenting obstacles to a user-friendly management of consent. Taking lessons from the overly granular interactions European users have with cookie consent banners on websites, there is not only evidence that people have learned to mindlessly give consent to cookies but that this automatic behavior persists over time and will be difficult to unlearn in the case of consent for data altruism.[126] Further, many empirical studies have shown that framing choices in a positive or negative light affects whether individuals disclose their personal data, especially when people are uncertain about the reasons why they are asked to share their data and the consequences of doing so.[127] In this respect, the European Data Protection Board states that loss-gain framing is an unfair practice[128] and the DGA indeed forbids the use of misleading marketing practices to solicit the provision of data. Not all design patterns that nudge users towards preferred behaviors are intrinsically evil, though. For instance, presenting the outcomes of decisions in a positive or negative manner can bolster data sharing for altruistic purposes. Underlining its benefits to the individual and to society may inspire the motivation to make one's data available, even though the risks of doing so should be spelled out transparently. Thus, the obligation to present fair and equal choices need to be prudently balanced with the necessity to incentivize data sharing for altruistic purposes. Hence, although there is an increasing awareness of the influence that interface design choices have on the disclosure of data, more research in the specific context of health data altruism needs to be done before empirically-based guidelines can be produced.

4.2 *Machine-Readable, Interoperable Semantics*

The need for semantic interoperability standards governing the exchange of health data is becoming urgent.[129] Further, another essential aspect of realizing the EU's vision of freely flowing data spaces concerns the necessary automation of data practices. For example, consent permissions need to be standardized, machine-readable, and actionable across organizations, sectors, and applications. To this end, open (i.e., free and non-proprietary) semantic web technologies and their integration with international standards represent a promising approach to addressing these requirements.

For a system to process, document, and verify data exchanges so as to comply with applicable laws, that system needs to be able to interpret various types of

[126] Bielova et al. (2024a).

[127] Bongard-Blanchy et al. (2023).

[128] European Data Protection Board (2023), pp. 19–20.

[129] Abboud et al. (2022).

information,[130] including obligations, permissions, and the requirements that govern the admissible use of data. A widely adopted standard for crafting such data use policies is W3C's Open Digital Rights Language (ODRL). Its Access Control (OAC) profile allows users like researchers or DAOs to create policies that govern how personal data is used based on a particular purpose. They can also restrict access to some data after a certain period of time has passed or authorize only certain types of entities to access the data.[131] ODRL by itself only provides the structure for expressing rules and policies like permissions and obligations, but lacks semantics: it needs a vocabulary that provides terms that identify legal concepts. The Data Privacy Vocabulary (DPV) published by the W3C DPVCG is one of such semantic resources that enables users to create legally relevant policies with the use of ODRL, when this is extended to represent legislations like the GDPR.[132] The DPV is an ontology that formally expresses a wide range of information concerning data, processing purposes, processing operations, legal bases, data subjects' rights, and more.[133] Formally expressing the requirements for altruistic reuse would allow users to easily query the public registers of data altruism organizations.[134] Additionally, data access requests could, in principle, be automatically matched to the available datasets held by DAOs in line with established conditions. In a similar manner to tiered consent, the data subjects themselves can set their preferences for the data uses they authorize, instead of needing to continuously engage in an overly granular deliberative process that may be overwhelming. Semantic specifications have also been matched with international standards on consent to tackle interoperability and machine-interpretability challenges. Notably, efforts such as these intend to foster the widespread adoption of a commonly recognized format.

Informed consent generally comprises two elements. First is a consent notice that contains relevant information about the data processing operations that will occur if consent is given. This fulfills the transparency obligations of the GDPR and the DGA. Second is a consent receipt that keeps a record of the decisions made, which fulfills the obligations mandated by the GDPR and the DGA to maintain a record of any consents given.[135] The ISO/IEC 29184:2020 "Privacy Notices and Consent" specifies how information is provided to individuals via consent request notices and largely covers the GDPR's requirements but not completely.[136] ISO 29184 is helpful for demonstrating compliance and can also provide a standard format for documenting consent. It also offers options for personalization, as machine-readable consent notices can be issued in text, visual, or graphic form

[130] Esteves et al. (2023), pp. 216–217.

[131] Esteves et al. (2023), p. 217.

[132] W3C DPVCG (2025).

[133] Pandit et al. (2024a).

[134] Esteves et al. (2023), p. 222.

[135] Pandit et al. (2024b), pp. 228–229 and 231.

[136] Pandit and Krog (2021), p. 203.

through a variety of user interface mediums, such as layered notices, icons, dashboards, or just-in-time notices.[137]

In terms of documenting consent, which involves creating, maintaining, communicating, and disclosing consent decisions in a machine-readable format, the ISO/IEC TS 27560 "Privacy technologies—Consent record information structure" specifies an interoperable, standardized information structure that defines how consent decisions should be recorded and documented.[138] The standard specifies common field requirements, such as a unique identifier for the consent record, the entities involved, the processing purposes, the data categories, the status of consent, and so on. It also stipulates the form the information can take, like the format.[139] Organizations can then use these records to determine whether certain processing is allowed and, therefore, whether data processing can start, continue, or should be terminated, such as when consent is withdrawn or has expired. Additionally, the standard is flexible enough to incorporate domain-specific labels or be extended to additional fields or information types that may become necessary, for example to relate to certain legislations and jurisdictions.[140] It can also be implemented in a machine-readable format (such as JSON), which could then be integrated with some standard interoperable semantics,[141] like the W3C's Data Protection Vocabulary which can be expanded to include legal terms that pertain to the DGA or the EHDS.[142]

Without these standardization efforts, it is impractical to implement data sharing, because there will be a multitude of ad hoc consent implementations which would result in fragmented ecosystems. Instead, a pan-European implementation needs to rely on semantic interoperability for consent to be widely accepted: standardizing semantics ensures that machines not only interpret the structure but also understand the meaning of information, thereby enabling reliable data access automation at scale. Additionally, this approach supports transparency and traceability of data access decisions, and thus accountability towards reusing data. It also makes it easy for data subjects to exercise their rights. Semantic specifications may support personalization in terms of both how the information notice is presented[143] and the consent permissions individuals can express. However, such an approach means that there needs to be an agreed upon semantic specification for all the relevant concepts, including for all possible processing purposes. Purposes need to be expressed in a highly precise manner to satisfy the GDPR's requirements over consent, though. Such a top-down approach may hardly be compatible with a bottom-up approach where researchers in the role of data users progressively refine the definition of the processing purpose on a case-by-case basis. That said, the Data

[137] Pandit and Krog (2021), p. 198.

[138] Pandit et al. (2024b), p. 230.

[139] Pandit et al. (2024b), p. 229.

[140] Pandit et al. (2024b), p. 229.

[141] Pandit et al. (2024b), p. 237.

[142] See the EHDS extension HealthDCAT-AP available at: https://healthdcat-ap.github.io/.

[143] Pandit et al. (2018).

Protection Vocabulary can accommodate for jurisdictional variance. For example, if the vocabulary contains the general concept "purpose", the DGA extension can support the specification "objective of general interest", which can be further specified at the national level or even by a specific data user. The semantic interoperability derives from the common parent concept contained in the Data Protection Vocabulary. However, the pathway to a consensus on the widespread adoption of these technologies may be long and uncertain, while declarative conditions of data use policies may also be ignored, leading to data misuse.[144]

5 Future Work and Conclusions

This chapter has examined consent for data altruism from the legal, design, and technical perspectives. As such, this work may offer early solutions to the challenges that implementing consent could pose. The chapter began by delineating the scenarios where health data altruism may still be meaningful, even though the EHDS regulation imposes the legal obligation to share health-related data. Next was to identify the requirements associated with the various consents that need to be requested for information to flow between entities. Here, I argued that the DGA establishes accountability and transparency safeguards that are necessary for strengthening the institution of consent as a means of self-determination. I also sketched out several challenges relating to the legitimacy, specificity, and usability of data altruism consent. Solutions to these issues include the dynamic consent embedded in emerging semantic web technologies, which enable the real-time interoperable exchange of data use permissions and automated access to datasets based on pre-specified conditions. Thanks to technological development, information disclosures and consent management could be more personalized in the near future, which may address some of the hurdles associated with contemporary digital consent, such as information fatigue and consent fatigue. That said, imposing one model of consent onto various contexts where different sensitivities are at play needs to be well-thought out as "choosing a model becomes a matter of finding an acceptable compromise"[145] and depends on factors such as the trustworthiness of the organization, whether the data subjects participate in determining what their data is being used for, and the surrounding safeguards that strengthen the institution of consent.

With the aim of informing the European Commission's work on a rulebook governing data altruism, the goal of future work is to draft some recommendations on how to design an empowering consent experience that encourages data sharing for altruistic purposes without exploiting the subject's cognitive biases. Part of this means considering the many types of human-computer interaction, including those

[144] Esteves et al. (2023), p. 224.

[145] Wiertz and Boldt (2022), p. 277.

with artificial agents. Future research will also need to address the open challenges identified in this chapter by exploring additional scenarios related to data altruism, such as collecting data directly from the data subjects and data processing for the purposes of general interest beyond that of scientific research. Topics that also need to be considered include the benefits of anonymizing data; the requirements for identity management and the security of consent-related data; the permissible processing of non-personal data, and how to implement permission management systems. Moreover, the legal and technical challenges arising from crossovers between the EHDS Regulation, the Open Data Directive,[146] the Medical Devices Regulation, and the Clinical Trials Regulation need to be further investigated.

This chapter concludes with a plea to ground the guidelines for implementing data altruism consent in the kind of interdisciplinary evidence that reflects how human beings make decisions about their data—evidence that realistically portrays the technological maturity of the proposed solutions. Consent can still be a substantial instrument of self-determination, but we need a concerted effort to seriously address the roots of disengagement, confusion, and deception caused by existing digital consent experiences.

Acknowledgments This research was financially supported by the "Biorobotics Research and Innovation Engineering Facilities" "IR0000036" - CUP J13C22000400007 (BRIEF) project. I would like to thank Federica Casarosa, Francesca Gennari and Harshvardhan Pandit for their precious comments on an early draft of this chapter. A special thanks goes to Andrea Parziale, who helps me to bring order to the rather confusing sketches I make on the whiteboard of our shared office and, therefore, to my thoughts. In this work I have managed to join insights from various past research studies that I have conducted with many colleagues, whom I thank for their enthusiasm, ideas and time.

Disclosure of Interests The author has no competing interests.

References

Abboud L, Bogaert P, Bowers S et al (2022) Report on secondary use of health data through European case studies. TEHDAS Towards European Health Data Space

Article 29 Data Protection Working Party (2018) Guidelines on Transparency under Regulation 2016/679, 17/EN WP260 rev.01. Adopted on 29 November 2017. As last Revised and Adopted on 11 April 2018

Article 29 Working Party (2013) Opinion 03/2013 on purpose limitation

Bielova N, Litvine L, Nguyen A et al (2024a) The effect of design patterns on (present and future) cookie consent decisions. In: Proceedings of the 33rd USENIX Security Symposium. Philadelphia USA, pp 1–9

Bielova N, Santos C, Gray CM (2024b) Two worlds apart! Closing the gap between regulating EU consent and user studies. Harv J Law Technol 37:1295–1333

[146] Directive (EU) 2019/1024 of the European Parliament and of the Council of 20 June 2019 on open data and the re-use of public sector information. PE/28/2019/REV/1. OJ L 172, 26.6.2019, pp. 56–83.

Bongard-Blanchy K, Sterckx J-L, Rossi A et al (2023) Analysing the influence of loss-gain framing on data disclosure behaviour: a study on the use case of app permission requests. In: Proceedings of the 2023 European Symposium on Usable Security. ACM, Copenhagen, Denmark

Bunnik EM, Janssens ACJW, Schermer MHN (2013) A tiered-layered-staged model for informed consent in personal genome testing. Eur J Hum Genet 21:596–601. https://doi.org/10.1038/ejhg.2012.237

Carolan E (2016) The continuing problems with online consent under the EU's emerging data protection principles. Comput Law Secur Rev 32:462–473

Chang K-C, Barber S (2023) Personalized privacy assistant: identity construction and privacy in the internet of things. Entropy 25:717

Chassang G, Feriol L (2024) Data altruism, personal health data and the consent challenge in scientific research: a difficult interplay between EU acts. Eur Data Prot Law Rev 10:57–68. https://doi.org/10.21552/edpl/2024/1/9

Commission Nationale de l'Informatique et des Libertés (n.d.) Design Patterns – Données & Design par LINC. https://design.cnil.fr/en/design-patterns/

Corona Datenspende (2025). https://corona-datenspende.github.io/en/#about

Creative Commons Italy, Garante per la Protezione dei Dati Personali (2025) White Paper - Rendere le informative privacy più comprensibili. Il legal design come approccio rivolto all'utente. GPDP, Roma

Dankar FK, Gergely M, Malin B et al (2020) Dynamic-informed consent: a potential solution for ethical dilemmas in population sequencing initiatives. Comput Struct Biotechnol J 18:913–921. https://doi.org/10.1016/j.csbj.2020.03.027

Decreto Legislativo 7 ottobre 2024, n. 144 Norme di adeguamento della normativa nazionale alle disposizioni del regolamento (UE) 2022/868 del Parlamento europeo e del Consiglio, del 30 maggio 2022, relativo alla governance europea dei dati e che modifica il regolamento (UE) 2018/1724. (24G00167). https://www.gazzettaufficiale.it/eli/id/2024/10/10/24G00167/SG

Doan X, Doğan FS, Rossi A (2024) Analysis of transparency and user-relevancy of DTC company policies. In: Hoepman J-H, Jensen M, Porcedda MG, Schiffner S, Ziegler S (eds) Privacy Symposium 2024. Springer Nature Switzerland, Cham, pp 191–215

Esteves B, Rodríguez Doncel V, Pandit HJ, Lewis D (2023) Semantics for implementing data reuse and altruism under EU's Data Governance Act. In: Acosta M, Peroni S, Vahdati S et al (eds) Knowledge graphs: semantics, machine learning, and languages. IOS Press, pp 210–226

European Commission (2020) Communication from the Commission to the European Parliament, the Council, the European Economic and Social Committee of the Regions. A European Strategy for Data

European Commission (2023) Logos for data intermediaries and data altruism organisations recognised in the Union. Available at: https://digital-strategy.ec.europa.eu/en/library/logos-data-intermediaries-and-data-altruism-organisations-recognised-union

European Commission (2024a) Joint Research Centre. The landscape of consent management tools: a data altruism perspective. Publications Office, LU

European Commission (2024b) EU register of recognised data altruism organisations. Available at: https://digital-strategy.ec.europa.eu/en/policies/data-altruism-organisations

European Data Protection Board (2020) Guidelines 05/2020 on consent under Regulation 2016/679

European Data Protection Board (2021) EDPB Document on response to the request from the European Commission for clarifications on the consistent application of the GDPR, focusing on health research

European Data Protection Board (2023) Guidelines 03/2022 on deceptive design patterns in social media platform interfaces: how to recognise and avoid them. Version 2.0. European Data Protection Board

Garante per la Protezione dei Dati Personali (2022) Parere ai sensi dell'article 110 del Codice e dell'article 36 del Regolamento - 30 giugno 2022 [9791886]

Gunawan J, Santos C, Kamara I (2022) Redress for dark patterns privacy harms? A case study on consent interactions. In: Proceedings of the 2022 Symposium on Computer Science and Law. pp 181–194

Kohane IS, Altman RB (2005) Health-information altruists — a potentially critical resource. N Engl J Med 353:2074–2077. https://doi.org/10.1056/NEJMsb051220

Lalova-Spinks T, Meszaros J, Huys I (2023) The application of data altruism in clinical research through empirical and legal analysis lenses Frontiers in Medicine 1010.3389/fmed.2023.1141685

Lay W, Gasparini L, Siero W, Hughes EK (2025) A rapid review of the benefits and challenges of dynamic consent. Res Ethics 21:180–202. https://doi.org/10.1177/17470161241278064

Lee AR, Koo D, Kim IK, Lee E, Kim HH, Yoo S, Kim J-H, Choi EK, Lee H-Y (2023) Identifying facilitators of and barriers to the adoption of dynamic consent in digital health ecosystems: a scoping review. BMC Med Ethics 24:107. https://doi.org/10.1186/s12910-023-00988-9

Mascalzoni D, Melotti R, Pattaro C et al (2022) Ten years of dynamic consent in the CHRIS study: informed consent as a dynamic process. Eur J Hum Genet 30:1391–1397. https://doi.org/10.1038/s41431-022-01160-4

Micheli M, Farrell E, Carballa SB, Posada SM, Signorelli S, Vespe M (2023) Mapping the landscape of data intermediaries. Joint Research Centre, Luxembourg

National Research Council (US) Committee on A Framework for Developing a New Taxonomy of Disease (2011) Toward Precision Medicine: Building a Knowledge Network for Biomedical Research and a New Taxonomy of Disease. National Academies Press (US), Washington (DC)

Nissenbaum H (2011) A contextual approach to privacy online. Daedalus 140:32–48. https://doi.org/10.1162/DAED_a_00113

Pandit HJ, Krog GP (2021) Comparison of notice requirements for consent between ISO/IEC 29184:2020 and General Data Protection Regulation. J Data Prot Priv 4:193–204

Pandit HJ, O'Sullivan D, Lewis D (2018) Personalised privacy policies. In: Benczúr A, Thalheim B, Horváth T et al (eds) New trends in databases and information systems. Springer International Publishing, Cham, pp 127–137

Pandit HJ, Esteves B, Krog GP et al (2024a) Data Privacy Vocabulary (DPV) – Version 2.0. In: Demartini G, Hose K, Acosta M et al (eds) The Semantic Web – ISWC 2024. Cham, Springer Nature Switzerland, pp 171–193

Pandit HJ, Lindquist J, Krog GP (2024b) Implementing ISO/IEC TS 27560:2023 consent records and receipts for GDPR and DGA. In: Jensen M, Lauradoux C, Rannenberg K (eds) Privacy technologies and policy. Springer Nature Switzerland, Cham, pp 228–251

Personalized Privacy Assistant Project (2025), available at: https://privacyassistant.org/

Robert Koch Institute & Research on Complex Systems of Humboldt University of Berlin (2025), Corona Data Donation Project, available at: https://corona-datenspende.github.io/en/

Rossi A, Haapio H (2021) Proactive legal design for health data sharing based on smart contracts. In: Smart contracts: technological, business and legal perspectives, Marcelo Corrales, Mark Fenwick and Stefan Wrbka. Hart Publishing, London, pp 101–122

Rossi A, Ducato R, Haapio H, Passera S (2019) When design met law: design patterns for information transparency. Droit de la Consommation = Consumenterecht: DCCR 79–121

Rossi G, Caso R, Castelli D, Giglia E (2022) Piano Nazionale per la Scienza Aperta. Ministero dell'Università e della Ricerca

Schweihoff J, Lipovetskaja A, Jussen-Lengersdorf I, Möller F (2024) Stuck in the middle with you: conceptualizing data intermediaries and data intermediation services. Electron Markets 34:48. https://doi.org/10.1007/s12525-024-00729-9

W3C DPVCG (2025) "DPV - EU General Data Protection Regulation (GDPR) version 2.1", available at: https://w3c.github.io/dpv/2.1/legal/eu/gdpr/

Wiedermann M, Rose AH, Maier BF, Kolb JJ, Hinrichs D, Brockmann D (2023) Evidence for positive long-and short-term effects of vaccinations against COVID-19 in wearable sensor metrics. PNAS nexus 2:pgad223

Wiertz S, Boldt J (2022) Evaluating models of consent in changing health research environments. Med Health Care Philos 25:269–280. https://doi.org/10.1007/s11019-022-10074-3

Redefining Anonymization: Legal Challenges and Emerging Threats in the Era of the European Health Data Space

Chiara Gallese

Abstract A 2023 case from the Court of Justice of the European Union, Case T-557/20, suggests a shift in how the concept of anonymization is defined. More specifically, the case introduces "subjective criteria" that must be used to differentiate between personal and anonymized data. Meanwhile, despite recent advancements in anonymization techniques, there has been an increase in cyber-attacks on healthcare facilities while the market for healthcare data is only growing. These trends pose significant risks to the rights and freedoms of citizens, particularly in the context of the regulations governing the European Health Data Space (EHDS), which allow for substantial volumes of health data to be shared at the EU level. In this chapter it is argued, however, that anonymization is not merely a technical procedure but rather a political decision. Decision-makers are responsible for determining who will perform anonymization, whose data will be anonymized, the techniques to be employed, and the level of data utility to be preserved. Thus, this chapter explores the legal issues surrounding the distinction between personal and anonymized data within the context of the EHDS. A redefinition of the concept of anonymization is also advocated.

1 Introduction

1.1 The Era of Big Data and the Health Data Market

As noted by Kitchin and Lauriault, processing data, both in terms of volume and variety, has seen a significant transformation since the seventeenth century. Four hundred years ago, creating and maintaining large datasets was predominantly the purview of governments. These public bodies conducted censuses and funded the

C. Gallese (✉)
University of Turin, Turin, Italy
e-mail: chiara.gallese@unito.it

F. Casarosa et al. (eds.), *Enabling and Safeguarding Personalized Medicine*, Data Science, Machine Intelligence, and Law 7,
https://doi.org/10.1007/978-3-031-99709-9_5

development of large administrative and natural resource databases.[1] In fact, according to Kitchin, in the EU, such datasets were typically generated every few years or so, or they were merely based on sample data, so as to provide a periodic but relatively static snapshot of various aspects of society and the natural world. The past 50 years, however, have marked the advent of big data, changing the way we relate to information[2] and posing challenges related to digital sovereignty.[3]

The current era is now characterized by the continuous and rapid generation of vast amounts of data across a range of diverse fields, including healthcare as is most relevant to this book. Unlike the traditional datasets of yore that were updated infrequently, big data is typically generated in real-time or near real-time.[4] This ongoing flow of data is driven by advancements in technology and the widespread adoption of digital devices like smartphones, smartwatches, laptops, and PCs.[5] The volume of data has exploded, with the proliferation of new technologies contributing to the massive scale of data being produced daily.[6] Big data also includes a wide variety of data types, including structured data (such as databases), semi-structured data (like JSON and XML files), and unstructured data (such as text, images, and videos). The use of big data extends across numerous fields, including business, healthcare, computer science, and social sciences, and different datasets can now be linked together to gain broader insights at the individual or societal level. The ability to analyze large datasets has led to new insights, innovations, and increased efficiency in many sectors.

Most recently, the growth of big data has been supported by significant technological advances in infrastructure and hardware, such as storage, processing power, and analytical tools. Technologies such as cloud computing and artificial intelligence have enabled the effective handling and analysis of such large amounts of data, bringing added value to large collections of data. The shift from traditional, periodically updated datasets to the dynamic, continuously generated big data of today represents a fundamental change in how data is conceived, collected, and used.[7] This transition means that more information can be extracted from data, leading to important knowledge gains. In this context, we are witnessing the increasing importance of data in contemporary society and the need for robust methods to criti-

[1] Kitchin and Lauriault (2015).

[2] Kitchin (2013, 2014).

[3] Pagallo (2022); Durante et al. (2022).

[4] Kitchin and Lauriault (2015), Kitchin and Lauriault (2018).

[5] Ibid.

[6] Ibid.

[7] Ibid.

cally manage, analyze, and interpret the vast amounts of information now available. However, as we explore this strange new world of data, we must not forget to take ethical principles and each citizen's right to privacy into account.[8]

1.2 The Economic Value of Health Data

Today's unparalleled growth in the health data being generated has significant implications for both healthcare services and research. According to the European Commission, in 2015, the EU's healthcare data market was valued at approximately €16 billion.[9] By 2020, this had nearly doubled, reaching around €31 billion.[10] Currently, the "reuse" of health data, i.e., using health data for secondary purposes, is alone estimated to be worth between €25–30 billion annually, with projections suggesting this value could reach approximately €50 billion within the next decade.[11] Notably, all these data originate from a vast range of different sources, including electronic health records, wearable devices, clinical trials, public health data, and more.[12]

Reusing health data offers numerous benefits. For example, secondary data research can lead to improved patient care through personalized treatment plans and more accurate diagnoses. It can also improve research by allowing analysts and AI systems to identify patterns and correlations in the data, which often leads to new medical discoveries and technological innovations in both the public and private sectors.[13] Reusing health data can also increase cost efficiencies by minimizing redundant medical testing and by exploiting AI for digital pathology.[14] It might also contribute to public health improvements through better disease monitoring, prevention strategies, and more informed funding allocations.

In 2019, pharmaceutical goods and other medical non-durable goods accounted for approximately 14% of total health expenditure in the EU, amounting to nearly €195 billion, according to Eurostat.[15] Additionally, therapeutic appliances and other medical durable goods made up about 4% of health expenditure, or around €60 billion.[16] Wearable medical devices, in particular, are an expanding market, valued in 2023 at US $81.15 billion in the US.[17] According to the EHDS Impact Assessment

[8] Ibid, Custers and Uršič (2016).

[9] European Commission (2022a).

[10] Ibid.

[11] Ibid.

[12] Ibid.

[13] Mancini (2014); Pavel et al. (2013).

[14] L'Imperio et al. (2024).

[15] European Commission (2022a).

[16] Ibid.

[17] Straits Research (2024).

study, the medical devices industry is also a significant sector in Europe, employing 760,000 workers across 33,000 companies, 95% of which are small-to-medium-sized enterprises (SMEs). This share of the industry represents almost 8% of total healthcare expenditure.[18] According to the study, the EU medical devices market, valued at €140 billion, has been growing since 2017 and is the second-largest market globally, following the US. It accounts for 28% of the world market for medical devices, and, in 2020, this sector contributed a €8.7 billion trade surplus to the EU's economy.[19]

All of those devices create a large amount of health data that can be reused and shared with third parties to gain insights into patients. Medical devices provide continuous, real-world, patient-specific insights that can drive improvements in healthcare delivery, research, and public health outcomes.[20] Moreover, access to diverse and high-quality health data speeds up the development of new medical devices, drugs, and AI systems,[21] leading to innovative healthcare solutions that can be sold and exploited.

However, there are some critical issues that depend on the economic, cultural, technical, and legislative circumstances surrounding the devices, particularly those that incorporate AI.[22] For example, the lack of standardization across different systems and data formats can hinder data use and analysis. Further, interoperability issues make effective data sharing through different healthcare systems and platforms across the EU very difficult. For this reason, the EU has established the Data Governance Act,[23] the Data Act,[24] and the European Health Data Space[25] as possible solutions. For an analysis of the differences between the EU and the US data spaces, see Pagallo's comprehensive discussions.[26]

2 Recent Cyberattacks on Healthcare Facilities

Due to the great value of health data, the healthcare industry has recently become the target of numerous worldwide cyberattacks.[27] In fact, according to 2023's Internet Crime report issued by the FBI, the healthcare sector experienced the highest number of organizations falling victim to ransomware attacks. Such attacks lead

[18] European Commission (2022a).

[19] Ibid.

[20] Kush (2023); Safran (2017).

[21] Pagallo et al. (2024a).

[22] Pagallo et al. (2024b).

[23] Carovano and Finck (2023).

[24] Gallese (2022).

[25] Terzis and Santamaria Echeverria (2023).

[26] Pagallo (2023a, b).

[27] Paul III et al. (2018); Kandasamy et al. (2022); Sekar et al. (2023); Devi (2023); Seh et al. (2020).

to disruptions in emergency services,[28] general patient services, and clinical trials.[29] They also often disclose patients' most sensitive data. This was especially true during the COVID-19 pandemic,[30] in part due to issues with due diligence and maladministration.[31] While public hospitals may have a policy that prevents them from paying cybercriminals, other facilities are willing to pay the ransom, which generally, and unfortunately, only serves to mark them as even more lucrative targets for these types of attacks.

There are two key security challenges that affect hospital computer systems in relation to cyberattacks: resource constraints and legacy system dependencies. Hospitals often prioritize medical quality, i.e., their primary business objective, over IT investments and cyber-security consultancy.[32] This, however, leaves them vulnerable to cyber threats. While this problem is not unique to healthcare,[33] it is very common in public-funded healthcare systems, and the consequences are more severe given the sensitivity of medical data and the critical nature of hospital operations. The problem of software and hardware compatibility with older equipment is an additional struggle for healthcare institutions. Many hospitals use specialized medical systems and equipment with a long operational lifespan and must amortize the investment over several years (such as is the case with positron emission tomography and MRI machines). These devices are often only compatible with older operating systems, which forces hospitals to delay software updates or continue using outdated systems.[34] This issue exposes hospitals to potential cyber-attacks, as legacy systems are often unsupported and lack the latest security patches.[35]

Recovering from such attacks costs healthcare facilities an average of over 10 million dollars,[36] reducing the funding available to deliver healthcare or conduct research. In a review of data breaches associated with healthcare security systems, Reddy et al. find that nearly 113 million data records were exposed in 2015 alone.[37] According to Looi et al., if stolen identity data is publicly released, patients and doctors may be subject to blackmail, fraud, identity theft, and targeted scams.[38] Sensitive information, such as terminating a pregnancy, mental illness, and substance abuse disorders, have already been published on the dark web following ransomware attacks.[39] The disclosure of such information can easily lead to dis-

[28] Ahmed et al. (2023).

[29] Harvey et al. (2023).

[30] Minnaar and Herbig (2021); Kolouch et al. (2021); Chigada and Madzinga (2021).

[31] Katagiri (2024); Stevens et al. (2017).

[32] Wernz et al. (2014).

[33] Fleischman et al. (2023).

[34] Narayana Samy et al. (2010).

[35] Nobile (2023a, b).

[36] Tarka et al. (2023); Lee et al. (2024).

[37] Reddy et al. (2023).

[38] Looi et al. (2024b).

[39] Looi et al. (2024b).

crimination, family conflict, stress, trauma, or even suicide, as happened following a hack into the Finnish therapy facility Vastaamo.[40]

There is no doubt that illegally acquired health data presents significant risks to patient privacy and security by exposing individuals to various forms of exploitation and harm.[41] Vulnerable patients, in particular, face heightened dangers as criminals may use this information to target them for phishing, social engineering attacks,[42] or targeted marketing practices.[43] These attacks can deceive individuals into revealing additional personal information, transferring money, or engaging in unfair contracts, exacerbating their vulnerabilities. Thus, disadvantaged patients, like inpatients, heavy drug users, and those with limited healthcare alternatives, are among those who suffer the most from breaches.[44]

In addition, data breaches facilitate identity theft, allowing perpetrators to impersonate patients and commit fraud.[45] For example, criminals might impersonate health insurance companies through phishing emails, tricking patients into clicking malicious links, paying undue sums, and so on. Health insurance numbers can also be exploited to cover someone else's medical expenses by impersonating a patient whose data has been stolen. Through the knowledge gained by the leaked information, criminals are even able to impersonate and exploit the victim in informal situations, such as asking for money from relatives. This can lead to financial losses, damage to credit scores, and also significant emotional distress for the affected individuals. The stolen data can also be used to access and manipulate other personal accounts, amplifying the scope of the damage.[46]

Banks and financial institutions might exploit health data to deny credit or mandate compulsory insurance to individuals with certain medical conditions, perceiving them as high-risk borrowers, as widely documented in the literature.[47] This discriminatory practice can severely limit their financial opportunities and stability, exacerbating their already vulnerable situation. Similarly, health insurance companies might use such data to deny coverage or increase premiums, especially for those with chronic or severe illnesses.[48] This practice can leave patients without essential health services, further endangering their well-being.

These potential abuses are the main reason that should lead to robust data protection and data governance measures, including anonymization practices. Ensuring the security of health data is important for safeguarding individuals from exploitation and discrimination that can significantly impact their lives. Enhanced

[40] Looi et al. (2024a); Ghanbari and Koskinen (2024).

[41] Garrison and Guy Posey (2012); Wairimu and Fritsch (2022).

[42] Salahdine and Kaabouch (2019).

[43] Guzelian et al. (2015).

[44] Ke et al. (2022).

[45] Kesari (2022).

[46] Halawa et al. (2016).

[47] Sarker (2020); Rice (1996); Dymski (2006); Bullington et al. (2022).

[48] Egan (1998); Crossley (2005); Kuschke (2018); Frey (2009).

cybersecurity measures, regular audits, and governance policies might help to mitigate these risks and protect vulnerable populations from the detrimental consequences of health data breaches.

However, as detailed in Sect. 3, protecting patient data is not merely a technical issue that can be solved by applying ordinary cyber-security measures. The concept of anonymization itself and its related practices are very complex. Hence, a thorough scholarly evaluation is needed.

3 The European Health Data Space

The EU recently approved a new regulation, titled the EHDS Regulation, that imposes obligations over the primary and secondary use of health data. The legislation also outlines a governance framework and some related infrastructure, building on the General Data Protection Regulation (GDPR),[49] the Data Governance Act (DGA),[50] the Data Act (DA),[51] and the Network and Information Systems Directive (NIS 2).[52]

This regulation represents the first common EU data space within the European strategy governing data and has three goals: (i) to facilitate the exchange of data for the delivery of healthcare at the European level; (ii) to create a single digital market for electronic health record systems; and (iii) to create a system through which companies, public institutions, and research entities can reuse health data.[53]

In the context of anonymizing health data in the EU, it is important to consider this new legislative framework, because, once enacted, it will entail a significant increase in anonymized data sharing.

[49] Regulation 2016/679 of the European Parliament and of the Council of 27 April 2016 on the protection of natural persons with regard to the processing of personal data and on the free movement of such data, and repealing Directive 95/46/EC (General Data Protection Regulation). Off J Eur Union L 59:1–88.

[50] Regulation 2022/868 of the European Parliament and of the Council of 30 May 2022 on European Data Governance and amending Regulation 2018/1724 (Data Governance Act). Off J Eur Union L 152:1–44.

[51] Regulation 2023/2854 of the European Parliament and of the Council of 13 December 2023 on harmonized rules on fair access to and use of data and amending Regulation 2017/2394 and Directive 2020/1828 (Data Act). Off J Eur Union L 49:1–71.

[52] Directive 2022/2555 of the European Parliament and of the Council of 14 December 2022 on measures for a high common level of cybersecurity across the Union, amending Regulation No 910/2014 and Directive 2018/1972, and repealing Directive 2016/1148 (NIS 2 Directive). Off J Eur Union L 133:1–80.

[53] European Commission (2022b).

Table 1 EHDS data categories and definitions

Term	EHDS Article	Definition
Data	Article 2	Definition borrowed from Article 2, point (1) of Regulation (EU) 2022/868
Personal data	Article 2	Definition borrowed from the GDPR.
Data concerning health	Article 2	Definition borrowed from the GDPR.
Genetic data	Article 2	Definition borrowed from the GDPR.
Electronic health data (EHD)	Article 2	Defined as personal or non-personal electronic health data.
Personal electronic health data (PEHD)	Article 2	Defined as data concerning health and genetic data as defined in Article 4, points (13) and (15), of Regulation (EU) 2016/679, processed in an electronic form.
Non-personal electronic health data (NPEHD)	Article 2	Defined as electronic health data other than personal electronic health data, encompassing both data that has been anonymized so that it no longer relates to an identified or identifiable natural person and data that has never been related to a data subject.
Person identification data/ Identification data	Article 2	Definition borrowed from Article 3, points (1), (2), and (3) of Regulation (EU) No 910/2014.
Health Data	Article 2	Definition borrowed from the GDPR.
Electronic health records	Article 2	Defined as "a collection of electronic health data related to a natural person and collected in the health system, processed for the purpose of the provision of healthcare".
Structured health data	Article 2 Recital 39a	Data in formats such as records in a relational database, XML documents or CSV files, and other files including free text, audio, video, and images provided as computer-readable files
Unstructured health data	Articles 2 and 15	Not defined.
Dataset	Article 15 and 36	Defined as "a structured collection of electronic health data".

3.1 *Data Definitions in the EHDS*

The EHDS contains several different categories of data, some defined and some not defined, as shown in Table 1. Thus, we have a wealth of terms that are not properly defined and could cause many interpretation issues. Further, applying anonymization techniques to those data might influence a definition, creating further confusion.

Health data are typically collected so as to deliver healthcare services to patients. For example, in hospitals, doctors may collect names, anamnesis, symptoms, and other relevant data to formulate a diagnosis. In some hospitals, these pieces of information are recorded on paper, then digitized later at the local, regional, or national level while, in others, they are digitized immediately through tablets and other smart devices.

Article 5 of the EHDS Regulation specifies that the primary uses of these data include (a) patient summaries; (b) electronic prescriptions; (c) electronic dispensations; (d) medical imaging studies and related imaging reports; (e) medical test results, including laboratory and other diagnostic results and related reports; and (f) discharge reports. These categories are then further described in Annex I.

3.2 *The Primary Use of Health Data*

The primary use is related to the original purposes of health data collection, which is mainly the delivery of health care services, "in order to assess, maintain or restore the state of health of the natural person to whom those data relate, including the prescription, dispensation and provision of medicinal products and medical devices, as well as for relevant social, administrative or reimbursement services" (Art. 2).

It is important to remember that in most cases consent is not needed to collect and process data for the delivery of healthcare primary use, as often the data processing falls within the exceptions provided by Article 9 GDPR, in particular the legal basis of the performance of an health care contract, the performance of a task carried out in the public interest, the compliance with a legal obligation, and the vital interest protection (Article 9(2), point (c) of GDPR). For this reason, the EHDS provides a soft opt-out mechanism, according to which "Member States' laws may provide that natural persons have the right to opt out from the access to their personal electronic health data registered in an EHR system through the electronic health data access services" (Art. 10).

The primary use of electronic health data under the EHDS is still to enhance healthcare at both the national and cross-border levels. Medical data, which is typically captured in electronic health records at the hospital level, contains segments of a patient's medical history that might be centrally managed or distributed across various healthcare providers. The EHDS will integrate three main sources of health data. First, electronic health records stored in healthcare facilities, such as hospitals and nursing homes, will form the backbone of this system, serving as the primary repository of patient information. Second, other health and medical software products, such as medical imaging software, e-prescribing software, medical diagnosis software, and telemedicine, will be incorporated into a single digital system to provide healthcare solutions in a much smoother manner. Third, wellness apps will be included, with a voluntary labeling scheme to inform consumers that their personal health management tools are being integrated with more formal electronic health records.[54]

Some of the key aspects of using health data under the EHDS rely on software and hardware components. For example, patients will have their electronic health data accessible through designated access points established by the Member States,

[54] European Commission (2022b).

ensuring a unified approach to data availability through a shared facility.[55] In fact, a cross-border digital infrastructure will be established, connecting Member States and enabling patients to share their health data across borders (hopefully) without technical issues. This system is aimed at empowering patients to control and share their electronic health records with healthcare providers of their choice, promoting patient autonomy and participation in their healthcare decisions—at least in theory.[56] The EHDS simply allows individuals to access their health data and share it with the healthcare professionals of their choice, including those located abroad.[57] This means that, say, any EU citizen can access their local data when visiting a doctor in a different Member State, which should help local hospitals provide better care. This is particularly important in places like Italy, where the different regions are highly fragmented. Yet, if implemented correctly, patients will be able to access and share their medical history in different parts of not only their own country but also the whole of the EU. This, of course, constitutes a great advancement for healthcare delivery.

In addition, Member States will be required to make "priority categories" of data available in a common European data exchange format. These categories include patient summaries, e-prescriptions, e-dispensations, medical images and image reports, laboratory results, and discharge reports.[58]

The only exemption is that Member States can choose not to convert personal health data into this particular electronic format if it was not collected electronically prior to the regulation coming into force. However, for the most part, health professionals will have access to a patient's electronic health records and will be expected to update the data of the patients they treat. Moreover, to enforce data sharing between healthcare providers, the regulation will introduce mandatory requirements for interoperability, security, safety, and anonymization.[59]

3.3 *The Secondary Use of Health Data*

Once collected, health data might also be used for non-clinical purposes, such as part of a statistical analysis, for epidemiology, or to train an AI model. These are classified as secondary uses. The ability to reuse these data for certain purposes is particularly crucial to research and development. For the survival of our civilization, we need to develop a better understanding of diseases, develop better treatments for the sick, and develop crucial insights into the epidemiology of diseases and conditions.

---

[55] Ibid.

[56] Ibid.

[57] European Commission (2022b).

[58] Ibid.

[59] Ibid.

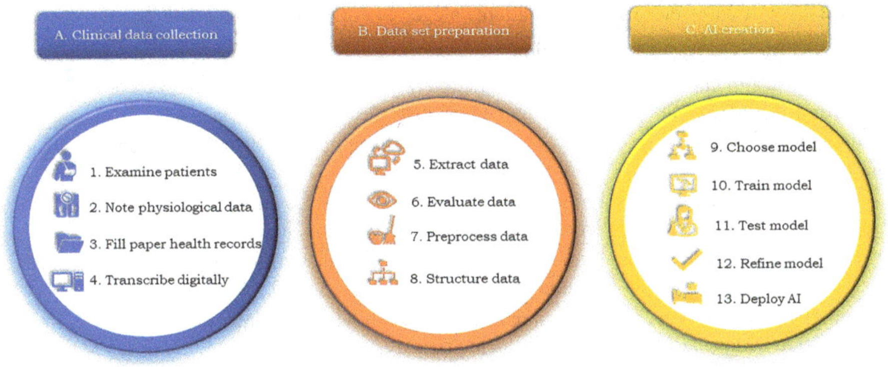

Fig. 1 The primary and secondary uses of healthcare data in an AI pipeline

Figure 1 shows an example of the different phases of data processing in health research with the aid of AI. First, the doctor collects data from patients as part of the course of delivering health care. She then uploads it to an electronic health record system. This falls into the primary use category. Then, the secondary use phase begins. The data are extracted and processed by IT experts to make it fit for use with AI. Finally, the data is used to train an AI model, which will be employed as a tool to improve patient care—at least as far as the legislators are concerned.

Section IV of the EHDS governs the secondary use of electronic health data. Article 51, for example, outlines the categories of electronic health data that the data holders are required to make available to third parties who request access for secondary use (i.e., the "data users"). This list provided in the Article ensures a wide range of data can be used to advance healthcare, research, and policymaking. The specified categories from Article 51 are shown in Table 2.

Article 53 of the Regulation outlines the secondary purposes for which health data can be shared. It describes a broad range of uses designed to improve public and individual health outcomes, support policymaking, and advance scientific research. One of the central aims is to promote public and occupational health. Health data can be shared to improve health outcomes at the population level, to respond to public health emergencies, or to enhance health in the workplace through targeted interventions. Sharing data can support the development of strategies to mitigate health risks and improve the overall well-being of the population. Health data can also be used to support policymaking and regulatory activities within public sector institutions, agencies, and bodies. Such data are also often used to help develop, implement, and evaluate health policies and regulations designed to benefit public health. If policy decisions are grounded in robust data, institutions across the EU can ensure that health policies are evidence-based and supported by actual data. In statistics, health data is instrumental for generating insights that inform and foster a deeper understanding of health trends, resource allocations, and how well health systems are performing. Such data-driven insights are important for optimizing how healthcare systems function and making informed decisions about resource

Table 2 Article 51 of the EHDS Regulation: categories of health data and their definitions

Term	Definition
Electronic health data from electronic health records	Patient information recorded in electronic health records, providing medical histories.
Data on factors impacting health	Socio-economic, environmental, and behavioral determinants that influence health outcomes.
Aggregated healthcare data	Data on healthcare needs, resource allocation, provision and access to healthcare, expenditure, and financing.
Pathogen data	Information about pathogens that affect human health is crucial for understanding and managing infectious diseases.
Healthcare-related administrative data	Data on medication dispensation, insurance claims, and reimbursement processes.
Genetic, epigenomic, and genomic data	Human genetic information is included, which is vital for personalized medicine and understanding genetic disorders.
Other human molecular data	Data from various 'omics' fields, such as proteomics, transcriptomics, metabolomics, and lipidomics, which are important for comprehensive molecular analyses.
Automatically generated personal health data	Data collected through medical devices that monitor and report health metrics automatically.
Data from wellness applications	Information from apps designed to track health and wellness metrics, such as fitness trackers and mobile health apps.
Professional data from health professionals	Data regarding the professional status, specializations, and institutional affiliations of healthcare providers involved in patient care.
Population-based health registries	Public health registries that collect health data at the population level.
Medical and mortality registries	Data from registries that record medical conditions and mortality statistics.
Data from clinical trials and studies	Data from clinical trials, studies, and investigations as regulated by EU regulations that provides insights into experimental treatments and their outcomes.
Other health data from medical devices	Any additional data collected from various medical devices not covered by other categories.
Registries for medicinal products and medical devices	Data from registries specifically tracking medicinal products and medical devices.
Research cohorts, questionnaires, and surveys	Data collected through research cohorts, health-related questionnaires, and surveys, made available after the initial publication of results.
Health data from biobanks and associated databases	Biological samples and associated health data stored in biobanks.

allocation. Health data also play an important role in education and teaching activities. Providing real-world data for educational purposes helps to train future healthcare professionals at both the vocational and higher education levels while integrating actual health data into educational curricula prepares students for the practical challenges they will face in their professional careers. Scientific research is another broad area where health data is used. Research related to public health,

health technology assessments, quality and safety standards, medicinal products, and medical devices, all benefit significantly from access to health data.

As such, the framework relies on creating a new, decentralized infrastructure for the secondary use of health data, known as HealthData@EU. This initiative will connect the types of bodies across all the Member States of the EU that have an interest in accessing health data. However, to be able to re-use health data, all applicants must obtain a permit from a "Health Data Access Body", which specifies the permissible uses of the data based on the entity's intended purposes for using the data. Moreover, the data can only be accessed and processed within closed environments provided by the Data Access Body, and those conditions must adhere to stringent cybersecurity standards. And lastly, users who obtain a data permit are only allowed to extract anonymous data from these secure environments. That said, if researchers, companies, or public institutions need access to personal electronic health data that is not anonymized, they may be able to access the data in a pseudonymized form. A pseudonymized form means the data will include information about diseases, symptoms, and medications without revealing any direct identifiers of the individuals. Of course, any attempt to re-identify the subjects in the data is strictly prohibited.

It is also prohibited to use the data for purposes that could harm individuals, such as increasing insurance premiums, marketing health products directly to patients or healthcare professionals, or designing harmful products or services. However, there is no definition of harm, and this provision remains vague at best.

The data access bodies must ensure transparency by publishing information about data access applications. Data users must also make their research results available to the public within 18 months, and they must inform their Data Access Body of any significant findings relevant to individual health. This requirement ensures that the knowledge generated from the use of health data contributes to scientific progress and is accessible to the broader community. However, data users are not required to publish the products, inventions, or tools developed using the data nor detailed technical information that could be used in a patent or might reveal a commercial advantage. In other words, while the scientific findings must be shared, the specifics that could form the basis for intellectual property (IP) protection do not have to be disclosed. As known, publishing detailed informations related to a patentable product will result in the rejection of the patent application for failing to meet the novelty criteria. In the most straightforward cases, users can directly request data from a single data provider, provided that privacy and security safeguards are maintained. Researchers and innovators from third-party countries can access the data for secondary uses under the same conditions as those from within the EU.

The secondary use of electronic health data under the EHDS framework is thus designed to advance healthcare research and innovation, but not specifically for patient needs. Rather, the intent is to maximize the benefits of using health data in cross-border collaborations within the EU so as to give the EU an advantage in its competition with international actors.

Against this normative background, and taking into consideration the risks of a data breach outlined in Sect. 2, anonymization becomes a primary factor for protecting patients' rights. In fact, once such a large-scale sharing infrastructure is in place, the majority of dataset brokers will have no choice but to anonymize and pseudonymize their data. Yet to accomplish this, several theoretical assumptions and practical considerations must be made, such as: What constitutes personal data? What data is considered to be a direct identifier? What anonymization techniques should be employed? What data should be anonymized and what should be pseudonymized? What are acceptable reasons to grant access to pseudonymized datasets as opposed to their anonymized versions?

As we will see in Sect. 4, these questions are not neutral and objective. Rather, they carry several political considerations. Additionally, despite the substantial potential benefits of data sharing under the EHDS framework, significant concerns have arisen regarding the protection of the data involved. The extensive sharing and use of health data increases the risk of cyber-attacks, data breaches, and data exploitation. For example, assume that Company A faces two cyber-security threats per year, such risks are multiplied for each company that has access to the same data.

Addressing these risks requires robust safeguards and security measures to protect health information from unauthorized access and misuse, which companies and institutions are not always ready to implement. To combat cyber-attacks, it is essential to continually update cybersecurity measures to address evolving threats, especially in the case of IoT medical devices.[60] This means, for example, implementing advanced encryption techniques, secure data storage solutions, and regular security audits to identify and mitigate vulnerabilities, in line with the recent EU legislation on cyber-security.[61] However, as noted by Saeed,[62] cyber-threats are becoming increasingly complex, so traditional security measures are no longer sufficient, and the requirements set out in Annex II are not detailed enough. On the other hand, it is not clear if the requirements of the Cyber-Resilience Act will be relevant to systems created by the EHDS. Additionally, such state-of-the-art measures are expensive to implement.

Data breaches pose a significant threat, even when the data are anonymized, due to the risk of linking with different datasets.[63] Mitigating this risk requires the data access bodies as well as other stakeholders to adopt appropriate data protection policies that not only comply with regulatory standards, such as the GDPR, but also keep pace with the most recent cyber-threats. These policies must include procedures for responding to data breaches, such as promptly notifying affected individuals in any case of any breach and taking corrective action to prevent future incidents. By contrast, the GDPR only requires notification in certain cases. Additionally, while larger entities might have the necessary means to enact such policies, SMEs

[60] Nobile (2023a, b).

[61] Ibid.

[62] Saeed et al. (2023).

[63] Sweeney (1997).

and individuals could face cyber-security challenges that are beyond their ability to defend against no matter how much awareness they have that such threats exist.[64]

It is clear from the sheer potential for data exploitation, that data use and reuse requires clear guidelines and some imposition of ethical standards, especially in the case of high-risk AI applications. Ensuring that health data is used legally, responsibly, and ethically requires transparent data-sharing practices. It also requires informed consent from the data subjects even when not required by law. The individuals whose data has been captured need to be involved in the processes of sharing data. Measures need to be implemented to prevent re-identifying individuals or misusing data for purposes beyond the intended scope, while also abiding by the new rules of the AI Act[65] in terms of data governance (Article 10) and transparency (Article 13).[66] For a more detailed analysis of the AI Act, we refer readers to Pagallo.[67]

Lastly, while sharing and using health data for public health, policymaking, education, and research purposes might offer substantial benefits, it also poses significant challenges in terms of exploitation and transparency, especially when used for training AI models and in continuous learning. Addressing these challenges requires an interdisciplinary approach[68] that involves lawyers, ethicists, IT specialists, and co-creation measures to promote effective stakeholder participation. Patients and other vulnerable groups need to be involved in policymaking as well as in data processing activities, where relevant. Ultimately, we need to adopt a critical perspective toward the multiple issues created by the EHDS and our techno-centric approaches to EU policies.[69]

4 Redefining Anonymization

4.1 Different Anonymization Techniques

The primary data protection guidance document in the field of law is the "Article 29 Working PartyOpinion 05/2014 on Anonymisation Techniques",[70] published by the Working Party on the Protection of Individuals with regard to the Processing of Personal Data (Article 29 WP) in 2014. To date, this remains the only official docu-

[64] Zwilling et al. (2022).

[65] Regulation 2024/1689 of the European Parliament and of the Council of 13 June 2024 laying down harmonized rules on artificial intelligence and amending Regulations (EC) No 300/2008, 167/2013, No 168/2013, 2018/858, 2018/1139 and 2019/2144 and Directives 2014/90/EU, 2016/797 and 2020/1828 (Artificial Intelligence Act). Off J Eur Union L 24:1–144.

[66] Pagallo (2023a, b).

[67] Pagallo (2023b).

[68] Nobile (2023a, b).

[69] Balayn and Gürses (2021).

[70] Working Party (2014).

ment on anonmization published by a data protection institution in the EU (now substituted by the EDPB—European Data Protection Board); therefore, itstill represents an important reference in the discipline.

It is important to discuss the information contained in the Opinion despite it being ten years old and pre-GDPR, because it offers insights into the legal concepts of anonymization, pseudonymization, and personal data that are still relevant today. Until the EDPB issues new guidelines on the topic offering a novel legal interpretation in light of the latest scientific developments, the Opinion remains the only legal interpretation tool with EU relevance.

The Art. 29 WP's Opinion discusses two primary categories of anonymization techniques in its guidelines: randomization and generalization. Randomization involves replacing sensitive data with random values, with the aim of obscuring individual data points through different methods.[71] One such method is adding noise, which introduces random noise to the data values, effectively masking the precise information of individual entries [55]. Another technique is permutation, which shuffles the data values within a dataset to break any direct links between the data and specific individuals.[72] Differential privacy is a more sophisticated approach that guarantees privacy preservation against many privacy attacks—such as differencing, linkage, and reconstruction attacks—by modifying data in a manner which ensures that removing or adding a single item does not significantly impact the overall analysis. In this way, it protects individual data points while maintaining the integrity of the entire dataset.[73] By contrast, generalization focuses on reducing the specificity of the data to protect individual identities. Aggregation is a straightforward generalization technique, summarizing data into broader categories, making it less specific.[74] K-anonymity ensures that each individual in the dataset is indistinguishable from at least k-1 others, providing a basic level of anonymity.[75] L-diversity extends k-anonymity by ensuring sufficient diversity in the sensitive attributes within each equivalence class, thus enhancing privacy protection.[76] T-closeness goes further by ensuring that the distribution of sensitive attributes in any equivalence class is close to their distribution in the overall dataset, offering a higher level of protection against re-identification.[77]

The Opinion draws some considerations regarding the robustness of each technique, following three criteria: (1) whether it is possible to single out an individual; (2) whether it is possible to link records relating to an individual; and (3) whether information can be inferred concerning an individual. If the answer is positive, the data is still considered personal data. It argues that the main strengths and

---

[71] Majeed and Lee (2020).

[72] Ibid.

[73] Ibid.

[74] Ibid.

[75] Rajendran et al. (2017).

[76] Ibid.

[77] Ibid.

weaknesses of each technique provide important contextual information for designing adequate anonymization processes and that such processes should be regularly updated in light of the latest advancements in the field.

This Opinion is not limited to the scope of anonymization but, rather, it addresses pseudonymization as well. Pseudonymisation is defined in Art. 4 of GDPR as "the processing of personal data in such a manner that the personal data can no longer be attributed to a specific data subject without the use of additional information, provided that such additional information is kept separately and is subject to technical and organisational measures to ensure that the personal data are not attributed to an identified or identifiable natural person". First, the Opinion clarifies a now consolidated concept that pseudonymization is not a method of anonymization but, rather, a security measure that merely reduces the links within a dataset to the original identity of an individual. This distinction is essential to the debate over what constitutes personal data, as case law leverages this very point to draw a line between personal and non-personal data.

Balancing the trade-off between data utility and the application of anonymization techniques is difficult. Overly aggressive anonymization can render data useless for analysis, defeating the purpose of sharing the data in the first place.[78] Moreover, it is essential to recognize that anonymization is not a one-time, single process but rather is made up of a spectrum of different protocols and procedures. Also, different levels of anonymization may be appropriate depending on the context and specific requirements of the task to be performed.

The very nature of real-world datasets, i.e., that they are constantly being enriched by additional sources of data, coupled with the increasing sophistication of re-identification techniques, demands a dynamic approach to anonymization and one that can adapt to new challenges while still balancing privacy with utility. Data utility can be defined as the degree to which anonymized data retains its usefulness for a specific purpose (or set of purposes) despite any alterations made to protect privacy. It measures the balance between privacy protection and the functionality of the data for analysis, decision-making, machine learning training, and other uses.

Figure 2 illustrates an example of different degrees of anonymization and data utility for research purposes on a large dataset containing biometric data, names, surnames, medical information, and other data. In this example, both anonymization and data utility are comprised between 0 and 1, with 0 denoting that the dataset contains unique identifiers (such as DNA or fingerprint data) but has maximum utility, and 1 denoting complete anonymization but minimum utility. For the sake of simplicity, we assume that identification and utility have a linear relationship such that the more identifiers, the higher the utility of the dataset.

The figure indicates some of the different ways data can be modified to preserve privacy, such as removing direct identifiers. It also illustrates how different degrees of anonymization can influence data utility.

[78] Rodriguez-Hoyos et al. (2018).

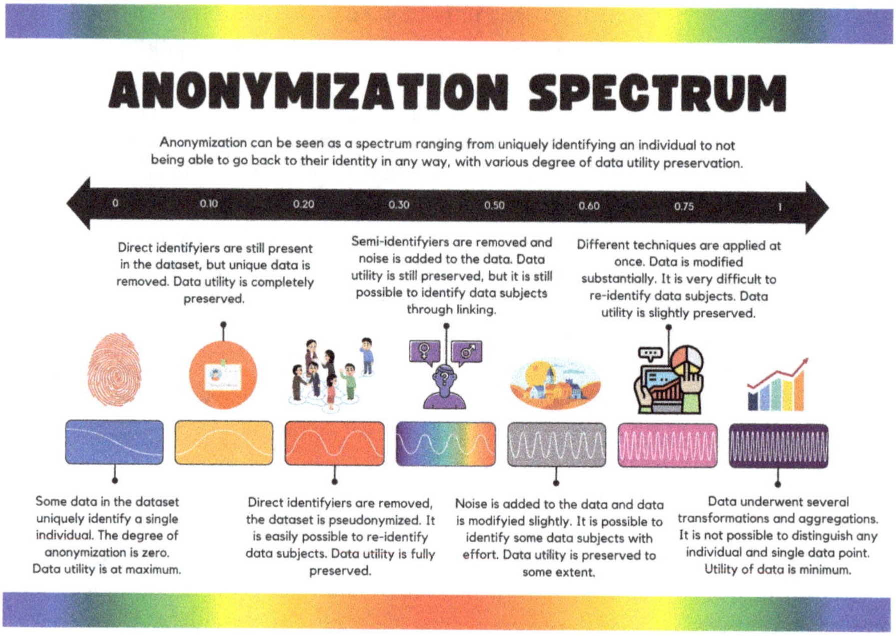

Fig. 2 An example of the anonymization spectrum

4.2 *The Role of Anonymization in the EHDS*

The topic of anonymized data is relevant in the EHDS from two perspectives. The first pertains to the data-sharing mechanism outlined in Article 66, which provides that health data access bodies should share electronic health data in an anonymized format if the user's processing objectives can be met with such data. If anonymized data are insufficient, pseudonymized data may be provided, with the key to re-identifying the data retained only by the Data Access Body or a trusted third party. As Article 66 states:

> Health data access bodies shall provide electronic health data in an anonymised format, where the purpose of processing by the health data user can be achieved with such data, taking into account the information provided by the health data user. Where the health data user has sufficiently demonstrated that the purpose of processing cannot be achieved with anonymised data in accordance with Article 68(1), point (c), health data access bodies shall provide access to electronic health data in pseudonymised format. The information necessary to reverse the pseudonymisation shall be available only to the health data access body or an entity that acts as a trusted third party in accordance with national law.

This provision enforces the principle of data minimization by defaulting to anonymization. However, this is problematic because the Regulation does not define the concept of "anonymization". Rather, the EHDS (Article 2, letter a9) simply refers to the GDPR for the following definitions: 'personal data', 'processing', pseudonymisation', 'controller', 'processor', 'third party', 'consent', 'genetic data', 'data concerning health', and 'international organisation',[79] but does not provide any guidance on how to achieve anonymity in this situation. The actual implementation of anonymization is left in the hands of the Data Access Bodies, which means different states will implement different protocols, likely leading to discrepancies across the EU.

In addition, deferring crucial definitions to the interpretation of the GDPR is not a good idea. There is already an ongoing decade-long discussion over the concept of personal data, which predates the GDPR and has never been solved. Since the EHDS will create a widespread data-sharing mechanism across the EU, it seems very dangerous for citizens' rights to have approved such a regulation without first solving the already contentious and outstanding issues regarding anonymization.

The second perspective involves patient opt-out options in relation to anonymized data. The mechanism is flawed because, if a patient chooses to opt out after their data have been anonymized, there is no way to identify the data for removal. Yet, according to Article 71:

> When the purposes of the processing of personal electronic health data by a health data holder do not or no longer require the identification of a data subject by the controller, that health data holder shall not be obliged to maintain, acquire or process additional information in order to identify the data subject for the sole purpose of complying with the right to opt out under this Article.

This provision is very problematic from an ethical point of view, firstly because it deprives citizens of exercising their will over their own health data, forcing them to be subject to third-party decisions, and secondly because of the data breach risks outlined in this chapter. Patients may be exposed to those risks against their consent, which might be legal but are unethical.

Additionally, the opt-out option is overridden by public interest, a concept that is not defined in the regulation and will thus be applied inconsistently across the EU. In fact, Article 71a provides that:

> By way of exception from the right to opt out provided for in paragraph 1, a Member State may provide in its national law for a mechanism to make data for which a right to opt out has been exercised available, provided that all the following conditions are fulfilled: (a) the health data access application or health data request is submitted by a public sector body or a Union institution, body, office or agency with a mandate to carry out tasks in the area of public health, or by another entity entrusted with carrying out public tasks in the area of public health, or acting on behalf of or commissioned by a public authority, and the processing of those data is necessary for any of the following purposes: (i) the purposes referred to in Article 53(1), points (a), (b) and (c); (ii) scientific research for important reasons of public interest; (b) those data cannot be obtained by alternative means in a timely and effective manner under equivalent conditions; (c) the health data applicant has provided the justification referred to in Article 68(1), point (g), or in Article 69(2), point (g) [...].

Despite these concerns, there is hope that the European Commission will issue guidance, as indicated in Recital 65:

[79] Regulation 2016/679, Article 4, points (1), (2), (5), (7), (8), (10), (11), (13), (15), (26).

> [Health Data Bodies] should apply tested state-of-the-art techniques that ensure electronic health data are processed in a manner that preserves the privacy of the information contained in the data for which secondary use is allowed, including techniques for pseudonymisation, anonymisation, generalisation, suppression and randomization of personal data. Health data access bodies can prepare datasets for the health data user as required under the issued data permit. In that regard, health data access bodies should cooperate across borders to develop and exchange best practices and techniques. This includes rules for pseudonymisation and anonymisation of micro datasets. When relevant, the Commission should set out the procedures and requirements, and provide technical tools, for a unified procedure for pseudonymising and anonymising electronic health data.

According to Article 66, sharing pseudonymized data necessitates a proper justification, demonstrating why processing cannot be pursued using anonymized data. This requirement is aimed at ensuring that the use of less secure pseudonymized data is only permitted when absolutely necessary for the processing objectives.

While the EHDS aims to facilitate data sharing and the secondary use of health data across the EU, it poses significant challenges regarding the definition and implementation of anonymization techniques. Clear guidance and a unified approach will be the only means to safeguarding privacy rights and maintaining consistency across Member States so that the benefits of the EHDS are realized without compromising individual rights.

4.3 *The Concept of Anonymization in Data Protection Law*

In its 2014 Opinion, the Working Party analyzed the effectiveness and limitations of anonymization techniques within the context of the EU's data protection laws. It highlighted several key points and recommendations regarding the concepts of both personal data and anonymized data.

The Working Party noted that anonymization can be a valuable strategy to balance the benefits of open data with the need to protect individual privacy. However, it acknowledged the inherent difficulties in achieving true anonymization while preserving the utility of the data. Various research studies have demonstrated the challenges of creating datasets that are both useful and irreversibly anonymized.[80]

According to the GDPR, as well as the previous Directive 95/46, that was in force in 2014, anonymization involves processing personal data in a way that *irreversibly* prevents identification. This must consider all means "likely reasonably" to be used for identification, either by the data controller or third parties. This process must consider all potential methods for re-identification, which can include sophisticated techniques and cross-referencing with other datasets. Importantly, anonymization constitutes further processing of personal data and must comply with legal grounds and account for the circumstances under which the original data was collected.

---

[80] Elliot et al. (2018); Eke et al. (2021).

A crucial distinction made by the Working Party in its Opinion is between anonymization and pseudonymization. Pseudonymized data, which still retains a potential means of re-identification, does not meet the threshold for anonymization and remains classified as personal data. Therefore, it continues to fall under the scope of data protection regulations.

In January 2025, the EDPB published the long-awaited "Guidelines 01/2025 on Pseudonymisation", a document that complements the Article 29 WP's Opinion and upholding its definitions regarding personal data. The Guidelines clearly state that "Pseudonymised data, which could be attributed to a natural person by the use of additional information, is to be considered information on an identifiable natural person, and is therefore personal. This statement also holds true if pseudonymised data and additional information are not in the hands of the same person. If pseudonymised data and additional information could be combined having regard to the means reasonably likely to be used by the controller or by another person, then the pseudonymised data is personal. Even if all additional information retained by the pseudonymising controller has been erased, the pseudonymised data becomes anonymous only if the conditions for anonymity are met".Recently, however, the case law has shifted towards a personalized concept of anonymization and pseudonymization, in contrast with Recital 26 of the GDPR and the previous Patrick Breyer case. Recital 26 states:

> To determine whether a natural person is identifiable, account should be taken of all the means reasonably likely to be used, such as singling out, either by the controller or by another person to identify the natural person directly or indirectly. To ascertain whether means are reasonably likely to be used to identify the natural person, account should be taken of all objective factors, such as the costs of and the amount of time required for identification, taking into consideration the available technology at the time of the processing and technological developments. The principles of data protection should therefore not apply to anonymous information, namely information which does not relate to an identified or identifiable natural person or to personal data rendered anonymous in such a manner that the data subject is not or no longer identifiable.

In Case C-582/14, Patrick Breyer v. Bundesrepublik Deutschland, in the judgment of 19 October 2016, the Court ruled that a dynamic IP address is considered personal data for a website operator if the operator has the legal means to combine it with other information to identify the individual (e.g., via cooperation with an ISP). This ruling gives precedence to the potential for identification over actual identification. Even if the website publisher cannot directly identify the visitor, the data qualifies as personal if they could do so through reasonable means, such as making a lawful request to an ISP. Further, in Case T-557/20,[81] Single Resolution Board (SRB) v European Data Protection Supervisor (EDPS) [2023], the Court ruled that the concept of personal data should be based on the position and data control of each party, a circumstance that results in different categorizations of the same dataset

[81] Case T-557/20, Single Resolution Board (SRB) v European Data Protection Supervisor (EDPS) (2023) ECLI:EU:T:2023:21. https://eur-lex.europa.eu/legal-content/EN/TXT/PDF/?uri=CELEX:62020TA0557.

depending on who holds it. This means that the data controller, before sharing the dataset, should consider the recipient's perspective and their ability to reidentify data subjects when deciding if the dataset is anonymized or not.[82]

The interpretation found in this judgment should be rejected in favor of a more objective one, since it exposes data subjects to more risks, due to the fact that anonymized datasets are not covered by the scope of the GDPR. If the original context determines whether data qualifies as "personal", the third party with whom the dataset is shared may argue that the GDPR does not apply because the data was shared as "non-personal". This creates a loophole for re-identification and potential privacy breaches. By contrast, qualifying the "personal" aspect of the data as inherently tied to the data itself, rather than contingent on the context of its processing or the entities involved, better aligns with the GDPR's intent to provide consistent protection. The implications of this judgment have been further discussed in a previous work.[83]

However, a key issue is that, once the data is anonymized, it generally falls outside the scope of data protection legislation. In some circumstances, individuals might still be protected under other provisions, such as doctor-patient confidentiality, but, for the most part, the anonymization process has the potential to draw a line between data protection and almost no protection.

4.4 A Shift in the Concept of Anonymized Health Data

The provisions in the EU Digital Strategy appear to treat anonymization as a black-or-white concept. At best, it allows "mixed datasets" to exist (i.e., datasets composed of both personal and non-personal data; see the Data Act).[84] This black-or-white thinking is found in several provisions—first and foremost, the GDPR.

In the GDPR, personal data is defined as any information that relates to an identified or identifiable living individual. This definition is open to interpretation, leading to several discussions among scholars regarding the implications of the word "identifiable", in that it is not clear as to whether the term also covers "the possibility" of being identifiable.[85] Since possibility has a qualitative nature, it depends on several factors, which might either be objective, like encryption keys, or subjective, like the ability of a person to identify someone in the dataset.

Case law and legal scholarship focus on the definition of personal data to understand when a dataset falls inside or outside the scope of the GDPR. However, this means a boundary between personal data and anonymized data (non-personal data) must be designed—and not one that is fuzzy but, rather, one that is clear and definite so that the law can be applied consistently. This is also because any discretion to

[82] Gallese (2024).

[83] Ibid.

[84] Gallese (2022).

[85] Finck and Pallas (2020).

interpret a law can result in a situation where the same patient providing the same exact data might be protected by the law in one case and not protected in another, even in the same country. For example, as often happens, one hospital might mistakenly consider pseudonymized data as anonymized, and share its datasets with multiple research groups, increasing the risk of a data breach. This was a major risk even before the EHDS, but the possibility of widespread cross-country data sharing increases the chances that patients' rights and freedoms will be violated.

Before the introduction of the GDPR, Ohm argued that the word "anonymize" should be abolished (Ohm, 2009). He recognized the failure of anonymization techniques and the subsequent harms given the ease with which an adversary can re-identify anonymized datasets. Subsequently, according to the author, the distinction between personal data and anonymized data is lost, and there is little point in keeping it alive.

The situation has not changed since the introduction of the GDPR. In fact, cyberattacks have only become more sophisticated and more frequent (see Sect. 2), as research has shown that anonymization techniques are fallible.[86]

In a constantly connected and globalized world, where most people actively share their information on social media and governments increasingly rely on online services to process citizens' data, the ease of combining different databases to re-identify supposedly "anonymized" data has significantly increased. This interconnectedness poses a substantial challenge to those wishing to protect data. The proliferation of digital footprints across various platforms means that data can often be cross-referenced with relative ease. For instance, social media profiles, public records, and online transactions can be amalgamated to reconstruct individual identities, even when those datasets were initially anonymized. The sheer volume and variety of data available as disparate pieces of information that can be linked together to form a whole picture of the data subject's life only serve to facilitate this re-identification process. This is particularly true in the case of health data since the information is often held by more than one public institution.

The ability to re-identify anonymized data thus raises significant privacy concerns. It shows the inadequacy of traditional anonymization methods, which may not account for the sophistication of modern data analytics and the extensive availability of auxiliary information. This situation is particularly concerning when sensitive personal data is involved, such as mental health data, as the implications of re-identification can be severe, leading to discrimination and exploitation. Moreover, this reality challenges the regulatory frameworks designed to protect personal data. The GDPR places great importance on anonymization to remove data from the scope of data protection laws. However, as demonstrated by recent case law, the effectiveness of anonymization must be continually assessed in light of evolving technological capabilities and the specific context of the data holders.

There is also a misconception about the true meaning of the word "anonymization". As already discussed, there are multiple technical solutions to mask the

[86] Sweeney (1997); Working Party (2014).

CLINICAL DATASET

HOSPITAL NAME

NAME OF DOCTOR DEPARTMENT DATE

NAME OF PATIENT	AGE	GENDER	DATE OF BIRTH	SYMPTOM	BLOOD TYPE	PRE-EXISTING ILLNESS	DATE OF STAY	CURRENT ILLNESS	BLOOD VALUES
NAME AND SURNAME	18	M	11/03	MIGRAINE	A	NONE	SPECIFIC DATES	NAME OF ILLNESS	203
NAME AND SURNAME	24	M	01/02	TIRED NESS	0-	NONE	SPECIFIC DATES	NAME OF ILLNESS	160
NAME AND SURNAME	60	F	04/12	HOT FLASHES	0+	DIABE TES	SPECIFIC DATES	NAME OF ILLNESS	220
NAME AND SURNAME	53	M	20/07	TIRED NESS	B	HIGH PRESSU RE	SPECIFIC DATES	NAME OF ILLNESS	93
NAME AND SURNAME	40	F	05/05	PAIN	AB	ENDOME TRIOSIS	SPECIFIC DATES	NAME OF ILLNESS	98
NAME AND SURNAME	35	M	09/06	RUSH	0+	NONE	SPECIFIC DATES	NAME OF ILLNESS	150

Fig. 3 An example of a clinical dataset

information of a person to different degrees, but there is no single definitive "anonymization". Figure 3 shows a simplified example of what a clinical dataset might look like, with the example based on my professional experience as a privacy expert and researcher working in several hospitals. Often, this type of table is shared in Microsoft Excel files by doctors with computer scientists or other IT experts for them to train an AI model. In the figure, only a few of the actual data columns are shown.

Looking at the figure, we see direct identifiers and semi-identifiers like name and surname, age, gender, and date of birth. While the date of birth is redundant with age, and the name-surname is not clinically relevant data, the other characteristics must generally be kept for training. Otherwise, depending on the specific situation, the AI model might not learn correctly. While some techniques might be able to retain some of the said characteristics and preserve the same accuracy in the model, there are instances in which the deep learning model needs the exact, unidentified data in order to avoid biases.

In this scenario, the stakeholders must decide what relevant security measures to apply to comply with the GDPR, such as encryption and anonymization. With the EDHS in force, such a dataset might be the object of the secondary data sharing provisions, which would mandate pseudonymization or anonymization. The matter then becomes one of how to anonymize the data without losing so much utility that, say, an AI model can no longer be trained, which might be the only reason for the sharing request. If the dataset is not helpful, there is no point in sharing it, and the EHDS provisions regarding the secondary use of data would be pointless.

However, because anonymization is not a solid, unique concept, the Data Access Body must choose one or more anonymization or pseudonymization measures before providing the data access to a permit holder. Depending on the specific request, some data might be removed, others might be masked, while others still will be left as they are. Yet because the combination of unique characteristics such as age at the time of data collection, blood type, gender, and dates of hospitalization can be found in different databases, the risk of linking this information together to reveal each patient's identity is high. For example, schools and workplaces likely have information regarding prolonged absences, while insurance companies and banks likely have information about periods of hospitalization, whether direct or inferred through payments. These can be used together with the names, ages, gender, date of birth, place of birth, and city of residence (which is usually the same as the hospital) to re-identify previously anonymized individuals. In some cases, these institutions may also have information about pre-existing conditions. Online cloud systems such as tax agencies or welfare fund databases also have the same information and more. It is not uncommon in many countries for these diverse pieces of information to be collected automatically and sent to different public authorities and other institutions.

If the clinical dataset is only "mildly" anonymized, it might be extremely easy to re-identify the patient and use the information for malicious purposes after a data breach. In a large field of research, such as genetics, data leading to unique identification such as DNA data are needed for the analysis, making it impossible to anonymize the dataset—and not because it is impossible to anonymize some gene sequences, but because the non-anonymized version is necessary to conduct the research.

Recital 92 of the EHDS notes that, as previously stated in Regulation (EU) 2022/868, some types of electronic health data may continue to be extremely sensitive even after being anonymized and rendered non-personal. There is always a chance that re-identification might happen or become accessible outside the scope of methods that are likely to be employed, even when cutting-edge anonymization techniques are being applied. According to this Recital, such residual risk particularly exists in the context of rare diseases (defined as a life-threatening or chronically debilitating condition that affects no more than five out of every 10,000 individuals in the EU).

The Recital argues that, due to the small number of cases, it is not possible to fully aggregate the published data in a way that protects individuals' identities while still retaining the necessary level of granularity for the data to convey meaningful information. Thus, the extent to which it affects different types of health data depends on the degree of granularity and description of the characteristics of the data subjects, the number of people affected, and other factors. The Recital uses the example of cases where the identification characteristics are broader and where the data is included in electronic health records, disease registries, biobanks, or person-generated data, etc. Other cases include where the technological advancement of methods that were not available at the time of anonymization can lead to re-identifying the data subjects using means beyond those reasonably considered. As a result, for these kinds of health data, there is still a chance of re-identification following anonymization or aggregation, which cannot be avoided.

Sharing this data type is very important for medical researchers because combining different datasets from different countries can increase the chances of extracting meaningful information about a disease, ultimately leading to a better chance of finding a cure or a treatment that improves patients' lives. The EHDS allows pseudonymized datasets to be shared, even though they are still considered to contain personal data and are protected by the GDPR. However, the requests for data must be adequately justified and can be turned down, leading to data users having access only to the "anonymized" form of the requested dataset, that is, the "non GDPR-protected" form. I argue that, if the law mandated the same standards of protection for anonymized datasets as it does for pseudonymized datasets, including them within the GDPR scope, patients' rights would be better protected.

It is important to consider that different institutions have different data practices and different conceptions of "anonymization", leading to very fragmented protection for patients. The current regulatory framework has led to a situation in which a patient's privacy depends on the luck of encountering an experienced IT professional who helps doctors with the anonymization process. This is how the risk of a data breach gets minimized. In this regard, the distinction between personal data and anonymized data in healthcare should be reconsidered, keeping in mind that data breaches might impact the fundamental rights of patients.

4.5 *Datafication and Anonymization*

The explosion of data over the past few decades has led to the phenomenon of "datafication".[87] This term, which is often used to describe the conversion of social factors into quantified data, refers to a range of big data challenges[88] that need to be examined through the lens of critical data theories. Corporations and states are increasingly using data mining to interrogate repositories of data, which has generated an intense debate about systematic surveillance and privacy invasion.[89] Accordingly, scholars like David Lyon[90] and Milan[91] have highlighted how these practices are threatening individual freedoms and the public's civil liberties.

Interdisciplinary research across social sciences, humanities, and computer science has increasingly focused on the potential for big data to perpetuate inequality,

[87] Mayer-Schönberger and Cukier (2013); Ruckenstein and Schüll (2017).

[88] Mayer-Schönberger and Cukier (2013).

[89] Milan (2019).

[90] Lyon (2014).

[91] Milan (2019).

discrimination, and exclusion.[92] For instance, the seminal works of Eubanks,[93] Gangadharan,[94] and Noble[95] have documented how data-driven systems can reinforce existing social biases and marginalize vulnerable populations. These scholars argue that the issues surrounding big data extend beyond technology, noting that it is also a "mythology" and an "ideology" that demands critical interrogation, as also noted by Boyd and Crawford,[96] van Dijck,[97] and Milan.[98]

Milan points out that the work of scholars like Aradau and Blanke[99] and Cheney-Lippold[100] demonstrate the narratives of modernization that surround big data but which often obscure the risks associated with the opaque regimes of population management and control. These critiques are essential for understanding how datafication can be used as a tool for surveillance and governance, potentially undermining democratic processes and principles.[101]

Moreover, there have been calls to consider the data produced by non-experts, as advocated by Gabrys et al.[102] and Kitchin and Lauriault.[103] This perspective accounts for the value of bottom-up practices and everyday forms of critical engagement with data,[104] a view that can be applied to the context of health data as well. As an example, patients produce their own data when they communicate their symptoms to healthcare professionals. Yet, often, this type of information is dismissed or diminished in value, especially in the case of women. However, the information provided by patients contributes to the health records that are ultimately turned into datasets and used to train AI systems. Therefore, it is important to involve non-experts in the data discourse. Scholars like Couldry and Powell[105] have encouraged a focus on these efforts, while Kennedy and Hill[106] highlight the importance of democratizing data practices and promoting inclusive, participatory approaches.

Feminist approaches to data, as discussed by D'Ignazio and Klein[107] and Fotopoulou,[108] provide additional critical lenses through which to examine the

---

[92] Ibid.

[93] Eubanks (2018).

[94] Gangadharan (2012).

[95] Noble (2018).

[96] Boyd and Crawford (2012).

[97] Van Dijck (2014).

[98] Milan (2019).

[99] Aradau and Blanke (2017).

[100] Cheney-Lippold (2011).

[101] Milan (2019).

[102] Gabrys et al. (2016).

[103] Kitchin and Lauriault (2015).

[104] Milan (2019).

[105] Couldry and Powell (2014).

[106] Kennedy and Hill (2018).

[107] D'ignazio and Klein (2023).

[108] Fotopoulou and Thornham (2020).

impacts of datafication in society. These perspectives advocate for inclusive, equitable data practices that consider the diverse experiences and needs of all individuals under an intersectional perspective,[109] particularly those from marginalized groups and those living in the so-called "global south".[110]

While the creation of big data has introduced significant opportunities for innovation and knowledge, it undoubtedly poses profound risks and challenges related to datafication and inequality. It is essential to study the mechanisms of datafication critically, exposing its underlying ideologies and studying anonymization and other data processing practices with a critical view.

In the discourse over health data, it is essential to acknowledge that anonymization is not merely a technical procedure but rather a political decision. Decision-makers are responsible for determining who will perform anonymization, whose data will be anonymized, the techniques to be employed, and the level of data utility to be preserved. These choices ultimately determine who will be protected and to what extent, highlighting the political nature of anonymization.

The EHDS places these critical decisions in the hands of Health Data Access Bodies, which will vary across Member States. There is no clear guidance on who these bodies should hire or the specific skills required, raising concerns about the consistency and effectiveness of anonymization practices. This variability can lead to significant disparities between wealthier and less wealthy countries, potentially fragmenting the protection offered by the EHDS and undermining its overall purpose.

Anonymization, often framed as a neutral or purely technical safeguard for privacy, is, in reality, deeply embedded in political and ethical considerations. As critical data studies scholars, we must consider the broader implications of anonymization practices, moving beyond the surface-level understanding of data protection to examine the power dynamics, social implications, and ethical questions that form the basis for these decisions. We must interrogate the assumptions underlying anonymization practices, to question who benefits from these processes, and to advocate for more equitable and transparent approaches to data processing. In this way, we can move towards a more profound understanding of data governance that protects the rights and interests of all individuals, not only those of the dominant groups.

Just like any other technical operation on data, anonymization is often perceived as a straightforward and neutral process of removing personal identifiers from datasets to protect privacy. However, this perception hides the inherently political nature of the process. Decision-makers, whether they are government bodies, corporations, health institutions, or other data controllers, will make crucial determinations about data. These decisions include selecting the methods used to anonymize data, choosing which datasets or individuals' data will be subject to anonymization, and deciding the extent to which the data will be ultimately modified.

These choices are not made in a vacuum; they are influenced by political, economic, and social factors. For instance, the decision to anonymize specific datasets

[109] Cho et al. (2013).

[110] Milan and Treré (2019).

may be driven by a peculiar interpretation of regulatory compliance, internal administrative procedures, or the pressure to publish results, but they always come from a position of power imbalance. The techniques chosen for anonymization—whether k-anonymity, differential privacy, or another method—reflect the priorities of those in power, often balancing the need to preserve data utility against the requirement to protect privacy. These decisions shape who benefits from the protections of anonymization and who might be left vulnerable.

At the heart of the process lie power dynamics over determining whose data is anonymized and to what extent. Anonymization can serve as a tool for protecting marginalized or vulnerable populations, but it can also be wielded in ways that reinforce existing inequalities. For example, if the anonymization process is biased—perhaps unconsciously prioritizing the privacy of certain groups over others—it can perpetuate social injustices. The decision about whose data is anonymized and whose is not can reflect broader societal biases and might further exacerbate power imbalances.

The ethics of anonymization thus extend beyond the data processing techniques and raise broader questions about the implications of these practices. We must ask crucial questions, such as what are the ethical responsibilities of those who anonymize data. Is it sufficient to anonymize data to meet legal requirements, or should there be a different approach that considers the needs and peculiarities of vulnerable groups? How do we ensure that anonymization practices do not inadvertently harm the very people they are meant to protect?

These perspectives have great relevance in the discourse regarding anonymization and data reuse. First of all, intersectionality[111] must be considered when defining anonymization and applying the related techniques. Intersectionality is an approach that considers how various forms of social categorizations, such as race, gender, class, sexual orientation, and others, intersect and overlap in the experiences of individuals, acknowledging that people's identities are complex and cannot be examined in isolation and that their intersecting identities can result in unique forms of discrimination, privilege, and social inequality.

In the context of anonymization, we must acknowledge that removing some data attributes from the datasets results in an "essentialization" of patients, that is, reducing their identities down to a core set of features while ignoring some features that could be relevant to the analysis when using the data for secondary purposes. The likely result is discrimination and harm. For example, by removing the race attribute from a dataset in an attempt to protect privacy, we could fail to notice that a certain disease is correlated to race.

In this regard, complex issues of feature selection, data protection, and health research intersect with each other. But solving issues such as intersectional discrimination is a matter of choice. For example, one can choose to hire an ethicist or

[111] Crenshaw (2013).

other expert to work with the IT professionals to perform a fairness assessment[112] on any data to be used for secondary purposes.

I advocate for a more nuanced understanding of anonymization, one that recognizes its political and ethical dimensions. When we critically examine anonymization practices, we can expose the power structures that influence these decisions and highlight the potential consequences for individuals and society. This perspective calls for greater transparency in how anonymization decisions are made and urges policymakers to consider the broader social implications of these practices, involving the relevant stakeholders in the process. In fact, there is a need for a more inclusive approach to data governance, where marginalized voices are considered in the decision-making process. This could involve engaging with communities whose data is being anonymized to understand their concerns and priorities, ensuring that anonymization practices do not exacerbate existing inequalities, just like other data processing practices.[113]

To address these challenges, it is important that legislators not only provide clear and detailed guidelines on anonymization standards and practices but that they also involve patients in the process. For instance, specifying the qualifications and expertise required for those performing the anonymization, as well as establishing consistent techniques and criteria for preserving data utility, and providing mandatory consultations with patients. By doing so, the EHDS can ensure a more uniform level of protection across Member States, reducing the risk of exploitation and harm to individuals. There should be a real effort to harmonize the approach to anonymization across the EU so as to reduce fragmentation. This harmonization could be achieved through EU-wide regulations or guidelines that provide clear, actionable instructions for Health Data Access Bodies.

5 Conclusion

The EHDS was borne out of a globalized and interconnected world in which health data is considered a precious asset, where healthcare facilities are increasingly being targeted by cybercriminals for malicious purposes, and where data brokers are exchanging health data like currency. The adoption of the regulation took place within a legal context already marked by significant fragmentation and unresolved tensions. Rather than seeking to resolve these shortcomings through the articulation of an independent conceptual framework, the regulation defers the definition of many of its key terms to earlier instruments, most notably the GDPR. While this reliance might appear to promote legal continuity, in practice it exacerbates existing complexities. The interplay between overlapping regimes—each shaped by its own historical contingencies and normative compromises—diminishes the regulation's

[112] Gallese (2023).

[113] Gallese (2024a).

effectiveness and renders its provisions difficult to interpret. Far from offering clarity, the resulting patchwork compels reliance on case law, doctrinal debate, and administrative guidance, layering interpretative demands on an already dense legal landscape. Unsurprisingly, this stratification has left fundamental questions unresolved. Basic yet crucial issues, such as the meaning of "anonymisation", have effectively fallen between the cracks, leaving both practitioners and scholars grappling with a regime whose coherence is more apparent than real.Against this background, the newly introduced mechanisms of digitalization, secondary use, and opt-out options have been undermined, rendered ineffective, and sometimes even given rise to dangerous mandates. Additionally, patients and vulnerable citizens, who do not have access to healthcare and who have little means through which to understand the consequences of the new provisions, have not been guaranteed the opportunity to participate in decisions that can gravely affect their rights to privacy. In general, the public's perception of the EHDS is partial and limited. For instance, the opt-out mechanisms available to patients have not been sufficiently publicized to ensure that the most impacted people are able to make informed decisions about how their data is used for "secondary purposes".

The first step to protecting citizens' rights in the context of sharing health data is to recognize the need for a redefined and properly accounted-for definition of anonymization. Given the high incidence of cyberattacks on the healthcare industry, it is foreseeable that the EHDS infrastructure will be targeted as soon as it is implemented. Consequently, legislators face a critical decision: either mandate a high standard of anonymization that may compromise data utility or abolish the distinction between "anonymized health data" and "personal health data". The latter approach would require data users to secure the datasets in accordance with GDPR's standards, ensuring robust data protection, thus reducing the related risks.

In addition, the very notion of "anonymization" can be problematic. Scholars like Ohm argue that anonymization often provides a false sense of security. With advances in data analytics and machine learning, re-identification, i.e., the process of matching anonymized data with other datasets to re-establish identities, has become more and more feasible. This raises important questions about the efficacy of anonymization as a protective measure and whether it truly serves the interests of those it aims to protect.

In conclusion, the protection of citizens' rights in the context of health data sharing requires a reevaluation of the definition and implementation of anonymization. Legislators must recognize the political dimensions of anonymization decisions. Clear guidelines and harmonized practices across Member States, that take into consideration the power relations involved, are not only essential to achieving the EHDS's goals but also to safeguarding individuals from the risks associated with data breaches and exploitation.

Acknowledgments This work was funded by the European Union, DataCom Project, Grant Agreement no. 101108151. This research was also financially supported by the "Biorobotics Research and Innovation Engineering Facilities" "IR0000036" – CUP J13C22000400007 (BRIEF) project. The views and opinions expressed are those of the author only and do not necessarily reflect those of the European Union or the European Commission. Neither the European Union nor the granting authority can be held responsible for them.

References

Ahmed NB, Daclin N, Olivaux M et al (2023) Cybersecurity challenges for field hospitals: impacts of emergency cyberthreats during emergency situations. Int J Emerg Manag 18(3):274–292

Aradau C, Blanke T (2017) Politics of prediction: security and the time/space of governmentality in the age of big data. Eur J Soc Theory 20(3):373–391

Balayn A, Gürses S (2021) Beyond debiasing: regulating AI and its inequalities. EDRi report

Boyd D, Crawford K (2012) Critical questions for big data: provocations for a cultural, technological, and scholarly phenomenon. Inf Commun Soc 15(5):662–679

Bullington K, Bills KL, Thomas DJ et al (2022) Above-average student loan debt for students with disabilities attending postsecondary institutions. J Postsec Educ Disabil 35(1)

Carovano G, Finck M (2023) Regulating data intermediaries: the impact of the data governance act on the EU's data economy. Comput Law Secur Rev 50:105830

Cheney-Lippold J (2011) A new algorithmic identity: soft biopolitics and the modulation of control. Theory Cult Soc 28(6):164–181

Chigada J, Madzinga R (2021) Cyberattacks and threats during COVID-19: a systematic literature review. S Afr J Inf Manag 23(1):1–11

Cho S, Crenshaw KW, McCall L (2013) Toward a field of intersectionality studies: theory, applications, and praxis. Signs J Women Cult Soc 38(4):785–810

Couldry N, Powell A (2014) Big data from the bottom up. Big Data Soc 1(2):2053951714539277

Crenshaw KW (2013) Mapping the margins: intersectionality, identity politics, and violence against women of color. In: The public nature of private violence. Routledge, pp 93–118

Crossley M (2005) Discrimination against the unhealthy in health insurance. Univ Kan Law Rev 54:73

Custers B, Uršič H (2016) Big data and data reuse: a taxonomy of data reuse for balancing big data benefits and personal data protection. Int Data Privacy Law 6(1):4–15

D'ignazio C, Klein LF (2023) Data feminism. MIT Press, Cambridge

Devi S (2023) Cyber-attacks on health-care systems. Lancet Oncol 24(4):e148

Durante M, Pagallo U et al (2022) La politica dei dati: Il governo delle nuove tecnologie tra diritto, economia e società. Mimesis, Milan

Dymski GA (2006) Discrimination in the credit and housing markets: findings and challenges. In: Handbook on the economics of discrimination, pp 215–220

Egan LE (1998) Genetic discrimination in health insurance. J Legis 24:237

Eke D, Aasebø IE, Akintoye S et al (2021) Pseudonymisation of neuroimages and data protection: increasing access to data while retaining scientific utility. Neuroimage Rep 1(4):100053

Elliot M, O'Hara K, Raab C et al (2018) Functional anonymisation: personal data and the data environment. Comput Law Secur Rev 34(2):204–221

Eubanks V (2018) Automating inequality: how high-tech tools profile, police, and punish the poor. St. Martin's Press, New York

European Commission (2022a) Commission Staff Working Document Impact Assessment Report accompanying the document Proposal for a regulation of the European Parliament and of the Council on the European Health Data Space. European Commission, Brussels

European Commission (2022b) Proposal for a regulation of the European Parliament and of the Council on the European Health Data Space. Off J Eur Union L Proposal:1–161

Finck M, Pallas F (2020) They who must not be identified—distinguishing personal from non-personal data under the GDPR. Int Data Privacy Law 10(1):11–36

Fleischman GM, Valentine SR, Curtis MB et al (2023) The influence of ethical beliefs and attitudes, norms, and prior outcomes on cybersecurity investment decisions. Bus Soc 62(3):488–529

Fotopoulou A, Thornham H (2020) Digital culture meets data: critical perspectives. Palgrave Macmillan, London

Frey T (2009) Your insurance does not cover that: disability-based discrimination where it hurts the most. Geo Wash Law Rev 78:636

Gabrys J, Pritchard H, Barratt B (2016) Just good enough data: figuring data citizenships through air pollution sensing and data stories. Big Data Soc 3(2):2053951716679677

Gallese C (2022) A first commentary to the proposal for a new regulation on fair access and use of data (Data Act). Media Laws 3:237–270

Gallese C (2024) The risks of health data commodification in the EU digital market. Yearb Antitrust Regul Stud

Gallese C (2024a) The reuse of health data in AI reproductive technologies: opening the door to a new form of colonialism? SSRN. https://ssrn.com/abstract=4817704

Gallese C, Scantamburlo T, Manzoni L et al (2023) Investigating semi-automatic assessment of data sets fairness by means of fuzzy logic. In: 2023 IEEE Conference on Computational Intelligence in Bioinformatics and Computational Biology (CIBCB). IEEE, pp 1–10

Gangadharan SP (2012) Digital inclusion and data profiling. First Monday

Garrison CP, Guy Posey O (2012) Medical identity theft: consequences, frequency, and the implication of electronic health records and data breaches. Int J Soc Health Inf Manag 5(11)

Ghanbari H, Koskinen K (2024) When data breach hits a psychotherapy clinic: the Vastaamo case. J Inf Technol Teach Cases. https://doi.org/10.1177/20438869241258235

Guzelian CP, Stein MA, Akiskal HS (2015) Credit scores, lending, and psychosocial disability. Boston Univ Law Rev 95:1807

Halawa H, Beznosov K, Boshmaf Y et al (2016) Harvesting the low hanging fruits: defending against automated large-scale cyber-intrusions by focusing on the vulnerable population. In: Proceedings of the 2016 New Security Paradigms Workshop. ACM, pp 11–22

Harvey H, Carroll H, Murphy V et al (2023) The impact of a national cyberattack affecting clinical trials: the Cancer Trials Ireland experience. JCO Clin Cancer Inform 7:e2200149

Kandasamy K, Srinivas S, Achuthan K et al (2022) Digital healthcare-cyberattacks in Asian organizations: an analysis of vulnerabilities, risks, NIST perspectives, and recommendations. IEEE Access 10:12345–12364

Katagiri N (2024) Defending medical facilities from cyber attacks: critical issues with the principle of due diligence in international law. Int Rev Law Comput Technol 38(1):1–20

Ke J, Wang W, Foutz NZ (2022) My data or my health? Examining patients' response to a healthcare data breach. SSRN. https://doi.org/10.2139/ssrn.4027459

Kennedy H, Hill RL (2018) The feeling of numbers: emotions in everyday engagements with data and their visualisation. Sociol 52(4):830–848

Kesari A (2022) Do data breach notification laws reduce medical identity theft? Evidence from consumer complaints data. J Empir Leg Stud 19(4):1222–1252

Kitchin R (2013) Big data and human geography: opportunities, challenges and risks. Dialogues Hum Geogr 3(3):262–267

Kitchin R (2014) The data revolution: big data, open data, data infrastructures and their consequences. Sage, London

Kitchin R, Lauriault TP (2015) Small data in the era of big data. GeoJournal 80:463–475

Kitchin R, Lauriault T (2018) Towards critical data studies: charting and unpacking data assemblages and their work. In: Thinking big data in geography: new regimes, new research. University of Nebraska Press

Kolouch J, Zahradnicky T, Kučínsky A (2021) Cyber security: lessons learned from cyber-attacks on hospitals in the COVID-19 pandemic. Masaryk Univ J Law Technol 15(2):301–341

Kuschke B (2018) Disability discrimination in insurance. De Jure 51(1):50–64

Kush RD (2023) Data sharing and reuse of health data for research. In: Clinical research informatics. Springer, pp 147–167

L'Imperio V, Coelho V, Cazzaniga G et al (2024) Machine learning streamlines the morphometric characterization and multiclass segmentation of nuclei in different follicular thyroid lesions: everything in a nutshell. Mod Pathol 37(12):100608

Lee J, Kim H, Choi SJ (2024) Do hospital data breaches affect health information technology investment? Digit Health 10:20552076231224164

Looi JC, Allison S, Bastiampillai T et al (2024a) Psychotherapy electronic health record data of 33,000 breached in Finland: tragically realised risks of harm to patients. Australas Psychiatry 32(4):288–289. https://doi.org/10.1177/10398562241259631

Looi JC, Looi RC, Maguire PA et al (2024b) Psychiatric electronic health records in the era of data breaches – what are the ramifications for patients, psychiatrists and healthcare systems? Australas Psychiatry 32(2):121–124

Lyon D (2014) Surveillance, Snowden, and big data: capacities, consequences, critique. Big Data Soc 1(2):2053951714541861

Majeed A, Lee S (2020) Anonymization techniques for privacy preserving data publishing: a comprehensive survey. IEEE Access 9:8512–8545

Mancini M (2014) Exploiting big data for improving healthcare services. J e-Learn Knowl Soc 10(2)

Mayer-Schönberger V, Cukier K (2013) Big data: a revolution that will transform how we live, work, and think. Houghton Mifflin Harcourt, Boston

Milan S (2019) Acting on data(fication). In: Citizen media and practice. Routledge, pp 212–226

Milan S, Treré E (2019) Big data from the south(s): beyond data universalism. Telev New Media 20(4):319–335

Minnaar A, Herbig FJ (2021) Cyberattacks and the cybercrime threat of ransomware to hospitals and healthcare services during the COVID-19 pandemic. Acta Criminol Afr J Criminol Victimol 34(3):155–185

Narayana Samy G, Ahmad R, Ismail Z (2010) Security threats categories in healthcare information systems. Health Inform J 16(3):201–209

Nobile CG (2023a) Legal aspects of the use of artificial intelligence in telemedicine. J Digit Technol Law 1(2)

Nobile CG (2023b) Regulating smart robots and artificial intelligence in the European Union. J Digit Technol Law 1(1)

Noble SU (2018) Algorithms of oppression: how search engines reinforce racism. In: Algorithms of oppression. New York Univ Press, New York

Ohm P (2009) Broken promises of privacy: responding to the surprising failure of anonymization. UCLA Law Rev 57:1701

Pagallo U (2022) The politics of data in EU law: will it succeed? Digit Soc 1(3):20

Pagallo U (2023a) Why the AI Act won't trigger a Brussels effect. In: AI approaches to the complexity of legal systems. Springer, Forthcoming

Pagallo U (2023b) Dismantling four myths in AI and EU law through legal information 'about' reality. In: Multidisciplinary perspectives on artificial intelligence and the law. Springer International Publishing, Cham, pp 251–261

Pagallo U, O'Sullivan S, Nevejans N et al (2024a) The underuse of AI in the health sector: opportunity costs, success stories, risks and recommendations. Health Technol 14(1):1–14

Pagallo U et al (2024b) Data protection in EU and US laws and AI: what legal changes we should expect in the foreseeable future? In: The Cambridge handbook of private law and artificial intelligence. Cambridge Univ Press, Cambridge, pp 599–617

Paul III DP, Spence N, Bhardwa N, Coustasse A et al (2018) Healthcare facilities: another target for ransomware attacks. Manag Fac Res

Pavel M, Jimison HB, Wactlar HD et al (2013) The role of technology and engineering models in transforming healthcare. IEEE Rev Biomed Eng 6:156–177

Rajendran K, Jayabalan M, Rana ME (2017) A study on k-anonymity, l-diversity, and t-closeness techniques. Int J Comput Sci Netw Secur 17(12):172

Reddy J, Elsayed N, ElSayed Z et al (2023) A review on data breaches in healthcare security systems. Int J Comput Appl 975:8887

Rice WE (1996) Race, gender, redlining, and the discriminatory access to loans, credit, and insurance: an historical and empirical analysis of consumers who sued lenders and insurers in federal and state courts, 1950–1995. San Diego Law Rev 33:583

Rodriguez-Hoyos A, Estrada-Jiménez J, Rebollo-Monedero D et al (2018) Does k-anonymous microaggregation affect machine-learned macrotrends? IEEE Access 6:28258–28277
Ruckenstein M, Schüll ND (2017) The datafication of health. Annu Rev Anthropol 46(1):261–278
Saeed S, Suayyid SA, Al-Ghamdi MS et al (2023) A systematic literature review on cyber threat intelligence for organizational cybersecurity resilience. Sensors 23(16):7273
Safran C (2017) Update on data reuse in health care. Yearb Med Inform 26(1):24–27
Salahdine F, Kaabouch N (2019) Social engineering attacks: a survey. Future Internet 11(4):89
Sarker D (2020) Discrimination against people with disabilities in accessing microfinance. Alter 14(4):318–328
Seh AH, Zarour M, Alenezi M et al (2020) Healthcare data breaches: insights and implications. In: Healthcare, vol 8. MDPI, p 133
Sekar JG, Chokkalingam A, Kesavan D (2023) Evolution of healthcare sector and evolving cyber-attacks—a summary. In: Smart distributed embedded systems for healthcare applications. CRC Press, pp 155–172
Stevens L, Dobbs C, Jones K et al (2017) Dangers from within? Looking inwards at the role of maladministration as the leading cause of health data breaches in the UK. In: Data protection and privacy: (in)visibilities and infrastructures, pp 205–239
Straits Research (2024) Wearable medical devices market size, share & trends analysis report
Sweeney L (1997) Weaving technology and policy together to maintain confidentiality. J Law Med Ethics 25(2–3):98–110
Tarka M, Blankstein M, Schottel P (2023) The crippling effects of a cyberattack at an academic level 1 trauma center: an orthopedic perspective. Injury 54(4):1095–1101
Terzis P, Santamaria Echeverria O (2023) Interoperability and governance in the European health data space regulation. Med Law Int 23(4):368–376
Van Dijck J (2014) Datafication, dataism and dataveillance: big data between scientific paradigm and ideology. Surveill Soc 12(2):197–208
Wairimu S, Fritsch L (2022) Modelling privacy harms of compromised personal medical data—beyond data breach. In: Proceedings of the 17th International Conference on Availability, Reliability and Security. ACM, pp 1–9
Wernz C, Zhang H, Phusavat K (2014) International study of technology investment decisions at hospitals. Ind Manag Data Syst 114(4):568–582
Working Party on the Protection of Individuals with regard to the Processing of Personal Data (2014) Opinion 05/2014 on anonymisation techniques. Article 29 Working Party
Zwilling M, Klien G, Lesjak D et al (2022) Cyber security awareness, knowledge and behavior: a comparative study. J Comput Inf Syst 62(1):82–97

Cybersecurity Perspectives on the Internet of Health Things

Federica Casarosa

Abstract Digitalization in the health sector is an ongoing process. New developments and emerging technologies, such as artificial intelligence, are instilling devices and applications with the potential to monitor health and make healthcare predictions. Further, this power is spreading beyond simple medical devices to products and services that can manage a person's overall wellness. However, the pervasive use of such devices in domestic settings like households and on personal devices like smartphones demands that some attention be given to the security vulnerabilities these products can create. Unfortunately, the EU's legal framework over cybersecurity is still piecemeal, requiring coordination between different legal Acts. This chapter, therefore, sheds light on the interplay between these pieces of legislation so as to provide a holistic understanding of the cybersecurity landscape surrounding today's wellness applications and devices. The analysis will clearly describe the challenges manufacturers face in complying with the EU's legal frameworks in both physiological and pathological terms. Overall, the chapter reveals that the current regulatory complexity can and should be simplified to ensure better coordination and systematization between all the stakeholders involved.

1 Introduction

The digitalization process today has become a pervasive part of all sectors of the economy and society, with the health sector being no exception. The number of software applications and devices developed to provide information, diagnose conditions, and manage diseases has increased substantially, demonstrating the importance of personalized care for patients.[1] Moreover, the development of emerging

[1] See the statistics of Confindustria – Dispositivi Medici, as regards the Italian market for medical devices, 2024, at https://www.confindustriadm.it/il-settore-in-numeri-2024/.

F. Casarosa (✉)
LIDER-Lab, DIRPOLIS, Sant'Anna School of Advanced Studies, Pisa, Italy
e-mail: federica.casarosa@santannapisa.it

F. Casarosa et al. (eds.), *Enabling and Safeguarding Personalized Medicine*, Data Science, Machine Intelligence, and Law 7,
https://doi.org/10.1007/978-3-031-99709-9_6

technologies, like artificial intelligence, is giving devices and applications even more potential for health monitoring and predictions based on the vast amounts of data being gathered from individuals through smartware and fitness apps.[2] The adoption of all these new products is not only being welcomed as a means to increase the efficiency and effectiveness of healthcare, but also as a way to tailor medical care to the distinctive molecular and genetic traits of individual patients.[3] At the individual level, these new devices are acting as tools that empower patients to decide on their own health.[4]

However, at the sector level, many medical devices and applications are simply grouped and categorized under a single concept, which is not particularly reflective of the legal frameworks present in the EU. For example, in one study, the European Parliament widely defines "medical AI" as a "type of AI which is focused on specific applications in medicine or healthcare".[5] The study then goes on to specifically refer to AI solutions for clinical practice, biomedical research, public health, and health administration.[6] Therefore, such a definition extends well beyond the qualification of medical devices. Hence, in this chapter, I will use the terminology set out in the Medical Device Regulation (MDR),[7] which defines "medical devices" as those devices and software applications that are intended to be used for one of the following objectives…

> … diagnosis, prevention, monitoring, prediction, prognosis, treatment or alleviation of disease; diagnosis, monitoring, treatment, alleviation of, or compensation for, an injury or disability; investigation, replacement or modification of the anatomy or of a physiological or pathological process or state; and providing information by means of in vitro examination of specimens derived from the human body, including organ, blood and tissue donations, and which does not achieve its principal intended action by pharmacological, immunological or metabolic means, in or on the human body, but which may be assisted in its function by such means.

Additional indications are also listed in the 'guidance documents' of several regulations.[8] Although the list of purposes is extremely detailed and covers a wide range of cases, it still leaves space for devices and applications with a more general health objective—for instance, objectives that are not connected with a disease, injury, or a disability but rather simply aimed at ensuring the wellbeing of the user. This last category will be the focus of this analysis.

---

[2] Chen et al. (2022).

[3] Emdin and Passino, in this volume.

[4] Corrales Compagnucci et al. (2022), p. 2; Fabbrizio et al. (2023).

[5] 'Artificial Intelligence in Healthcare: Applications, Risks, and Ethical and Societal Impacts' (2022).

[6] Palmieri (2024), p. 4.

[7] Regulation (EU) 2017/745 of the European Parliament and of the Council of 5 April 2017 on medical devices, amending Directive 2001/83/EC, Regulation (EC) No 178/2002 and Regulation (EC) No 1223/2009 and repealing Council Directives 90/385/EEC and 93/42/EEC. OJ L 117, 5.5.2017, pp. 1–175.

[8] 'Guidance on Qualification and Classification of Software in Regulation (EU) 2017/745 -MDR and Regulation (EU) 2017/746- IVDR' (MDCG 2019) 11 and Ludvigsen et al. (2022).

There are many examples of health devices and applications outside the realm of medicine—for instance, nutrition tracking applications that help people monitor their food consumption, calculate nutrients or count calories for a balanced diet. The most advanced applications contain embedded AI systems where you can identify the components of food dishes via an image recognition system.[9] Other examples include apps for menstrual tracking, where women can monitor their bodily functions and reactions to birth control and fertility conditions. Again, some come with embedded AI-based chatbots that provide personalized replies about health issues, fitness programs, and nutrition plans. Notably, these apps have raised several concerns regarding ethical issues and data protection.[10]

Another example at the boundary between health and medical devices is the case of social care or assistive robots.[11] These types of robots help users with a range of task, both physical and social.[12] As an example, they can be used to conduct educational and recreational activities for elderly people to help keep them company, avoid depression, or even monitor for signs of Alzheimer's before the disease is even diagnosed.[13] The robots can have varying degrees of autonomy and may integrate several different technologies from sensor systems to algorithms for processing data to cloud computing services and AI systems designed to react, chat, and respond to human emotions.

These three examples show the pervasiveness of health devices and applications outside the medical settings. But their use in domestic settings, such as in households and on personal devices, requires attention in terms of the security vulnerabilities these devices can create—not just in terms of personal data breaches but also in terms of physical safety. According to Fosch and Mahler,[14] the type of impact that a cybersecurity incident with a social care robot may have depends on several factors: the origin of the incident, the target, the effect on the device, and the effect on the user. For instance, a malicious attack launched via a social care robot may target the device itself through a fault injection that partially damages the internal control system. Consequently, the robot may no longer react to requests or it could trigger unexpected behaviour. This could result both in physical and psychological harm to the user.

It is easy to transpose this analysis to the other examples mentioned above. For instance, a malicious attack could allow a third party to take control of the application, compromising private information. Although this type of attack may have limited physical impact, the incident may cause mental or emotional harm to the user.[15]

As reported elsewhere,[16] the legal framework for cybersecurity in the EU is still piecemeal. Protection is only afforded through various interactions between differ-

[9] Héritier et al. (2023); Mohanty et al. (2022).

[10] Amelang (2022); Hammond and Burdon (2024).

[11] Fosch-Villaronga and Drukarch (2023), p. 35.

[12] Fosch-Villaronga (2019).

[13] Maibaum et al. (2022); Sawik et al. (2023).

[14] Fosch-Villaronga and Mahler (2021).

[15] Hammond and Burdon (2024).

[16] Casarosa (2024a).

ent legal Acts that not only address cybersecurity but also numerous other facets of the digital world. For example, there is the Cyber Resilience Act,[17] which covers the cybersecurity requirements of connected products; the General Data Protection Regulation,[18] which covers data processing security; the recent Artificial Intelligence Act (AI Act),[19] which governs the security of embedded systems; and the European Health Data Space Regulation, which pertains to certain security aspects of wellness devices and applications.[20]

The purpose of this chapter is to shed light on the interplay between these pieces of legislation so as to provide a holistic understanding of cybersecurity in the context of healthcare applications and devices. The ensuing analysis will clearly describe the challenges manufacturers face in complying with the EU's regulatory provisions both in terms of physiological and pathological situations. The chapter ends with a discussion on the complexity of this regulatory landscape, which I argue should be simplified to ensure better coordinate and systematise all the stakeholders involved.

2 Applicable Legal Frameworks

2.1 The General Data Protection Regulation

The General Data Protection Regulation (GDPR) is the main framework covering the processing of health data. Further, according to the definition provided in Article 4 (15), the scope of this legislation is extremely wide.[21] This is also confirmed by Recital 35, which clarifies that health data covers a subject's past, current, and future health conditions.[22]

The three examples provided in the previous section all fall under the scope of the GDPR. More specifically, the social care robot collects and processes data related to a person's ability to react to queries. It also processes data to acknowledge improvements or deteriorations in their user's abilities. Although not all data collected qualifies as health data, they are still related to the *health status* of the subject.

[17] Regulation (EU) 2024/1689 of the European Parliament and of the Council of 13 June 2024 laying down harmonised rules on artificial intelligence and amending Regulations (EC) No 300/2008, (EU) No 167/2013, (EU) No 168/2013, (EU) 2018/858, (EU) 2018/1139 and (EU) 2019/2144 and Directives 2014/90/EU, (EU) 2016/797 and (EU) 2020/1828 (Artificial Intelligence Act).

[18] Regulation (EU) 2016/679 of the European Parliament and of the Council of 27 April 2016 on the protection of natural persons with regard to the processing of personal data and on the free movement of such data, and repealing Directive 95/46/EC (General Data Protection Regulation).

[19] Regulation (EU) 2024/2847 of the European Parliament and of the Council of 23 October 2024 on horizontal cybersecurity requirements for products with digital elements and amending Regulations (EU) No 168/2013 and (EU) No 2019/1020 and Directive (EU) 2020/1828 (Cyber Resilience Act).

[20] Regulation (EU) 2025/327 of the European Parliament and of the Council of 11 February 2025 on the European Health Data Space and amending Directive 2011/24/EU and Regulation (EU) 2024/2847.

[21] Schäfke-Zell (2022).

[22] Tzanou (2021).

Similarly, images of food collected by the nutrition tracking application are processed to reveal information about a person's dietary habits. Period tracking applications collect information about sleep, mood, and sexual behavior. Consequently, such data allows the embedded system to infer health conditions and even create a profile of the user.

According to Article 32 of GDPR, devices that collect personal data should comply with certain security requirements. These requirements include technical and organizational measures aimed at guaranteeing "a level of security appropriate to the risk". This risk-based approach relegates the task of identifying which measures are appropriate to the data controller, who must consider a specific set of criteria when making their decisions. These include: the current state-of-the-art and best practices in data and communications security, such as industry standards and certifications, the costs of implementation, the nature of the data processing, and reasonably foreseeable threats to the rights and freedoms of individuals.[23] Thus, given that health data qualify as a special category of data, data processing tends to carry a higher degree of risk and, consequently, data processing tasks typically require a higher level of security.[24]

Although the ultimate choice over which security measures to implement is left to the data controller, the legislation does provide some guidelines on the types of measures that could be implemented. These span both data-specific measures, such as pseudonymization and encryption, along with more general security measures, such as safeguarding confidentiality, protecting the integrity of the data, and ensuring that the processing systems are resilient. It is also worth noting that the European Data Protection Board has published some guidance documents.[25] However, the technology is evolving so rapidly that the value of these guidance documents is somewhat limited.[26]

References to the state-of-the-art imply the possibility of adopting standards developed at the international or European level, assuming that these reflect the most basic knowledge shared by the technical community and are therefore updated more often.[27] Note that, according to Micklitz,[28] the 'state of the art' refers to the lowest levels of knowledge in a research field—i.e., it relates to findings that are generally accepted by the whole scientific community. This level is the one considered in the international standards. The state of science and technology sit at a higher level, which is then followed by pure scientific findings and scientific knowledge. In particular, scientific knowledge addresses research that has not yet become established wisdom and, therefore, might not have yet found its way into consumer-ready technological devices. For instance, existing international standards include

[23] Burton (2020), p. 636.

[24] Koolen et al. (2023).

[25] EDPB (2021); Kosta (2023).

[26] Koolen et al. (2023).

[27] Kamara (2021).

[28] Micklitz (2023), p. 107.

the OWASP's Software Assurance Maturity Model,[29] the Building Security In Maturity Model,[30] and the NIST Privacy Framework.[31] These standards provide a detailed analysis of the different phases through which data security strategies can be adopted, endorsing a recurring process that evaluates the maturity level of the company adopting them. However, adopting any of these standards does not guarantee compliance with Article 32. Moreover, it does not exclude liability in case of damages.

First, Article 32(3) of the GDPR limits the opportunity to prove compliance with "an approved code of conduct [...] or an approved certification mechanism". The two cases listed in the provision literally do not include international standards, leaving only the possibility of relying on certifications at European level.[32] However, according to Article 32(1), international standards become relevant when looking at the state-of-the-art in a specific field.[33] Consequently, a manufacturer that decides to adopt one of these standards will still have to justify their choice on the basis of the other criteria; namely, the cost of implementation, the nature of the data processing, reasonable foresight of a threat, and so on. Such evaluations are crucial if a data breach occurs.[34]

The GDPR also provides a set of rules for what to do in the event of a data breach. First, the data controller needs to notify their relevant national data protection authority without undue delay and, when feasible, within 72 hours of the controller becoming aware of the breach.[35] That a data breach has occurred does not automatically imply that the controller has not complied with the provisions of the GDPR.[36] However, the data protection authority will evaluate whether any measures taken were appropriate and sufficient to prevent or mitigate the breach on a case-by-case basis. According to a recent study on the decisions made by the various data protection authorities,[37] there does not seem to be a common methodology; although, some important elements are highlighted. For example, data controllers should be conducting regular risk management exercises to test their security measures. Those responsible for data processing should also be using the most up-to-date tools and software. Lastly, the processing procedures should include authentication measures and logs should be kept to record all activities associated with the data.

---

[29] See https://owasp.org/www-project-samm/.

[30] See https://www.blackduck.com/glossary/what-is-bsimm.html.

[31] See https://www.nist.gov/privacy-framework.

[32] See art. 42 GDPR.

[33] See, for instance, the ISO standards dedicated to health at https://www.iso.org/sectors/health, and in particular, ISO 22857:2013 on Health informatics (Guidelines on data protection to facilitate trans-border flows of personal health data) or the forthcoming ISO/DIS 27799 on Health informatics — Information security management in health using ISO/IEC 27002.

[34] According to Article 4(12) of GDPR, a data breach affects the accessibility, integrity or confidentiality of personal data that results in a risk of adverse effects on data subjects.

[35] EDPB (2023).

[36] CJEU, Case C-340/21, VB v Natsionalna agentsia za prihodite, 14 December 2023.

[37] Kosta (2023), p. 10.

2.2 The Artificial Intelligence Act

The AI Act is the result of a long negotiation process aimed at establishing a legal framework for protecting the values, fundamental rights, and moral principles of EU residents when designing, developing, and deploying AI-based systems.[38] These principles are listed as including human agency and oversight, technical robustness and safety, privacy and data governance, transparency, diversity, non-discrimination and fairness, and social and environmental well-being.[39]

The AI Act adopts a risk-based approach that distinguishes three types of AI systems: the ones bearing (i) an unacceptable risk; (ii) a high risk; and (iii) a low or minimal risk. The first category is prohibited, as it includes AI systems whose risks contravene EU values or violate fundamental rights. The bulk of the regulation is focused on high-risk AI systems, which are defined based on their intended purpose and modality of use—for instance, AI systems intended to be used as safety components within other products or stand-alone AI systems with implications to fundamental rights.

The AI Act explicitly acknowledges that AI-based systems can be embedded into medical devices.[40] As such, the legislation prescribes that any medical devices classified as high risk under the MDR will have the same classification under the AI Act, if they have an AI component. This implies that some devices classified as low-risk under the MDR or In Vitro Device Regulation (IVDR) will fall under the limited risk category of the AI Act.[41] However, these classifications become less clear when one looks at non-medical devices, such as our three health device examples. Healthcare devices may still fall under the scope of the AI Act when looking at the list of cases in Annex III of the regulation. For instance, social robots are generally equipped with sensors, cameras, and microphones that are not only able to identify types of movements and facial expressions but can also be used to infer human emotions.[42] Notably, emotion recognition is explicitly included in Annex III, point 1, (c).[43] Palmieri, however, suggests a different interpretation of the Act, suggesting that social care robots might be subject to the Machinery Regulation as such AI systems may actually qualify as a product or safety component.[44]

More doubtful is the application of the AI Act to the other two examples. Neither the nutrition tracking app or the menstrual tracking app contain emotion recognition and none of the other cases listed in Annex III apply. Thus, these examples would fall into the low-risk category defined in Article 50. Here, manufacturers of AI

---

[38] Pehlivan (2024).

[39] Busch et al. (2024); Demková (2024); Ebers (2024).

[40] AI Act, Annex I.

[41] Palmieri (2024), p. 12.

[42] Fosch-Villaronga and Drukarch (2021); Palmieri and Goffin (2023); Pierce and Fosch-Villaronga (2022).

[43] Durovic and Corno (2024); Raposo (2024).

[44] Palmieri (2024).

systems "intended to interact directly with natural persons" are required to inform the users interacting with such an AI-based system. However, this obligation may be circumvented if the interaction with the AI system is "obvious from the point of view of a natural person who is reasonably well-informed, observant and circumspect, taking into account the circumstances and the context of use".[45] Apart from this disclosure, and the general obligation regarding AI literacy envisaged in Article 4, the Act applies no additional requirements to the design, development, or deployment of the AI system. Interestingly, this interpretation applies to a wide range of non-medical devices that still provide a health function, not only from a cybersecurity perspective but more generally in terms of the overall objective of building a landscape populated with trustworthy and secure AI systems.[46]

For those applications that fall into the scope of high-risk AI systems, the AI Act sets out a suite of legal requirements, including a risk management system (Article 9), data governance (Article 10), documentation and record-keeping (Articles 11 and 12), transparency and provision of information to users (Article 13), human oversight (Article 14), and robustness, accuracy and cybersecurity (Article 15). This last provision addresses the cybersecurity perspective by distinguishing between different, yet intertwined perspectives.

Article 15 requires that AI systems be resilient to any "errors, faults or inconsistencies that may occur within the system or the environment in which the system operates, in particular, due to their interaction with natural persons or other systems". This clause mainly refers to the robustness of the AI system. Additionally, the system must be protected "against attempts by unauthorised third parties to alter their use, outputs or performance by exploiting system vulnerabilities". This refers to cybersecurity. It is important to stress that the approach adopted in this provision does not clearly converge with the wider definition of cybersecurity, which involves defending against any threats designed to compromise a computer system or the security of the information it holds, without distinguishing between threat types and sources.[47] In fact, Article 2(1) of the Cybersecurity Act[48] defines cybersecurity as "the activities necessary to protect network and information systems, the users of such systems, and other persons affected by cyber threats". As clearly described by Nolte et al.,[49] the distinction between robustness and cybersecurity is puzzling as the former is not a distinct feature but rather a dimension of the latter. Moreover, the provision increases the dichotomy between these two overlapping concepts. For one, the Act demands different thresholds for each of the concepts. Second, different measures need to be adopted to ensure robustness on the one hand and cyberse-

---

[45] AI Act, Article 50(1).

[46] Gennari (2024).

[47] See Carovano and Meinke (2023); Papakonstantinou (2022).

[48] Regulation (EU) 2019/881 of the European Parliament and of the Council of 17 April 2019 on ENISA (the European Union Agency for Cybersecurity) and on information and communications technology cybersecurity certification and repealing Regulation (EU) No 526/2013 (Cybersecurity Act) OJ L 151, 7.6.2019, pp. 15–69.

[49] Nolte et al. (2024), p. 4.

curity on the other. As a case in point, Article 15(4) requires that any AI systems should be "as resilient as possible", while Article 15(5) also requires that AI systems should "be resilient" in terms of cybersecurity. Moreover, to ensure robustness. i.e., resilience, the manufacturer should adopt both organizational and technical measures, whereas, to ensure cybersecurity, only technical measures need to be adopted.[50]

This distinction has also been translated into a request for standardization that the EU Commission presented to CEN/CENLEC. The Commission wanted to draft a European standard that would provide guidance to the manufacturers of AI systems on how to comply with the requirements of the Act.[51] Article 40 states that any AI system complying with the harmonized standards shall be presumed to conform to the requirements set out in Articles 9–15. Additionally, Article 41(2) provides for coordination between the compliance with cybersecurity certification schemes adopted pursuant to the Cybersecurity Act and compliance with art. 15.[52]

Once an AI system has passed its conformity assessment, it can be put on the market with the CE marking. Notably, according to Article 43 of the AI Act, the manufacturer of any AI system described under point 1 of Annex III can choose between a self-assessment (defined in Annex VI) or a conformity assessment to be conducted by a third-party called a Notifying Body (as described in Annex VII). But the obligations do not stop there. In the post-market surveillance phase, manufacturers still have obligations to ensure that they continue to comply with the requirements of the AI Act. For example, Article 72 prescribes that the manufacturer establish and document a post-market monitoring system that operates throughout their product's lifetime. From a cybersecurity perspective, this monitoring system must check to determine whether any vulnerabilities have or are likely to emerge and, if so, whether those vulnerabilities will impact the device's safety or performance. Accordingly, manufacturers have to create processes to provide users with mitigation measures, such as issuing patches or updates. Moreover, manufacturers are expected to adopt an incident response plan with clear protocols for addressing cybersecurity events and notifying stakeholders of potential mitigation measures when necessary.

In case of a serious incident, the manufacturer must inform their national market surveillance authority within 15 days of becoming aware of the event (or from the

---

[50] Biasin et al. (2023), p. 50.

[51] https://ec.europa.eu/transparency/documents-register/detail?ref=C(2023)3215&lang=en. See also Junklewitz et al. (2023).

[52] It must be noted that, in principle, the recently adopted cybersecurity certification scheme on European Common Criteria (Commission Implementing Regulation (EU) 2024/482 of 31 January 2024 laying down rules for the application of Regulation (EU) 2019/881 of the European Parliament and of the Council as regards the adoption of the European Common Criteria-based cybersecurity certification scheme) could be applicable to AI based systems. However, its scope does not fully converge with the features and challenges emerging in AI-based systems, in particular as regards ethical issues as well as risks for discriminatory baheviour. Rampášek et al. (2025), p. 106093.

moment that a causal link between the event and the AI system has reasonably been established). Article 2(49) defines a serious incident as…

> … an incident or malfunctioning of an AI system that directly or indirectly leads to any of the following: (a) the death of a person, or serious harm to a person's health; (b) a serious and irreversible disruption of the management or operation of critical infrastructure; (c) the infringement of obligations under Union law intended to protect fundamental rights; (d) serious harm to property or the environment.[53]

Additionally, different timelines are provided in case of a person's death (10 days) versus the case of a widespread infringement or a serious incident leading to irreversible disruption of critical infrastructure (2 days). Along with notifying the authorities, the manufacturer will also need to conduct investigations and eventually take corrective action to resolve any harm caused.

2.3 The Cyber Resilience Act

Increased awareness at the European level over the security risks emerging from rising levels of interconnectedness between devices triggered the adoption of the Cyber Resilience Act (CRA). This issue was first identified in the EU's Cybersecurity Strategy for the Digital Decade presented in 2020.[54] At that time, the European Commission presented a legislative intervention aimed at preventing and mitigating the impact of malicious attacks designed to exploit vulnerabilities in any product that uses a remote data connection to a device or network, whether that device operates within a closed, dedicated network or can be accessed via the Internet. As a matter of clarity, Article 3(2) of the CRA defines remote data processing as "data processing at a distance for which the software is designed and developed by the manufacturer […] and the absence of which would prevent the product with digital elements from performing one of its functions".

Meanwhile, Article 1 of the CRA defines the scope of the regulation as ensuring the cybersecurity of 'products with digital elements' made available on the European market. Article 3(1) goes on to define such products as "any software or hardware product and its remote data processing solutions, including software or hardware components to be placed on the market separately". It is important to stress that the scope of the regulation excludes products with digital elements that fall under the definition of medical devices.[55] This is an important distinction that allows the manufacturers of medical devices to focus solely on the safety and security requirements prescribed in the MDR. Still, our three examples fall under the scope of the CRA. The social care robot, which processes data and connects to the cloud, can be

---

[53] See also AI Act, Art. 73.

[54] Commission 'The EU's Cybersecurity Strategy for the Digital Decade' JOIN(2020) 18 final. See also Burri and Zihlmann (2023); Chiara (2023); Shaffique (2024).

[55] Article 2 (2) and recital 25 CRA.

accessed by the manufacturer to verify the device is operating correctly or by a medical expert to check the conditions of the patient. As such, the robot is clearly a connected product. Similarly, the nutrition and the period tracking apps are not only connected to the cloud in order to store, collect, and process data, but they are also able to connect directly to other devices. For instance, the nutrition-tracking application might be connected to a smartwatch or even a smart fridge to identify the user's dietary habits. Similarly, the period-tracking app can be shared with a partner's smartphone to share decisions about pregnancy.

Further, these products must comply with both the pre-market and post-market requirements set out in the CRA. The Act addresses both the design and development phases, as well as the monitoring and updating activities carried out after the product is available on the market.

Manufacturers are required to design, develop and manufacture any product with digital elements in such a way as to ensure an appropriate level of cybersecurity; this necessarily means that no known exploitable vulnerabilities should be present and that secure default configurations should be available. Such obligations also extend across the supply chain, as the manufacturer is responsible for any third parties that participate in the design or development of any part of the products—whether they do so collaboratively or independently.[56] The basic requirements are set in Annex II and include stipulations related to both security and handling vulnerabilities. In terms of security, the list consists of "security-by-default" measures, confidentiality protection, integrity, the availability of the data and the networks, data minimization measures, resilience measures (particularly against DoS attacks), safeguards against network effects, records of internal activity, and data portability. Additionally, products should be protected from unauthorized access through appropriate control mechanisms. Plus, the data should be kept confidential through methods likes encryption, etc.

As emerges clearly from the list in Annex II, the requirements are not sufficiently detailed to identify all the technical and organizational measures that should be adopted at each stage of a product's design and development. However, the Annex does set out a preliminary framework that can be further defined through risk management systems—especially those that evaluate the readiness of products towards different types of cybersecurity threats.[57] Already, the technical documentation that manufacturers need to prepare before any products can be placed on the market must contain an assessment of any relevant cybersecurity risks and a description of the means by which the manufacturer intends to mitigate those risks. This documentation is not only passed on to the Notified Body as part of the third-party assessment procedure but must also be kept up-to-date by the manufacturer and provided to the market surveillance authority on request.

The role of standards is also crucial here, and the CRA directly acknowledges that fact. Article 27 indicates two possible approaches to standardizing the field. The

[56] Article 13 (5) CRA

[57] Casarosa (2024b); Rampášek et al. (2025).

first is to have the EU Commission ask European standard-setting organizations to draft harmonized standards. The second is for each manufacturer to adopt of common specifications drafted by the EU Commission. However, this second option is only a fallback situation if the first one is not accepted. The first option is more reliable and transparent, as the process envisaged for developing European standards is based on consensus, openness, transparency, national commitment, and technical coherence principles.[58]

At the end of the conformity assessment procedure, the manufacturer should receive a "Declaration of Conformity" for its product. This is simply a document that confirms the product complies with the requirements set out in Annex II.[59] Depending on the class of risk of the product, the type of conformity assessment may vary, ranging from an internal control procedure to a full conformity assessment based on quality assurance. The examples considered by this analysis are excluded from the possibility of adopting an internal control procedure. According to Article 7(2) of the CRA, certain products are deemed to be "important". These important products are defined as those with digital elements that…

> … perform a function which carries a significant risk of adverse effects in terms of its intensity and ability to disrupt, control or cause damage to a large number of other products or the health and safety of a large number of individuals through direct manipulation, such as a central system function, including network management, configuration control, virtualization, processing of personal data.

Point (19) of Annex III goes on to specify the following as a Class I important product: "personal wearable products to be worn or placed on a human body that have a health monitoring (such as tracking) purpose and to which Regulation (EU) 2017/745 or (EU) No 2017/746 do not apply". Therefore, wearable health devices are subject to the conformity assessment procedures referred to in Articles 32(2) and (3) of the CRA—this being the third-party assessments evaluating conformity conducted by a Notified Body. All these Articles, Annexes, and Points serve to guarantee that the compliance certifications procedures are both transparent and conducted according to harmonized standards.

Moreover, the manufacturer's obligations do not end after a Declaration of Conformity is issued. Once compliant, the product is subject to post-market surveillance controls by specifically defined authorities, which can take all appropriate corrective actions to bring it (back) into compliance, withdraw it from the market, or recall it within a reasonable period. Further, manufacturers are also obliged to notify their national Computer Security Response Team (CSIRT) of any exploited vulnerabilities or incidents impacting the product's security within 24 hours of becoming aware of such events. CSIRTs are national bodies created according to

---

[58] CEN/CENLEC, 'What is a standard?', available at https://www.cencenelec.eu/european-standardization/european-standards/. For a critical appraisal, Volpato and Eliantonio (2020).

[59] Article 32 CRA.

NIS 2 Directive[60] and designated to ensuring measures that create a high common level of cybersecurity across the Union. Such notifications should provide all essential information about the event along with any corrective and/or mitigating measures taken. This should allows the informed CSIRT to provide appropriate support to resolve the event while also disseminating relevant information about cybersecurity incidents to the various market surveillance authorities and, other national CSIRTs—especially in the case of cross-border cybersecurity events. Users might also be informed but, generally, only where their collaboration is required to deploy corrective measures.

2.4 *The European Health Data Space*

The Regulation governing the European Health Data Space (EHDS) was first presented in May 2022 and adopted in January 2025. There are two main purposes to this Regulation. The first is to expand the use of electronic health data so as to deliver health care to individuals by collecting data from them. The second is to assist and improve research, innovation, policymaking, patient safety, personalized medicine, official statistics, and regulatory activities by sharing health datasets. Both of these objectives should be able to be achieved by creating a 'data space' where health data are stored, managed, and operationalized to support research, overcome the challenges of limited data interoperability, and bridge the historically fragmented rules allowing access to data for scientific purposes. This Regulation also imposes barriers on individuals who wish to access or exercise control over their health data.[61]

The EHDS Regulation is relevant to all three of our examples as each meets the definition of a wellness application. Article 2(2)(ab) defines this as…

> … any software, or any combination of hardware and software, intended by the manufacturer to be used by a natural person, for the processing of electronic health data, specifically for providing information on the health of natural persons, or the delivery of care for purposes other than the provision of healthcare.

This definition acknowledges the fact that wellness applications may collect several types of data that can be used to infer the health conditions of the user. It is important to highlight that wellness applications have been purposefully included within the scope of the EHDS so as to incorporate any data collected through interoperable exchange systems, i.e., electronic health record (EHR) systems. In fact, the EHR system was put into place in 2008 to encourage the shift from paper-based patient

---

[60] Directive (EU) 2022/2555 of the European Parliament and of the Council of 14 December 2022 on measures for a high common level of cybersecurity across the Union, amending Regulation (EU) No 910/2014 and Directive (EU) 2018/1972, and repealing Directive (EU) 2016/1148 (NIS 2 Directive).

[61] EU Commission (2020).

documentation to digital. Ultimately, the objective is to make each patient's EHR accessible all throughout Europe. However, this goal has not yet been achieved as many of the information systems used at the national level are incompatible both format-wise and in terms of the technical standards used.[62]

Notably, the manufacturers of wellness applications are under no mandatory obligations to certify their products. The only exception is if the manufacturer wants to include their product within the infrastructure of electronic health data for primary uses. Under these circumstances, the manufacturer will then be required to comply with the requirements outlined in Article 30 and Annex II of the EDHS Regulation.[63] These requirements pertain to processing data in a way that ensures the data are safe and secure; that no unauthorized access is possible; that identification and authentication mechanisms (including role-based controls) are robust; that activity involving the data are logged in accessible records; that access to personal data is restricted; that digital signature mechanisms are in place; and that data retention periods are advised to relevant stakeholders. To receive a "Declaration of Conformity", the manufacturer only needs to conduct a self-assessment. But, although this idea of self-assessment is designed to enhance the autonomy and responsibility of the manufacturer, it does carry the risk of producing low-reliability evaluations.[64]

In the EDHS Regulation, monitoring and enforcement powers are allocated to the various market surveillance authorities.[65] These bodies that are in charge of verifying compliance with essential requirements after a wellness application is put on the market.[66] Yet a step in the system of control is missed here as wellness applications seem to be excluded from any obligations to notify anyone of a serious incident. Serious incidents are defined as …

> … any malfunction or deterioration in the characteristics or performance that directly or indirectly leads, might have led or might lead to the death of a natural person or serious damage to a natural person's health; a serious disruption of the management and operation of critical infrastructure.

That said, Article 44 of the EHDS Regulation prescribes that any manufacturer who contributes to an EHR is required to notify no later than 15 days after becoming aware or immediately after establishing a causal link between the application and the serious incident (or the reasonable likelihood of such link). Conversely, Article 47 of the Regulation focuses on the interoperability perspective and, if this narrow interpretation is adopted, the offending wellness application does not have any obligation to conduct subsequent monitoring or correct its harm in the case that the product does affect the health and safety of patients.[67]

---

[62] Casarosa (2024b), p. 4.

[63] Terzis and Santamaria Echeverria (2023).

[64] Casarosa (2024b).

[65] Article 43 EHDS Regulation.

[66] Article 47 EHDS Regulation.

[67] Casarosa (2024b).

3 The Way Forward Between Overlapping Obligations

The above overview shows that the current legal frameworks applicable to health devices that fall outside the definition of medical devices is still extremely piecemeal. They variously impose different requirements and notification obligations that are overlapping, if not duplicating, depending on the type of event affecting the security of the device or application.

As depicted in Table 1, the cybersecurity requirements applicable are scattered across the different regulations, leaving the task of identifying the more detailed standards that might ensure compliance to the manufacturers. From the perspective of technological neutrality, this approach might be justified given that legislative requirements can quickly become irrelevant in the face of rapid technological developments. However, this approach also paves the way for a process of standardization that strongly relies on the ability of the standard-setting bodies, whether international or European, to translate the principles and general definitions outlined in the legislation into operational requirements.[68]

From another perspective, assessing compliance with the selected standards will fall under the purview of the authorities or Notified Bodies indicated in each legislative instrument. Except for the case of data protection, where no ex-ante assessment by third parties is needed, plus the case of self-assessment, Notified Bodies will have the task of verifying that any product placed on the market complies with all the various regulations in place.

Moreover, in a pathological situation, i.e., when an incident which may affect the device's functioning occurs, manufacturers may have to clearly identify the event according to the different definitions of what constitutes an 'incident'. Consequently, the relevant authorities may need to be notified as soon as the event is classified, as Table 2 shows.

Table 1 Coordination issues—requirements and assessment procedures

Legislation	Cybersecurity requirements	Standards value	Type of assessment	Authority/ Notified Body
GDPR	Article 32	To be adapted to risk assessment	No ex-ante assessment	N/A
AI Act (only high risk)	Article 15	Compliance (Article 40)	Self-assessment or third-party evaluation	Notified bodies
CRA	Annex II	Compliance (Article 27)	Third-party evaluation	Notified bodies
EHDS	Article 30 and Annex II	N/A	Self-assessment	Notified bodies

[68] Cantero Gamito (2018); Cuccuru (2020); Micklitz (2023); Rampášek et al. (2025).

Table 2 Coordination issues—incident handling

Legislation	Incident definition	Notification content	Timeline	Notification bodies
GDPR	Article 4(12)—Data breach	Article 32	72 hours from becoming aware	Data protection authority
AI Act	Article 3 (49)—Serious incident	Article 73	15 days from the moment the causal link is established	Market surveillance authority
CRA	Article 3 (43)—Incident	Article 14	24 hours from becoming aware	CSIRT
EHDS	Article 2 (2) (r)—Serious incident	Article 44	15 days from becoming aware	Market surveillance authority

This obligation to notify the authorities has a twofold objective. First, in the short term, the aim is to discover attacks and identify underlying vulnerabilities so as to allow a coordinated response to a cybersecurity incident. However, in the long term, the aim is to improve the level of security over data and enhance cyber preparedness.[69] The underlying assumption, then, is that acquiring information related to a cybersecurity incident could help to reveal other (potential or ongoing) incidents involving other actors in the sector. Yet, if this is the case, duplicating the notification obligations to different authorities without also imposing information-sharing obligations reduces the likelihood of achieving such results.

This picture clearly shows the results of stratifying different sets of regulations. Although the objectives of each piece of legislation are legitimate, a lack of coordination has paved the way for overlaps and duplication. This critical appraisal has also been acknowledged by the EU Commission, which, in its latest work programme[70] included among the objectives a proposal "to remove inefficient requirements for paper formats in product legislation and build synergies and consistency for data protection and cybersecurity rules". It remains to be seen how this will be achieved, as coordination should consider several aspects. One crucial element will be the compliance assessments, which are delegated to the Notified Bodies. Here, it will be important to ensure that the expertise and competence of the Notified Bodies are up to the task. As a matter of fact, it is more than probable that such bodies will be providing services across different technologies and sectors. Therefore, their expertise and knowledge will be crucial to provide a reliable assessment as regards compliance with the legislation.[71]

Moreover, the legislation places different authorities in charge of reporting tasks. Yet centralizing the notification procedures through one unified platform could

---

[69] Casarosa (2024c).

[70] Communication, Commission Work Programme 2025 - Moving forward together: A Bolder, Simpler, Faster Union. Strasbourg, 11.2.2025, COM(2025) 45 final, p. 2.

[71] Burden et al. (2024).

simplify a manufacturer's obligations in case of incidents. Such a platform could also help the different authorities communicate and coordinate their efforts depending on the type of event. It could also help with any subsequent monitoring required, and even be used to sanction activities. Note that the initial proposal outlining the CRA originally included a step toward centralization. Here, the notification mechanism was envisaged as a central point of reference for collecting notifications across all EU member states. Further, the national CSIRT bodies only needed to be informed in a limited number of cases. However, this approach was later modified to where the role of ENISA became ancillary.[72] A less ambitious intervention would be a coordination effort to create a common but flexible template for notifications that could bend to different types of incidents but contained all the information any notification body required. This would allow manufacturers to avoid duplicating effort while ensuring all information was reported consistently.

In any case, the choices to achieve a simplified and more consistent cybersecurity framework must consider the impact on all the actors involved, from the manufacturers to the Notified Bodies to the market surveillance authorities and beyond.

Acknowledgments The research was conducted within the framework of the PNRR project "SoBigData.it: Strengthening the Italian RI for Social Mining and Big Data Analytics" (CUP B53C22001760006).

Disclosure of Interests The authors have no competing interests to declare that are relevant to the content of this article.

References

Amelang K (2022) (Not) safe to use: insecurities in everyday data practices with period-tracking apps. In: Hepp A, Jarke J, Kramp L (eds) New perspectives in critical data studies: the ambivalences of data power. Springer International Publishing, Cham, pp 297–321. https://doi.org/10.1007/978-3-030-96180-0_13

Biasin E, Yaşar B, Kamenjašević E (2023) New cybersecurity requirements for medical devices in the EU: the forthcoming European Health Data Space, Data Act, and Artificial Intelligence Act. Law Technol Hum 5:43–58. https://doi.org/10.5204/lthj.3068

Burden H, Stenberg S, Flink K (2024) When AI meets machinery – the role of the notified body. Rise rapport 56

Burri M, Zihlmann Z (2023) The EU Cyber Resilience Act – an appraisal and contextualization. Zeitschrift für Europarecht (EuZ):B1–B45

Burton C (2020) Article 32 Security of processing. In: Kuner C, Bygrave LA, Docksey C, Drechsler L (eds) The EU General Data Protection Regulation (GDPR). Oxford University Press, New York, pp 630–639. https://doi.org/10.1093/oso/9780198826491.003.0068

[72] See Article 11, Proposal for a Regulation on horizontal cybersecurity requirements for products with digital elements and amending Regulation (EU) 2019/1020, COM(2022) 454 final, Brussels, 15.9.2022.

Busch F, Kather JN, Johner C, Moser M, Truhn D, Adams LC, Bressem KK (2024) Navigating the European Union Artificial Intelligence Act for Healthcare. npj Digit Med 7:1–6. https://doi.org/10.1038/s41746-024-01213-6

Cantero Gamito M (2018) Europeanization through standardization: ICT and telecommunications. Yearb Eur Law 37:395–423. https://doi.org/10.1093/yel/yey018

Carovano G, Meinke A (2023) Improving Fairness and Cybersecurity in the Artificial Intelligence Act

Casarosa F (2024a) Cybersecurity of Internet of Things in the health sector: understanding the applicable legal framework. Comput Law Secur Rev 53:105982. https://doi.org/10.1016/j.clsr.2024.105982

Casarosa F (2024b) European Health Data Space – is the proposed certification system effective against cyber threats? Eur J Risk Regul:1–11. https://doi.org/10.1017/err.2024.25

Casarosa F (2024c) L'armonizzazione degli obblighi di notifica: il DDL Cybersicurezza verso la NIS 2. Rivista italiana di informatica e diritto 6:4–4. https://doi.org/10.32091/RIID0146

Chen T, Carter J, Mahmud M, Khuman AS (eds) (2022) Artificial intelligence in healthcare: recent applications and developments, brain informatics and health. Springer Nature Singapore, Singapore. https://doi.org/10.1007/978-981-19-5272-2

Chiara PG (2023) Il Cyber Resilience Act: la proposta di regolamento della Commissione europea relativa a misure orizzontali di cybersicurezza per prodotti con elementi digitali. Rivista italiana di informatica e diritto 5:11. https://doi.org/10.32091/RIID0108

Corrales Compagnucci M, Wilson ML, Fenwick M, Forgó N, Bärnighausen T (eds) (2022) AI in eHealth: human autonomy, data governance and privacy in healthcare, 1st edn. Cambridge University Press. https://doi.org/10.1017/9781108921923

Cuccuru P (2020) Regulating by request: on the role and status of the standardisation mandate under the new approach. In: The legitimacy of standardisation as a regulatory technique. Edward Elgar Publishing, pp 48–63

Demková S (2024) The EU's artificial intelligence laboratory and fundamental rights. In: Finck M (ed) Redressing fundamental rights violations by the EU: the promise of the 'complete system of remedies. Cambridge University Press

Durovic M, Corno T (2024) The privacy of emotions: from the GDPR to the AI Act, an overview of emotional AI regulation and the protection of privacy and personal data. In: Privacy, data protection and data-driven technologies. Routledge

Ebers M (2024) Truly risk-based regulation of artificial intelligence how to implement the EU's AI Act. Eur J Risk Regul:1–20. https://doi.org/10.1017/err.2024.78

EDPB (2021) Guidelines 01/2021 on Examples regarding Personal Data Breach Notification.

EDPB (2023) Guidelines 9/23 on personal data breach notification under GDPR. https://doi.org/10.5040/9781782258674

EU Commission (2020) 'Digital health data and services – the European health data space' (Consultation) 23 December 2020 - 04 February 2021. <https://ec.europa.eu/info/law/better-regulation/have-your-say/initiatives/12663-Digital-health-data-and-services-the-European-health-data-space_en>

Fabbrizio A, Fucarino A, Cantoia M et al (2023) Smart devices for health and wellness applied to tele-exercise: an overview of new trends and technologies such as IoT and AI. Healthcare 11:1805. https://doi.org/10.3390/healthcare11121805

Fosch-Villaronga E (2019) Robots, healthcare, and the law: regulating automation in personal care, 1st edn. Routledge. https://doi.org/10.4324/9780429021930

Fosch-Villaronga E, Drukarch H (2021) On healthcare robots: concepts, definitions, and considerations for healthcare robot governance

Fosch-Villaronga E, Drukarch H (2023) Accounting for diversity in robot design, testbeds, and safety standardization. Int J Soc Robot 15:1871–1889. https://doi.org/10.1007/s12369-023-00974-6

Fosch-Villaronga E, Mahler T (2021) Cybersecurity, safety and robots: strengthening the link between cybersecurity and safety in the context of care robots. Comput Law Secur Rev 41:1–13. https://doi.org/10.1016/j.clsr.2021.105528

Gennari F (2024) O Complementarity, Where Art Thou? Wading through the Medical Device Regulation and the AI Act Compliance: the case of software as a medical device. A primer. BioLaw J - Rivista di BioDiritto:411–453. https://doi.org/10.15168/2284-4503-3207
Hammond E, Burdon M (2024) Intimate harms and menstrual cycle tracking apps. Comput Law Secur Rev 55:106038. https://doi.org/10.1016/j.clsr.2024.106038
Héritier H, Allémann C, Balakiriev O et al (2023) Food & You: a digital cohort on personalized nutrition. PLOS Digital Health 2:e0000389. https://doi.org/10.1371/journal.pdig.0000389
Junklewitz H, Hamon R, André A et al (2023) Cybersecurity of Artificial Intelligence in the AI Act. Publications Office of the European Union, Luxembourg. https://doi.org/10.2760/271009, JRC134461
Kamara I (2021) Data protection standardisation: the role and limits of technical standards in the EU data protection law. Vrije Universiteit Brussel – LSTS
Koolen C, Wuyts K, Joosen W et al (2023) From insight to compliance: the concept of 'appropriate technical and organisational measures' in EU cybersecurity law. https://doi.org/10.2139/ssrn.4459481
Kosta E (2023) One-stop-shop case digest on security of processing and data breach notification
Ludvigsen K, Nagaraja S, Daly A (2022) When is software a medical device? Understanding and determining the "intention" and requirements for software as a medical device in European Union Law. Eur J Risk Regul 13:78–93. https://doi.org/10.1017/err.2021.45
Maibaum A, Bischof A, Hergesell J et al (2022) A critique of robotics in health care. AI Soc 37:467–477. https://doi.org/10.1007/s00146-021-01206-z
Micklitz H-W (2023) The role of standards in future EU digital policy legislation. BEUC; ANEC
Mohanty SP, Singhal G, Scuccimarra EA et al (2022) The food recognition benchmark: using deep learning to recognize food in images. Front Nutr 9. https://doi.org/10.3389/fnut.2022.875143
Nolte H, Rateike M, Finck M (2024) Robustness and cybersecurity in the EU Artificial Intelligence Act
Palmieri S (2024) The renewed EU legal framework for medical AI. Eur J Law Technol 15
Palmieri S, Goffin T (2023) A blanket that leaves the feet cold: exploring the AI Act safety framework for medical AI. Eur J Health Law 30:406–427. https://doi.org/10.1163/15718093-bja10104
Papakonstantinou V (2022) Cybersecurity as praxis and as a state: the EU law path towards acknowledgement of a new right to cybersecurity? Comput Law Secur Rev 44:105653. https://doi.org/10.1016/j.clsr.2022.105653
Pehlivan CN (2024) Report: the EU Artificial Intelligence (AI) Act: an introduction. Global Priv Law Rev 5
Pierce RL, Fosch-Villaronga E (2022) Medical robots and the right to health care: a progressive realization. In: Ienca M, Pollicino O, Liguori L, Stefanini E, Andorno R (eds) The Cambridge handbook of information technology, life sciences and human rights. Cambridge University Press, pp 70–85. https://doi.org/10.1017/9781108775038.008
Rampášek M, Mesarčík M, Andraško J (2025) Evolving cybersecurity of AI-featured digital products and services: rise of standardisation and certification? Comput Law Secur Rev 56:106093. https://doi.org/10.1016/j.clsr.2024.106093
Raposo VL (2024) Facial recognition AI technology in healthcare and the law. In: Research handbook on health, AI and the law. Edward Elgar Publishing, pp 41–56
Sawik B, Tobis S, Baum E et al (2023) Robots for elderly care: review, multi-criteria optimization model and qualitative case study. Healthcare (Basel) 11:1286. https://doi.org/10.3390/healthcare11091286
Schäfke-Zell W (2022) Revisiting the definition of health data in the age of digitalized health care. Int Data Priv Law 12:33–43. https://doi.org/10.1093/idpl/ipab025
Shaffique MR (2024) Cyber Resilience Act 2022: a silver bullet for cybersecurity of IoT devices or a shot in the dark? Comput Law Secur Rev 54:106009. https://doi.org/10.1016/j.clsr.2024.106009

Terzis P, Santamaria Echeverria (Enrique) OE (2023) Interoperability and governance in the European Health Data Space regulation. Med Law Int 096853322311656. https://doi.org/10.1177/09685332231165692

Tzanou M (ed) (2021) Health data privacy under the GDPR: big data challenges and regulatory responses, Routledge research in the law of emerging technologies. Routledge, New York; Milton Park, Abingdon, Oxon

Volpato A, Eliantonio M (2020) The contradictory approach of the CJEU to the judicial review of standards: a love–hate relationship? In: The legitimacy of standardisation as a regulatory technique. Edward Elgar Publishing, pp 91–109

Scoping Challenges Through the Players of the Personalized Medicine Ecosystem

Personalized Medicine: A Medical Perspective

Michele Emdin and Claudio Passino

Abstract The doctor who arms himself in his profession with curiosity and interest in others must not fear the complexity of his task; he must love it. This is a complexity that has always been present in the disease of patients, but today is revealed more than ever by sophisticated magnifying glasses, engraved by robotic hands, enumerated and codified by digital folders. It is a complexity veiled by an entropy of information to which no artificial intelligence other than the mind of doctors, nurses, and health professionals in teamwork can bring order. Indeed, he complexity of the individual phenotype requires a personalized approach that must pair the most advanced scientific knowledge and the most effective diagnostic and therapeutic tools with the empathy that should characterize the patient-doctor/care provider mutual relationships. Primary care and the hospital should be dedicated to the management of biological disease while keeping humanity on both sides of the therapeutic alliance. Today's challenge is to get an early diagnosis and an appropriate treatment by putting together -omics and the Hippocratic approach. Only in this way, we will align classical medical reasoning with artificial intelligence algorithms in a way that does not leave the patient alone.

1 Personalized Medicine: Lessons from the Past

> ...Into whatsoever houses I enter, I will enter for the relief of the sick... recites the Hippocratic oath.

M. Emdin (✉)
Health Science Interdisciplinary Center, Sant'Anna School of Advanced Studies, Pisa, Italy

Fondazione Toscana Gabriele Monasterio, Pisa, Italy
e-mail: michele.emdin@santannapisa.it

C. Passino
Health Science Interdisciplinary Center, Scuola Superiore Sant'Anna, Pisa, Italy

Fondazione Toscana Gabriele Monasterio, Pisa, Italy
e-mail: michele.emdin@santannapisa.it

F. Casarosa et al. (eds.), *Enabling and Safeguarding Personalized Medicine*, Data Science, Machine Intelligence, and Law 7,
https://doi.org/10.1007/978-3-031-99709-9_7

Anton Pavlowitsch Chekhov (1860–1904) counted Grigorii Antonovich Zakharin (1829–1887) among his teachers at the Moscow Medical School. Zakharin, who was a professor, an internist, and a doctor at the tsarist court, and was also a friend to Rudolf Wirchow, Armand Trousseau, and Claude Bernard, advocated the concept that "thinking like a doctor" means individualizing each case; the disease does not exist, only the patient, whose history and living and working environment must be known by the physician in addition to the symptoms, and whose emotional as well as physical suffering must be investigated. While a caress cannot heal, every patient will feel better if the medical relationship is empathic. This notion supports the goal of understanding and treating the complexity of the individual health problem, using at the bedside the most advanced clinical knowledge, the modern diagnostic technology, the most effective treatment, combining drugs, device implantation, surgery, rehabilitation (the téchne to use the Greeks' words) to improve quality and expectancy of life. It is here, at the bedside of the sick, that genetics, biology, evidence-based diagnostics, and therapeutics meet allowing physicians to draw diagnosis and treatment in the individual patients. To this end, the impressive amount of knowledge, which continues to grow every day, allows us to treat and sometimes cure diseases that until yesterday were hopeless. Though the patient's path is still heartbreaking and sometimes questions remain without an answer, empathy (empatheia) will be always there.

2 The Basis of Personalized Medicine Today

Conventional medicine has long relied on empirical therapies, which have evolved into treatments based on the recognition of disease mechanisms.[1] while the current evidence-based, guideline-recommended medicine is based on randomized controlled trials (RCTs). RCTs, which represent the highest level of scientific evidence achieved up-to-date, identify therapies[2] through a translational research approach[3] which first assesses the biological plausibility and safety of a particular remedy, and finally tests its efficacy and dose response. The knowledge achieved is then summarized by Medical Guidelines, which are periodically updated by expert consensus with the endorsements of Scientific Societies and Independent Agencies. Regulatory Institutions and policymakers should then adapt constantly the Health System framework and action, in order to advance the diagnostic and therapeutic offers.

However, RCTs, which are usually conducted on heterogeneous patient populations with predefined characteristics, leave their findings open to a tailored attempt to meet the needs of individuals. Physicians must not fall into the error of considering the results of the RCT as an excuse to pursue the concept of "one size fits all" approach. In facts, the recognition of distinctive inherent molecular or genetic traits

[1] Jain (2009), pp 10–12.

[2] Hariton and Locascio (2018), pp. 1716–1720.

[3] Woolf (2008), pp. 211–213.

in individual patients, causing differential disease patterns and progression, as well as diverse response to drug therapy, and different incidence of adverse reactions, pointed out the need for tailoring medical effort by an intervention based on the knowledge of the individual, unique molecular/genetic mapping.[4]

On this basis, the idea of personalized medicine (PM) was first proposed in 1999 as a way of overcoming the constraints of the current approach associated with disregarding the distinct individual variations and was defined by the American National Research Council Toward Personalised Medicine as follows "The tailoring of medical treatment to the individual characteristics of each patient … to classify individuals into subpopulations that differ in their susceptibility to a particular disease or their response to a specific treatment" (see Fig. 1).[5]

Personalized medicine is also often referred to as "precision medicine" or "P4 medicine", the latter term being used to include 4 components—predictive, preventive, personalized, and participatory—as first proposed by Leroy Hood, founder of the Institute for Systems Biology in Seattle and a pioneer in systems approaches to biology and medicine. P4 is a medical model that proposes healthcare be customized, with medical decisions, treatments, practices, or products being tailored to subgroups of patients, instead of a one-drug-fits-all model.[6,7] Predictive medicine demands a proactive role not only of health care systems and professionals but also of the healthy subjects and patients involved in trials. It is based on identifying genetics and other risks for disease and assumes knowing and planning in advance for the effects of illnesses and for the efficacy and adverse effect of treatment. Examples include neonatal screening for phenylketonuria and congenital

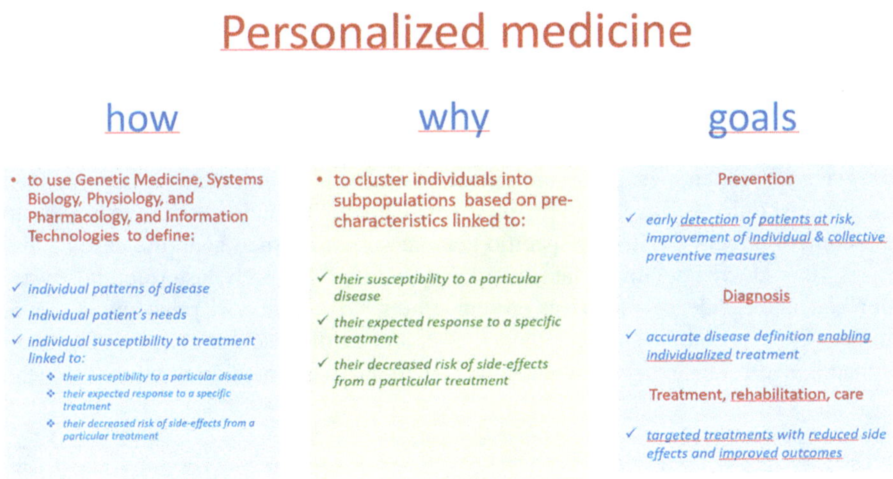

Fig. 1 Rationale, methods, and final goals of personalized medicine

[4] Goldberger and Buxton (2013), pp. 2559–2560.

[5] National Research Council (2011), p. 12.

[6] Weston and Hood (2004), p. 179.

[7] Hood and Friend (2011), pp. 184–187.

hypothyroidism, fecal occult blood tests for colorectal cancer, and screening for cervical cancer through Pap smears.

In preventive medicine, individuals are empowered to adopt measures to prevent or reduce the risk of developing a disease or to recognize early disease when it could be reversed or more easily treated. Some preventive measures such as vaccinations, healthy eating, regular physical exercise, and quitting smoking have been highly successful in reducing the individual risk of developing life-threatening diseases. anticipation is an essential component of personalized medicine. Patients need to be deeply involved and actively participate in their own care to reap the benefits of patient-physician relationships by inspiring trust and cooperation and in the efficacy and efficiency of a medical intervention.

The modern concept of personalized medicine mostly stands on recent advances in Genetic Medicine, Systems Biology, Physiology, and Pharmacology, and, ultimately, Information Technologies. The Human Genome Sequencing Project, which identified up to 23,000 genes was completed in 2003.[8] The sheer variety in human genomes, as a result of single-nucleotide polymorphisms, insertions, deletions, structural variants, and variations in the number of copies, significantly helps to explain the individual variability in disease development and progression, as well as the different responses to treatment experienced by different patients. Systems Biology describes the changes in biology associated with transcriptomics, proteomics, and metabolomics, as well as physiological changes triggered by gene expressions at the cell, tissue, organ, and body level. Both biological and physiological perturbations can be evaluated by using biomarkers (e.g. peptides, deoxyribonucleic acid (DNA), ribonucleic acid (RNA) or imaging parameters) which apply to areas of clinical disease management. Additionally, System Biology can explain the mechanisms of a disease's development even in its very early stages. It can also provide the tools for disease screening, diagnosis, prognosis, implementing preventative procedures, and guides to treatment.[9,10]

Systems Pharmacology aims to identify the genes and proteins responsible for drug responses and eventual individual resistance.[11] Nonetheless, personalized medicine should be considered distinct from Genetic Medicine, which is limited to the clinical effect of a single, specific genetic variation, such as in the case of diseases like Duchenne muscular dystrophy, familial hypercholesterolemia, cystic fibrosis, and sickle cell anemia, among others.[12] As concerns prevalent diseases such as cancer, diabetes, neurodegenerative, and cardiovascular disease, all greatly impacting on morbidity and mortality, personalized medicine must face the

[8] https://www.genome.gov/human-genome-project.

[9] Mohr (2024), p. 1496.

[10] Cong and Endo (2024), pp. 257–260.

[11] Tan (2022), pp. 849–851.

[12] Cutting (2015), pp. 45–56.

complex nature of the disease phenotype and the individual treatment response which are not only associated with genetic factors but also with environmental ones.[13]

Personalized medicine has a role in drug discovery and development alongside clinical trials and the practice of medicine. One of the earliest examples pertains to trastuzumab, a monoclonal antibody used to treat breast and stomach cancer, that are Human Epidermal Growth Factor Receptor 2 (HER2) positive. For most of the twentieth century, all women affected by breast cancer received similar chemotherapy; however, up to 30% of breast cancers were unresponsive to standard treatment due to an over-expression of HER2. Nowadays, assessments for HER2 overexpression routinely drive which therapeutic approach could be used in women affected by breast cancer.[14] As another example, up to 60% of melanomas carry an activating mutation in the gene encoding the serine-threonine protein kinase B-RAF (BRAF), V600E being the most frequent. The discovery of vemurafenib, a potent inhibitor of BRAF with the V600E mutation, has thus prompted an active search for this mutation in melanoma patients.[15]

In clinical trial design, personalized medicine has gradually redefined the traditional RCT, such that today trials are conducted with no control or placebo arms. An example of this is the success of crizotinib, a selective inhibitor of the anaplastic lymphoma kinase (ALK). ALK-EML4 fusion is the driver for lung cancer progression. The crizotinib trial included 82 lung cancer patients who tested positive for the biomarker ALK with no control group. Inhibiting ALK in lung tumors with the ALK rearrangement resulted in tumor shrinkage or stable disease in most patients with only minor side effects.[16]

Besides efficacy, personalized medicine also allows to test for adverse drug reactions and appropriate dosing based on genetics. For example, abacavir, a medication used to treat HIV, though generally well tolerated, may be associated with severe side effects that may include liver damage and lactic acidosis. A study by Mallal et al. proved a genetic association with the hypersensitivity identifying the driving gene as the major histocompatibility complex class I allele HLA-B*5701. Consequently, the recommendation now is to screen for HLA-B*5701 in order to reduce the risk of a hypersensitive reaction to abacavir.[17] The goal of gathering this type of genetic information is to individualize the risk factors, biological characteristics, and personal ancestries associated with a disease. Accordingly, the incidence of genome-wide association studies (GWAS), a research methodology used to identify genomic variants that are statistically associated with a risk for a disease or a particular trait is on the increase. Such studies have already found genetic-based variations in the risk factors for diseases such as Type 2 diabetes, heart disorders,

[13] Carlsten (2014), pp. 736–739.

[14] Hudis (2007), pp. 39–51.

[15] Flaherty et al. (2019), pp. 809–819.

[16] Kwak (2010), pp. 1693–1703.

[17] Mallal (2008), pp. 3227–2336.

Parkinson's disease, obesity, prostate cancer, and Crohn's disease. GWASs involve surveying the genomes of many people and looking for genomic variants that occur more frequently in those with a specific disease or trait compared to those without that disease or trait. Once such genomic variants are identified, they are typically used to search for nearby variants that directly contribute to the condition.

The first GWAS was published in 2005 on patients with age-related macular degeneration (ARMD).[18] Two different gene mutations were found, each containing a variation in only one nucleotide (called single nucleotide polymorphisms, associated with ARMD). Since then, the popularity of GWASs has only grown: historically, the typical sample size of a GWAS was several thousand individuals compared to now when the sample sizes can number in the hundreds of thousands. The GWAS Catalog is a consistent, searchable, and freely available collection of all human genome-wide association studies, produced by a collaboration between the European Bioinformatics Institute and the NIH-National Human Genome Research Institute.[19] The methods and results of GWAS have also informed other applications in epidemiologic research, such as gene-environment studies, Mendelian randomization studies, and polygenic risk score approaches.

3 Translational Research and Personalized Medicine: The Impact on Patients, Physicians, and Industry-Driven Drug Development

Translational research has long been concerned with converting preclinical technologies into clinical applications. Recently, however, translational researchers have become interested in implementing methods associated with personalized medicine. These applications include developing animal models that mimic human disease patterns, using biomarkers to assess the effectiveness and/or toxicity of treatments, using bioinformatics and analysis software in both preclinical and clinical studies to reduce failure rates in the later stages of drug development, as well as conducting post-implementation studies related to drug distribution and patient acceptability.[20]

All in all, the ultimate goal of personalized medicine is to provide a tailored treatment for patients without a cure. As an example, newer chemotherapies such as panitumumab and cetuximab have been developed to target patients with metastatic colorectal cancer and the KRAS gene who do not do well with the conventional chemotherapies, such as 5-fluorouracil, irinotecan, and oxaliplatin.[21] The improvement in life quality, and expectancy, and in patient satisfaction from personalized

[18] Rivera et al. (2005), pp. 3227–3236.

[19] https://www.ebi.ac.uk/gwas/.

[20] Lee (2023), pp. 4687–4696

[21] Heinemann (2013), pp. 592–601.

medicine not only benefits those being treated, but also physicians. For example, they no longer need to toil with trial-and-error approaches to diagnose and treat the sick. Instead, they can base remedies on the molecular and genetic causes of a disease. Further, personalized medicine can minimize the risk of any adverse effect, while the biopharmaceutical industry benefits from any procedures that minimize costs and the time it takes to develop drugs.

3.1 The Fall and Rise of Failed Drugs

Another advantage of personalized medicine is that, on occasion, it can salvage failed drugs. For instance, during initial testing, a drug may have presented with an unacceptable level of toxicity and/or poor efficacy. However, when genetically tested over very large populations, the drug may prove useful to a peculiar set of patients. Consider thalidomide: despite its stigma following fetal deformities in pregnant women, its usefulness has been revived as a result of proven efficacy and safety in treating certain forms of myeloma, light chain amyloidosis, and also Crohn's disease.[22] Accordingly, in July 1998, the US Food and Drug Administration approved thalidomide as safe for the treatment of cutaneous manifestations of erythema nodosum. The manufacturer instituted a comprehensive program to control how the drug is prescribed, dispensed, and used so as not to expose fetuses to the teratogenic agent (System for Thalidomide Education and Prescribing Safety—S.T.E.P.S. [Celgene Corporation, Warren, New Jersey]).[23] The program was in part based on experiences gained with other drugs, specifically isotretinoin and clozapine, that offer important clinical benefits but carry the potential for serious harm. Clozapine, which has also been associated with life-threatening side effects, as agranulocytosis still on the market due to its safety and efficacy in some patient populations with schizophrenia. Current investigations of clozapine are targeted at Parkinson's disease and Huntington's chorea.[24,25]

3.2 Is Personalized Prevention and Care Sustainable?

While personalized medicine promises to revolutionize pharmacotherapy, its potential extends beyond already sick populations, to identify healthy individuals at risk, to prevent disease through targeted therapies. If such "precision prevention" were to be practiced on a broader scale, we may see significant reductions in healthcare

[22] Franks (2004), pp. 1802–1811.

[23] Zeldis (1999), pp. 319–330.

[24] Friedman (2022), pp. 1021–1024.

[25] Factor and Friedman (1997) pp. 483–485.

spending. Thus, it would be entirely worthwhile trying to measure the true cost-effectiveness of these novel interventions.[26]

Nonetheless, personalized medicine, if not adequately guided, carries several risks in terms of efficacy and sustainability:[27] (1) overtesting, i.e., testing done because it is technically possible, not because it has proven useful; (2) overdiagnosis, i.e., diagnosing a disease that would otherwise never become clinically significant or threaten patient's life; (3) overtreatment, i.e. the consequence of overdiagnosis; (4) overcharging, i.e.—the composite result of overtesting, overdiagnosis, and overtreatment impacting on the healthcare systems.

For all these reasons, further development of personalized medicine requires a multidisciplinary effort involving health systems, the pharmaceutical industry, biotechnology companies, Universities, and Research Organizations, as well as other social, political, and economic actors, including patients' associations. One example is the Personalized Medicine Coalition (PMC), located in Washington DC.[28] PMC is a nonprofit organization involving the pharmaceutical industry, biotechnology companies, universities, government agencies, patient groups, information technology companies, and healthcare providers. It…

> … promotes the understanding and adoption of concepts, services, and products that can provide physicians with a better understanding of the molecular characteristics influencing a patient's health….-with the goal …to advance more informed prevention and early detection strategies, more precise diagnoses, and tailored treatment recommendations that work for patients and their families.[29]

As the documentation provided by the Coalition highlights, the cost of sequencing a human genome in 2024 was $1000 versus $100 million in 2001. Further, there was a 75% increase in biopharmaceutical industry investments in developing new personalized medicines from 2005 to 2010, and, as a result, 38% of all the new drugs approved by the U.S. Food and Drug Administration in 2023 were personalized medicine. PMC advises policymakers on how to regulate, pay for, and encourage the clinical adoption of personalized medicine and advises organizations on the development of evidence-based standards and measures that are used to help assess the quality of health care. In 2021, for example, PMC encouraged the National Committee for Quality Assurance (NCQA) to adopt changes to its colorectal cancer screening measure. The idea was to help align the existing measures with the value that molecularly-guided testing strategies can provide for these patients in the era of personalized medicine.

Health Information Technology also makes a huge contribution to advancing personalized medicine. Standout technologies include central electronic systems for managing health data as these not only enable the flow of information (such as medical images, genomics, biospecimens, and patient outcomes) guaranteeing data

---

[26] Berndt (2019).

[27] Fiala (2019), pp. 108–119.

[28] https://www.personalizedmedicinecoalition.org.

[29] caBIG (2007), pp, 330–334.

protection. One such system of communication was effectively applied within the Cancer Biomedical Informatics Grid Project, launched in 2003 by the National Cancer Institute (NCI) in the USA. Through this network, more than 50 NCI cancer units, engaging over 900 clinicians, scientists, and patient advocates as developers, adopters, and workspace participants together with academic and commercial institutions shared biomedical information in an integrated way with an open source software application.[30]

Finally, political and socioeconomic players are also driving the integration between personalized medicine and healthcare systems. The most notable of these players is the general public, who are placing enormous pressure on governments and the pharmaceutical industry to provide safer and more effective treatments. Additionally, National and International Public Agencies as well as health insurance companies, are supporting the shift toward personalized medicine in order to minimize expenditure on ineffective treatments.

3.3 Are There Any Boundaries to Personalized Medicine?

Personalized medicine holds good reason to become a mantra for patients and physicians, and it is also highly attractive to health systems. Still, a number of limitations are an obstacle to an apparent success story. First, the advancing knowledge of disease biology recognized unexplored territories, and though innovative research methodologies, data science and artificial intelligence implementation are a promise for speeding the process, much unknown is there both for rare diseases and for those pathologies with major epidemiological impact. Further, the currently available data on pharmacogenetics does not provide comprehensive information on why drug responses can vary between different people because the data are largely biased toward adult Caucasian males. Second, the genotype/phenotype relationship requires an extraordinary research effort. Beyond monogenic diseases, -omics and multimodal imaging might be of great help in this respect. Third, factors other than genes can contribute to drug responses, including diet, voluptuary habits, lifestyle, and infections.[31] Fourth, there is still limited support for personalized medicine from many of the world's governments and other healthcare organizations. In developed countries, such as the USA and Europe, personalized medicine has been acknowledged and implemented in health policies to foster its development. However, developing countries are lagging behind due to limited resources, even when it comes to conventional medicine. Another challenge facing personalized medicine is ethical, legal, and social concerns. Issues have been raised over stratifying patients into ethnic groups because this is likely to result in a form of social segregation, which policymakers strive to avoid. Furthermore, denying patients

[30] https://health.ec.europa.eu/medicinal-products/personalised-medicine_en.

[31] Agyeman and Ofori-Asenso (2015), pp. 239–244.

treatment based on genetic classification may be poorly understood by the general public and could be interpreted as treatment denial.

Finally, local drug/device approval, prescription, and distribution regulation impact on differences in time/population availability.

4 Final Remarks

> The doctor who arms himself in the profession with curiosity and interest in others must not fear the complexity of his task, he must love it. This is a complexity that has always been present in the disease of patients, but today is revealed more than ever by sophisticated magnifying glasses, engraved by robotic hands, and enumerated and codified by digital folders. This is a complexity veiled by an entropy of information to which no artificial intelligence can bring order other than through the minds of doctors, nurses, and health professionals working in teams.

He will use the heuristic approach to observe and intuit, the scientific method to formulate the diagnostic hypothesis and contradict it without prejudice with the acquisition of new evidence. He will use every diagnostic tool evaluating its appropriateness and accuracy, without ever mistaking the means for the aim. He will weigh therapeutic advice on a prognosis and carefully evaluate the risks and benefits of a drug, device, or surgical option. He will do that by considering an individual patient, of that age, with those comorbidities, and in light of other drugs or organ dysfunctions that can foster side effects. He will also consider the possible fragilities to be found in emotions, cognition, culture, and family support, which can inexorably compromise the efficacy of what the textbooks and guidelines describe as the perfect treatment (*primum non nocere*). Finally, he will always pursue the objective of "bringing relief"—improving the patient's quality of life and life expectancy by nourishing the therapeutic alliance of sympathy and friendship.

Personalised medicine is not an oxymoron. while the patient asks for a relief which is based not only on a prompt, exact diagnosis and treatment, but also on a personal relationship with the care provider made of in the form of listening, an explanation, or empathy at each stage of medicine. It can involve preventive efforts for people with the risk factors of a disease, screening symptomatic patients with silent diseases, early diagnosis and treatment of acutely symptomatic patients, secondary prevention and care of chronic patients, till the final effort for blunting physical and emotional suffering for improve the quality of death at the end of one's life.

The complexity of the individual phenotype requires a personalised approach that combines the most advanced and effective diagnostic and therapeutic tools with the empathy which should characterize the special relationship between a doctor and a patient. Primary care and hospitals should be dedicated to managing biological diseases while keeping humanity on both sides of the therapeutic alliance. We also need an introspective knowledge of the evolution of sickness, which should be object of a narrative medicine to avoid a dehumanized care of patients. Getting an early diagnosis and an appropriated treatment by putting together -omics with the clinical Hippocratic approach, refining classical medical reasoning with the implementation of the artificial intelligence algorithms without leaving the patient lone is the today's challenge.

Acknowledgements This research was financially supported by the "Biorobotics Research and Innovation Engineering Facilities" "IR0000036" – CUP J13C22000400007 (BRIEF) project.

References

Agyeman AA, Ofori-Asenso R (2015) Perspective: does personalized medicine hold the future for medicine? J Pharm Bioallied Sci 7:239–244

Berndt ER, Goldman DP, Rowe JW (2019) Economic dimensions of personalized and precision medicine. University of Chicago Press

caBIG (2007) Strategic Planning Workspace. The Cancer Biomedical Informatics Grid (caBIG): infrastructure and applications for a worldwide research community. Stud Health Technol Inform 129:330–334

Carlsten C, Brauer M, Brinkman F et al (2014) Genes, the environment and personalized medicine: we need to harness both environmental and genetic data to maximize personal and population health. EMBO Rep 15:736–739

Cong Y, Endo TA (2024) Quadruple revolution: deciphering biological complexity with artificial intelligence, multiomics, precision medicine, and planetary health. OMICS 28:257–260

Cutting GR (2015) Cystic fibrosis genetics: from molecular understanding to clinical application. Nat Rev Genet 16:45–56

Factor SA, Friedman JH (1997) The emerging role of clozapine in the treatment of movement disorders. Mov Disord 12:483–496

Fiala C, Taher J, Diamandis EP (2019) P4 medicine or O4 medicine? Hippocrates provides the answer. J Appl Lab Med 4:108–119.

Flaherty KT, Puzanov I, Kim KB et al (2019) Inhibition of mutated, activated BRAF in metastatic melanoma. N Engl J Med. 2010 Aug 26 363:809–819

Franks ME, Macpherson GR, Figg WD (2004) Thalidomide. Lancet 363:1802–1811

Friedman JH (2022) Clozapine is severely underused in Parkinson's disease patients. Mov Disord Clin Pract 9:1021–1024

Goldberger JJ, Buxton AE (2013) Personalized medicine vs guideline-based medicine. JAMA 309:2559–2560

Hariton E, Locascio JJ (2018) Randomised controlled trials - the gold standard for effectiveness research: Study design: randomised controlled trials. BJOG 125:1716–1720

Heinemann V, Douillard JY, Ducreux M et al (2013) Targeted therapy in metastatic colorectal cancer – an example of personalised medicine in action. Cancer Treat Rev 39:592–601

Hood L, Friend S (2011) Predictive, personalized, preventive, participatory (P4) cancer medicine. Nat Rev Clin Oncol 8:184–187

Hudis CA (2007) Trastuzumab--mechanism of action and use in clinical practice. N Engl J Med 357:39–51

Jain KK (2009) Textbook of personalised medicine. Springer, Netherlands

Kwak EL, Bang YJ, Camidge DR et al (2010) Anaplastic lymphoma kinase inhibition in non-small-cell lung cancer. N Engl J Med 363:1693–1703

Lee GA, Durante A, Baker EE et al (2023) Patients' perceptions on the facilitators and barriers using injectable therapies in dyslipidaemia: an empirical qualitative descriptive international study. J Adv Nurs 79:4687–4696

Mallal S, Phillips E, Carosi G et al (2008) PREDICT-1 Study Team. HLA-B*5701 screening for hypersensitivity to abacavir. N Engl J Med 358:568–579

Mohr AE, Ortega-Santos CP, Whisner CM, Klein-Seetharaman J, Jasbi P (2024) Navigating challenges and opportunities in multi-omics integration for personalized healthcare. Biomedicine 12:1496

National Research Council (2011) Toward precision medicine: building a knowledge network for biomedical research and a new taxonomy of disease. The National Academies Press, Washington, DC. https://doi.org/10.17226/13284

Rivera A, Fisher SA, Fritsche LG et al (2005) Hypothetical LOC387715 is a second major susceptibility gene for age-related macular degeneration, contributing independently of complement factor H to disease risk. Hum Mol Genet 14:3227–3236

Tan RK, Liu Y, Xie L (2022) Reinforcement learning for systems pharmacology-oriented and personalized drug design. Expert Opin Drug Discov 17:849–863

Weston AD, Hood L (2004) Systems biology, proteomics, and the future of health care: towards predictive, preventative, and personalized medicine. J Proteome Res 3:179–196

Woolf SH (2008) The meaning of translational research and why it matters. JAMA 299:211–213

Zeldis JB, Williams BA, Thomas SD et al (1999) S.T.E.P.S.: a comprehensive program for controlling and monitoring access to thalidomide. Clin Ther 21:319–330

Navigating the Increasing Complexity of Health Technology Assessments in the Digital Era: How to Support Value-Based Personalized Healthcare?

Ciro Pappalardo, Floriana d'Ambrosio, and Giovanna Elisa Calabrò

Abstract The evolution of healthcare systems towards value-based care has prompted the need for integrated approaches to personalized care. Digital health technologies (DHTs) hold promise to address challenges such as aging populations, rising healthcare costs, and disparities in access. However, ensuring DHTs are cost-effective, equitable, and responsibly implemented requires robust evaluation frameworks. Health technology assessment (HTA) is a multidisciplinary process for evaluating the value of technologies across their lifecycle—focusing on clinical, economic, ethical, and social aspects. The rapid development and unique features of DHTs challenge current HTA models, which were designed for an era when DHTs were not widespread. Incorporating real-world data and evidence into dynamic, iterative assessment models could yield timely and relevant insights into DHT value production. New frameworks must also address ethical, privacy, and cybersecurity challenges essential for building trust and safeguarding patient autonomy. This chapter explores the evolving role of HTA in the digital era, identifies gaps in existing frameworks across development, implementation, and post-market evaluation, and discusses strategies for methodological improvement and innovation. By fostering a more flexible, risk-based, and multidisciplinary approach, HTA can ensure DHTs are integrated safely and effectively into existing healthcare systems, aligning with the broader goal of delivering value-based, patient-centered healthcare.

C. Pappalardo (✉) · F. d'Ambrosio
Section of Hygiene, University Department of Life Sciences and Public Health, Università Cattolica del Sacro Cuore, Rome, Italy

G. E. Calabrò
Department of Human Sciences, Society and Health, University of Cassino and Southern Lazio, Cassino, Italy

VIHTALI (Value in Health Technology and Academy for Leadership & Innovation), Spin-Off of Università Cattolica del Sacro Cuore, Rome, Italy

F. Casarosa et al. (eds.), *Enabling and Safeguarding Personalized Medicine*, Data Science, Machine Intelligence, and Law 7,
https://doi.org/10.1007/978-3-031-99709-9_8

1 Introduction and Background

Around the world, healthcare systems are evolving towards value-based models that not only emphasize personalized care but also aim to maximize the benefits and efficiency of the overall system. To date, optimizing the limited resources that are generally available to healthcare systems has been a major focus.

Porter and Teisberg first articulated this approach—defining value as outcomes achieved per dollar spent—to guide systems toward better health outcomes and greater efficiency.[1] Value-based healthcare, as introduced by Michael Porter in 2010, attempts to maximize the value of care delivered to patients by prioritizing the outcomes that matter to them most. In this way, healthcare is tailored to the patient's individual characteristics, preferences, and needs.[2] Sir Muir Gray's triple value paradigm, which comprises allocative, technical, and personal values integrated with modern population medicine, has worked to further refine such approaches.[3] Indeed, in 2019, the European Commission's "Expert Panel on Effective Ways of Investing in Health (EXPH)" expanded this concept to include four pillars of value to guide solidarity-based healthcare systems, these being personal value, allocative value, technical value, and societal value.[4] Fortunately, this quest for efficiency has driven innovations that have enhanced patient engagement and outcomes and have also helped to ensure sustainable healthcare for all.[5]

Interestingly, digital health technologies (DHTs), which include a broad spectrum of tools and applications, such as telemedicine, wearable devices, and health information systems, might be pivotal in this transformation. The World Economic Forum,[6] in collaboration with the the Boston Consulting Group[7] have stated that harnessing data and the digital world to "digitize the front-end" and "augment the back-end" is vital to sustainable healthcare. Accordingly, DHTs are showing significant promise in addressing major healthcare challenges, such as issues with progressively aging populations, the increasing demand for health and long-term care services, the rising costs of healthcare, and challenges with accessing appropriate healthcare.[8] In these ways, DHTs have a very real possibility to enhance the sustainability, efficiency, and quality of healthcare systems, and even potentially becoming a health determinant in their own right.[9]

However, to fully exploit the transformative potential of DHTs and mitigate issues like the digital divide, it is crucial to ensure they are implemented both

[1] Porter and Teisberg (2006).

[2] Porter 2010.

[3] Gray (2013); Gray (2016).

[4] EXPH (2019), p. 5.

[5] The World Economic Forum (2017); Chen et al. (2023a); Nguyen et al. (2023).

[6] World Economic Forum, Boston Consulting Group (2024).

[7] Boston Consulting Group (2024).

[8] Kickbusch et al. (2019).

[9] Chidambaram et al. (2024).

responsibly and cost-effectively. The World Health Organization (WHO) emphasizes that DHTs should be developed under the principles of transparency, accessibility, scalability, privacy, security, and confidentiality to harness their potential and avoid unintended consequences.[10]

In this context, health technology assessment (HTA) can play a crucial role. Defined as a "multidisciplinary process that uses explicit methods to determine the value of a health technology at different points in its life cycle" and also as a "bridge between the world of research and the world of decision-making", HTAs have become a widely accepted tool to inform decision-making.[11] Overall, these assessments work as a method of synthesizing evidence in a way that considers the clinical effectiveness, safety, and cost-effectiveness of a technology and, when broadly applied, they also include the social, ethical, and legal aspects of using health technologies.[12] To ensure the assessments are both comprehensive and standardized, the reports tend to be structured according to a specific framework, such as the HTA Core Model of the European Network for Health Technology Assessment (EUnetHTA) or The International Network of Agencies for Health Technology Assessment (INAHTA) framework.[13] The EUnetHTA project, which developed the HTA Core Model, officially concluded in 2021 after nearly two decades of collaboration among European HTA agencies. The project's legacy continues through the European Regulation on Health Technology Assessment (Regulation (EU) 2021/2282), which aims to further harmonize HTA processes across the EU. Alternatively, the International Network of Agencies for Health Technology Assessment, established in 1993, provides a framework to facilitate collaboration among the world's assessment agencies. This organization offers guidance and shares resources to support evidence-based decision-making in healthcare. Evaluating DHTs under these HTA or value-based healthcare principles could ensure that digital innovations are integrated into healthcare systems both efficiently and effectively, promoting personalized, value-driven care.

However, while current HTA frameworks have proven to be effective at assessing traditional health technologies, many struggle to comprehensively evaluate DHTs. Vukovic et al. identify some of the limitations with the current assessment frameworks in terms of dynamic technologies, noting gaps in transparency and methodological rigor that mean the clinical and economic impacts of e-health and m-health technologies simply cannot be assessed.[14] Currently, most HTA evaluations primarily rely on published evidence being appraised. This includes comprehensive clinical trials, analyses of a technology's cost-effectiveness, and long-term impact studies. This process is often both time-consuming and resource-intensive and is therefore misaligned with the rapid development cycles that are characteristic of

[10] WHO (2021a).

[11] O'Rourke et al. (2020).

[12] Luce et al. (2010).

[13] INAHTA (2021).

[14] Vukovic et al. (2018).

DHTs.[15] Hence, while stringent requirements are essential to ensuring the safety and efficacy of these technologies, they may also pose barriers to innovation. It is therefore crucial to find a balance between conducting rigorous assessments and producing foundational evidence. Here, rigorous assessments will differentiate digital products with a high level of efficacy from products that are simply produced to leverage commercial opportunism, while foundational evidence is necessary to realize the full potential of digital medicine.[16] Achieving such a balance could help enact transformational changes in health and care, delivering broader economic benefits.

Moreover, addressing this challenge will require a comprehensive strategy from healthcare stakeholders. Primarily, there is an urgent need to develop enhanced methodologies and frameworks specifically designed to accommodate the unique requirements of DHTs. Such tools are essential for defining what constitutes 'good evidence'—the type of evidence necessary to demonstrate that DHTs are both clinically sound and cost-effective. Given the fast-paced nature of DHT development, it has been suggested that the evaluation of DHTs could benefit from relying more on different types and levels of evidence, such as real-world data. As an example, The Lancet (2018) highlights the potential of the real-world data DHTs generate to support alternative methods of evaluation, given that traditional randomized trials may not align with the iterative nature of digital product design.

Further, these tools can help developers understand the kind of evidence that needs to be generated to ensure their DHTs can be effectively integrated into different healthcare systems.[17]

In recent years, various initiatives have been launched to adapt existing methodological frameworks or to develop new ones. The aim is to incorporate additional domains to address the inherent characteristics of DHTs. Some successful examples of these initiatives are the Evidence Standard Framework of the National Institute for Health and Care Excellence (NICE) and the Model for Assessment of Telemedicine Applications (MAST). NICE (2024) developed the Evidence Standards Framework to guide evaluations of DHTs, emphasizing a structured approach to assessing their effectiveness and economic impact. Similarly, Kidholm et al. introduced the Model for the Assessment of Telemedicine Applications to provide a comprehensive framework for evaluating telemedicine by considering multidisciplinary domains such as safety, clinical effectiveness, and patient perspectives.[18] Nonetheless, most of these frameworks have limitations. They are often designed for particular socioeconomic or national contexts, which limits their transferability to other countries. Additionally, their specificity and the exclusion of certain DHTs often results in limited applicability. In response to these challenges, stakeholders introduced the Europe Research and Innovation Action project in

[15] Guo et al. (2020).

[16] Bates et al. (2018).

[17] Mathias et al. (2024).

[18] Kidholm et al. (2012).

January 2024, designed to operate over a 4-year horizon. The aim of the initiative is to develop a flexible, inclusive, validated, and ready-for-use European HTA framework. The resulting European Digital Health Technology Assessment (EDiHTA)[19] project was designed to assess various DHTs, including telemedicine, mobile applications, and artificial intelligence, across different technology readiness levels and territorial scopes. The project involves collaborations between multiple stakeholders, such as HTA agencies, healthcare providers, technology developers, and patient organizations, each ensuring the comprehensive evaluation and adoption of DHTs in European healthcare systems. Overall, this project seeks to assess and overcome the existing limitations of the current HTA frameworks by suggesting new features for an adaptable framework that can comprehensively evaluate a wide range of DHTs.

To better navigate the increasing complexities of HTAs in this era of digital healthcare, we aim to report some of the potential challenges with the assessment process. Part of this includes exploring some of the tools that could potentially support the assessment of DHTs. Another part includes advocating for the use of HTAs as an instrument to support the transition towards a more digital, value-based, personalized version of healthcare. In this introduction, we have described the foundational concepts associated with value-based healthcare, DHTs, and HTAs, with a view to establishing a solid foundation for understanding the current landscape and the potential future directions of HTAs in the realms of society, the environment, and governance. The next section explores the existing HTA landscape, providing a comprehensive analysis of the current frameworks and practices that define today's assessment processes. Section 3 addresses some of the specific challenges posed by DHTs, highlighting the potential gaps and limitations that arise when applying traditional HTA principles to these innovative technologies. Moreover, Section 3 underscores the need for new approaches to conducting HTAs that are tailored to the unique attributes of DHTs. Section 4 focuses on several potential strategies and tools to overcome these challenges. We discuss how modifying today's HTA methodologies might mean DHTs can be used more effectively in contemporary healthcare systems. We also look at how ensuring rigorous evaluation processes might simultaneously foster innovation. Finally, Section 5 reflects on the future of HTA in the digital age. Here, we envision some of the features that a modified HTA framework could introduce, while emphasizing the importance of a multidisciplinary approach and the continuous evolution of methodologies to keep pace with technological advancements.

Through these sections, our hope is to provide a comprehensive analysis of how HTAs might evolve to better assess DHTs and to ensure that these technologies can be safely and effectively integrated into existing healthcare systems. Ultimately, the goal is to enhance the quality and efficiency of healthcare delivery for all stakeholders while fostering innovation. By emphasizing the continuous integration of real-world data and evidence, by advocating for a flexible, risk-based assessment model,

[19] EDiHTA (2024).

and by promoting a multidisciplinary approach that involves a broader range of stakeholders, this work seeks to provide a foundation for more responsive and adaptive HTA processes.

2 Current HTA Evaluations and Frameworks

HTA has become an indispensable tool in modern healthcare systems for guiding policy and practice. This is because HTAs can provide comprehensive evaluations of the medical, social, economic, and ethical implications of a wide array of health technologies.

Official assessments are generally regulated at both the continental and national levels, with national and regional agencies and ministries typically conducting HTAs themselves or delegating this task to specialized institutions, such as university units or dedicated research centers. For example, in Italy, industries typically rely directly on universities, research centers, or specialized institutions to conduct the assessments. In 2021, the WHO identified 60 different HTA agencies around the world capable of undertaking an assessment.[20] At the European level, several countries have both national and regional agencies. However, in all European countries, HTAs are regulated by the European Union (EU) through the new Regulation 2021/2282.[21] This regulation aims to harmonize HTA processes across member states as a way to enhance the efficiency of healthcare systems by sharing HTA reports and collaborating on joint clinical assessments. The regulation, which entered force on 11 January 2022 and applies from 12 January 2025, establishes a framework for joint clinical assessments of health technologies at the EU level. It mandates collaborative evaluations of new medicinal products and certain high-risk medical devices, aiming to streamline assessments and reduce duplication across member states. The regulation also introduces joint scientific consultations and a system for the voluntary exchange of information among national authorities. While member states are required to consider the outcomes of these joint assessments in their national decision-making processes, the final decisions on pricing and reimbursement remain under national jurisdiction.

The United States has also witnessed a growing interest in HTAs, particularly through the activities of the Institute for Clinical and Economic Review (ICER), providing independent evaluations of medical interventions through a value framework.[22] Canada also has an HTA body operating under its drug agency—the CDA-AMC.[23] In Asia, countries like South Korea have also established formal HTA

---

[20] WHO (2021b).

[21] Regulation (EU) 2021/2282 of the European Parliament and of the Council of 15 December 2021 on health technology assessment and amending Directive 2011/24/EU.

[22] ICER (2023).

[23] CDA-AMC (2024).

agencies, such as the National Evidence-based Healthcare Collaborating Agency,[24] which play a pivotal role in evaluating new technologies and informing reimbursement decisions. Similarly, Australia's Medical Services Advisory Committee conducts evaluations to determine the value of medical technologies and as a way of helping to guide funding decisions.[25]

Moreover, in 1993, the International Network of Agencies for Health Technology Assessment (INAHTA) was established as an umbrella organization for all these separate HTA agencies. The idea is to support global collaboration and reduce any duplication of effort. INAHTA, which now consists of 53 agencies from 33 countries, provides a platform for sharing HTA reports, expertise, and best practices in evidence-based decision-making. The network supports health system decision-making through working groups and joint projects and by developing critical resources such as guidelines, glossaries, and surveys, all aimed at advancing global HTA practices.

In this context, HTA frameworks have long served as foundational tools, providing a standard structured approach to evidence synthesis.[26] For example, the HTA Core Model, developed by EUnetHTA between 2006 and 2008, was one of the milestones needed to prepare the EU for its impending HTA regulations.[27] Because standardized evidence is shared across countries, this model significantly improves the efficiency of conducting assessments. It also leads to faster and more equitable access to innovative healthcare technologies for patients across the EU. Its development marks a key advancement in harmonizing HTA practices, making it one of the most important currently used methodological frameworks in the field.[28] Overall, this model is characterized by two salient features. First, it is multidisciplinary and, second, it relies on explicit methods to determine the value of a technology at various points in that technology's lifecycle. In total, the model is designed to assess nine core domains:

- **Health problem and current use of technology**: This domain concerns the epidemiological burden of the health problem and the current use of the technology under review. It involves thoroughly analyzing the prevalence and incidence of the target disease and the existing healthcare practices used to manage the condition.
- **Description and technical characteristics**: Assessing this domain requires developing a detailed description of the technology, including its technical specifications, intended use, and underlying principles of operation. It also includes an examination of the technology's innovation compared to existing alternatives.

[24] NECA (2024).

[25] Medical Services Advisory Committee (2024).

[26] O'Rourke et al. (2020).

[27] EUnetHTA (2018).

[28] Emergency Medicines Agency (2023).

- **Safety**: The safety domain refers to the potential risks and adverse effects of using the technology. This includes assessing the frequency and severity of adverse events and the overall safety profile of the intervention.
- **Clinical effectiveness**: This domain concerns the technology's efficacy and effectiveness at achieving desired health outcomes. It involves a comprehensive review of clinical trials, observational studies, and other relevant evidence to determine the intervention's impact on patient health.
- **Costs and economic evaluation**: The economic evaluation domain involves assessing the technology's cost-effectiveness, including both direct and indirect costs. This generally requires undertaking cost-utility, cost-benefit, and cost-effectiveness studies to determine the financial implications of adopting the technology.
- **Ethical, social, and legal aspects**: These domains address the broader implications of the technology, ensuring the innovation aligns with ethical standards, societal values, and legal requirements.
- **Organizational aspects**: This domain covers the impact of the technology on healthcare organizations and their ability to deliver healthcare. It includes an assessment of the required infrastructure, changes in healthcare processes, and the implications for healthcare professionals.

By systematically addressing these domains through a structured set of items and questions, the HTA Core Model ensures a comprehensive evaluation of health technologies that can be used to both inform decision-making and promote high-quality healthcare.

3 Challenges with Assessing DHTs

A significant body of literature shows how, when evaluating DHTs, HTA frameworks often struggle to effectively address the unique challenges these technologies present. As an example, Vis et al., Moshi et al., and Farah et al. collectively illustrate the various challenges within existing HTA frameworks.[29] Vis et al. point out how eHealth frameworks struggle to assess usability and clinical outcomes, while Moshi et al. highlight that mobile medical applications tend to demand more dynamic and iterative evaluation processes. Lastly, Farah et al. rightly argue that AI-based medical devices need to be assessed by frameworks that incorporate measures of algorithmic performance and ethical considerations.

Vukovic et al. hypothesize that inconsistencies in HTA reports, particularly when it comes to the ethical, social, organizational, and legal implications of a technology, are likely due to the inherent challenges of assessing these elements in the rapidly evolving fields of e-Health and m-Health.[30] They note that the lack of a

[29] Vis et al. (2020), Moshi et al. (2018), and Farah et al. (2024).

[30] Vukovic et al. (2018).

universally accepted methodology and the fast-paced nature of developing these technologies contribute to these difficulties. But, without careful evaluation, these challenges may mean innovative digital health technologies are not taken up by healthcare systems, which could potentially affect value-based care. For example, given the potential for very broad implications, assessment frameworks often exclude ethical evaluations of a DHT.[31] Yet ethics represents a crucial part of a comprehensive assessment, particularly when viewed from the current cultural perspective that sees science and technology as democratized fields. In this sense, identifying and assessing ethical issues early can better prepare society for future moral dilemmas and guide research, development, and usage practices to avoid or reduce ethically undesirable outcomes. In fact, von Hippel highlights the role democratized innovation plays in fostering broader societal participation in science and technology.[32] Such participatory approaches mean ethical issues tend to be identified earlier, helping to prepare society to navigate emerging moral dilemmas and guiding researchers and developers to mitigate undesirable ethical outcomes.

3.1 Privacy, Transparency, and Accountability

One primary ethical concern is the privacy and protection of each patient's personal data.[33] Integrating big data into DHTs generally brings together diverse patient-specific information from a range of sources, including new types of data like genomics. Hence, this debate predominantly revolves around privacy issues, as the standard methods of protection might prove inadequate in new digital environments. Anonymization, for example, is vulnerable to re-identification techniques, which can potentially expose sensitive information. Instruments such as informed consent face challenges like a lack of transparency, data repurposing, and limited user alternatives, complicating the individual's control over how their data is used.[34] Therefore, navigating the ethical landscape of how patient data is used by DHTs requires a novel approach—one that recognizes the inherent unpredictability of how data are and will be used, especially in future secondary applications.[35]

Another significant issue is the transparency and accountability with which these technologies function, especially when evaluating AI-based technologies. A lack of transparency can undermine trust and accountability, as patients and healthcare professionals may struggle to understand or accept the technology's recommendations.[36] The lack of explainability associated with many DHTs further highlights the

[31] Vukovic et al. (2018).

[32] von Hippel (2006).

[33] Davis and Osoba (2016).

[34] Andreotta et al. (2022).

[35] Chenthara et al. (2019), pp. 1487–1495; OECD (2019).

[36] Amann et al. (2020); Durán and Jongsma (2021).

need for robust regulatory frameworks. To this end, in 2024, the EU approved the AI Act which establishes comprehensive guidelines for developing, deploying, and monitoring AI technologies. The Act, which entered force on 1 August 2024, establishes a comprehensive regulatory framework for AI systems within the EU. The framework follows a risk-based classification approach, categorizing AI applications into four levels: unacceptable risk (prohibited applications), high risk (subject to strict obligations), limited risk (transparency requirements), and minimal risk (no specific requirements). High-risk AI systems, particularly those used in critical sectors like healthcare, are mandated to comply with stringent criteria, including robust risk management systems, high-quality data sets, detailed technical documentation, human oversight mechanisms, and adherence to transparency and accuracy standards. The Act also introduces the European Artificial Intelligence Board to oversee the legislation's implementation and ensure its consistent application across member states. Notably, the AI Act's extraterritorial scope means it applies to providers and users outside the EU if their AI systems are used within the Union. Further, the AI Act builds upon the ethical principles outlined by earlier "Trustworthy AI" guidelines, operationalizing these charters into specific legal requirements. Ethical and legal issues related to transparency are addressed in the Act, such as a mandate that obligates practitioners to inform patients when AI-enabled technologies are being used as well as providing clear explanations of how AI decisions are made, alongside accountability frameworks to ensure responsible use. However, while the AI Act provides a legal framework for enhancing transparency and accountability, particularly in healthcare, it is crucial that HTA processes ensure compliance with these regulations, regardless of whether the Act explicitly covers the technologies being assessed. This approach should help foster trust and enable informed decision-making within the healthcare system.

Algorithmic fairness and bias also pose substantial ethical challenges. AI algorithms can inadvertently perpetuate discrimination depending on the data that was used to train the model. This can result in inequitable treatment or access to healthcare resources, exacerbating existing health disparities.[37] The AI Act also stresses the importance of data governance, requiring that data used by AI systems in healthcare is not only of high quality but is also representative to avoid bias and inaccuracies in AI-driven healthcare decisions. However, achieving this could be particularly challenging in healthcare, where the data are often heterogeneous and inherently sensitive. Ideally, training data should reflect great variations in genetic diversity, socioeconomic status, and cultural background. Thus, HTAs should rigorously assess whether these technologies have undergone and will continue to undergo cyclical evaluations for fairness and bias by relevant experts while ensuring that all stakeholders, including patients, are consulted about the risks, consequences, and mitigation measures associated with the deployment of new digital technologies.

The nature of DHTs also raises concerns about our dependency on technology and its impact on patient autonomy. While these tools are generally intended to

[37] Chen et al. (2023b).

increase empowerment, their effects must be carefully evaluated.[38] For instance, although digital clinical communication can improve interactions between patients and clinicians, potentially increasing autonomy, it paradoxically risks fostering a dependency on clinical advice that can hinder independent decision-making and disempower patients.[39] Ignatowicz et al.'s study particularly highlights the dual ethical implications of digital communication when attempting to manage chronic conditions.[40] Further, as Wies et al. point out, commercial chatbots are often targeted toward vulnerable individuals, such as those experiencing loneliness, and these devices are fundamentally designed to create dependency behaviors that may be later carried over to other digital healthcare tools.[41]

3.2 *Equity and Accessibility*

In a world where digital technologies are having a major impact on shaping societies, social evaluations are indispensable. HTAs must assess the impact of DHTs on healthcare disparities, evaluating whether these innovations have the potential to worsen existing inequalities or help reduce them, particularly for underserved populations.[42]

One significant challenge is the cultural resistance and hesitancy often seen toward digital health solutions. Frequently, this reluctance to use DHTs is driven by concerns like resistance to change, difficulty understanding the technology, and the perception of reduced human interaction. Additionally, healthcare personnel themselves may struggle to adapt to digital systems without extensive practice or training.[43] Using DHTs can therefore negatively impact clinical effectiveness, especially during initial implementation periods.[44]

Moreover, the digital divide remains a pressing concern, with much of the world still lacking access to the internet and technological devices, or suffering from poor digital literacy.[45] DHTs frequently rely on significant levels of digital infrastructure, such as substantial computing power and storage capacity, which are not universally available. Evaluating whether the necessary infrastructure is accessible to all intended users is crucial to ensure that DHTs do not exacerbate these existing inequalities, but rather contribute to more equitable healthcare outcomes.

---

[38] WHO (2023).

[39] Ignatowicz et al. (2018).

[40] Ignatowicz et al. (2018).

[41] Wies et al. (2021).

[42] Cristopher Gibbons (2011); Samarasekera (2022).

[43] Borges do Nascimento et al. (2023a).

[44] Vallo Hult et al. (2020).

[45] World Bank (2023).

Another aspect to consider is the sustainability of the digital infrastructure required for DHTs. As the adoption and usage of DHTs grow, the demand for computing power, storage, and energy may increase exponentially. Schlieter et al. emphasize that, as the adoption of new technologies increases, sustainability concerns become critical, particularly in terms of energy consumption, storage, and the infrastructure demands required for scaling health-IT systems.[46] These authors advocate for integrating sustainable practices into the design and implementation of digital health solutions to address these challenges. Ensuring that the necessary infrastructure can be scaled and maintained in a sustainable and equitable manner is crucial, particularly in resource-constrained regions.

The governance and decision-making processes surrounding the development and deployment of DHT-based technologies should also be examined from an equity perspective. It is important to ensure that the voices and needs of diverse stakeholders, including marginalized communities, are represented and considered in the design, implementation, and ongoing management of these technologies. Patient engagement and trust in digital health solutions are vital to a technology's success but are often influenced by previous experiences, perceived reliability, and data transparency.[47] Intergenerational differences can also play a role, with older adults potentially facing greater barriers to adopting DHTs due to lower digital literacy and resistance to change.[48] Socioeconomic factors, including the affordability of digital health devices and services, also slow their widespread adoption.[49] Lastly, general health literacy impacts how patients engage with DHTs, with lower health literacy potentially hindering effective use. Few studies have adequately examined the effectiveness of digital solutions among other marginalized populations, such as those differentiated by ethnicity, language, frailty, and rural populations. The World Economic Forum (2021) underscores how too little focus has been placed on the effectiveness of digital health solutions for marginalized groups. The report highlights the need for inclusive design and evaluation practices to ensure equitable access across diverse communities. Considering the inherent differences with traditional health technologies, conventional HTA frameworks might not sufficiently capture the perspectives of these groups, Therefore, their experiences, attitudes, habits, values, motivations, and expectations regarding the technology might be falling by the wayside.

The infrastructure requirements might also present challenges to organizations. Previously, most health technologies relied on standard infrastructures, such as electricity. Today, with the advent of DHTs, there is a heavy dependence on more advanced infrastructure, such as internal servers and a fast, stable internet connection. The need for continuous software updates and real-time data integration might also further complicate the ability to provide accurate assessments over time.

---

[46] Schlieter et al. (2024).

[47] Birnbaum et al. (2015).

[48] Hargittai and Dobransky (2017); Hargittai et al. (2019).

[49] Patel et al. (2022).

DHTs can also have an impact on workflows and processes. Several studies have found that introducing DHTs can disrupt existing workflows, change process dynamics, and shift power structures and hierarchical relationships within healthcare organizations. Menachemi and Collum and Alami et al. each examine the benefits and drawbacks of electronic health record systems, noting that while these systems can improve efficiency and communication, they often disrupt existing workflows by introducing new procedural requirements and altering established practices.[50] They also highlight how these disruptions may lead to resistance among healthcare professionals, particularly when changes challenge traditional hierarchical structures. Alami et al., for example, provide a broader perspective on telehealth technologies, identifying unintended consequences across multiple areas, such as shifts in organizational power dynamics, creating new dependencies on technology, and exacerbating inequalities among users with varying degrees of digital literacy.[51] They emphasize that these changes can affect trust, collaboration, and the overall integration of telehealth solutions into existing healthcare processes, underscoring the importance of addressing these factors in implementation strategies. The need for extensive and continuous training and issues with interoperability have also been reported as factors impacting the delivery of healthcare.[52]

3.3 Organizational Considerations

The constantly evolving nature of these technologies also introduces significant economic implications. Conventional frameworks frequently overlook the full lifecycle costs of DHTs, including the expenses associated with continuous updates, staff, algorithm training, and maintenance.[53] This oversight can not only profoundly influence how cost-effective DHTs are, it can also alter an organization's decision-making processes. Therefore, to ensure DHTs are implemented successfully, effective change management processes should be integrated into HTA frameworks, including any changes needed to the roles and responsibilities of staff and stakeholders.

User acceptance and engagement are also vital for the successful uptake of DHTs. These are factors generally influenced by both organizational culture and perceptions of how easy the devices are to use.[54] Proper allocation of financial and human resources, compliance with data security and privacy regulations, and interdepartmental coordination are essential. Additionally, continuous education and

[50] Menachemi and Collum (2011); Alami et al. (2019).

[51] Alami et al. (2019).

[52] Borges do Nascimento et al. (2023b); Mensah et al. (2023).

[53] Vukovic et al. (2018).

[54] Hennemann et al. (2017).

training for healthcare professionals is necessary to keep pace with technological advancements and should be considered when evaluating new technologies.[55]

Data quality and integration are other aspects to consider when describing and assessing the utility of DHTs in each context. Poor data quality can lead to detrimental outcomes, including compromised continuity of care, patient safety issues, and reduced clinician productivity. Syed et al. show how poor data quality in digital health can be a significant barrier to effective implementation.[56] Their 2023 systematic review highlights issues like data inaccuracies, missing information, and platform inconsistencies, all of which can disrupt the continuity of care, endanger patient safety, and hinder clinician productivity. Furthermore, digital devices often rely on accessing and analyzing diverse sets of data, including electronic health records, medical images, genetic data, and data from wearable devices. Evaluating their interoperability and ability to seamlessly integrate and exchange data with existing healthcare systems is therefore paramount.[57] From an organizational perspective, ensuring high-quality data involves implementing rigorous data governance frameworks, providing regular staff training, and maintaining an IT infrastructure that supports data integration. HTA frameworks could assess whether the devices can handle different data types, formats, and resolutions and whether they can effectively integrate and harmonize data from disparate sources, spanning regional, national, continental, and global data platforms.

3.4 Environmental Impact

Another big theme is the environmental impact of DHTs. As previously stated, some energy-intensive processes might potentially lead to negative environmental consequences.[58] However, DHTs are also often mentioned as having positive effects on the overall carbon footprint of the healthcare systems. For instance, telemedicine can reduce emissions by minimizing the need for travel by healthcare professionals and patients.[59] Sustainable healthcare systems must consider environmental impacts across the entire lifecycle of the system and the technologies within it when assessing the added value of these technologies for patients and the population. This includes evaluating the carbon footprint of manufacturing, deploying, and disposing of digital health devices and software. This is an essential part of developing sustainable healthcare solutions that align with global efforts to mitigate climate change.

[55] Borges do Nascimento et al. (2023a).

[56] Syed et al. (2023).

[57] WHO (2019).

[58] Schlieter et al. (2024).

[59] Alami et al. (2023); Pickard Strange et al. (2023).

3.5 Data Protection and Cybersecurity

The conformity and regulatory aspects of DHTs present significant complexities too, mostly due to rapid technological advancements and their consequent regulations. Many existing HTA frameworks often lack the agility and adaptability required to keep pace with these changes, leading to regulatory gaps that not only hinder effective evaluations but also stop DHTs from being properly integrated into healthcare systems.[60]

In the European context, recent regulations have introduced new items to consider when evaluating DHTs. For example, the General Data Protection Regulation (GDPR) is one of the cornerstones of the EU's legal framework for data protection. Implemented on 25 May 2018, this regulation is actually a comprehensive legal framework governing the collection, processing, and storage of personal data within the EU. It establishes stringent principles to safeguard the rights of individuals, such as lawfulness, fairness, transparency, data minimization, and purpose limitation. Particularly relevant to DHTs, the GDPR mandates robust mechanisms for protecting sensitive health data, including encryption, pseudonymization, and anonymization. Additionally, explicit and informed patient consent is required before data can be collected and used. Non-compliance can result in fines of up to €20 million or 4% of the annual global turnover of the offending organization, whichever is higher. Further, the GDPR also applies to organizations outside the EU that process data related to individuals within the EU. Hence, since its implementation in 2018, the GDPR has set stringent standards for how personal data, including health data, must be handled. Moreover, its principles are critical for ensuring that personal health data is collected, processed, and stored in a manner that respects the privacy and rights of individuals.

DHTs, which often involve collecting and processing large volumes of personal and health-related data, must comply with the GDPR to ensure that patient data is adequately protected. This includes implementing robust data anonymization and encryption techniques, securing explicit consent from patients for data processing, and ensuring that the data is only used for the purposes it was collected for. Any failure to comply with GDPR can result in severe penalties along with damage to the reputation of the healthcare providers and technology developers concerned.

The AI Act, enacted by the European Commission which became effective on 1 August 2024, addresses some of the specific challenges posed by AI systems.[61] As mentioned previously, the AI Act categorizes AI systems into different levels of risk—unacceptable risk, high risk, low risk, and minimal risk—imposing strict requirements on high-risk systems, which are particularly prevalent in the digital

[60] Vukovic et al. (2018).

[61] Regulation (EU) 2024/1689 of the European Parliament and of the Council of 13 June 2024 laying down harmonised rules on artificial intelligence and amending Regulations (EC) No 300/2008, (EU) No 167/2013, (EU) No 168/2013, (EU) 2018/858, (EU) 2018/1139 and (EU) 2019/2144 and Directives 2014/90/EU, (EU) 2016/797 and (EU) 2020/1828 (Artificial Intelligence Act).

health sector. High-risk AI systems, including those used for diagnosing diseases, personalizing treatment plans, and managing patient data, must undergo rigorous testing and validation to ensure their accuracy, robustness, and reliability. The Act mandates transparency in AI decision-making processes, requiring that the outcomes of AI systems be explainable to users and that there be clear documentation of how these systems process personal data. Furthermore, the AI Act imposes obligations for continuous monitoring and risk management, ensuring that any AI system in use remains compliant with evolving standards and that any risks to data protection or patient safety are promptly identified and mitigated.

The European Health Data Space (EHDS) further builds on these regulations by establishing a comprehensive framework for sharing and using health data across the EU's member states.[62] The EHDS is designed to create a unified European approach to health data that ensures the secure exchange of this data for research, innovation, and policy-making purposes. It supports the interoperability of health data systems by setting standards for data formats, exchange protocols, and access rights. Additionally, the EHDS includes provisions for data governance, requiring that health data is managed in a way that ensures its quality, accuracy, and security while respecting the privacy rights of patients as established in the GDPR.[63]

Cybersecurity in healthcare is another topic of the utmost importance that is directly linked to patient safety. Cyberattacks can paralyze health systems and even threaten human life. Giansanti, for example, underscores the critical importance of cybersecurity in healthcare, particularly as DHTs are becoming more and more integral to clinical decision-making and managing patient data.[64] The study highlights that cyberattacks can not only jeopardize sensitive health information but also bring healthcare systems to a standstill while directly threatening patient safety. Giansanti goes on to emphasize the need for comprehensive measures, including data encryption, multi-layered authentication protocols, and regular cybersecurity audits, to mitigate risks and protect the integrity of patient data and healthcare operations.

Therefore, as DHTs handle sensitive patient data and influence healthcare decisions, it is crucial to assess the security measures implemented to prevent unauthorized access, data breaches, and tampering. The European Union's NIS 2 Directive establishes a high and common level of cybersecurity across the Union, introducing more stringent requirements for protecting network and information systems in key sectors, including healthcare.[65] Under the NIS 2 Directive, healthcare providers are classified as essential entities that are subject to robust cybersecurity risk manage-

[62] Regulation (EU) 2025/327 of the European Parliament and of the Council of 11 February 2025 on the European Health Data Space and amending Directive 2011/24/EU and Regulation (EU) 2024/2847.

[63] Regulation (EU) 2016/679 of the European Parliament and of the Council of 27 April 2016 on the protection of natural persons with regard to the processing of personal data and on the free movement of such data, and repealing Directive 95/46/EC (General Data Protection Regulation).

[64] Giansanti (2021).

[65] Directive (EU) 2022/2555 of the European Parliament and of the Council of 14 December 2022 on measures for a high common level of cybersecurity across the Union (NIS2 Directive).

ment measures and reporting obligations. These entities must implement state-of-the-art security practices, conduct regular risk assessments, and ensure the protection of stored, transmitted, and processed data. The Directive also emphasizes the need for cooperation among member states and across sectors to effectively manage cybersecurity threats. Thus, healthcare organizations are required to follow standard cybersecurity protocols while also participating in information sharing and other coordination efforts.

It is worth noting that DHTs ultimately carry the risk of medical errors and malpractice liabilities. However, the current frameworks are only built to assess well-established and often heavily regulated technologies. Yet, where DHTs are concerned, the numerous differences between traditional technologies and their new digital counterparts may well challenge these frameworks. As it stands, there are significant gaps between the two paradigms, and regulations over digital technologies around the globe are constantly evolving. This can make it difficult to determine liability when adverse events involving DHTs occur. At the least, such events can undermine the trust of users and slow down the adoption of such technologies. Rowland et al., who examined the specific risks associated with DHTs in the context of medical malpractice liability, highlight that the dynamic nature of digital technologies, combined with gaps in global regulations and the absence of standardized evaluation frameworks for complex digital devices, complicates the who should be held liable in the case of errors or adverse events.[66] They argue that this uncertainty could undermine user trust, making patients and practitioners more reluctant to use such technologies. As such, these authors emphasize the urgent need for robust regulatory mechanisms and clear legal guidelines to address these emerging challenges. Overall, HTAs should consider the legal frameworks and liability guidelines that pertain to the target DHT. Further, this consideration must include whether clear guidelines exist over the responsibility of manufacturers, healthcare providers, and users in the case of adverse events.

4 New Tools and Recommendations to Navigate the Complexities of DHTs HTA Processes

In order to face the challenges mentioned above, scientists conducting HTAs should be equipped with new instruments that can help overcome the limits of previous frameworks, ensuring reports meet the goals of truly personalized, value-based healthcare.

[66] Rowland et al. (2022).

4.1 Dynamic HTAs and the Integration of Real-World Evidence and Data

As discussed in the previous section, one of the main features of DHTs is the possibility for technologies to substantially change over time. In fact, given that software constitutes one of the fundamental components of digital health technologies, software updates can substantially change the functionality and clinical impact of a DHT in a very short period of time. Conventional HTA models are typically designed for static technologies like drugs or catheters. Reassessments for non-digital technologies are typically conducted a long time after the initial assessment and aim to evaluate whether a product remains effective and continues to provide value for its cost, while also monitoring for any new risks or side effects that may have emerged post-launch. A dynamic HTA framework could support continuous and more frequent evaluations using both qualitative and quantitative research methods to address the unique challenges posed by DHTs throughout their lifecycle.[67] For example, these frameworks could be adapted to ongoing developments while incorporating mechanisms for periodic assessments and real-time data integration. This approach might also allow for a more accurate and timely understanding of a technology's effectiveness, safety, and value in real-world settings, ensuring that product customizations are tailored to patients' needs.

One of the pivotal characteristics of a dynamic HTA framework would be leveraging real-world evidence and real-world data. The U.S. Food and Drug Administration defines real-world data as "data relating to patient health status and/or the delivery of healthcare routinely collected from various sources". These may include data from electronic health records, claims and billing activities from a healthcare delivery system, data from product or disease registries, patient-generated data, or data/metadata from mobile devices. Similarly, real-world evidence is clinical evidence of the use and potential benefits or risks of a medical product derived from analyzing real-world data. Real-world evidence can be generated by randomized trials, large simple trials, pragmatic trials, observational studies, or other such means (prospective and/or retrospective).[68]

Using real-world data allows for the ongoing collection of real-time information about how DHTs are used and how they perform across diverse real-world contexts. This continuous stream of data can be analyzed to generate real-world evidence and to provide insights into the actual benefits and risks associated with these digital tools. For instance, data on patient adherence, health outcomes, and even usage patterns captured through the apps themselves could be used to inform dynamic reassessments of their value.

Currently, real-world data and evidence are increasingly being integrated into HTA processes, although their use remains somewhat limited. Regulatory agencies like the Food and Drug Administration and European Medicines Agency have

[67] Tarricone et al. (2021); Segur-Ferrer et al. (2024).

[68] Food and Drug Administration (2024).

historically employed randomized control trials for approval purposes and real-world evidence for post-marketing safety evaluations. Today, given the increased quantity of data available, the increasing number of new technologies, and, ultimately, the high costs associated with randomized control trials, national and regional HTA bodies such as NICE are beginning to incorporate real-world evidence into their frameworks as a complement to traditional evidence. This is particularly so for technology reassessments where randomized control trials are impractical. However, standard frameworks for routinely integrating real-world evidence across all HTA processes are largely still under development.[69]

These approaches not only adapt well to the cyclical necessities of the kinds of evaluations DHTs require, but they also leverage the amounts and types of data produced to fully utilize the capacity of digital solutions. For example, real-world evidence can help manufacturers improve their products by making them safer or more effective in specific local contexts. Evaluations of this nature involve selecting suitable endpoints for continuous measurement and assessing the financial savings or costs linked to any change. This process is therefore connected to the creation of scientific methods designed to assess both clinical outcomes and economic health metrics using real-world evidence. In turn, this is fostering the advancement of value-based healthcare models.[70] As just one example, some DHTs might be designed to record data that is helpful for evaluating the positive care effects administered to users over time. Metadata from apps can track the duration and frequency with which a prescribed treatment regimen has been used, thereby effectively measuring adherence to the treatment. Improvements in health status could then be documented via sensors and other connected devices. Smart glucometers for patients with Type I diabetes are a good example. Other positive care effects can be identified from existing data sources. For instance, the data from health insurance claims could be used to document reductions in the duration of illnesses or increases in patient survival. Features such as in-app questionnaires lend themselves well to the digital environment, providing a standardized framework for collecting data within the context of a product's use. Such questionnaires can document several relevant categories of positive care effects, ranging from established scales that measure a patient's quality of life to measures of facilitating access to care, health literacy, patient sovereignty or autonomy in health management, and/or reducing therapy-related expenses and other burdens for patients and their relatives.

Real-world data and real-world evidence might also have the potential to support initial evidence generation in the approval process. Real-world evidence from claims data, for example, could deliver initial evidence at costs far below those associated with traditional randomized control trials. This might benefit small-to-medium-sized enterprises that often push innovation in this sector, instead of the much larger actors that previously assumed this role.[71]

---

[69] Hogervorst et al. (2022); Khosla et al. (2021).

[70] Brönneke et al. (2023).

[71] The Lancet (2018); Brönneke et al. (2023).

Of course, the use of real-world evidence still has many limitations, including concerns about data quality, the lack of standardized methodologies, and challenges with implementation. Issues such as patient selection, data representativeness, and data privacy and security are critical if we are to successfully integrate real-world evidence into HTAs.[72] Additionally, broader challenges such as ensuring the acceptability, reliability, and generalizability of real-world data, as well as addressing data heterogeneity and linking diverse data sources, complicate the use of these valuable data repositories. Transparency in data handling and sticking to rigorous standards is also essential but difficult to achieve, especially when dealing with unsupervised models.[73] Yet, despite these barriers, the literature highlights how the potential added value of real-world evidence could still outweigh its downsides. For example, Graili et al. delved into the complexities of integrating real-world evidence into HTAs, emphasizing both its potential and its limitations.[74] They highlight that real-world evidence, which is derived from diverse sources such as electronic health records, claims databases, and patient registries, provides valuable insights into the real-world effectiveness and safety of DHTs. However, they also point out several barriers, including inconsistent data quality, the lack of standardized methodologies, and challenges to ensuring data representativeness and privacy. Additionally, the study underlines the difficulty of harmonizing heterogeneous datasets and ensuring the interoperability of data sources, which are crucial for drawing reliable and generalizable conclusions. The lack of transparency in data handling and the challenges of addressing biases inherent to unsupervised data sources are also noted as significant concerns. Yet, despite these limitations, Graili et al. argue that when rigorous standards are applied, using real-world evidence can substantially enhance HTA processes by offering complementary insights into randomized controlled trials and by helping to bring about more informed decision-making.

4.2 Risk Model for DHTs Evaluation

Incorporating a risk model similar to the frameworks established by the EU AI Act and the NHS Evidence Standards Framework for DHTs could markedly enhance the sophistication and precision of HTAs for digital health interventions.

High-risk DHTs, particularly those that could significantly influence clinical outcomes or patient safety, would necessitate rigorous evidence and comprehensive evaluation. On the other hand, low-risk DHTs could undergo a more streamlined assessment process, giving rise to faster deployment without compromising safety or efficacy.

72 Claire et al. (2024).

73 Catwell and Sheikh (2009).

74 Graili et al. (2023).

Such a model would not only optimize resource allocation within HTA processes but also promote greater regulatory consistency and transparency. By ensuring that the depth of assessment correlates with the potential risk, a tiered approach could enhance stakeholder trust and support the accelerated integration of innovative DHTs into clinical practice. Additionally, this alignment with existing risk-based regulatory frameworks could simplify the interoperability of assessments across jurisdictions, fostering an ecosystem where digital health technologies are evaluated with a rigor proportional to their impact on public health and safety.

4.3 Patient Involvement and New Outcome Measures

Historically, most HTA methods were primarily designed for standardized, self-contained curative treatments like pharmaceuticals, which aim to improve both the length and quality of a patient's life. The most commonly used metric in cost-utility analyses, Quality-Adjusted Life-Years (QALYs), exemplifies this approach by measuring the incremental benefit of a health intervention through the additional years of healthy life it offers, adjusted for quality.[75]

However, new methods of data collection have emerged, and these more patient-centered sets of measures, such as the Patient-Reported Outcomes Measurement Information System (PROMIS), could now be integrated into evaluations. PROMIS, for example, encompasses a set of measures that evaluate and monitor physical, mental, and social health in adults and children. Further, this is a system that can be used with both the general population and on individuals living with chronic conditions. Collecting the patients' own views of their symptoms reflects a more holistic picture of health and wellbeing, ensuring a more comprehensive evaluation of a DHT's effectiveness. It also helps patients and clinicians make the best healthcare decisions together.[76]

Integrating new outcome measures aligns with the principles of value-based healthcare by emphasizing patient-centered care and enhancing healthcare outcomes in relation to the cost of delivering them (Fig. 1)[77].

4.4 New Expertise and Multidisciplinary Approaches

Evaluating DHTs additionally presents an opportunity to expand the traditional boundaries of HTAs to include multidisciplinary assessments. Such an expansion would not only broaden the scope of HTAs but also provides the potential to

---

[75] EuroQol Group (1990).

[76] von Huben et al. (2021).

[77] Segur-Ferrer et al. (2024).

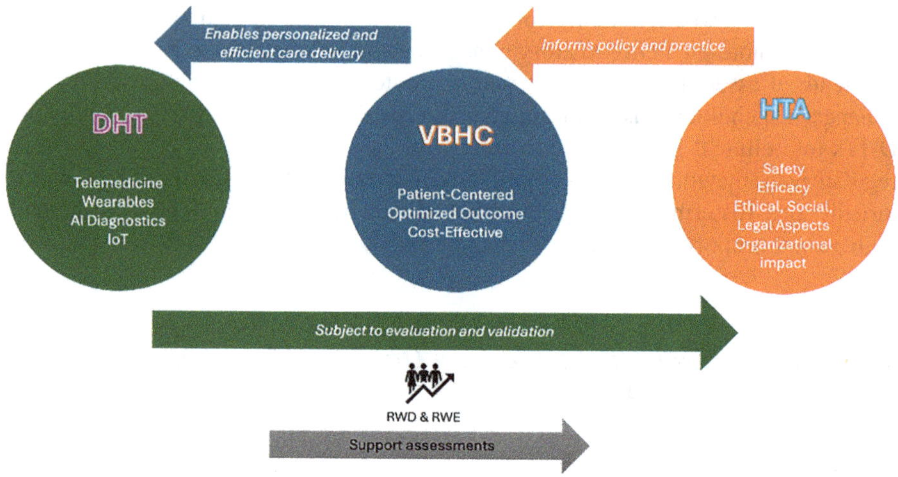

Fig. 1 Integration of Value-Based Healthcare (VBHC), Digital Health Technologies (DHTs), and Health Technology Assessment (HTA)

establish new framework domains tailored specifically for the unique challenges posed by DHTs. The assessments made in the traditional domains could be enriched with fresh perspectives and expertise on legal, ethical, social, and other considerations. Overall, the result would be a more comprehensive and nuanced evaluation process.

Involving cybersecurity specialists, for example, is fundamental to the evaluation of DHTs. As these technologies handle sensitive patient information and are vulnerable to cyber threats, cybersecurity experts could assess the security protocols of DHTs, identifying potential vulnerabilities and recommending strategies to safeguard patient data.[78]

Similarly, health informatics specialists and interoperability architects could play a pivotal role in the HTA process. Interoperability encompasses more than just technical compatibility. It involves seamless integration and bidirectional communication across diverse healthcare systems, devices, and platforms. These specialists could rigorously assess whether a DHT can effectively share, interpret, and use data across various electronic record systems, medical devices, and external databases, ensuring compliance with standards such as Health Level Seven (HL7) and Fast Healthcare Interoperability Resources (FHIR). In addition, their expertise is likely to be vital in cultivating a cohesive, interoperable healthcare ecosystem – one that can enhance continuity of care and reduce redundancy but also facilitate the rapid adoption and effective deployment of technologies across diverse healthcare environments.[79]

[78] Giansanti (2021).

[79] Lehne et al. (2019).

User-centered design (UCD) principles are also critical in addressing the complex needs of healthcare users. According to De Vito Dabbs et al., involving end-users in the design process is critical for ensuring interactive devices are usable, accessible, and aligned with the patient's needs.[80] Their study highlights that, in healthcare, user-centered design must go beyond traditional usability considerations to address the emotional, cognitive, and behavioral factors that influence patient engagement. While traditional user-centered design frameworks typically focus on general user needs, the healthcare domain necessitates a more nuanced approach that accounts for the high stakes and regulatory constraints inherent to medical contexts. As van Velsen et al. state, user-centered and human-centered design methodologies in the eHealth domain often fall short of addressing the inherent complexities of healthcare environments, such as highly variable user needs, stringent regulatory requirements, and the dynamic nature of healthcare systems.[81] They argue that today's frameworks tend to focus on static usability requirements, which may not fully capture the evolving and context-specific demands of eHealth applications. To overcome these challenges, they suggest that frameworks be built with more adaptive and agile design practices, including iterative testing and stakeholder co-creation, to better align eHealth solutions with real-world healthcare needs.

Moreover, when adapting these frameworks for digital health, designers must not only consider usability and accessibility but also the integration of human factors and ergonomics to enhance the overall patient experience. Sujan et al. emphasize eight core principles of human ergonomics specifically tailored to the healthcare context, with a particular focus on the design of AI systems.[82] This approach ensures that DHTs are designed with a holistic understanding of users' cognitive and emotional states, thus optimizing both the functionality and safety of these technologies.

Further, involving environmental scientists in the framework design process might address the sustainability aspects of DHTs, helping to tackle the multifaceted challenges posed by these technologies. Several authors have noted the importance of incorporating environmental considerations into HTAs, citing factors like the environmental footprint of DHTs, the levels of energy consumption, the use of rare-earth minerals, and the reliance on extensive data infrastructures.[83] Researchers like Hensher has comprehensively explored how to integrate environmental impacts into the economic evaluation of healthcare systems, emphasizing the need for HTA methodologies to consider ecological sustainability alongside traditional economic and clinical metrics.[84] This particular study highlights the potential for ecological economics to provide a framework for evaluating the environmental consequences of healthcare interventions, such as resource use and carbon emissions. However,

[80] De Vito Dabbs et al. (2009).

[81] van Velsen et al. (2022).

[82] Sujan et al. (2022).

[83] Kaack et al. (2022); Wang et al. (2024).

[84] Hensher (2020).

the author is careful to note that no consensus has been reached on standardized methods for incorporating these factors into HTAs.

5 Conclusion and Future Directions

DHTs are transforming healthcare by not only by paving the way to value-based personalized care, but also by addressing several critical challenges across the domain, including the increasing need for healthcare and the inequity of general access to it. Yet, despite the potential of DHTs, traditional HTA frameworks often fall short when attempting to evaluate their dynamic and unique features. The rapid development cycles, data privacy issue, and algorithmic transparency demands of DHTs often challenge contemporary HTA frameworks. Therefore, to truly harness the potential of DHTs in delivering personalized care, new and better assessment frameworks are essential.

Navigating the complexity of the digital health era requires new tools alongside real-world data and evidence to support enhanced HTA frameworks. Such tools could leverage new data resources, like the metadata in apps, data from sensors, and the built-in features of DHTs, to track clinical outcomes, ensure patient involvement throughout the evaluation process, and align healthcare interventions with individual patient needs. Also, by expanding the current scope of HTAs to include new professionals, the resulting evaluations could ensure a more nuanced and more comprehensive understanding of the value of DHTs. However, significant challenges remain, and addressing them will be critical for the successful implementation of new HTA models.

In conclusion, collaborative efforts will be fundamental to creating an environment that promotes a holistic approach to healthcare. Tomorrow's HTA models need to involve many stakeholders; they also need to foster consensus at the national and continental levels. This includes defining common terminology, harmonizing and enriching existing HTA frameworks, and creating an open repository of frameworks, guides, articles, and HTA methodologies. Optimizing assessment processes throughout the DHT lifecycle, adopting a multi-stakeholder, multi-domain, and modular approach, and ultimately providing a validated and ready-for-use digital HTA framework for DHTs are essential steps forward. These efforts will drive the successful integration of digital health solutions into modern healthcare systems, supporting the transition towards value-based personalized healthcare, and ultimately improving patient outcomes and experiences.

Acknowledgements This research was financially supported by the "Biorobotics Research and Innovation Engineering Facilities" "IR0000036" – CUP J13C22000400007 (BRIEF) project.

References

Alami H, Gagnon M-P, Fortin J-P (2019) Some multidimensional unintended consequences of telehealth utilization: a multi-project evaluation synthesis

Alami H, Rivard L, Lehoux P et al (2023) Integrating environmental considerations in digital health technology assessment and procurement: Stakeholders' perspectives. Digital Health 9:20552076231219113. https://doi.org/10.1177/20552076231219113

Amann J, Blasimme A, Vayena E et al (2020) Explainability for artificial intelligence in healthcare: a multidisciplinary perspective. BMC Med Inf Dec Making 20(1):310. https://doi.org/10.1186/s12911-020-01332-6

Andreotta AJ, Kirkham N, Rizzi M (2022) AI, big data, and the future of consent. AI & Soc 37(4):1715–1728. https://doi.org/10.1007/s00146-021-01262-5

Bates DW, Landman A, Levine DM (2018) Health apps and health policy: what is needed? JAMA 320(19):1975–1976. https://doi.org/10.1001/jama.2018.14378

Birnbaum F, Lewis DM, Rosen R, Ranney ML (2015) Patient engagement and the design of digital health. Acad Emerg Med 22(6):754–756. https://doi.org/10.1111/acem.12692

Borges do Nascimento IJ, Abdulazeem H, Vasanthan LT et al (2023a) Barriers and facilitators to utilizing digital health technologies by healthcare professionals. NPJ Dig Med 6(1):1–28. https://doi.org/10.1038/s41746-023-00899-4

Borges do Nascimento IJ, Abdulazeem HM, Vasanthan LT et al (2023b) The global effect of digital health technologies on health workers' competencies and health workplace: an umbrella review of systematic reviews and lexical-based and sentence-based meta-analysis. Lancet Dig Health 5(8):e534–e544. https://doi.org/10.1016/S2589-7500(23)00092-4

Brönneke JB, Herr A, Reif S, Stern AD (2023) Dynamic HTA for digital health solutions: opportunities and challenges for patient-centered evaluation. Int J Technol Assess Health Care 39(1):e72. https://doi.org/10.1017/S0266462323002726

Catwell L, Sheikh A (2009) Evaluating eHealth interventions: the need for continuous systemic evaluation. PLoS Med 6(8):e1000126. https://doi.org/10.1371/journal.pmed.1000126

CDA-AMC (2024) Canada's Drug Agency. https://www.cadth.ca/

Chen C, Ding S, Wang J (2023a) Digital health for aging populations. Nat Med 29(7):1623–1630. https://doi.org/10.1038/s41591-023-02391-8

Chen RJ, Wang JJ, Williamson DFK et al (2023b) Algorithmic fairness in artificial intelligence for medicine and healthcare. Nat Biomed Eng 7(6):719–742. https://doi.org/10.1038/s41551-023-01056-8

Chenthara S, Wang H, Ahmed K (2019) Security and privacy in big data environment. In: Sakr S, Zomaya AY (eds) Encyclopedia of big data technologies. Springer International Publishing, Cham, pp 1487–1495

Chidambaram S, Jain B, Jain U et al (2024) An introduction to digital determinants of health. PLOS Digital Health 3(1):e0000346. https://doi.org/10.1371/journal.pdig.0000346

Claire R, Elvidge J, Hanif S et al (2024) Advancing the use of real world evidence in health technology assessment: insights from a multi-stakeholder workshop. Front Pharmacol 14. https://doi.org/10.3389/fphar.2023.1289365

Cristopher Gibbons M (2011) Use of health information technology among racial and ethnic underserved communities. Persp Health Inf Manage 8(Winter):1f

Davis JS, Osoba OA (2016) Privacy preservation in the age of big data: a survey, 23 September 2016

De Vito DA, Myers BA, Mc Curry KR et al (2009) User-centered design and interactive health technologies for patients. Comput Inf Nurs CIN 27(3):175. https://doi.org/10.1097/NCN.0b013e31819f7c7c

Durán JM, Jongsma KR (2021) Who is afraid of black box algorithms? On the epistemological and ethical basis of trust in medical AI. J Med Ethics 47(5):329–335. https://doi.org/10.1136/medethics-2020-106820

EDiHTA (2024) European Digital Health Technology Assessment (EDiHTA) Framework. https://edihta-project.eu/

EUnetHTA (2018) HTA Core Model®. https://www.eunethta.eu/hta-core-model/.

European Medicines Agency (2023) Towards a permanent collaboration framework for EMA and Health Technology Assessment bodies | European Medicines Agency (EMA). https://www.ema.europa.eu/en/news/towards-permanent-collaboration-framework-ema-and-health-technology-assessment-bodies

EuroQol Group (1990) EuroQol--a new facility for the measurement of health-related quality of life. Health Policy (Amsterdam, Netherlands) 16(3):199–208. https://doi.org/10.1016/0168-8510(90)90421-9

EXPH (2019) Defining Value in 'Value-Based Healthcare', 2019

Farah L, Borget I, Martelli N, Vallee A (2024) Suitability of the current health technology assessment of innovative artificial intelligence-based medical devices: scoping literature review. J Med Internet Res 26(1):e51514. https://doi.org/10.2196/51514

Food and Drug Administration (2024) Real-world evidence. https://www.fda.gov/science-research/science-and-research-special-topics/real-world-evidence

Giansanti D (2021) Cybersecurity and the digital-health: the challenge of this millennium. Healthcare 9(1):62. https://doi.org/10.3390/healthcare9010062

Graili P, Guertin JR, Chan KKW, Tadrous M (2023) Integration of real-world evidence from different data sources in health technology assessment. J Pharm Pharm Sci 26:11460. https://doi.org/10.3389/jpps.2023.11460

Gray JAM (2013) The shift to personalised and population medicine. Lancet (London, England) 382(9888):200–201. https://doi.org/10.1016/s0140-6736(13)61590-1

Gray M (2016) Designing healthcare for a different future. J R Soc Med 109(12):453–458. https://doi.org/10.1177/0141076816679781

Guo C, Ashrafian H, Ghafur S et al (2020) Challenges for the evaluation of digital health solutions—A call for innovative evidence generation approaches. NPJ Digital Medicine 3(1):1–14. https://doi.org/10.1038/s41746-020-00314-2

Hargittai E, Dobransky K (2017) Old dogs, new clicks: digital inequality in skills and uses among older adults. Can J Commun 42(2):195–212. https://doi.org/10.22230/cjc.2017v42n2a3176

Hargittai E, Piper AM, Morris MR (2019) From internet access to internet skills: digital inequality among older adults. Univ Access Inf Soc 18(4):881–890. https://doi.org/10.1007/s10209-018-0617-5

Hennemann S, Beutel ME, Zwerenz R (2017) Ready for eHealth? Health professionals' acceptance and adoption of eHealth Interventions in Inpatient Routine Care. J Health Commun 22(3):274–284. https://doi.org/10.1080/10810730.2017.1284286

Hensher M (2020) Incorporating environmental impacts into the economic evaluation of health care systems: perspectives from ecological economics. Resour Conserv Recycl 154:104623. https://doi.org/10.1016/j.resconrec.2019.104623

Hogervorst MA, Pontén J, Vreman RA et al (2022) Real world data in health technology assessment of complex health technologies. Front Pharmacol 13. https://doi.org/10.3389/fphar.2022.837302

Ignatowicz A, Slowther A-M, Elder P et al (2018) Ethical implications of digital communication for the patient-clinician relationship: analysis of interviews with clinicians and young adults with long term conditions (the LYNC study). BMC Med Ethics 19(1):11. https://doi.org/10.1186/s12910-018-0250-0

INAHTA (2021) INAHTA Framework. https://www.inahta.org/download/fwk/

INAHTA. The International Network of Agencies for Health Technology Assessment. INAHTA. https://www.inahta.org/

Institute for Clinical and Economic Review (2023) 2023 Value Assessment Framework. https://icer.org/wp-content/uploads/2023/10/ICER_2023_VAF_For-Publication_101723.pdf

Kaack LH, Donti PL, Strubell E et al (2022) Aligning artificial intelligence with climate change mitigation. Nat Clim Chang 12(6):518–527. https://doi.org/10.1038/s41558-022-01377-7

Khosla S, Tepie MF, Nagy MJ et al (2021) The alignment of real-world evidence and digital health: realising the opportunity. Therap Innov Regul Sci 55(4):889–898. https://doi.org/10.1007/s43441-021-00288-7

Kickbusch I, Agrawal A, Jack A et al (2019) Governing health futures 2030: growing up in a digital world—a joint The Lancet and Financial Times Commission. Lancet 394(10206):1309. https://doi.org/10.1016/S0140-6736(19)32181-6

Kidholm K, Ekeland AG, Jensen LK et al (2012) A model for assessment of telemedicine applications: mast. Int J Technol Assess Health Care 28(1):44–51. https://doi.org/10.1017/S0266462311000638

Lehne M, Sass J, Essenwanger A et al (2019) Why digital medicine depends on interoperability. NPJ Digital Medicine 2(1):1–5. https://doi.org/10.1038/s41746-019-0158-1

Luce BR, Drummond M, Jönsson B et al (2010) EBM, HTA, and CER: Clearing the Confusion. Milbank Quart 88(2):256–276. https://doi.org/10.1111/j.1468-0009.2010.00598.x

Mathias R, McCulloch P, Chalkidou A, Gilbert S (2024) Digital health technologies need regulation and reimbursement that enable flexible interactions and groupings. NPJ Dig Med 7(1):1–4. https://doi.org/10.1038/s41746-024-01147-z

Medical Services Advisory Committee (2024). http://www.msac.gov.au/

Menachemi N, Collum TH (2011) Benefits and drawbacks of electronic health record systems. Risk Management and Healthcare Policy 4:47–55. https://doi.org/10.2147/RMHP.S12985

Mensah NK, Adzakpah G, Kissi J et al (2023) Perceived impact of digital health technology on health professionals and their work: a qualitative study in Southern Ghana. Digital Health 9:20552076231218838. https://doi.org/10.1177/20552076231218838

Moshi MR, Tooher R, Merlin T (2018) Suitability of current evaluation frameworks for use in the health technology assessment of mobile medical applications: a systematic review. Int J Technol Assess Health Care 34(5):464–475. https://doi.org/10.1017/S026646231800051X

National Evidence-based Healthcare Collaborating Agency (NECA) (2024). https://www.neca.re.kr/eng/index.do

Nguyen AM, Rivera AM, Gualtieri L (2023) A new health care paradigm: the power of digital health and E-patients. Mayo Clinic Proc Dig Health 1(3):203–209. https://doi.org/10.1016/j.mcpdig.2023.04.005

NICE (2024) Evidence standards framework (ESF) for digital health technologies. NICE. https://www.nice.org.uk/about/what-we-do/our-programmes/evidence-standards-framework-for-digital-health-technologies

O'Rourke B, Oortwijn W, Schuller T, Group the IJT (2020) The new definition of health technology assessment: A milestone in international collaboration. Int J Technol Assess Health Care 36(3):187–190. https://doi.org/10.1017/S0266462320000215

OECD (2019) Enhancing Access to and Sharing of Data. OECD. https://www.oecd.org/en/publications/enhancing-access-to-and-sharing-of-data_276aaca8-en.html

Patel SP, Sun E, Reinhardt A et al (2022) Social determinants of digital health adoption: pilot cross-sectional survey. JMIR Formative Res 6(12):e39647. https://doi.org/10.2196/39647

Pickard Strange M, Booth A, Akiki M et al (2023) The role of virtual consulting in developing environmentally sustainable health care: systematic literature review. J Med Internet Res 25:e44823. https://doi.org/10.2196/44823

Porter ME (2010) What is value in health care? N Engl J Med 363(26):2477–2481. https://doi.org/10.1056/NEJMp1011024

Porter ME, Teisberg EO (2006) Redefining health care: creating value-based competition on results. Harvard Business Press

Rowland SP, Fitzgerald JE, Lungren M et al (2022) Digital health technology-specific risks for medical malpractice liability. NPJ Dig Med 5(1):1–6. https://doi.org/10.1038/s41746-022-00698-3

Samarasekera U (2022) The rise of racial minority health apps. Lancet Digital Health 4(4):e218–e219. https://doi.org/10.1016/S2589-7500(22)00043-7

Schlieter H, Gand K, Marsch LA et al (2024) Editorial: Scaling-up health-IT—sustainable digital health implementation and diffusion. Front Dig Health 6:1296495. https://doi.org/10.3389/fdgth.2024.1296495

Segur-Ferrer J, Moltó-Puigmartí C, Pastells-Peiró R, Vivanco-Hidalgo RM (2024) Methodological frameworks and dimensions to be considered in digital health technology assessment: scoping review and thematic analysis. J Med Internet Res 26(1):e48694. https://doi.org/10.2196/48694

Sujan M, Pool R, Salmon P (2022) Eight human factors and ergonomics principles for healthcare artificial intelligence. BMJ Health Care Inf 29(1):e100516. https://doi.org/10.1136/bmjhci-2021-100516

Syed R, Eden R, Makasi T et al (2023) Digital health data quality issues: systematic review. J Med Internet Res 25:e42615. https://doi.org/10.2196/42615

Tarricone R, Petracca F, Ciani O, Cucciniello M (2021) Distinguishing features in the assessment of mHealth apps. Expert Rev Pharmacoecon Outcomes Res 21(4):521–526. https://doi.org/10.1080/14737167.2021.1891883

The Lancet (2018) Is digital medicine different? Lancet 392(10142):95. https://doi.org/10.1016/S0140-6736(18)31562-9

Vallo Hult H, Hansson A, Gellerstedt M (2020) Digitalization and physician learning: individual practice, organizational context, and social norm. J Contin Educ Heal Prof 40(4):220–227. https://doi.org/10.1097/CEH.0000000000000303

van Velsen L, Ludden G, Grünloh C (2022) The limitations of user-and human-centered design in an eHealth context and how to move beyond them. J Med Internet Res 24(10):e37341. https://doi.org/10.2196/37341

Vis C, Bührmann L, Riper H, Ossebaard HC (2020) Health technology assessment frameworks for eHealth: A systematic review. Int J Technol Assess Health Care 36(3):204–216. https://doi.org/10.1017/S026646232000015X

von Hippel E (2006) Democratizing innovation. The MIT Press

von Huben A, Howell M, Howard K et al (2021) Health technology assessment for digital technologies that manage chronic disease: a systematic review. Int J Technol Assess Health Care 37(1):e66. https://doi.org/10.1017/S0266462321000362

Vukovic V, Favaretti C, Ricciardi W, de Waure C (2018) Health technology assessment evidence on E-Health/M-Health technologies: evaluating the transparency and thoroughness. Int J Technol Assess Health Care 34(1):87–96. https://doi.org/10.1017/S0266462317004512

Wang T, Zhu H, Qian S et al (2024) Designing digital patient experiences: the digital health design framework. Appl Ergon 119:104289. https://doi.org/10.1016/j.apergo.2024.104289

Wies B, Landers C, Ienca M (2021) Digital mental health for young people: a scoping review of ethical promises and challenges. Front Dig Health 3. https://doi.org/10.3389/fdgth.2021.697072

World Bank (2023) Digital Progress and Trends Report 2023. https://www.worldbank.org/en/publication/digital-progress-and-trends-report

World Economic Forum (2017) Value in Healthcare: Laying the Foundation for Health System Transformation, 2017

World Economic Forum (2021) Why tech needs to focus on the needs of marginalized groups. World Economic Forum. https://www.weforum.org/agenda/2021/07/tech-focus-needs-marginalized-groups/.

World Economic Forum, Boston Consulting Group (2024) Transforming Healthcare: Navigating Digital Health with a Value-Driven Approach, 2024

World Health Organization (2019) WHO guideline Recommendations on Digital Interventions for Health System Strengthening. WHO Guidelines Approved by the Guidelines Review Committee. World Health Organization, Geneva

World Health Organization (2021a) Global strategy on digital health 2020-2025, 2021

World Health Organization (2021b) National Agencies for Health Technology Assessment. https://cdn.who.int/media/docs/default-source/health-economics/nationalagenciehta.pdf.

World Health Organization (2023) Empowerment through Digital Health. https://www.who.int/europe/initiatives/empowerment-through-digital-health.

The Evaluative, Economic, and Organizational Dimensions of Personalized Medicine

Leopoldo Trieste and Giuseppe Turchetti

Abstract The chapter analyzes the implications of personalized medicine for a range of stakeholders. Specifically, we analyze the challenges associated with evaluating personalized medical strategies while focusing on the limitations of the methodologies in use today, such as whether and how traditional constructs like pharmaco-economics and health technology assessments still apply. We also explore the technological solutions available within "standard" medicine, discussing the possible economic implications of personalized medicine and the different remuneration mechanisms that are currently used to compensate technology and service providers. The chapter concludes with a discussion on the organizational implications of adopting a personalized medical approach for healthcare systems as well as individual healthcare facilities. The corresponding analysis should help readers fully appreciate the perspectives of the various stakeholders in personalized medicine while also helping to encourage healthcare systems to adopt this "new" medicine.

1 The Four Steps (and Technologies) of Personalized Medicine

Personalized medicine is an evolving approach to healthcare that involves tailoring medical treatments to the individual characteristics of each patient.[1] It spans principles, techniques, organizational strategies, institutions, and technologies related to four interconnected steps: deep patient profiling, diagnosis, advanced patient

[1] Green and Guyer (2011), pp. 209–2011; Wolf et al. (2012), p. 361; Schleidgen et al. (2013), pp. 6–7 (Table 1), and p. 8 (Table 2); Verma (2012), pp. 2–8; Collins and Varmus (2015), p. 794. See also the National Academies of Sciences, Engineering (2017).

L. Trieste (✉) · G. Turchetti
Institute of Management, Sant'Anna School of Advanced Studies, Pisa, Italy
e-mail: leopoldo.trieste@santannapisa.it

F. Casarosa et al. (eds.), *Enabling and Safeguarding Personalized Medicine*, Data Science, Machine Intelligence, and Law 7,
https://doi.org/10.1007/978-3-031-99709-9_9

monitoring, and personalized treatments. However, within this realm, it is important to distinguish between the complexity and customizability of the technology embedded in healthcare services and the complexity and customizability of healthcare services themselves.

The first step in delivering personalized medical care, profiling and screening, typically involves undertaking a comprehensive and detailed profile of a patient's characteristics and health conditions. This is a process that often includes gathering genetic and genomic data to inform treatment decisions.[2] This is because genetic testing can identify specific mutations or variations in a person's DNA that affects how a patient will respond to certain medications and therapies.

Personalized medicine may also involve molecular profiling techniques, like proteomics and metabolomics, to delve into the molecular mechanisms underlying a patient's disease. This detailed molecular information helps to tailor treatment plans.

Diagnoses generally emerge from managing large amounts of data. The profiling and screening step typically allows practitioners to identify and forecast a comprehensive risk profile, which is used to inform a diagnosis, personalized communication, and newly programmed screenings. While forming a diagnosis often follows a standard set of criteria, albeit with minor variations based on the characteristics, skills, experience, and culture of patients), personalization may involve how that information is summarized and tailored to suit the characteristics of both medical professionals and patients.

Monitoring relates to biomarkers, which are measurable indicators of the presence or severity of a disease state. Biomarkers can predict the progression of a disease or indicate how a patient is responding to treatment, both of which help to customize therapeutic strategies.[3]

Technological advancements mean there are now a number of ways to monitor patients. At a micro level, miniaturized devices can detect and measure biological information, providing real-time data. Alternatively, wearable devices worn on or implanted within the body also allow continuous monitoring of specific health conditions.

Patients can also be remotely monitored through telehealth platforms that not only provide comprehensive health data to clinicians and but also interact with connected medical devices and mobile applications, helping patients to track their health metrics. During this monitoring phase, personalization may involve providing customized feedback to patients, such as offering tailored advice or alerting the patient to health dangers based on the individual's data. One of the key benefits of personalized medicine is that treatments can be proactive as well as reactive. Genetic screening identifies individuals with genetic predispositions to diseases, enabling early interventions such as increased surveillance or prophylactic surgeries. Genetic tests can also inform personalized lifestyle modifications. For example, individuals with a genetic predisposition to obesity might receive tailored diet

[2] Schleidgen et al. (2013), pp. 6–7; Hejblum et al. (2015), pp. 16–17.

[3] Green and Guyer (2011), pp. 209–211; Wolf et al. (2012), p. 361; Hejblum et al. (2015), ibid.

and exercise plans. Similarly, understanding the genetic factors that influencing a person's immune response can optimize vaccination schedules and formulations for better efficacy. Further, biomarker-based screening tests can detect diseases at earlier stages when treatments are more effective and less costly and, if a disease is identified, profiling and screening allow for personalized treatment.

Supported by advanced technologies, deep profiling and monitoring can enhance healthcare delivery through personalized risk assessments, prevention strategies, genetic counseling for hereditary conditions, and tailored drug prescriptions based on genetic profiles. For instance, in cancer treatment, personalized services often involve the genomic profiling of tumors to identify specific mutations and target immunotherapies based on the tumor's specific characteristics.

Notably, the extent to which a medical treatment will be personalized will generally depend on how effectively heterogeneity is managed when delivering healthcare services.

Services such as personalized nutrition plans give rise to customized dietary advice and interventions based on genetic markers. Personalized wellness programs provide tailored fitness and wellness plans based on individual health data. Lifestyle and behavioral coaching are personalized according to individual needs. Mental health apps offer customized therapy and support.[4] AI-based algorithms analyze patient data to predict disease risks, while machine learning models optimize treatment plans and rehabilitation sessions. For more details on how AI can help healthcare professionals deliver custom services, see Topol.[5]

2 The Real Degree of Personalization

The true measure of personalized medicine lies not merely in the quantity or complexity of information collected for each patient, but in the ability to effectively manage this heterogeneity so as to provide tailored solutions. As such, personalization does not mean reducing the information or knowledge used to inform a personalized treatment simply because each patient is a one-off exception. Nor does it mean abandoning evidence-based practices that are based on "average" measures. In personalized medicine, patients are not treated in isolation; emerging evidence and statistical analyses derived from large datasets and clinical studies are definitely considered.

Therefore, personalized medicine is still deeply rooted in statistical methodologies. In fact, personalized medicine is an approach that relies on large volumes of data to enhance our ability to identify, classify, and predict a disease's progression. However, personalized medicine enables more precise patient stratification and more effective, individualized care.

[4] Johnson and Choi (2022), p. 1.

[5] Topol (2019).

2.1 Bottlenecks in Managing and Delivering Personalized Solutions

What is particularly relevant is how to address the bottlenecks caused by heterogeneity that arise at various levels of the personalized medicine supply chain and how healthcare services are responding to heterogeneity. At each level of the supply chain, technologies are constrained by specific limits to personalization. Additionally, medical services have varying capacities to manage heterogeneity. In this sense, deep profiling and patient segmentation are pointless if the associated service technology cannot support highly personalized solutions.

2.1.1 Profiling

Screenings are often undertaken in groups involving patients with relatively homogeneous epidemiologies and medical histories. Here, personalization refers more to tailoring communications based on the information derived from comprehensive profiling and non-health-related data, such as language skills and social characteristics. As a more specific example, medicine now has the ability to (text) mine and then assess active and bidirectional social cues through the frequency of words used, how individuals use and assign meanings to words in different contexts, and which words trigger specific answers or reactions that improve engagement. Table 1 provides more detail.

In this table, core technology refers to the technology integrated into a healthcare service that is essential for the service to be effective. Importantly, the table does not refer to specific services, but rather classifies different types of healthcare services according to the degree to which the service and the embedded core technology are personalized. At this level, the degree of personalization is higher for services than for the associated technologies. In other words, how diagnoses, personalized treatments, and guidelines are communicated is more tailored than how ultrasounds or wearable devices are administered. This is typical of communication-based services. Further, if personalization involves several technologies, the personalization does not relate to a single one, but rather to the combination of technologies chosen for profiling.

Table 1 Degree of technology and service personalization—profiling

		Degree of personalization: embedded core technology	
		Low	**High**
Degree of personalization: Service	**High**	Traditional screening, and personalized communication	Personalized screening, and personalized communication
	Low	Traditional screening	Personalized screening, traditional communication

Table 2 Degree of technology and service personalization—monitoring

		Degree of personalization: embedded core technology	
		Low	**High**
Degree of personalization: Service	**High**	Traditional screening, personalized and non-technologically mediated interactions between doctor and patient	Advanced personalized screening
	Low	Traditional screening	Advanced ICT screening, standardized communication

2.1.2 Monitoring

Heterogeneity at the monitoring level is influenced by the types of technologies used to supply information about the patient's condition. The level of personalization depends, of course, on the treatments planned and the regimens followed, e.g., inpatient, outpatient, at home. Thus, in general, the types of services offered, and the technologies used primarily depend on the particular organization delivering the healthcare. See Table 2.

2.1.3 Personalized Treatments

The degree to which personalized treatments vary significantly and largely depends on the type of technology involved and the nature of the services they support. While personalized drug therapies involve a high degree of personalization, the associated service delivery is typically standardized. By contrast, medical devices, such as health robots, tend to be characterized by less customizable technologies where the degree of personalization depends more on hardware constraints than software. Therefore, customization is often achieved through the particular modules included in the treatment. That said, by combining programmed modules and communication capabilities, these technologies can provide complex services with a high degree of personalization. Table 3 provides more details.

2.2 *Why Medical Devices Are Not Pills*

Personalized medicine involving drugs differs significantly from cases that simply involve medical devices, and this difference has significant implications for identifying the economic and organizational impacts of personalized medicine.[6] Table 4 summarizes the main differences between personalized drug therapies and personalized care using medical devices.

[6] Pecchia and Craven (2013), p. 3.

Table 3 Degree of technology and service personalization—treatment/training

		Degree of personalization: embedded core technology	
Degree of personalization: Service		**Low**	**High**
	High	Medical devices	Technology based on patient/ healthcare operator interaction
	Low	Traditional drug therapy	Personalized drug therapy

Table 4 Personalized drug therapies versus medical devices: a comparison[a]

Dimensions	Personalized drug therapy	Personalized medical device
Principal action	Immunologic/metabolic chemical based	Mechanical, control, EEE, software…
Product life cycle	No life cycle	Short life cycle changing versions depending on technical characteristics
Clinical evaluation	Easy to blind	No placebo
	Usually, one end-user	Multiple end-users
	Short learning curve	Long learning curve
	Less dependent by settings/ organizations	Strongly dependent by settings/ organizations
	Short learning curve	Long learning curve
	Associated service easy to standardize	Associated service complex to standardize
Use issues	Usually does not require training for patients and healthcare professionals	Usually requires training for patients and healthcare professionals
Diversity	Mainly large multinationals	Extremely specialized SME and experts
Costs	High costs for screening and preparation and low costs for delivery and care	High costs for screening and unit average costs of delivery depending on the number of users
	No amortization	Amortization
	No maintenance/installation	Maintenance costs

[a]Developed and expanded from Pecchia and Craven (2013), p. 3

3 The Economic and Organizational Impacts of Personalized Medicine

3.1 Implications for Patients

The most significant benefits of personalized medicine for patients include improved treatment outcomes, preventive care, empowerment, and engagement.[7] However, the economic impacts of personalized medicine are not as clear. On the one hand, personalized medicine will typically increase costs related to screening, preparing

[7]Hickmann et al. (2022), pp. 4–8.

therapies, and treatments, potentially reducing access to care.[8] On the other hand, it can reduce the number of ineffective treatments and adverse drug reactions, and may also be more effective and preventing a disease's progression.[9]

The primary challenges of personalized medicine from the perspective of patients revolve around equity of access, privacy, and data security. Equity of access concerns the high costs associated with preparing and testing personalized solutions. Further, the collection and use of genetic information raises significant privacy and data security issues.[10] Therefore, protecting patient data from unauthorized access and ensuring informed consent are crucial for maintaining trust in personalized medicine. Thus, one can expect additional costs for designing, implementing, and maintaining the digital infrastructures that support personalized healthcare.

3.2 Implications from a Clinical Perspective for Healthcare Organizations

The primary distinction between personalizing medical devices versus personalizing drug therapies lies in how the service is delivered. Pills typically involve standardized service delivery, whereas healthcare services involving medical devices generally entail relatively high heterogeneity due to the diversity of patients involved.

Consequently, implementing new solutions involving medical devices often necessitates organizational changes, with these changes being more pronounced than those associated with drug therapies.[11]

3.3 Implications for Healthcare Professionals

Personalized medicine has the potential to enhance diagnostic and treatment capabilities. However, for these remedies to reach their fullest potential, healthcare professionals must become proficient in interpreting complex genetic and molecular data. This requires specialized training in genomics and bioinformatics so as to accurately diagnose conditions and tailor treatments. Physicians must understand pharmacogenomics to prescribe medications based on a patient's genetic profile,

[8] Lu et al. (2023), pp. 3–6.

[9] See the contribution of the Personalized Medicine Coalition (2014) available at: https://www.personalizedmedicinecoalition.org/Userfiles/PMC-Corporate/file/pmc_the_case_for_personalized_medicine.pdf.

[10] See Lunshof et al. (2008), p. 407.

[11] See Hickmann et al. (2022), ibid.

which involves staying up-to-date on the latest advancements and integrating genetic testing into routine practice.[12]

Personalized medicine also necessitates continued education and training not only in genetics, molecular biology, and bioinformatics, but also in personalized communication. Tailoring medicine to the individual frequently requires collaboration between various specialists,[13] which means healthcare professionals must work closely with different experts to develop and implement personalized treatment plans.

Yet another consequence of personalized medicine is that obtaining informed consent will become more complex, and healthcare professionals must be skilled in communicating these complexities to patients. As such, the roles and duties of healthcare professionals will inevitably expand in future to encompass the additional tasks associated with personalized medicine, such as genetic counseling, coordinating care, and developing efficient workflows. Already, personalized medicine requires healthcare professionals to clearly and empathetically communicate complex information. This includes explaining genetic risks, test results, and personalized treatment plans in a way that patients can understand.

3.4 Implications for Industry

Personalized drug therapies are poised to transform the pharmaceutical industry. By identifying which patient populations are most likely to benefit from a specific drug, pharmaceutical companies can concentrate on developing treatments targeting specific genetic markers or disease subtypes. This approach narrows the scope of clinical trials, ensuring that only relevant patients are involved, which can speed up the development process and lower costs. Further, modular services and training delivered through medical devices, apps and robotics are expanding the market for health apps, software, and engaging solutions (e.g., advanced gamification).[14]

Personalized medicine is expected to drive the expansion of healthcare services, including genetic counseling, advanced diagnostics, and specialized treatment plans.[15] Healthcare providers need to adapt to these changes by investing in new technologies and training. This includes integrating big data analytics and artificial intelligence to effectively manage and interpret complex genetic information.[16]

---

[12] See Formea et al. (2015), pp. 130–131.

[13] Xu et al. (2021) explore the intrinsic interdisciplinarity of personalized medicine.

[14] See, among others, Johnson and Choi (2022), p. 1.; Yeung et al. 2023, pp. 6–7; Kasoju et al. (2023), p. 12.

[15] Goetz and Schork (2018), pp. 955–958.

[16] See Challen (2019).

3.5 *Organizational Implications: Towards Personalized Care Pathways*

Integrated profiling, monitoring, and personalized care in medicine all increase the complexity of the services delivered to patients. While the industry is striving for a healthcare model that places the patient at the center, the proliferation of technologies enabling personalized care may inadvertently create a situation where the patient finds themselves at the center of a complex labyrinth of treatments and tests by a plethora of healthcare professionals.

Therefore, sustainable personalized medicine requires the design of new, more advanced, and more personalized diagnostic and therapeutic care pathways, i.e., patient-centered pathways[17] that support personalized medicine without adding complexity for the patient. Defining and designing personalized patient-centered pathways involves integrating all relevant dimensions within a health technology assessment approach.[18] In turn, this means these personalized patient-centered pathways must:

(1) clearly define the objectives and key elements of evidence-based care (the clinical dimension);
(2) facilitate communication among team members, caregivers, and patients, with a positive impact on patient-reported outcome measures, patient-reported experience measures, consumer satisfaction, quality of work, usability, and acceptability;[19]
(3) coordinate the care process by defining roles and implementing the activities usually performed by multidisciplinary care teams (organizational issues);
(4) document, monitor, and evaluate outcomes (in line with health technology assessment definitions); and
(5) identify the resources needed to implement the process (the economic dimension).

Traditionally, healthcare pathways aim to increase the efficiency of healthcare services by rationalizing patient characteristics and needs—that is, by assembling patients into homogeneous groups. But this is the opposite of personalized medicine. Today, however, with the help of advanced diagnostic and treatment technologies, ICT and AI algorithms, we can add a sixth dimension to personalized care pathways in that they must:

[17] See Redaelli et al. (2019).

[18] See Garrison et al. (2007); Trosman et al. (2011), pp. e25–e28; O'Rourke et al. (2020), p. 188.

[19] Kingsley and Patel (2017), pp. 138–142; Rudolph et al. (2019), pp. 5–10; Benson (2020) p. 10 and Tables 1–4; Lowry et al. (2024), pp. 1, 9–10.

(6) identify technological solutions to enhance the personalization of services without compromising efficiency.

Assessing patient-centered pathways clearly requires a substantial effort in terms of selecting and/or developing new qualitative and quantitative approaches to measure and monitor the organizational impacts of personalized medicine.

3.6 *Technological Implications*

From a technological perspective, personalized medicine involves integrating profiles, monitoring data, treatments, and managing large amounts of data, which will invariably require efficient solutions such as multi-user decision support systems and ICT platforms. Fortunately, today numerous technologies are available to help make healthcare services more accessible, especially for patients in remote areas or those with mobility issues, including telemedicine and chronic disease platforms, electronic health record systems, personal health management apps, health information exchange platforms, and clinical trials platforms. These facilities can empower patients to actively participate in their own healthcare, promote adherence to treatment plans, and encourage healthier behaviors. Moreover, integrating big data and analytics into health platforms can support more informed clinical decisions and improved public health strategies. Similarly, digital health platforms can facilitate faster and more efficient clinical trials, aiding the development of new treatments and medical technologies.

However, while personalized diagnostic and therapeutic care pathways can address organizational issues across the phases of personalized medicine from profiling to treatment, digital platforms work to enhance service efficiency and integration. Thus, there is a risk that emphasizing technological efficiency when attempting to integrate personalized medical services might overshadow the interpersonal relationships at play, thereby increasing the distance between patients and their healthcare providers (Fig. 1). Additionally, prioritizing the technological efficiency of services over their effectiveness is likely to significantly impact the outcomes of patient care.

It is therefore important to remember that the goal of technological innovation in the field of personalized health is not to push the technological frontier, but to address the questions and needs that the current standard of care is unable to meet. Ignoring this fundamental premise often leads to solutions in search of a problem, whereas, ideally, technologies—at least those with the most immediate impact—should be built around recognized needs.

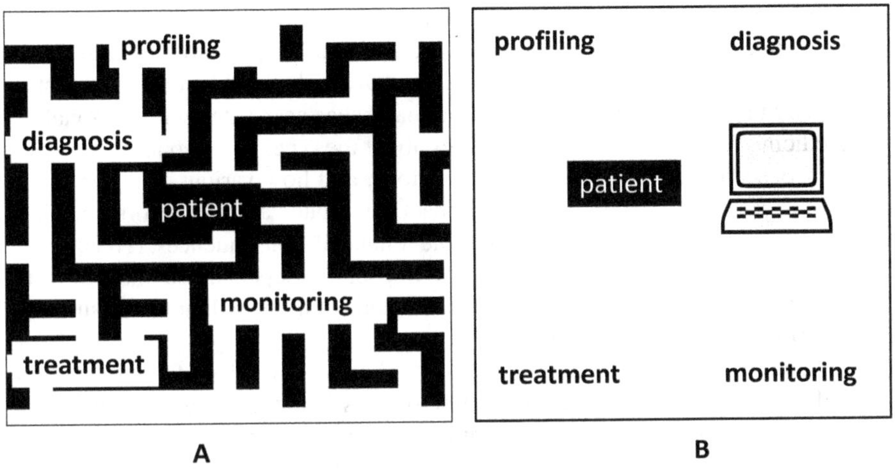

Fig. 1 Risks of personalized medicine. The patient is at the center, but... (**a**) The patient at the center of a labyrinth of non-integrated, effective but inefficient healthcare services. (**b**) The patient at the center of an artificially interactive ICT platform of integrated and technologically efficient (but clinically effective?) healthcare services

4 Assessing the Economic and Organizational Dimensions

4.1 Why Assessing Economic and Organizational Impacts Is Important

There are several reasons for why we need to assess the economic and organizational impact of personalized medical solutions.

(1) When assessing the impact of personalized medicine, one must look beyond the efficacy of the treatment alone. This is particularly relevant in the case of medical solutions that involve alternative forms of disease management, such as telemedicine. Even in cases of personalized drug therapies, where the impacts for an organization tend to be limited, profiling, screening, diagnosis, monitoring, and so on necessitate that one reconsiders the way personalized healthcare services are currently organized across the entire supply chain. Specifically, the organizational implications of personalized medicine also affect the satisfaction of patients and healthcare professionals with their treatments, alongside the long-term sustainability of healthcare services.

(2) To achieve efficiency, personalized medicine will invariably involve patient-centered diagnostic therapeutic pathways and highly modular services offered through medical devices and digital platforms.[20] These platforms will likely

[20] Rochet and Tirole (2003), pp. 90–94.

involve different stakeholders, such that assessing personalized medicine will not differ much from analyzing the organizational implications of digitizing a service, whether or not these services are delivered by public or private institutions. Further, assessing the organizational issues associated with personalized medicine will inform hospital facilities about the types of personalized services they can implement, under what conditions, and how various types and numbers of personalized solutions will impact key organizational performance indicators, which also have economic and financial consequences. Thus, unless someone analyzes the organizational impact of personalized medicine, the stakeholders involved in guiding personalized solutions will not have sufficient information to make informed decisions.

(3) Personalized medicine aims to improve the effectiveness of treatments and reduce their costs. Note here that effectiveness is not the same as clinical efficacy, given that effectiveness integrates dimensions that a patient can subjectively feel like pain, discomfort, quality of service, quality of life, and so on. However, preparing personalized therapies has economic consequences that require thorough analysis. Beyond the costs of any technologies embedded in personalized solutions, the economic issues depend on how the associated services are managed and organized. And only an organizational analysis of personalized medicine can determine how these costs are generated.

4.2 How to Assess the Economic and Organizational Impacts of Personalized Medicine

There are two principles that should guide any assessment of the economic and organizational impact of personalized medicines:

(1) Personalized medicine has diverse impacts on clinical and non-clinical factors.
(2) The impacts of personalized medicine are heterogeneous because they vary across different stakeholders.

These principles necessitate a health technology assessment (HTA). A HTA is a multi-stakeholder, multidimensional tool for assessing the value of a health technology. By 'value', we mean its effectiveness, its cost-effectiveness, its acceptability, usability, and organizational impact, along with any legal or ethical issues associated with its use.[21]

[21] O'Rourke et al. (2020), p. 188 offer an updated definition of Health Technology Assessment.

5 Methodological Challenges of Personalized Medicine in a HTA Framework

Let us focus on the economic and organizational dimensions of HTA for personalized medicine.[22] To better understand the consequences of personalized medicine on the methods adopted in the HTA framework, consider the principles underlying the current economic analysis of health programs. This process is usually based on the following main assumptions:[23]

(1) Resource scarcity;
(2) Technology (drugs or medical devices) as given goods;
(3) Constant or decreasing returns to scale for health resource allocation. This assumption prevents the switching phenomena, where increased investment could transform a previously dominated solution into a dominant alternative. Decreasing returns allow one to identify an optimal quantity of resources to allocate to a specific program;
(4) Unlike traditional cases of contagion, the behavior of a single patient does not affect the conditions of other patients;
(5) Finite and fixed states of nature, numbered over time; and
(6) Rationality of preferences.

Under these and other more sophisticated hypotheses, which arise from conditions for perfect competition and produce a full isomorphism between individually observed properties and those inferred from samples and the general population, an optimal criterion exists for resource allocation. This criterion orders alternative solutions according to their efficiency, based on the ratio between costs and effects or the ratio between cost and effectiveness differences of a specific solution compared with the standard of care.

5.1 The Challenges Associated with Digital Platforms and AI-Based Solutions

Digital platforms will likely support the delivery of personalized medical services going forward. Yet assessing the economic impact of these platforms is set to become a significant methodological challenge. Because the value and utility of digital platforms[24] tends to increase with the number of users, it is easy to presume that there is no optimal quantity of resources that should be allocated to a given service.

---

[22] See Redaelli et al. (2019). See also O'Rourke et al. (2020), ibid.

[23] For more details see Cannizzo et al. (2018), p. 3; Turchetti et al. (2014), pp. 147–148.

[24] See Rochet and Tirole (2003), ibid.; Evans and Schmalensee (2016); Hagiu and Wright (2020); Parker et al. (2016); Ezrachi and Stucke (2016); Manyika et al. (2016).

Moreover, as digital platforms are often designed to serve multiple user groups, the value of a platform to one group can easily depend on the size and engagement of the other groups on the platform, in a phenomenon commonly known as cross-side network effects.[25] As such, patients and users can influence each other in many ways beyond those experienced as part of a diagnosed disease. In the case of increasing returns there is not an optimal allocation of healthcare resources: the more one invests in a healthcare program, the more it produces positive outcomes in proportional terms.

Additionally, the most common good shared on these platforms is information. Information increases in value with use (increasing returns), while medical devices depreciate with use. Hence, the information these devices collect and share increases in value with use.[26]

5.2 *Clinical and Statistical Challenges of Personalized Medicine*

Personalized medicine transforms the nature of clinical trials through which we assess the effectiveness and cost-effectiveness of alternative solutions. Table 5 reports the main differences between traditional randomized controlled trials and trials involving the assessment of personalized solutions.

Personalized medicine must address and solve statistical problems arising from the complexity and variability of biological systems, the vast amounts of data generated, and the need for robust analytical methods.

The first problem is the high dimensionality of data and its related computational complexity.[27] Genomic, proteomic, and other omics data often involve thousands or millions of variables compared to a relatively small number of samples—e.g. genetic markers as opposed to patients. High dimensionality can lead to overfitting, where models perform well on training data but poorly on unseen data, reducing the generalizability of findings.

The analysis of large-scale, high-dimensional data requires significant computational resources and sophisticated algorithms. Developing efficient computational methods and leveraging high-performance computing infrastructures are essential to managing and analyzing big data effectively.

A second problem deals with multiple testing. Analyzing thousands of genetic variants or biomarkers simultaneously increases the risk of false positives due to

[25] See Katz and Shapiro (1994); Economides (1996); Gawer and Cusumano (2002); Economides and Katsamakas (2006); Gawer (2009); Rysman (2009).

[26] On the effect of increasing returns on economic theory, see, among others, David (1985), Arthur (1989), and Bresnahan and Greenstein (1999).

[27] See Freidlin et al. (2010), pp. 153, 155; Belle et al. (2015), p. 5; Alyass et al. (2015); Reza Soroushmehr and Najarian (2016), Rubin and van der Laan (2018). See also the recent review of Molla and Bitew (2024).

Table 5 Traditional RCTs vs. Personalized Medicine Trials, a comparison

Aspect	Traditional RCTs	Personalized Medicine Trials
Population homogeneity vs. heterogeneity	Seek to minimize variability by including a homogeneous population.	Embrace heterogeneity to explore treatment effects in diverse subpopulations.
Treatment uniformity vs. customization	Apply a single treatment regimen to all participants in the treatment group.	Tailor treatments based on individual characteristics.
Endpoints and outcome measures	Uniform endpoints for all participants.	Multiple, tailored endpoints based on individual patient profiles.
Adaptive vs. fixed protocols	Typically follow a fixed protocol throughout the study.	Often use adaptive protocols that can evolve based on interim results and individual responses.
Generalizability	Results are intended to be broadly applicable.	Aim to provide insights specific to subgroups with certain genetic or biomarker characteristics.

multiple comparisons. This necessitates rigorous statistical corrections, e.g., Bonferroni corrections or false discovery rates, which can reduce the data's statistical power and the ability of analysts to detect true associations.

A third problem is related to population stratification. Genetic differences between populations can confound the results of genomic studies if not properly accounted for. This can lead to spurious associations between genetic markers and diseases, making it essential to use methods that control for population structures, such as principal component analysis. Additionally, combining heterogeneous data types poses significant statistical and computational challenges. Effective methods of integrating genomic data with clinical and other health data are needed to create comprehensive models that can leverage all available data while managing noise and discrepancies between data sources.

Many personalized medicine studies, especially those involving rare diseases, have limited sample sizes due to the difficulty of recruiting participants. Small sample sizes can reduce statistical power and increase the risk of both false positive and false negative errors. Additionally, monitoring patients over time generates longitudinal data, which can be complex to analyze due to within-subject correlations and time-varying covariates. Advanced statistical methods, such as mixed-effects models and time-series analysis, are often required to correctly analyze and interpret longitudinal data.

Also, patient data may be incomplete due to non-compliance, dropouts, or technical issues during data collection. Missing data can bias results if not properly handled, necessitating the use of imputation techniques or models robust to missingness.

Ensuring that predictive models are validated and reproducible across different cohorts and settings is challenging. Over-reliance on a single dataset can lead to models that do not generalize well, highlighting the need for rigorous validation techniques.[28] Additionally, personalized medicine often involves sensitive genetic and health data, raising concerns about privacy and data security.[29] Therefore, statistical methods must include strategies for anonymizing data and protecting patient confidentiality while still allowing for meaningful analysis.

Establishing causality, rather than mere association, between genetic variants, biomarkers, and health outcomes is complex. Advanced statistical techniques like Mendelian randomization or instrumental variable analysis are required to infer causality and guide effective treatment decisions.

Addressing these statistical challenges is crucial for successfully implementing personalized medicine. Progress will require the development of robust statistical methods, interdisciplinary collaboration, and the continuous refinement of analytical techniques to ensure that personalized treatments are both effective and reliable.

5.3 *The Need for Simulation and Continuous Monitoring*

Using technologies and goods that give rise to increasing returns, alongside costly devices for delivering personalized training and rehabilitation, means we must inevitably correlate the cost-effectiveness of the technological solutions with the number of patients served. This is because these technologies only become sustainable for clinics and healthcare facilities as the number of cared-for individuals increases (i.e. economies of scale). While simulations can help assess the sustainability of personalized medicine as a condition for market entry, this is not the case for the administration of personalized medicine. For this reason, dynamic health technology assessments that allow for real-time evaluations of personalized solutions as they are administered is advisable.

5.4 *Organizational and Economic Issues*

Different key performance indicators (KPIs) can be assessed as a part of considering the organizational issues related to delivering personalized solutions.[30] In addition to these scholars, Brenner et al. (2023) identify specific KPIs for assessing the value of digital health interventions. Table 6 is based on the KPIs indicated in the literature.

[28] See Ramspek et al. (2021).

[29] See Lunshof et al. (2008), p. 407, Box 1.

[30] See Hrebiniak and Joyce (1984), Lynch and Cross (1991), Kaplan and Norton (1996), Neely et al. (2002), Parmenter (2015), and Marr (2015). See also Burlea-Schiopoiu and Ferhati (2020).

Table 6 Potential key performance indicators for different stakeholders

Stakeholder	Key Performance Indicators
Healthcare Providers*	Patient treatment success rate, diagnostic accuracy, time to diagnosis, adverse event rate, cost per patient, turnaround time for genetic testing, resource utilization, staff training and competency, patient satisfaction, patient adherence to treatment plans, access to personalized medicine services, revenue from personalized medicine, cost savings from reduced complications
Patients*	Patient treatment success rate, diagnostic accuracy, time to diagnosis, adverse event rate, cost per patient, patient satisfaction, patient adherence to treatment plans, access to personalized medicine services
Diagnostic companies	Diagnostic accuracy, turnaround time for genetic testing, collaboration and partnerships, intellectual property generated
Payers*	Cost per patient, cost savings from reduced complications
Laboratories	Diagnostic accuracy, turnaround time for genetic testing, resource utilization
Pharmaceutical companies	Patient treatment success rate, adverse event rate, investment in R&D, number of new personalized treatments, collaboration and partnerships, intellectual property generated
Biotechnology firms	Investment in R&D, number of new personalized treatments, collaboration and partnerships, intellectual property generated
Research institutions	Number of new personalized treatments, collaboration and partnerships, intellectual property generated
Hospitals/Clinics*	Cost per patient, resource utilization, staff training and competency, access to personalized medicine services, revenue from personalized medicine, cost savings from reduced complications
Medical schools/ training institutions	Staff training and competency

* Stakeholders involved in clinical trials

These KPIs vary according to the involved stakeholders, including healthcare providers, patients, diagnostic companies, hospitals and clinics, laboratories, pharmaceutical industries, and technology providers.[31]

Notably, this list of KPIs should be updated when medical devices are involved. For instance, Table 7 only lists the main KPIs related to medical devices from the perspective of a hospital facility.

The economic impacts of personalized medicine refer to both the direct health and non-health costs, as well as any associated indirect costs, such as productivity losses. That said, these indirect costs are expected to decrease with personalized treatment, as a result of technologies like remote monitoring solutions. The types and levels of costs to be assessed may vary significantly depending on the

[31] See Brynjolfsson and Hitt (2000); Brenner et al. (2023).

Table 7 KPIs for medical devices—a hospital facility perspective

Category	Kpi	Description	Measurement Method
Operational efficiency	Equipment utilization rate	The percentage of time medical devices are in use compared to available time, indicating efficiency and demand.	Equipment logs, utilization reports
	Maintenance downtime	The total downtime of medical devices due to scheduled and unscheduled maintenance, affecting operational continuity.	Maintenance logs, downtime tracking
	Equipment turnaround time	The average time taken to repair and return a medical device to service after it has been taken out of operation.	Repair logs, turnaround time tracking
	Inventory management	The accuracy and adequacy of medical device inventory levels to meet patient needs and minimize excess stock.	Inventory records, stockouts reports
Quality and safety	Device reliability	The reliability of medical devices in terms of uptime and failure rates, ensuring consistent performance.	Failure rate analysis, uptime tracking
	Compliance with regulatory standards	Adherence to regulatory requirements and standards for medical device safety and performance.	Regulatory audit results, compliance reports
	Adverse events	The number and severity of adverse events related to medical device usage, impacting patient safety.	Incident reports, adverse event tracking
Financial performance	Cost per procedure	The average cost incurred per procedure involving medical devices, including maintenance and depreciation costs.	Procedure cost analysis, financial records
	Return on investment (ROI)	The financial return achieved from investments in medical devices, considering costs and revenue generated.	ROI calculations, financial reports
Patient experience	Device effectiveness	The effectiveness of medical devices in achieving desired patient outcomes and satisfaction.	Patient outcome assessments, satisfaction surveys
	Waiting time for device usage	The average waiting time patients experience before receiving care involving specific medical devices.	Patient wait time records, process time tracking
Environmental impact	Energy efficiency	The energy consumption of medical devices and efforts to minimize environmental impact through efficiency measures.	Energy usage data, efficiency improvements
	Waste management	The management of medical device-related waste, ensuring proper disposal and recycling practices.	Waste disposal records, recycling metrics

Table 8 Types and expected levels of costs of personalized medicine

	Hospital Facilities	Patients	Healthcare Service Providers	Payers
Health Costs				
Genomic Sequencing and Analysis				
Personalized Treatment Plans				
Medical Devices for Personalized Treatments				
Advanced Diagnostics and Treatment Services				
Coverage for Genetic Testing and Treatments				
Regular Monitoring and Follow-ups				
Coverage for Medical Devices				
Non-Health Costs				
IT Infrastructure and Data Security				
Staff Training and Development				
Administrative and Integration Costs				
Insurance Premiums and Out-of-Pocket Expenses				
Time and Travel				
Policy Development and Implementation				
Data Management and Security				

The different shades of grey indicate the level of costs: from dark (high) to light (moderate)

stakeholder. Synthesizing the different perspectives on all the economic dimensions of AI-based solutions,[32] Table 8 reports the expected levels of health and non-health costs.

[32] Among others, Kasztura (2019); Jiang et al. (2017); Gavan et al. 2018; Vellekoop et al. (2022); Khanna (2022) discuss the expected costs of personalized medicine. Table 8 is based on this literature. See also Shabaruddin et al. (2015).

5.5 A Check List for Performing HTAs on Personalized Medicine Solutions

Following is an initial list of questions that should be considered when performing health technology assessments on personalized healthcare services. Answering these questions should help technology and healthcare service developers, as well as HTA experts to: identify the stakeholders involved; overcome constraints and barriers to adopting, spreading, and receiving reimbursements for health technologies; and choose the impacts worth assessing.

(1) Which types of technologies are embedded in healthcare solutions?
(2) Which types of services are involved?
(3) Which elements of personalized medicine are integrated: profiling? diagnosis? monitoring? treatment?
(4) Where are the sources of heterogeneity in the technological solutions offered and the and patient characteristics observed?
(5) What differences exist between the degree to which the involved technologies are personalized and the related healthcare services?
(6) Who are the primary and secondary stakeholders involved in profiling, monitoring, delivering, and receiving personalized treatment/training?

For each identified stakeholder:

(7) What is the role of the stakeholder?
(8) What value does the stakeholder associate with the technology and related services? This not only includes any improvement or positive impact of the personalized solutions beyond the current scenario, but also the stakeholder's willingness to pay for this improvement.
(9) What factors drive or limit the stakeholder's actions in achieving their specific objectives? For example, the primary objective of a patient might be to improve their state of their health, whereas a hospital might be aiming to provide sustainable healthcare services while achieving a positive balance between costs and reimbursements. Technology developers and service providers often seek to generate returns sufficient to compensate for their investments in technology and personalized services, while healthcare systems generally strive to enhance the overall health and quality of life of their citizens by increasing access to care without compromising on essential quality standards or exceeding their resource constraints.
(10) Which other stakeholders drive or limit each player's ability to achieve their objectives?
(11) How do the identified factors that limit or drive the stakeholder's actions increase or reduce the value of the proposed solution from the stakeholder's perspective?

Questions 1–4 define the level to which the services are personalized. The answers to questions 7–11 need to be formulated in terms of variables, i.e., a list of dimensions from each identified perspective that must be unambiguously defined to determine how to measure them.

For example, let us consider the value of personalized medicine from the perspective of a healthcare professional, a patient, and a hospital facility.

From the perspective of a patient, the value produced by a personalized solution refers to the increase in quality of life due to the lack of side effects or reduced pain. In general, patient reported outcome measures and patient reported experience measures[33] depend on how the healthcare service is organized. Additionally, in terms of costs, a patient is also interested in how the new solution reduces out-of-pocket expenses. Alternatively, healthcare professionals tend to assess personalized solutions in terms of clinical outcomes and the improvements the solution makes to their work, while hospitals are generally more interested in how a personalized solution reduces the patient's length of stay, the average unit costs for treating each patient, and the difference the treatment makes to the organization's key performance indicators.

Identifying and understanding the stakeholders' underlying needs and priorities and distinguishing between positions and interests, however, may trigger opposite or conflicting interests. To resolve these conflicts, managers must build strong relationships and maintain regular engagement. Additionally, practice cultures must support open communication to ensure transparency and foster trust. Neutral mediators can help with this when circumstances demand. Teams must focus on common goals and emphasize the bigger picture to align stakeholders around shared objectives. Collaborative problem-solving and brainstorming win-win solutions coupled with decision-making frameworks like consensus-building or weighted matrices for fair evaluations can help in this regard. Moreover, initiatives like this are more likely to be successful when the desire to reach a common agreement that overcomes conflicts takes precedence over the individual interests of stakeholders. This dynamic is driven more by political considerations than economic ones, as it demands a shared vision, effective mediation, and a collective commitment to prioritize the common good over personal agendas.

6 Conclusions

Personalized medicine represents a transformative approach to healthcare, where medical treatments and interventions are tailored to individual genetic, environmental, and lifestyle factors. However, taking a personalized medical approach often raises some significant economic and organizational implications that require careful consideration.

A primary concern is often the cost-effectiveness of personalized medicine. While targeted therapies and diagnostics can potentially improve outcomes and reduce long-term healthcare costs by preventing ineffective treatments, initial costs

[33] See Benson (2020).

such as genetic testing and specialized treatments can be substantial. Assessing economic impacts involves comparing these upfront costs with the potential long-term savings from reduced hospitalizations and complications.

The complexity of personalized medicine can also pose challenges in terms of market access and reimbursement. Pharmaceutical companies and medical device manufacturers often find it difficult to charge full price for novel, personalized treatments given the need to demonstrate both clinical and economic efficiency. Evaluating these impacts requires understanding the regulatory landscape and payer perspectives. Yet reimbursement is not the only criteria to consider when thinking about taking a personalized medical approach. Turchetti et al. discuss why health technologies, such as robotic-mediated rehabilitation, do not suffice on their own for use in clinical practice.[34] Acceptability, usability, ethical and legal organizational barriers may all reduce the effectiveness of personalized medicine. As a multidimensional, multistakeholder approach, HTAs can identify which factors, conditions, and even stakeholders drive or limit the capability of modern healthcare systems to overcome technological, cultural, and organizational barriers to market.

Personalized medicine also demands shifts in healthcare delivery models. Hospitals and clinics must integrate advanced diagnostic technologies, genomic data analysis, and specialized personnel trained in interpreting genetic information.

This organizational change requires investments in infrastructure, staff training, and IT systems and platforms capable of managing and analyzing large datasets. In terms of personalized drug therapies, assessing impact involves evaluating improvements in treatment efficacy, reduced adverse reactions, and overall patient outcomes compared to standard treatments.

Personalized medical devices also need to be underpinned by novel metrics—metrics capable of assessing the effectiveness and cost of personalized treatments, how well patients are sticking to their treatment plans, and whether the devices are generally being accepted and used. Lastly, from an industrial perspective, assessing the sustainability of personalized medicine means, among other things, analyzing R&D costs, potential market share gains, and returns on investment.

In conclusion, while personalized medicine holds promise for improving patient care and outcomes, its economic and organizational implications are complex and multifaceted. Successful adoption requires careful assessment of cost-effectiveness, market dynamics, regulatory challenges, and organizational readiness. By understanding and addressing these issues proactively, stakeholders can face the complexities involved and improve the potential benefits of personalized medicine while ensuring sustainable healthcare delivery.

Since personalized solutions involve a system of various devices, technologies, algorithms, and interacting stakeholders (not only healthcare professionals and patients but also payers, technology providers, monitoring and regulatory

---

[34] Turchetti et al. (2014), pp. 147–148.

institutions, etc.), their implementation and impact should be regarded as a health system transformation rather than as a discrete set of technological tools.[35]

Acknowledgement This research was financially supported by the "Biorobotics Research and Innovation Engineering Facilities" "IR0000036" – CUP J13C22000400007 (BRIEF) project. The authors would like to thank Federica Casarosa, Francesca Gennari, and Arianna Rossi for their relevant comments, which have greatly contributed to improving their work.

Disclosure of Interests The authors have no competing interests to declare that are relevant to the content of this chapter.

References

Alami H, Lehoux P, Auclair Y, de Guise M, Gagnon MP, Shaw J et al (2020) Artificial intelligence and health technology assessment: anticipating a new level of complexity. J Med Internet Res 22(7):e17707

Alyass A, Turcotte M, Meyre D (2015) From big data analysis to personalized medicine for all: challenges and opportunities. BMC Med Genomics 8(33) https://doi.org/10.1186/s12920-015-0108-y

Arthur WB (1989) Competing technologies, increasing returns, and lock-in by historical events. Econ J 99(394):116–131

Belle A, Thiagarajan R, Soroushmehr SM, Navidi F, Beard DA, Najarian K (2015) Big data analytics in healthcare. Biomed Res Int. 2015:370194

Benson T (2020) Measure what we want: a taxonomy of short generic person-reported outcome an experience measures (PROMs and PREMs). BMJ Open Quality 9:e000789

Brenner M, Weir A, McCann M, Doyle C, Hughes M, Moen A, Ingvar M, Nauwelaerts K, Turk E, McCabe C (2023) Development of the key performance indicators for digital health interventions: a scoping review. Digit Health 22(9). https://doi.org/10.1177/20552076231152160. PMID: 36714542; PMCID: PMC9880566

Bresnahan TF, Greenstein S (1999) Technological competition and the structure of the computer industry. J Ind Econ 47(1):1–40

Brynjolfsson E, Hitt LM (2000) Beyond computation: information technology, organizational transformation and business performance. J Econ Persp 14(4):23–48

Burlea-Schiopoiu A, Ferhati K (2020) The managerial implications of the key performance indicators in healthcare sector: a cluster analysis. Healthcare 25;9(1):19. https://doi.org/10.3390/healthcare9010019. PMID: 33375693; PMCID: PMC7823544.

Cannizzo S, Lorenzoni V, Palla I, Pirri S, Trieste L, Triulzi I, Turchetti G. (2018) Rare diseases under different levels of economic analysis: current activities, challenges and perspectives. RMD Open. 4(Suppl 1): e000794

Challen R, Denny J, Pitt M, Gompels L, Edwards T, Tsaneva-Atanasova K (2019) Artificial intelligence, bias, and clinical safety. BMJ Quality Saf 28(3):231–237

Collins FS, Varmus H (2015) A new initiative on precision medicine. New England J Med 372(9):793–795

David PA (1985) Clio and the economics of QWERTY. Am Econ Rev 75(2):332–337

Economides N (1996) Network externalities, complementarities, and invitations to enter. Eur J Polit Econ 12(2):211–233

[35] See Alami et al. (2020).

Economides N, Katsamakas E (2006) Two-sided competition of proprietary vs. open source technology platforms and the implications for the software industry. Manage Sci 52(7):1057–1071

Evans DS, Schmalensee R (2016) The antitrust analysis of multi-sided platform businesses. Yale J Regul 33(2):417–514

Ezrachi A, Stucke ME (2016) Virtual competition: the promise and perils of the algorithm-driven economy. Harvard University Press, Cambridge

Formea CM, Nicholson WT, Vitek CR (2015) An inter-professional approach to personalized medicine education: one institution's experience. Per Med Mar 12(2):129–138

Freidlin B, Korn EL, George SL, Gray R (2010) Randomized clinical trials with biomarkers: design issues. J Natl Cancer Inst 102(3):152–160

Garrison LP Jr, Neumann PJ, Erickson P, Marshall D, Mullins CD (2007) Using real-world data for coverage and payment decisions: The ISPOR Real-World Data Task Force Report. Value in Health 10(5):326–335

Gavan SP, Thompson AJ, Payne K (2018) The economic case for precision medicine. Exp Rev Precis Med Drug Dev 8;3(1):1–9

Gawer A (2009) Platform dynamics and strategies: from products to services. In: Gawer A (ed) Platforms, markets and innovation. Edward Elgar Publishing, pp 45–62

Gawer A, Cusumano MA (2002) Platform leadership: how Intel, Microsoft, and cisco drive industry innovation. Harvard Business Review Press, Cambridge

Goetz LH, Schork NJ (2018) Personalized medicine: motivation, challenges, and progress. Fertil Steril 109(6):952–963

Green ED, Guyer MS (2011) Charting a course for genomic medicine from base pairs to bedside. Nature 470(7333):204–213

Hagiu A, Wright J (2020) Multi-sided platforms. Ann Rev Econ 12:243–268

Hejblum BP, Skinner J, Thiebaut R (2015) Time-course gene set analysis for longitudinal gene expression data. PLoS Comput Biol 11(6):e1004310

Hickmann E, Richter P, Schlieter H (2022) All together now – patient engagement, patient empowerment, and associated terms in personal healthcare. BMC Health Serv Res 22(1116)

Hrebiniak LG, Joyce WF (1984) Implementing strategy: the role of structural change. Columb J World Bus 19(2):27–41

Jiang F, Jiang Y, Zhi H, Dong Y, Li H, Ma S, Wang Y et al (2017) Artificial intelligence in healthcare: past, present and future. Stroke Vasc Neurol 2(4):230–243

Johnson AK, Choi SW (2022) Stakeholder engagement, proper planning and modular design for mHealth apps: lessons from Quest Explore and working toward standards for mHealth app design. Mhealth 8(29):1–4

Kaplan RS, Norton DP (1996) Using the balanced scorecard as a strategic management system. Harv Bus Rev 74(1):75–85

Kasoju N, Remya NS, Sasi R, Sujesh S, Soman B, Kesavadas C et al (2023) Digital health: trends, opportunities and challenges in medical devices, pharma and bio-technology. CSIT 11(1):11–30

Kasztura M, Richard A, Bempong NE, Loncar D, Flahault A (2019) Cost-effectiveness of precision medicine: a scoping review. Int J Public Health 64(9):1261–1271

Katz ML, Shapiro C (1994) Systems competition and network effects. J Econ Persp 8(2):93–115

Khanna NN, Maindarkar MA, Viswanathan V, Fernandes JFE, Paul S, Bhagawati M, Ahluwalia P, et al (2022) Economics of artificial intelligence in healthcare: diagnosis vs. treatment. Healthcare 9;10(12):2493. https://doi.org/10.3390/healthcare10122493. PMID: 36554017; PMCID: PMC9777836

Kingsley C, Patel S (2017) Patient-reported outcome measures and patient-reported experience measures. BJA Educ 17(4):137–144

Lowry V, Tremblay-Vaillancourt V, Beaupré P et al (2024) How patient-reported outcomes and experience measures (PROMs and PREMs) are implemented in healthcare professional and patient organizations? An environmental scan. J Patient Rep Outcomes 8(133)

Lu CY, Terry V, Thomas DM (2023) Precision medicine: affording the successes of science. NPJ Precis Onc 7(3):1–8

Lunshof JE, Chadwick R, Vorhaus DB, Church GM (2008) From genetic privacy to open consent. Nat Rev Genet 9(5):406–411

Lynch RL, Cross KF (1991) Measure up!:Yardsticks for continuous improvement. Blackwell, Oxford

Manyika J, Chui M, Bisson P, Woetzel J, Dobbs R, Bughin J et al (2016) Digital America: a tale of the haves and have-mores. McKinsey Global Institute

Marr B (2015) Key performance indicators: the 75 measures every manager needs to know. Financial Time Press, Upper Saddle River (NJ)

Molla G, Bitew M (2024) Revolutionizing personalized medicine: synergy with multi-omics data generation, main hurdles, and future perspectives. Biomedicines 12(12):2750. https://doi.org/10.3390/biomedicines12122750

National Academies of Sciences, Engineering, and Medicine; Health and Medicine Division; Board on Health Care Services; Board on the Health of Select Populations; Committee on the Evidence Base for Genetic Testing (2017) An Evidence Framework for Genetic Testing. National Academies Press (US), Washington, DC

Neely A, Adams C, Kennerley M (2002) The performance prism: the scorecard for measuring and managing business success. Prentice Hall Financial Times, London

O'Rourke B, Oortwijn W, Schuller T (2020) The new definition of health technology assessment: a milestone in international collaboration. Int J Technol Assessment Health Care 36(3):187–190

Parker G, Van Alstyne MW, Choudary SP (2016) Platform revolution: how networked markets are transforming the economy—and how to make them work for you. W.W. Norton & Company, New York

Parmenter D (2015) Key performance indicators (KPI): developing, implementing, and using winning KPIs. Wiley, New York

Pecchia L, Craven MP (2013) Early stage health technology assessment (HTA) of biomedical devices: the MATCH experience. In: Long M (ed) World Congress on Medical Physics and Biomedical Engineering, Beijing, China 26–31 May, 2012

Personalized Medicine Coalition (2014) The Case for Personalized Medicine, 4th edn. Retrieved from https://www.personalizedmedicinecoalition.org/Userfiles/PMC-Corporate/file/pmc_the_case_for_personalized_medicine.pdf

Ramspek CL, Jager KJ, Dekker FW, Zoccali C, van Diepen M (2021) External validation of prognostic models: what, why, how, when and where? Clin Kidney J 14(1):49–58

Redaelli T, Moro S, Corica G, Garbelli C, Traversi E (2019) Percorsi diagnostico terapeutici assistenziali anche riabilitativi o riabilitazione "da scarico"? [Diagnostic and therapeutic therapeutic pathways, including rehabilitative ones or only "discharge" rehabilitation?]. G Ital Med Lav Ergon 41(2):105–111

Reza Soroushmehr SM, Najarian K (2016) Transforming big data into computational models for personalized medicine and health care. Dialogues Clin Neurosci 18(3):339–343

Rochet JC, Tirole J (2003) Platform competition in two-sided markets. J Eur Econ Assoc 1(4):990–1029

Rubin DB, van der Laan MJ (2018) Statistical issues and limitations in personalized medicine research with clinical trials. Int J Biostat 20(8):18

Rudolph C, Petersen GS, Pritzkuleit R et al (2019) The acceptance and applicability of a patient-reported experience measurement tool in oncological care: a descriptive feasibility study in northern Germany. BMC Health Serv Res 19(786):1–13

Rysman M (2009) The economics of two-sided markets. J Econ Persp 23(3):125–143

Schleidgen S, Klingler C, Bertram T, Rogowski WH, Marckmann G (2013) What is personalized medicine: sharpening a vague term based on a systematic literature review. BMC Med Ethics 14(1):55

Shabaruddin FH, Fleeman ND, Payne K (2015) Economic evaluations of personalized medicine: existing challenges and current developments. Pharmgenomics Pers Med 8:115–126. https://doi.org/10.2147/PGPM.S35063. PMID: 26309416; PMCID: PMC4538689

Topol EJ (2019) Deep medicine: how artificial intelligence can make healthcare human again. Hachette Books, New York

Trosman JR, Van Bebber SL, Phillips KA (2011) Health technology assessment and private payers' coverage of personalized medicine. J Oncol Pract 7(3_suppl):18s–24s

Turchetti G, Vitiello N, Trieste L, Romiti S, Geisler E, Micera S (2014) Why effectiveness of robot-mediated neurorehabilitation does not necessarily influence its adoption. IEEE Rev Biomed Eng 7:143–153

Vellekoop H, Versteegh M, Huygens S, Corro Ramos I, Szilberhorn L, Zelei T et al (2022) The net benefit of personalized medicine: a systematic literature review and regression analysis. Value Health 25(8):1428–1438. https://doi.org/10.1016/j.jval.2022.01.006. Epub 2022 Mar 2. PMID: 35248467

Verma M (2012) Personalized medicine and cancer. J Pers Med 30; 2(1):1–14. https://doi.org/10.3390/jpm2010001. PMID: 25562699; PMCID: PMC4251363

Wolf SM, Crock BN, Van Ness B, Lawrenz F, Kahn JP, Beskow et al (2012) Managing incidental findings and research results in genomic research involving biobanks and archived datasets. Genet Med 14(4):361–384

Xu X, Hu J, Lyu X, Huang H, Cheng X (2021) Exploring the interdisciplinary nature of precision medicine: network analysis and visualization. JMIR Med Inform 9(1):e23562

Yeung AWK, Torkamani A, Butte AJ, Glicksberg BS, Schuller B, Rodriguez B, et al. (2023) The promise of digital healthcare technologies. Front Public Health 11:1196596. doi: https://doi.org/10.3389/fpubh.2023.1196596. PMID: 37822534; PMCID: PMC10562722.

New Perspectives in Research and Development for Patients and Caregivers: The Challenges of Digital Health Competencies in Europe for Personalized Medicine

Sabrina Grigolo, Renza Barbon Galluppi, and Milena Sirtori

Abstract The European Health Data Space is an opportunity to promote the sharing of health data across borders. In turn, this should enable more personalized diagnoses, more innovative medical treatments, and more digital technologies to improve our health. However, any policies to share health data need to contain strong legal safeguards that not only ensure the security of the data but also ensure that the people managing these digital therapies—patients and caregivers as well as practitioners—are equipped with the appropriate skills. The already well-known Digital Competence Framework for Citizens (DigComp) has provided a common understanding across the EU and beyond of what digital competence is. One of the aims of this framework is to describe the perspectives of patients and caregivers to those involved in the R&D associated with digital health, personalized medicine, and rehabilitation therapies. This chapter therefore provides a review of the contexts in which patients are actively involved in administering healthcare. The key themes covered include: digital education, digital skills, preventing cyber and physical risk, the factors mediating digital competency, and the daily impact of digital therapies. In addition, we identify the current challenges in personalized medicine and define the needs of patients and caregivers in response. Overall, we find the "digital transformation" in health requires a cultural approach that can empower all those involved, from the patients, caregivers, and their families to practitioners and politicians. Digital skills for health are not optional; they are a necessary requirement for a conscious process of improving everyone's quality of life. Hence, following the "All Digital Weeks" held annually in Italy, we advocate for a Digital Health Literacy Space at the national and European levels.

S. Grigolo (✉) • M. Sirtori
Patient Expert EUPATI, Rome, Italy
e-mail: sabrina.grigolo@unito.it

R. B. Galluppi
Associazione Rete Malattie Rare, Venice, Italy

F. Casarosa et al. (eds.), *Enabling and Safeguarding Personalized Medicine*,
Data Science, Machine Intelligence, and Law 7,
https://doi.org/10.1007/978-3-031-99709-9_10

1 Introduction

Digital health and care refers to the tools and services that use information and communication technologies to prevent, diagnose, treat, monitor, and manage health-related issues. This also includes therapies that monitor and manage the lifestyle habits impacting health.[1] Digital medicine is a subset of digital health, comprising any software and hardware built on clinical evidence that measures and/or intervenes in the service of human health.[2] Although the term digital health is often used to refer to well-being and digital medicine to illness, in this chapter, we use these terms interchangeably as a way of referring to the singular concept of health.

Today, digital medicine is presenting important opportunities for patients and healthcare professionals to communicate and share choices about healthcare decisions, both face-to-face and remotely. Thanks to technology, people are increasingly leaving a digital footprint as they go about their daily lives. Consequently, enormous quantities of data are being collected that provide evidence of one's lifestyle and numerous applications are leveraging this data to benefit our general health. However, with this in mind, we need to ask ourselves some questions: Today, are digital skills for citizens' health still optional? Or have they become a necessary requirement?

In Europe at least, we can unequivocally say that having digital skills is an essential requirement for many activities. In fact, Alldigital EU, and international non-profit association based in Belgium, runs an annual campaign called "Alldigital Skills" that aims to train EU citizens in the digital skills for needed for living life. In terms of health, as another example, Mission 6 of Italy's National Recovery and Resilience Plan (PNRR) has sought to strengthen its National Health System in response to COVID-19 through new applications of telemedicine, tele-rehabilitation, and tele-assistance. Additionally, remote monitoring of therapeutic treatments, including vital signs, physiological, and lifestyle-related parameters are now implementable realities, made possible by advances in sensors, the Internet of Things (IoT) and the widespread diffusion of connectivity. Thus, most of Europe's citizens are "always on", i.e., always connected to the internet no matter where they go.

The purpose of this chapter is to represent the position of the patient and caregiver cohorts that are experts in digital health technologies. Today, patients and caregivers need to acquire specific skills to be able to use digital health technologies in line with DigComp 2.2.[3] Moreover, being digitally competent is not just about having IT skills, but also about a growing awareness of managing one's own data and how to access health services and health information. Critical thinking, therefore, becomes one of the foundations for creating empowerment in healthcare. This perspective is not representative of the entire broader community of patients and caregivers, but it certainly represents an important and useful point of observation for improving the quality of healthcare services in general.

---

[1] EU COM (2018), pp. 11–12.

[2] Recchia (2021), p. 6.

[3] Vuorikari et al. (2022), pp. 3–5.

2 The Italian Contest on Digital Field

According to a report on the state of the "Digital Decade",[4] Italy has untapped potential to contribute further to Europe's collective efforts to meet the Union's Digital Decade targets. Given the size of the Italian economy and its population, these efforts could significantly contribute to increasing the digital skills of Europe's citizens. Notably, Italy has made significant advances to its digital infrastructure in recent years, but still performs below the EU average in terms of skills and digitalizing some of its public services. The strategies adopted involving cloud technologies, blockchain, AI, and more recently cybersecurity, together with numerous reforms and substantial investments made under the nation's Resilience and Recovery Plan (PNRR), create a solid framework for achieving a sustainable and inclusive digital transformation.[5]

Yet, in terms of digital skills, Italy's progress remains slow, contributing only modestly to the Digital Decade target. For example, only 46% of the population have basic digital skills. This undermines their capacity to benefit from digital opportunities and to exercise their digital citizenship. It also has a negative impact on Italy's inclusiveness. However, although the government recognizes developing new skills and updating job profiles as a priority, too few enterprises are actually offering training to their employees. Additionally, at 1.5% of all graduates, the number of IT graduates in Italy not only remains significantly below the ambitions set out in the Digital Decade plan and the EU average of 4.2%, but also the country is not even able to meet its own demand for qualified professionals. Further, these numbers prevail despite newly expanded and flexible training offers focusing on STEM. The share of women among IT specialists is also low at 16%, well below the EU average of 18.9% as are Italy's scores in providing digital public services for its citizens (68 for Italy vs. 77 for Europe) and for businesses (75 vs. 84).

Despite Italy's sluggish performance in recent years, the government has been exerting increased effort in: the availability, efficiency, and security of digital infrastructure; the interoperability of data and information across public administrations; implementing the once-only principle; increasing its use of digital identities; and finalizing a national system for electronic health records. Recent measures taken to ensure more user-centric public services, and to improve the accessibility of the digital public services there already are, are likely to further encourage the public to "go digital". According to the National Institute of Statistics of Italy (ISTAT), one of the objectives of the European program is to increase the share of 16–74 year-olds with at least basic digital skills to 80% by 2030.[6] As of 2023, only 45.9% of adults had adequate skills; over a third (36.1%) had insufficient skills; and 5.1%, despite being Internet users, had no skills at all. In the European panorama, these

[4] The second annual report on the State of the Digital Decade (2024) https://digital-strategy.ec.europa.eu/en/library/report-state-digital-decade-2024.

[5] EU (2023), p. 18.

[6] Across the five domains defined by the current Digital Skills Reference Framework.

statistics place Italy among the lowest scoring countries, with a distance from the EU27 average of almost 10 percentage points.

In Italy, as is the case in other European countries, digital skills are associated with the socio-cultural characteristics of the population. In particular, in Italy, 59.1% of young people between 16 and 24 years old have at least basic skills compared to just 19.4% of adults between 65 and 74 years old. The distance between young people and the elderly is in line with the European average, but Italy has values significantly lower than the EU27 in all age groups.

The large amount of data that Italy's health system produces today could be managed more effectively and more efficiently thanks to the development of new products and services.

At the moment, as regards digital technologies for health, only telemedicine is regulated, all other National Health Service (SSN) data in particular are subject to Italian privacy regulations. The application of the new European regulation will promote data interoperability aimed to improve the quality of life. Interoperable data deriving from information flows of different dimensions, such as health, assistance, socio-health and social care, the environment, epidemiological and disease registers for safe economic sustainability. Assistance refers to the full range of healthcare and social care services provided to citizens, including preventive, diagnostic, therapeutic, rehabilitative, and palliative care. Environmental data can be correlated with health data because they help to understand and prevent diseases and contribute to an integrated vision of health (the 'One Health' approach). The environment also impacts rehabilitation, patients' quality of life, and the logistics and sustainability of healthcare services. Healthcare services provided by the National Health Service (SSN), delivered by doctors, nurses, healthcare professionals, and both public and accredited facilities.

Therefore, the challenge is to try to correlate research, care, environment, quality of life and sustainability in order to unify the information collected for different purposes. The information generated by the patients themselves is added to the data produced directly by the healthcare system.

For example, people are increasingly managing their own health proactively through monitoring and information apps on smartphones. These data constitute an incredibly valuable medical history that institutions could draw on to not only improve treatment plans but also the quality of healthcare services. For example, increased data sharing should allow for far more cohesive healthcare systems that are better able to respond to the needs of patients, their caregivers, and their families. Heath systems will also benefit from more innovative models that bring together the perspectives of different segments of society, including academia, business, public administrations, and civil society. Overall, we should also see a more effective process of empowerment based active participation by more communities.

More effective use of data, from a legal, ethical and regulatory perspective, will only support the opportunities offered by new digital technologies in promoting better coordination of care between providers and the social/health services sector. First, services can be more easily and more effectively updated, inevitably conditioned by scientific and technological progress. Second, technologies and products can be developed based on diverse empirical data that guarantee high-value healthcare services and services to all citizens.

Yet, in order to understand the impact of digital tools on daily life, it is necessary to define the contexts in which digital medicine fits. These contexts comprise the living environments of the patients, caregivers, and families, plus the doctor's profession. We therefore propose a care relationship model that combines the 'world' of families, patients, and caregivers, the 'world' of healthcare workers, professionals, scientists and researchers. Here, the realm of those receiving care is characterized by an experiential knowledge derived from living with a disease in everyday life, whereas the realm of the care deliverers is characterized by scientific knowledge acquired from books and in-field training. We argue that only together can these two perspectives identify and develop therapies and care paths that guarantee full autonomy to sick people and their caregivers.

Today the patient and the caregiver no longer play a passive role in care. Rather, they are increasingly sharing in healthcare decisions and administering therapies. These are signs of a change in how a person's fundamental right to self-determination are being expressed. No longer merely identified as fragile subjects whose health is to be protected, patients and caregivers can now be true agents of change, responsible for their own care. However, all this transformation demands new skills, including digital ones for both medical professionals as well as patients, caregivers, and citizens.

3 Digital Literacy in Health: Temporary Need or Permanent Requirement?

The realm of digital health is not yet served by a standard lexicon, and the many disciplines and fields that it comprises, such as education, employment, and so on, are often divided by their own particular jargon. Within the large and complex category of digital health technologies, there are hundreds of thousands of apps and services that, en masse, serve a diverse range of purposes, from diagnosis to monitoring clinical conditions to supporting doctors' decisions, to interventions against a disease.[7] The main critical success factors of digital technologies are:[8]

- The "centrality of the care relationship" as a new paradigm for how the actors of a system interact;
- The "culture of data and its value" as a clear, shared, transparent concept between all actors and at different levels of management;
- "digital skills" as a continuous stream of learning and development for all actors, including the identification of new roles;

[7] Gussoni (2021), p. 6.

[8] Santarelli and Di Carlo (2013), p. 34.

- "financial investments" as an integrated and convergent strategy for the "conceptual and technological" transformation of a new interoperable system that allows the widespread diffusion of digital tools, ease of access, and equity;
- "governance" through a holistic and systemic vision of e-health in which the enormous potential of new technologies is integrated into a new design for the engagement process.

The foundations of health's "digital transformation" are mainly cultural. Further, this process involves many parties: patients, caregivers, families, society in a broad sense, healthcare professionals, NGOs, institutions, private companies, and politicians. However, many healthcare workers, institutions, and politicians do not seem to be aware that all these actors need to operate within a process that supports "organizational empowerment". As defined by Wallerstein, organizational empowerment refers to the capacity of groups/organizations to build transparency, share power, and collaborate when making decisions. It concerns how effective an organization is at exerting social and political influence over a community or over society in general. Within these groups, people not only gain skills and capacities, they facilitate bonds of belonging and social identity as they develop a sense of trust and community. As mediating structures of social relations, groups and organizations can offer emotional, material, cognitive, and informational support, in addition to being part of a social network that enables knowledge, resource sharing, and the mutual strengthening of capacities.[9]

Redefining the concept of health and care requires making a profound interconnection between scientific and experiential knowledge. This creates an all-encompassing, circular system in which true innovation binds the relationships between the parties as a cohesive element of each interlocutor, with the patient first and foremost. Here, technology provides a perspective of care that enhances a patient's history in a way that can help to overcome the biomedical paradigm still present in healthcare realities today. There is therefore a collective need to guarantee forms of digital healthcare that are guided by the human touch and that can generate multidisciplinary value. Additionally, digital health systems must be able to communicate in an interoperable way, facilitating the movement of data rather than moving patients and their families. A "digitally-oriented" data culture, investments into infrastructure, and training for healthcare personnel and patients all represent the fundamental axes of a sustainable and democratic digital health system. Moreover, by undertaking usability tests, we, as a society, should be able to reduce the digital divide, offering opportunities for a true healthcare democracy. To this end, the process of defining policies in digital health will have to take some essential factors into account, including:[10]

(a) Guaranteeing that digital technologies will be used effectively, safely, and only for their intended purposes;

[9] Wallerstein (2006); ICPHR (2021).

[10] Flowers et al. (2024), p. 2.

(b) Providing an authorization path for specific therapeutic indications through regulatory agencies;
(c) Protecting equity and universalism by eliminating the factors of discrimination and inequality;
(d) Engaging expert patients in R&D from the onset of co-design through to drafting informed consent; and
(e) Ensuring that innovative digital therapies are accessible to all patients and caregivers so as to reduce the gap between research and practical use.

Lastly, digital health literacy is a permanent structural requirement in a real-world healthcare democracy as without the right competencies, any systems built will likely fail.

4 Digital Skills for Patients and Caregivers

According to the Digital Literacy Taskforce of the American Library Association (2011), digital literacy is "the ability to use information and communications technologies (ICT) to find, evaluate, create, and communicate information. This requires both cognitive and technical skills." Digital literacy, as applied to medicine, is defined as "e-health literacy" or the ability to search, find, understand and evaluate health information obtained from the use of information technologies and apply the knowledge acquired to address or solve a health problem. Digital literacy, and consequently e-health literacy, are therefore fundamental tools for allowing individuals—and patients and caregivers in particular—to not only benefit from the advantages of digital medicine but to also effectively access health services within modern digital medicine frameworks.

The European Health Data Space (EHDS) is a health-specific ecosystem comprised of rules, common standards and practices, infrastructures, and a governance framework. The aims of building this ecosystem are to: (1) empower individuals through increased digital access to and control of their electronic personal health data; (2) foster a single market for electronic health records, relevant medical devices, and high-risk AI systems; and (3) provide a trustworthy and efficient framework for using health data for research, innovation, policy-making and regulatory activities.[11] Here, digital health literacy is an important strategy in reaching the first objective. As a baseline, DigComp 2.2[12] is the reference framework designated by the European Commission for establishing the digital skills that citizens must possess to actively adjust to the technological changes taking place inside and outside the EU. The framework states citizens must:

[11] https://www.european-health-data-space.com/.

[12] Vuorikari et al. (2022), pp. 3–5.

- know and understand the use of digital equipment (PCs, mice, keyboards, tablets or smartphones, touchscreens, cameras, thumb drives, etc.). This includes a computer's operating system and its software;
- know how to navigate the internet and search and filter information using the main web browsers and search engines;
- know what digital data are, what formats exist, and how to view their contents to access information;
- know how to manage digital identities (i.e., how to create and store passwords);
- know how to evaluate the terms, conditions, and privacy rules set by IT service providers.

A patient with knowledge and skills in the use of digital resources is a patient with the ability to make decisions, satisfy needs, and solve problems. As such, they are likely to demonstrate critical thinking and exert greater control over their health.

Digital skills for work and for life are at the top of the European Policy Agenda.[13] The EU digital skills strategy and related policy initiatives aim to equip its citizens with the skills and competencies needed to successfully navigate today's digital transformation. For example, the European Skills Agenda of 1 July 2020 supports digital skills for all, including by supporting the objectives of the Digital Education Action Plan. It aims to "enhance digital skills and competencies for digital transformation", while also fostering the development of a high-performing digital education system.[14] Similarly, the Digital Compass and the European Pillar of Social Rights Action Plan both set the ambitious policy targets of reaching a minimum of 80% of the population with basic digital skills and having 20 million IT specialists by 2030.[15] Additionally, digital competence is one of the "key competencies for lifelong learning". First defined in 2006, the European Council's "Recommendation on Key Competences for Life-long Learning" was since updated in 2018. It now reads as follows:[16]

> Digital competence involves the confident, critical and responsible use of, and engagement with, digital technologies for learning, at work, and for participation in society. It includes information and data literacy, communication and collaboration, media literacy, digital content creation (including programming), safety (including digital well-being and competencies related to cybersecurity), intellectual property-related questions, problem-solving and critical thinking.

As we know, competencies are a combination of knowledge, skills, and attitudes. In other words, they are composed of concepts and facts, i.e., knowledge, skills, e.g., the ability to carry out processes, and attitudes, e.g., a disposition, a mindset to act. "Key" competencies are developed throughout life. Work on operationalizing digital competencies, following the 2006 Council Recommendation[17], started in 2010.

[13] Ibid.

[14] Ibid.

[15] Ibid.

[16] Council Recommendation on Key Competences for Life- long Learning, 201.

[17] Ibid.

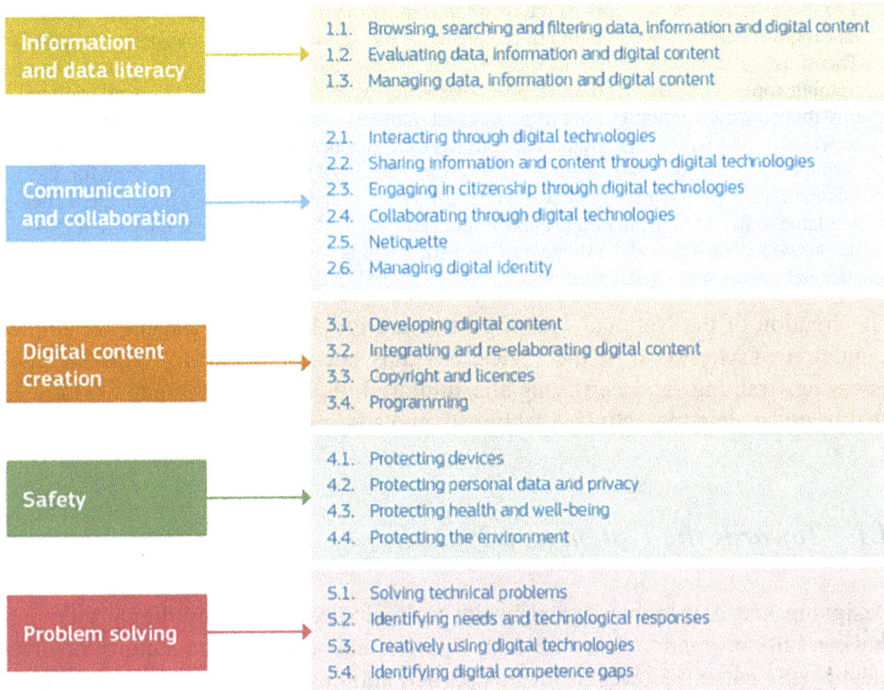

Fig. 1 The DigiComp reference model illustrates the digital competences organized in information and data literacy; communication and collaboration; digital content creation; safety; problem-solving

In 2013, the first DigComp reference framework came out defining digital competence as a combination of 21 competencies grouped into five main areas (see Fig. 1). Since 2016, these five main areas have comprised: information and data literacy, communication and collaboration, digital content creation, safety, and problem-solving.[18] The last update of DigComp 2.2 focuses on "examples of the knowledge, skills and attitudes applicable to each competency" (Dimension 4). For each of the 21 competencies, 10–15 statements are given to illustrate timely and updated examples that highlight contemporary themes.

The Decree of the Italian Ministry of Health of 21 September 2022 "Approval of the guidelines for telemedicine services—Functional requirements and service levels"[19] describes, for the first time in a standard, the skills necessary for patients to use telemedicine. Annex A of the Decree states:

[18] Vuorikari et al. (2022), pp. 3–5.

[19] Approvazione delle linee guida per i servizi di telemedicina - Requisiti funzionali e livelli di servizio. (22A06184) (GU Serie Generale n.256 del 02-11-2022) https://www.gazzettaufficiale.it/eli/id/2022/11/02/22A06184/sg.

> The use of telemedicine services requires the acquisition of skills and the presence of certain requirements for those who are recipients of the service (patients and/or caregivers). Therefore, telemedicine solutions must include simple and easily accessible information/training tools for users, such as video tutorials, infographics, paper brochures as well as possible coaching activities both in person and remotely to ensure that all the technologies provided to the patient, including medical devices, can be used appropriately, safely, and autonomously by the patient and/or caregiver. The PN-DT (National Platform for the Dissemination of Telemedicine) also makes information and training tools on telemedicine available to patients to encourage appropriate and informed use. Further, if the patient uses the service from home, she will have to have sufficient access to the internet to guarantee a stable connection to digital platforms.

The creation of the National Training Plan in Digital Health regarding the implementation of Mission 6 of the PNRR has thus become a priority. This includes assessing, training, and certifying the digital skills of all personnel working in healthcare (managerial, clinical, technical, and administrative).

4.1 Towards the Patient as a Partner

Designing and developing digital health technologies, especially digital therapies that can fully respond to the needs and requirements of the patient, requires involvement by the patient. However, for this participation to be optimal, the patient must be an expert, having not only acquired experience with a condition but also expertise. Most health technologies today are developed without any real involvement by the patient. Rather, they emerge from top-down approaches that are essentially "techno-centric". The end user, i.e. the patient, is referred to as the "human factor"—at most an informant, not so much a real partner in the design process. In this model, patients are not equal to the other members of the project team, i.e., the software developers, engineers, and healthcare professionals who make decisions about the form and content of technologies. As a result, patients are merely consulted by the developers to express their opinions on an already-designed technology. Often the patient is involved only to validate an already-defined project—to give it legitimacy and make it more socially appealing. In the best cases, patients with the most experience are selected as prototype "testers" at an advanced stage of development. Fortunately, the idea of the patients themselves being involved in the design of digital therapies is becoming increasingly widespread. At least some now see this a critical success factor in improving the quality and application of digital technologies.[20]

To this end, a participatory approach that includes patients in the design process seems the most effective way to acquire their input into a product's development. In this model, patients are regularly invited to share ideas, opinions, and points of view on the design of the new technology, taking a place in periodic meetings with all other members of the team. That said, this happens very rarely in Italy, as the patient is not recognized as having the ability to make a real contribution of knowledge or experience to the development of digital health technology. On the one hand, this is

[20] Coravos et al. (2019), p. 46.

due to a lack of awareness. However, on the other, there are few appropriate training paths for patients to become experts in their own care. The "Patient Expert in Digital Technologies for Health" training course[21] intends to encourage this path. Its single objective is to improve the quality of the technology offered to patients through the contribution of the patient expert in digital therapy so as to be able to lead their lives in the best possible state of health. In 2022, the first 53 expert patients graduated from the course.

5 The New Role of the Patient in the Innovation Process: From the Expert Patient to the Patient Partner

A patient that is aware and informed about their condition has a greater chance of understanding an illness and following a treatment. This not only has a favourable impact on the need for assistance and cost, but also on the emotional and psychological state of the individual. In 2012, European training for expert patients involved the R&D of new drugs took shape thanks to the EUPATI project[22] and finance by the IMI Programme. A few years later, in 2014, a national platform was born in Italy, named the Patient Academy, which later transformed into the EUPATI Expert Patient Academy. This result had been in the making for several years, starting from the first concept of the expert patient articulated by Prof David Tuckett of the University of Cambridge in 1985. Tuckett stated that medical care would be more effective if doctors viewed patients as experts on their own pathologies.[23] He advocated the notion that the patient actually adds the experience of their own pathology and the changes that occur during therapy, but always in a close relationship with their doctors, their doctors' skills, and those of all the other healthcare professionals involved.

The concept of the "expert patient" therefore derives from applying innovation models that consider the involvement of all stakeholders—especially civil society—to sustainable development. It also involves a way of thinking that moves beyond the logic of only seeing the end user as a consumer to reach that of the patient becoming partner in a co-production and co-design process.

According to the Food and Drug Administration, the definition of a patient is…

> … any person with, or at risk for, a specific health condition, whether or not receiving therapy to prevent or treat that condition. Patients are also the people who directly experience the benefits and harms associated with medicinal products.[24]

---

[21] Created by UnitelmaSapienza in collaboration with the Eupati Expert Patient Academy and the Smith Kline Foundation, thanks to contributions by Polifarma spa.

[22] https://eupati.eu/.

[23] Tuckett (1985).

[24] Patient-Focused Drug Development Glossary Standardized nomenclature and terminologies related to patient-focused medical product development (2018).

However, patient partners include individual patients, caregivers, and/or patient advocacy groups, who ensure that the patients' wants, needs, and preferences are represented in activities related to medical product development and evaluation.[25] This refined definition of the patient moves them beyond being a stakeholder and into the realm of being a new "value holder". Porter argues that the value of health services remains largely unmeasured and misunderstood.[26] Value must be defined "around the customer", and the creation of value for patients should determine the rewards for all other actors in the system. Additionally, as value depends on results, not inputs, value in health care should be measured by the outcomes achieved, not the volume of services delivered. While Health-Related Quality of Life still has a role to play in describing the impact of a patient's health status (from their perspective), modern healthcare systems also need a new type of outcome measure—one that provides unidimensional, patient-centric, valid, and reliable assessments of patient value.[27]

The individual patient's voice in many performance measures, however, has largely been missing. At the organizational level, there are still too few ways to assess performance, even though patients are often the best source available for reporting on the experiences and results of individual care (Cella, 2015). Patient-reported outcomes are measures of how patients feel or what they are able to do in the context of their health status. These reports usually take the form of questionnaires that ask the patient directly about their health conditions, behaviors, and experiences. Importantly clinicians and others are not given the opportunity to modify the responses; thus, they directly reflect the voice of the patient. Patient-reported outcomes span physical, mental, and emotional health; a person's functioning; symptoms and symptom burden. They are relevant to many activities, including: helping patients and their clinicians make informed decisions about health care, monitoring the progress of care, setting policies for the coverage and reimbursement of health services, improving the quality of healthcare services, and tracking and reporting on the performance of healthcare delivery organizations.[28]

6 Best Practices for Patient and Caregivers as New "Value Holders"

Table 1 presents the results of a literature search on the experiences of patients and caregivers in digital health. These reflections were identified for their relevance and because they describe the impact of digital therapies on daily life. The statements are grouped into themes for ease of reading.

---

[25] Wilson et al. (2018), p. 8.

[26] Porter (2010).

[27] McKenna and Wilburn (2018), p. 478.

[28] Cella (2015), p. 5.

Table 1 results of a literature search on the experiences of patients and caregivers in digital health

Area	Practices and experiences
Formative	Organizing competencies in a consistent format across the course of a patient's life gives rise to a highly flexible tool that different actors in telehealth can easily refer to. This includes high-level decision-makers, digital technology firms, middle management, and clinical teams. The patient learning pathway (PLP) is a new telehealth reference framework focused on increasing each patient's competence in self-management, shared decision-making, and empowerment. This tool attempts to identify the needs of patients and caregivers, while defining their role as valuable actors in healthcare. Overall, this pathway integrates patients and caregivers into organizational processes as a high-priority need. If supported, it could substantially impact the quality, safety, and value of healthcare and services. It could also ensure that patient priorities are known and included, rather than assumed.[a] The intention is not to add responsibility to the patients' shoulders, but rather to shine a light on what they have already or could learn to do to better support themselves with targeted resources and tools throughout the arduous journey of life with an illness. The PLP methodology comprises five chronological phases: (1) identifying and engaging the main stakeholders; (2) exploration; (3) involving patients as partners; (4) co-developing the first PLP draft; and (5) validation and consensus building regarding competencies.[b]
Use of digital tools	Digital caregivers have primarily been developed for use in the homes of older patients. Much of the research on this topic explores how the participants (including the researchers) cope with and navigate the 'human' aspects of the technology. Factors like personalisation and friendliness focus on creating human-like interactions between digital caregiver and the patient. Hence, the participants are involved in a balancing act between making the digital caregiver sufficiently person-like and friend-like without compromising the health of the patient. Simultaneously, the researchers are trying to make the patients feel as if they are interacting with some*one* rather than some*thing*, while at the same time not making the digital caregiver seem like a real person or a real friend. This illustrates the participants' discursive negotiations about the degree of humanisation the digital caregiver needs in order to promote the health of the patient. In this particular study, there was a conflict between the patients' discourse of self-determination versus the healthcare professionals' discourse of authority and medical responsibility. In other words, the question was raised: Should the digital caregiver follow the patient's preferences or the healthcare professionals' rules? With this in mind, we must be aware that possible conflicts between the patient and the digital caregiver might arise due to different understandings of friendliness and health as well as between friendliness as a health-enhancing practice governed by the patient versus the professional obligations of taking responsibility for someone's healthcare.[c] Factors such as demographics, socioeconomic resources, and the caregiving context may play a role in caregivers' willingness to pay for digital support services. Moreover, the digital and social divide may negatively affect caregivers' willingness to pay for digital support services. Policymakers and insurance providers should consider innovative policies to fund digital support services that are effective at supporting and improving caregivers' health outcomes via subsidies or other incentives. Future research that evaluates the cost-effectiveness of digital support services is needed in the context of a growing number of informal caregivers and ever-scarcer resources.[d] Video conference-based group education for patients and caregivers is now both feasible and acceptable and may improve several outcomes for both groups. Although these researchers found that their field had seen several positive developments over the last 5–7 years, they advised that future researchers should increase the number of high-quality randomized controlled trials with larger samples to establish the effectiveness of group education via video conferences for several patient and caregiver cohorts, particularly children and adolescents. Research should also investigate how to train facilitators so as to identify the important elements of facilitating group education via video conferences.[e]

(continued)

Table 1 (continued)

Area	Practices and experiences
User's experience	Patient satisfaction surveys provide an opportunity for monitoring the effectiveness of virtual care and can guide ongoing enhancements. While virtual care holds great promise, educators must address some barriers. For example, many vulnerable patients are at risk of reduced access to care due to limited proficiency in English, a lack of digital literacy skills, and poor access to the internet. In addition, studies have demonstrated disparities in virtual care readiness by age, race, education, income, and community. However, three core interventions might support improved equity in virtual care: access to platforms and technology, patient education, and addressing privacy concerns.[f]
Experience related to diseases	Collaboration between clinicians, patients, and caregivers is key to developing high-quality digital educational resources. The project discussed in this paper followed a patient-centered approach to developing a comprehensive online educational resource for patients with cirrhosis. By having patients with cirrhosis as a key part of their team, they ensured the site met the needs of this unique population. Lessons from their process may help other organizations looking to address disease-specific knowledge gaps. The next steps with www.cirrhosiscare.ca include continued iterative refinement and structured impact evaluation.[g]
Usability	This study discusses the process of evaluating the acceptability and efficacy of a newly developed app, along with the feasibility of involving and retaining 50 caregivers to children having been discharged during an acute phase of illness post hematopoietic stem cell transplant (HCT). Based on the theories of behavioural economics theories and adherence, this novel intervention should help families to manage post-discharge medications, increase adherence to medical regimens, and mitigate the onset of graft versus host disease and, in turn, subsequent readmissions. This is the first prospective, longitudinal randomized control trial examining the effects of an intervention delivered as a smartphone app on adherence to immunosuppressant medications in the pediatric HCT population. The study's outcomes should address critical gaps in non-adherence knowledge and inform future studies of digital intervention outcomes in pediatric HCT.[h]
Assessment	The current digital literacy assessment instruments targeting older adults have both strengths and weaknesses, relative to their study design, administration method, and ease of use. Certain instrument modalities like the MDPQ (Mobile Device Proficiency Questionnaire) are more generalizable and inclusive and thus, more favourable for measuring the digital literacy of older adults. More studies focusing on the suitability of such instruments for older populations are warranted, especially for areas like "digital content creation" and "safety" that currently lack assessment. Evidence-based discussions regarding the implications of digitalization for the treatment of older adults and how healthcare professionals may benefit from this phenomenon are encouraged.[i]

[a]Jackson et al. (2023), pp. 4–5
[b]Jackson et al. (2023), pp. 4–5
[c]Hallqvist (2022), p. 346
[d]Hassan et al. (2023), p. 4
[e]Vaagan et al. (2023), pp. 5–6
[f]Bolster et al. (2022), p. 840
[g]Johnson et al. (2023), p. 7
[h]Ralph et al. (2023), pp. 8–9
[i]Oh et al. (2021)

7 Conclusion

Following the success of Italy's annual All Digital Weeks in 2023 and 2024, particularly in the "Health" and "Healthcare and Accessibility" sectors, we recommend promoting a center of excellence that can coordinate skills training and projects in e-health, digital health literacy, and related sectors. These programs would include solutions and IT-based organizational processes to support the above topics. Ideally, the central government would sponsor a national training plan to help professionals, patients, caregivers, and citizens acquire the digital skills needed to use telemedicine services, consistent with the national guidelines.[29] Digital health literacy is not just a necessity but, today, represents a fundamental requirement for a participatory health democracy, including access to health services. Action for citizens is urgently needed to reach a level of digital competence that will allow Italy to move from a position at the bottom[30] to a champion of society's ongoing digital transformation. In Italy, digital health technologies could not only represent a development opportunity but an essential necessity for exercising the right to health.

On the whole, e-health services are designed to enhance people's quality of life. However, the efficacy of public e-health services in achieving this objective remains uncertain, as does their adoption. So, to improve both the quantity and quality of e-health services, it is crucial for e-health researchers and healthcare providers to seriously consider the willingness of older users to adopt such services. For example, the older population faces more barriers to using new technologies, leading to lower awareness of effort expectancy and performance expectancy, which are internal technological factors. Consequently, their intentions to adopt e-health services are more likely to be swayed by social influence and facilitating conditions, both of which are external environmental factors.[31] We therefore propose to modify the United Theory of Acceptance and Use of Technology (UTAUT) model such that older adults find it easier to use e-health services. We aim for this to serve as a bridge between technology engineering and health promotion research, paving the way for future research directions that can enrich the work of e-health specialists. We also underline the necessity for e-health services to be perceived as beneficial, popular, and socially and culturally accepted within the cohort of older adults. Here, it is important to emphasize the role of the government in providing user-friendly service interfaces and guiding the design flow to assist older users.[32]

Another challenge is to optimize how complex services are organized as soon as possible to support faster management and better accessibility. Notably, this must not only include people with chronic diseases but also rare diseases and not just adults but also young people. As a society, we must begin to draft useful and innovative treatment paths that integrate scientific knowledge with the experiences of those

[29] GU General Series n.256 of 02-11-2022.

[30] DESI Index 2022 (2023).

[31] Lu and Tsai-Lin (2024), p. 3.

[32] Lu and Tsai-Lin (2024), p. 4.

who live with a pathology on a daily basis if we are ever to enhance the quality of patient lives.

Last but not least, AI can influence medical decisions. In fact, a clinician must first identify all potential decisions and probabilities associated with each outcome and then incorporate the utilities of the patient (or other party) that are attached to each outcome in order to select the most appropriate choice. As a result, the validity of a decision analysis depends on how comprehensively the outcomes are specified, as well as how well the utilities are measured and the probabilities are estimated. Ideally, this method would help ensure that decisions are evidence-based and aligned with patient preferences, thereby bridging the gap between objective data and personal values.[33]

Acknowledgements This research was financially supported by the “Biorobotics Research and Innovation Engineering Facilities” “IR0000036” – CUP J13C22000400007 (BRIEF) project.

References

Bolster MB, Chandra S, Demaerschalk BM et al (2022) Crossing the virtual chasm: practical considerations for rethinking curriculum, competency, and culture in the virtual care era. Acad Med 97(6):839–846

Cella D, Hahn EA, Jensen SE, et al. (2015) Patient-Reported Outcomes in Performance Measurement. Research Triangle Park (NC). RTI Press. Available from: https://www.ncbi.nlm.nih.gov/books/NBK424378/. https://doi.org/10.3768/rtipress.2015.bk.0014.1509

Coravos A, Goldsack JC, Karlin D et al (2019) Digital medicine: a primer on measurement. Digit Biomark 2019(3):31–71. https://doi.org/10.1159/000500413

Digital Economy and Society Index (DESI) (2023). https://digital-strategy.ec.europa.eu/en/policies/desi-human-capital)

European Commission (2023) 2030 Digital Decade Report. Report on the state of the Digital Decade

European Commission Brussels (2018) Communication from the Commission to the European Parliament, The Council, the European Economic and Social Committee and the Committee of the Regions on enabling the digital transformation of health and care in the Digital Single Market; empowering citizens and building a healthier society, COM(2018) 233

Flowers E, Saha S, Allum L, Rose L (2024) An environmental scan of online resources for informal family caregivers of ICU survivors. J Crit Care 80:154499

Gussoni G (2021) Terapie digitali, una opportunità per l’Italia, Tendenze nuove, Numero Speciale 1/2021: 3–7, https://doi.org/10.32032/TENDENZENS202101EXECUTIVESUMMARY.PDF

Hallqvist J (2022) The making of a professional digital caregiver: personalisation and friendliness as practices of humanisation. Med Human 48(3):347–356

Hassan AYI, Cucculelli M, Lamura G (2023) Caregivers’ willingness to pay for digital support services: Comparative survey. Health Policy 130:104751

International Collaboration for Participatory Health Research (ICPHR) (2021) Position Paper 5: Empowerment and Participatory Health Research. Version: August 2021. International Collaboration for Participatory Health Research, Baltimore

Jackson M, Clovin T, Montiel C et al (2023) Adopting a learning pathway approach to patient partnership in telehealth: a proof of concept. PEC Innov 3:100223

[33] Yu et al. (2024), p. 1897.

Johnson E, Hyde A, Drager D et al (2023) Collaborating with patients and caregivers to create web-based educational resources for people affected by cirrhosis. PEC Innov 3:100201

Lu C-C, Tsai-Lin T-F (2024) Are older adults special in adopting public eHealth service initiatives? The modified model of UTAUT. Sage Open 14(1). https://doi.org/10.1177/21582440241228639

McKenna SP, Wilburn J (2018) Patient value: its nature, measurement, and role in real world evidence studies and outcomes-based reimbursement. J Med Econ 21(5):474–480. https://doi.org/10.1080/13696998.2018.1450260

Oh SS, Kim KA, Kim M et al (2021) Measurement of digital literacy among older adults: systematic review. J Med Inter Res 23(2):e26145

Porter ME (2010) What is value in health care? N Engl J Med 363:2477–2481

Ralph JE, Sezgin E, Stanek CJ et al (2023) Improving medication adherence monitoring and clinical outcomes through mHealth: A randomized controlled trial protocol in pediatric stem cell transplant. Plos One 18(8):e0289987

Recchia G (2021) Terapie Digitali, una Opportunità per l'Italia. Una Call to Action per l'adozione nella pratica medica, Tendenze Nuove Numero Speciale n.1 – 2021; 13–20: 10.32032/TENDENZENS202101Editoriale.PDF https://www.fondorepubblicadigitale.it/wp-content/uploads/2024/06/Report-on-the-State-of-the-Digital-Decade-2023-Italy.pdf

Santarelli E, Di Carlo C (2013) La sanità elettronica in Italia: evidenze dall'indagine LITIS. Rivista di economia e statistica del territorio 1:34–61

Tuckett D (1985) Meetings between experts : an approach to sharing ideas in medical consultations / by David Tuckett [and Others]. Tavistock Print, London

Vaagan A, Haaland-Øverby M, Eriksen AA et al (2023). Group-based patient education via videoconference: a scoping review. Patient Education and Counseling, 108026

Vuorikari R, Kluzer S, Punie Y (2022) DigComp 2.2: The Digital Competence Framework for Citizens - With new examples of knowledge, skills and attitudes, EUR 31006 EN, Publications Office of the European Union, Luxembourg, ISBN 978-92-76-48883-5, https://doi.org/10.2760/490274, JRC128415

Wallerstein N (2006) What is the evidence on effectiveness of empowerment to improve health?, Copenhagen, WHO Regional Office for Europe (Health Evidence Network report; http://www.euro.who.int/Document/E88086.pdf, December 2007)

Wilson H, Dashiell-Aje E, Anatchkova M et al (2018) Beyond study participants: a framework for engaging patients in the selection or development of clinical outcome assessments for evaluating the benefits of treatment in medical product development. Qual Life Res 27:5–16. https://doi.org/10.1007/s11136-017-1577-6

Yu KH, Healey E, Leong TY, Kohane IS et al. (2024) Medical artificial intelligence and human values. N Engl J Med 390(20):1895–1904 https://doi.org/10.1056/NEJMra2214183

Motivating Corporations: Compliance and Responses in the Medical Devices Sector

Georgios Christou

Abstract Until recently, the Medical Device Directive (MDD) 93/42/EEC (1993) and the Active Implantable Medical Device Directive (AIMDD) 90/385/EEC (1990) made up the European Union's regulatory model governing medical devices. However, the medical devices sector has vastly developed over the past 20 years, and these Directives have now been replaced by the Medical Device Regulation (MDR) 2017/745 (2021). Already under fire for their shortcomings in enforcing quality and safety standards, part of the impetus for replacing the old regulations was a scandal involving breast implants made by the company Poly Implant Prostheses (PIP). A lack of safeguards imposed by PIP resulted in severe injuries and deaths when the implants failed. The repercussions of these malpractice cases spanned nearly 20 years and included criminal investigations, product recalls, bankruptcy, and reprisals given the toothlessness of the prevailing legislation. Framed by this saga, this chapter examines responses by the medical device industry to the new regulations, analyzing how this stance came to be through the corporation's own motivations. A series of Nielson-Parker models map these corporate responses to the new framework revealing how this clash between the medical devices industry and the EU ultimately conciliated a balance capable of achieving both their goals—at least to some extent. For the manufacturers, these goals centered around economic interests while, for the regulators, the imperative was to ensure increased product safety going forward.

1 Introduction

Until recently, the Medical Device Directive (MDD) 93/42/EEC (1993) and the Active Implantable Medical Device Directive (AIMDD) 90/385/EEC (1990) made up the European Union's regulatory model governing medical devices. However,

G. Christou (✉)
Sant'Anna School of Advanced Studies, Pisa, Italy
e-mail: georgios.christou@santannapisa.it

F. Casarosa et al. (eds.), *Enabling and Safeguarding Personalized Medicine*, Data Science, Machine Intelligence, and Law 7,
https://doi.org/10.1007/978-3-031-99709-9_11

the medical devices sector has vastly developed over the past 20 years, and these Directives have now been replaced by the Medical Device Regulation (MDR).[1] Already under fire for their shortcomings in enforcing quality and safety standards, part of the impetus for replacing the old regulations was a scandal involving breast implants made by the company Poly Implant Prostheses (PIP). A lack of safeguards imposed by PIP resulted in severe injuries and deaths when the implants failed. In addition to malpractice cases such as this, critics also decried the lack of oversight built into the Directives. For example, as of 2021, there were 39,844 in vitro devices circulating in the market. But, of those, only 8% needed to be certified by a "Notified Body" under Annex II of the old Directive.[2] This chapter will therefore examine the corporate responses to these new regulations made by the medical devices industry. It will look at how and why device manufacturers developed the stances they did through their own motivations. Additionally, Nielson-Parker models will be used to map the EU's new legislative framework to the industry's responses. Ultimately, the results reveal how the inevitable clash between the medical devices industry and the EU eventually conciliated a balance capable of achieving both their goals—at least to some extent. For the manufacturers, these goals centered around economic interests while, for the regulators, the imperative was to ensure increased product safety going forward. Overall, this paper should provide some clarity as to how corporations in this field think about the industry in the hopes of facilitating more effective policymaking in the future.

Section 2 provides a brief history of this tumultuous landscape, while Sect. 3 outlines the models used for the analysis. The results of the analysis are provided in Sects. 4, 5, and 6. Section 7 then concludes the chapter with a short summary of the material covered.

2 A Short History

Until May 2021, the medical device industry was regulated by two directives: the MDD 93/42/EEC and the AIMDD 90/385/EEC. The most fundamental aspect of these Directives appeared in Article 9 of the MDD, where providers first classify a technology as a medical device according to 18 rules set out in Annex IX. Under rule 2.1, a technology becomes a medical device based on its intended purpose, which must include one or more medical functionsaccording to the Directive. Once classified as a medical device, the rules go on to identify the risk associated with the device, which moves the device into one of different six classes, and then Article 11 then prescribes a "conformity assessment" to confirm the risk classification. These

[1] Regulation (EU) 2017/745 of the European Parliament and of the Council of 5 April 2017 on medical devices, amending Directive 2001/83/EC, Regulation (EC) No 178/2002 and Regulation (EC) No 1223/2009 and repealing Council Di-rectives 90/385/EEC and 93/42/EEC (Medical Device Regulation).

[2] MedTech (2021).

conformity procedures, essentially boiled down to meeting a few particular standards and requirements, including: (1) compliance with ISO 13485 (a quality management standard); (2) providing a technical file; (3) hiring a "Notified Body" to assess and certify the device; and (4) appointing an authorized EU representative for regulatory affairs (that is not a member of the company's sales and marketing team).[3] This representative's role was to share information with the authorities so as to, first, prove their device complied with the MDD and, second, to register the device and ensure that the technical file was always available to the authorities.[4] Notably, ISO 13485 dictates a harmonized standard over quality management for the medical device industry. While it was not an explicit part of the MDD itself, it was essential for manufacturers in practice, as complying with this standard afforded the manufacturer a high level of confidence that their device would conform to the regulatory requirements. For more on this, we refer readers to BSI.[5]

However, during the 2000s, there were increasing concerns that the MDD and its sister regulation for in-vitro devices, the IVD Regulation,[6] were becoming outdated. Medical technologies, including medical devices, were advancing quickly. Software-driven solutions were on the rise,[7] as were robotics.[8] Then a scandal broke out involving Poly Implant Prothese's (PIP) breast implants. Instead of using its originally-specified materials to make the implants, PIP had switched to an industrial-grade silicone, resulting in severe injuries and deaths when the implants failed. An investigation ensued, and PIP's implants were found to have a high rate of ruptures. Consequently, the French Health Products Safety Agency took these products off the market in March 2010.[9] The physicians involved were completely unaware that PIP's implants were not only low-grade but also somewhat defective. Rather, they trusted the product because, in 2000, it had been endorsed with a Conformité Européene (CE) mark of quality by the German Notified Body TUV Rheinland.[10] The BMJ reported that:

> Some time in 2001 [...] the PIP implant went on to differ in two key respects from its original regulatory application: the company dispensed with the protective outer skin and replaced the silicone contents with lower grade material.[11]

---

[3] Halpaus (2015), p. 2.

[4] Ibid.

[5] BSI (2024).

[6] Regulation (EU) 2017/746 of the European Parliament and of the Council of 5 April 2017 on in vitro diagnostic medical devices and repealing Directive 98/79/EC and Commission Decision 2010/227/EU.

[7] Xue et al. (2008).

[8] Agrawal et al. (2024).

[9] Lampert et al. (2012), p. 243.

[10] Lampert et al. (2012), p. 244.

[11] House of Commons Health Committee (2012), p. 19.

This "lower grade material", which was cheap industrial silicone meant for use in mattresses, was allegedly substituted in order to cut costs and boost profits.[12] In 2010, PIP went bankrupt after its implants were banned and its founder fell under investigation by the French police, being charged with involuntary injury.[13]

While the substitution was in violation of the MDD, this supposed safety framework lacked sufficient checkpoints to prevent it from happening. The defects were simply due to the use of an unapproved silicone material, which did not comply with manufacturing specifications. Yet the manufacturers could successfully able to evade liability due to PIP's bankruptcy.[14] This caused severe ripples throughout the entire industry. The Medicines and Healthcare Regulatory Authority had completely failed to safeguard the women who had received these implants despite first receiving a report of potential problems with PIP implants nearly a decade before the scandal broke out. This included a case of premature rupture of both implants in the same patient.[15]

Multiple suggestions for how to fix the broken legislation were given by scholars, political figures, and committees, including the Committee on the Environment and the Committee on Public Health and Food Safety, who stated that the PIP case revealed failures at both the European and the national levels. They particularly highlighted the lack of cooperation and inadequate means of tracing the raw materials used in medical devices. Furthermore, the PIP implants case, alongside another case involving hip implants, demonstrated shortcomings in the certification system, as well as deficiencies in the oversight of the Notified Bodies and their regulation by national authorities.[16] In light of this scandal, the EU introduced the In-Vitro Device Regulation (IVD Regulation) as well as the EU Medical Device Regulation (MDR) to try and prevent such a tragedy from happening again.[17] In fact, the European Medicines Agency cited the PIP scandal as well as the Johnson & Johnson toxic hip scandal as the reasons why these new regulations needed to be introduced.[18] A notable aspect of the MDR was the sheer lobbying pressure that it received from the industry during the deliberation period, which lasted from 2008 to 2013. MedTech, self-described as "Europe's biggest trade association for medical technology and health devices"[19] was a particularly outspoken voice.[20] MedTech Europe was established in October 2012 as an alliance formed by two organizations—the European Diagnostic Manufacturers Association, representing the European in vitro diagnostic industry, and Eucomed, representing the European medical devices industry.

---

[12] Jones (2012).

[13] Ibid.

[14] Gennari (2023), p. 148.

[15] Martindale and Menache (2013).

[16] Committee on the Environment, Public Health and Food Safety (1993).

[17] Maher and Price (2022).

[18] Frias (2019).

[19] MedTech 'About Us' (2024).

[20] Boch-Andersen (2018).

Lobbying by MedTech led to several of the stricter amendment options being rejected, such as additional requirements for premarket clinical trials and a transfer of the responsibility for certifying high-risk devices to the European Medicines Agency.[21] It is also notable that MedTech still continues to alter the course of these new regulations even now that they have been implemented.[22]

The European Parliament and the Council of the EU passed the MDR on 5 April 2017, and it entered into force on 25 May 2017, replacing both the AIMDD and the MDD. The new regulation was due to become fully applicable on 26 May 2020 after a three-year transition period but was postponed by a year due to the Covid-19 pandemic.[23] Since they are regulations of the European Union, under Article 288 of the Treaty on the Functioning of the European Union (TFEU) they become binding in all Member States automatically after being adopted by the European Parliament and the Council of the European Union, unlike a directive that requires adoption by the national parliaments of each member state to take force. As such, all medical and in vitro devices will need to be recertified in order to stay on the market, although there are some exemptions for certain medical devices with certificates already issued by Notified Bodies that could continue to be sold until 27 May 2024.

The biggest initial change of the MDR is the increase in scope. The scope of the MDR has been expanded to include certain products that were previously not covered by the MDD, such as certain aesthetic products, software, and devices that incorporate nanomaterials.[24] The MDD previously classified software and specific groups of products without an intended medical purpose as consumer goods, not medical devices. This was likely a response to the PIP scandal that preceded it.[25]

3 The Nielsen-Parker Model

Much like policymakers, corporations also react and respond in their own ways. What motivates corporate behavior has been part of a long-standing debate in the regulatory literature. Scholars like Ayres and Braithwaite argue that both individuals and firms have "multiple selves" with different motives that operate both serially and simultaneously.[26] Accordingly, they also recommend that regulators deploy plural regulatory strategies "responsively" to activate plural motives.[27] The idea of plural motives behind compliance has also been discussed by other researchers.[28] One

---

[21] Bowers and Cohen (2018).

[22] Maxwell (2024).

[23] Shatrov and Blankart (2022), p. 1234.

[24] MDR Article 2 & Annex XVI.

[25] Kirsh (2012).

[26] Ayres and Braithwaite (2018).

[27] Ibid.

[28] Perez et al. (2009).

such elaboration is the Nielsen-Parker holistic compliance model,[29] which synthesizes different lessons from the regulatory literature and various disciplines into 14 questions. The model builds on previous efforts to incorporate the findings of this field into a comprehensive yet simple model and seeks to make a unique proposal.[30] The model emphasizes the interaction between the different factors and the different actors that can enforce or encourage compliance.[31] It seeks to provide insights into "how individuals' and businesses' everyday motivations, characteristics and business models interact to influence their perceptions of their regulatory obligations, enforcement and, ultimately, their compliance".[32] The model considers interests and motives to be a mix of both economic and normative social factors, while also differentiating between direct and indirect factors that can have an impact on a corporation's decision-making. The model's purpose is to "guide the collection of information about potential reasons why people do or do not comply with particular obligations".[33] However, it is important to note here that a company might be influenced by all factors at the same time.[34] As seen in Ayres and Braithwaite's responsive regulation theory and Gunningham, Kagan, and Thornton's conception of competing "social", "economic", and "legal" licenses to operate,[35] both theorists assume that most businesses are motivated by all three factors at once and that the actions of regulators and stakeholders can influence which motive comes to the fore at any particular time.[36] Nielsen and Parker build on the conception of these factors from Winter and May:

> Economic (material) motivations are defined as the extent to which the firm is committed to maximizing its own economic or material utility. Social motivations are defined as the extent to which the firm is committed to earning the approval and respect of others, and finally, normative motivations are the extent to which the firm is committed to obeying the law (in general) for its own sake and the relevant regulatory regime (in particular) because it sees it as legitimate.[37]

The Nielsen–Parker holistic compliance model also acknowledges that economic, social, and normative motives to comply or not comply are "activated" through the behavior and attitudes of the many individuals, firms, and organizations that surround each business or individual. Official regulators also activate these motives, as indicated by the "enforced" dimensions of compliance below.

There are three advantages to using this model. First, it can be used prospectively to help design effective legislation and/or predict where there might be future

[29] Nielsen and Parker (2012).

[30] Parker and Nielsen (2017), p. 217.

[31] Parker and Nielsen (2017), p. 219.

[32] Parker and Nielsen (2017), p. 219.

[33] Parker and Nielsen (2017), p. 220.

[34] Ibid.

[35] Gunningham et al. (2003).

[36] Ayres and Braithwaite (2018).

[37] Winter and May (2001).

compliance issues. Second, it can be used during implementation to help design and target effective regulatory education programs, compliance monitoring schemes, and/or enforcement strategies. Lastly, it can be used to conduct a risk assessment of target populations to help determine which regulatory strategies—i.e., education, monitoring, &/or enforcement—should be used with which subgroups, while also helping in the post-implementation monitoring and evaluation phases to examine the impact of existing regulatory strategies.[38] The factors examined in this paper should assist with policy design and evaluation, too.

While it is of course important to examine all 14 questions of the model to come to a full and holistic perspective of a particular industry and its regulator(s), this is impossible to do in one short paper. It is however important to note that not all questions might be relevant to every given industry.[39] Hence, not every question will be examined in this chapter. Rather, the discussion will focus on the interests and motives of the corporations involved in medical device manufacturing, along with any other questions that might be relevant in explaining the motivations of these corporations. Additionally, the model provides guidance on "spontaneous compliance factors" and the "characteristics and capacities of members of the target population", which should be another valuable avenue of investigation as there are enough data here to make a reasonable analysis. Conversely, there are not enough available data to draw useful insights for model components like "enforced compliance factors" or "deterrence factors" given the recency of the new regulations. Ultimately, it would be too difficult to draw inferences about these areas without an in-depth examination of historical data and in-depth interviews with industry figures in order to come to conclusive data.

4 Model Analysis: Spontaneous Compliance Factors

4.1 Economic considerations

First, it is worthwhile considering the interests and motives that drive these companies to make decisions in response to regulatory pressure. The Nielsen-Parker model asks the following questions to determine whether economic motives are at play:

> Does the target group believe that it costs too much time, money and effort to comply? Does the target group believe that there are tangible advantages to be gained from breaking the rules? Does the target group see any advantage to them in complying with the rules?[40]

Nielsen and Parker define economic and material considerations as "an understanding of the business firm as an economic entity whose main focus and priority is to expand the business, make (and sell) more products and services, earn more money,

---

[38] Parker and Nielsen (2017), p. 220.

[39] Nielsen and Parker (2012), p. 431.

[40] Parker and Nielsen (2017), p. 222.

and return a greater profit to its owners".[41] These factors, of course, may not be purely financial but may also involve physical and material effects (e.g., imprisonment of an individual, closing down a plant, etc).[42] They acknowledge the fact that corporations often engage in "calculative thinking", or "rational choice".[43]

On that front, unfortunately, the new MDR has not been without its growing pains. A big issue has been that of the transitionary period. More specifically, on 27 May 2024, all certificates issued under the former two Directives would expire, requiring all devices on the market to be re-certified under the MDR. But, as of July 2022 with less than two years left to this deadline, MedTech reported that the vast majority of medical devices on the market did not yet comply with the new legislation.[44] By "the vast majority", MedTech was referring to "more than 85% of the > 500,000 devices estimated to be covered by (AI)MDD certificates".[45] At the time, some scholars estimated that a full transition would "probably take even longer than this to complete, and devices certified under the former directives [would] continue to be used during this time and perhaps for decades if they are put into service or made available on the market on 26 May 2025 at the latest",[46] which is why there has been such a reluctance to assess the impact of the MDR.

A big contributor to this problem seems to be the time taken to certify the devices. Complying with this requirement costs both money and effort. Respondents to the MedTech survey indicate that, although for some this process might be completed relatively quickly (say, six months), the vast majority of manufacturers would be waiting 13 to 18 months for a Notified Body to certify their product.[47] This is especially true for new devices and class III devices.

Access to Notified Bodies is generally difficult, with five of the old Notified Bodies withdrawing from the market, likely due to the more stringent requirements imposed by the MDR.[48] Further, as of 2022, only 20 of the 49 existing Notified Bodies had been listed under the MDR.[49] These long and unpredictable certification cycles, combined with a lack of binding timelines for conformity assessments and non-responsive Notified Bodies, have formed a devastating blow to both innovation and supply in the EU's medical device industry. MedTech's survey reveals that, as of 26 May 2021, 101 companies had already chosen to launch 4,306 new devices

---

[41] Nielsen and Parker (2012), p. 431.

[42] Ibid.

[43] Ibid.

[44] MedTech Survey (2022a), p. 6.

[45] Ibid.

[46] Shatrov and Blankart (2022), p. 1235.

[47] MedTech (2022a), p. 8.

[48] OrielSTAT (2021).

[49] Shatrov and Blankart (2022), p. 1237.

outside of the EU instead of within it.[50] And since 2021, manufacturers, particularly large manufacturers, have shown a preference for getting their first regulatory approvals in the US, not the EU.[51] Similarly, many EU-based SMEs are prioritizing approvals for new products in the EU and the US equally. Consequently, around half of the EU's medical device innovations will benefit US patients first.[52]

SMEs have definitely borne the brunt of the new legislation's impact. As of 2022, only 6% of the devices manufactured by SMEs had been re-certified, compared to 16% for large manufacturers. Further, only 7% of the certifications for SMEs had passed through technical file and quality management, compared to an overall average of 13% according to the MedTech survey.[53] The survey also reports that, while SMEs would be responsible for producing 26% of the devices requiring certification expected on the market by 26 May 2024, they would actually require 40% of the total certificates needed. This circumstance is especially problematic since, as mentioned, SMEs are lagging behind the larger companies in terms of submitted applications for MDR certification. In fact, between 15% and 30% of SMEs reported having no access to an MDR-designated Notified Body as yet.[54] So, despite being traditionally seen as the backbone of European industry,[55] most SMEs lack the financial capability to transition their devices into the new market given their resource constraints.[56] Further, although the MDR does make some concessions for SMEs, such as freeing them from the obligation of directly employing a person responsible for regulatory compliance under Article 13, the survey clearly indicates that implementing these new harmonized strategies has proven to be very difficult for SMEs. This could have drastic results on the industry. For example, it could lead to potential shortages of vital medical devices in the EU.[57]

The response by industry so far has been that of lobbying and bargaining with the regulator. MedTech, the primary industry body in the field has released multiple reports on the subject, concerning both medical devices and in vitro devices, given similar worries about the MDR's sister regulation, the IVD Regulation. The economic factors and long certification times associated with compliance seem to be the most contentious points simply because they have the potential to be truly financially devastating for some industry players.

---

[50] MedTech Survey (2022a), p. 17.

[51] Ibid.

[52] Ibid.

[53] MedTech Survey (2022a), p. 15.

[54] MedTech Survey (2022a), p. 15.

[55] MedTech (2019).

[56] Sorenson and Drummond (2014).

[57] Martelli et al. (2019).

4.2 Social Considerations

Secondly, it is vital to also examine the social interests that the Nielsen-Parker model guides us through. Social motives refer to "earning the approval and respect of significant others with whom an actor interacts".[58] These "significant others" could be other businesses, trading partners, employees, customers, local communities, the public, family and friends, but also the regulators themselves—the goal being to build better relationships with these stakeholders, particularly in industries where interactions between the companies and the regulator are frequent.[59] Some scholars combine social and economic motives together based on the rationale that social stigma might lead to economic and other kinds of losses over the long term.[60] However, Nielsen and Parker take care to distinguish between the two on the grounds that:

> If a firm is primarily economically motivated, then large fines might be necessary to ensure compliance. Whereas, if the firm is more socially motivated, then quite a small fine might be effective as long as firm leaders believe a breach of the law will become known and lead to social opprobrium.[61]

Question 2 of the model is particularly relevant:

> Does the target group agree with the policy objectives and the principles that underpin the rules surrounding their licensed activity? Do they agree with how the policy and principles have been put into practice—for example, do they think particular obligations are unacceptable?[62]

With this in mind, it is interesting to explore the social benefits of complying with the new Directive. Despite the negative implications and growing pains of the MDR, it is difficult to ignore the potential positive impacts it could have, particularly on the primary goal it set out to achieve, which is increasing patient safety. Another benefit might be a closer relationship between the regulator and industry. In turn, this would create more trust between corporations and the public, especially in the wake of the scandals that preceded it. For example, MDR Recitals 44–47 and Articles 33–34 give rise to EUDAMED,[63] a common medical devices database that aggregates post-market data on the potential adverse effects of medical devices. Sponsors can use the database on a voluntary basis to report serious adverse events, device deficiencies, and related updates. Recital 44 of the MDR describes it as a platform for collaboration among Member States—the idea being to detect problems early and, ideally, prevent them from happening again. Clearly, this database could become much more proactive in the future, once stakeholders become more

---

[58] Nielsen and Parker (2012), p. 431.

[59] Kagan and Scholz (1984).

[60] Nielsen and Parker (2012), p. 431.

[61] Ibid.

[62] Parker and Nielsen (2017), p. 221.

[63] EUDAMED (2025).

familiar with how it works.[64] The electronic vigilance system should enable manufacturers to report serious incidents and other similar events, while also coordinating incident evaluations by the authorities and serving as a means of information exchange.

Another sticking point has been the equivalence test, which was retained from the MDD. This test has long been criticized by scholars for providing the wrong incentives to manufacturers—the consensus being that it deters manufacturers from gathering new clinical evidence.[65] Also, it does not properly track the incremental changes made to a device that ultimately lead to the product substantially departing from its original form.[66] Still, the MDR might reconcile this problem through its more stringent post-market surveillance. Such efforts on the part of manufacturers have not been observed as yet, but the MDR is still fairly new and, who knows, stricter requirements might encourage manufacturers to work towards improved levels of patient safety in the EU.

That said, some scholars remain skeptical about just how effective post-market surveillance will be. Shatrof and Blankart, for example, argue that postmarket evidence holds limited value for assessing the safety and effectiveness of medical devices over time, as continuous modifications and replacements reduce how relevant the data are to the original device.[67] They add that many health professionals view adverse events as normal and see reporting them as unnecessary or futile, which is why industry often fails to address safety concerns.[68] They also point out that "many users also do not have sufficient knowledge of adverse event reporting systems, even in large hospitals".[69] Finally, they highlight that, since interpreting the reports of any problems falls to the relevant authorities in each Member State, the effectiveness of whatever response is deemed necessary will naturally vary from country to country.[70] Considering the origins of the MDR and a general reluctance by industry to comply with these new frameworks, it is unclear whether the social motives are as strong as the economic ones. While there are clear benefits to the corporations complying with the MDD, such as forming closer ties with the regulator, it does not seem that post-market surveillance on its own will be enough to induce compliance—at least not currently. This is unfortunate since more stringent post-market surveillance could easily lead to greater trust between manufacturers and their customers and, by extension, the regulators as well. However, given the very low certification rates and the threats by industry to de-prioritize Europe as a market, it does not appear that corporations will readily accept the new Directive. Moreover, while MedTech may cite patient safety as a primary concern in their

[64] Shatrov and Blankart (2022), p. 1237.

[65] Sorenson and Drummond (2014).

[66] Shatrov and Blankart (2022), p. 1237.

[67] Ibid.

[68] Ibid.

[69] Ibid.

[70] Ibid.

press releases, it is worth noting that their actions do not seem to show the same level of resolve. Particularly telling of their disagreement with the Directive's vision is the fact that "major blockers to innovation" had to be "deleted or balanced".[71] Since the beginning of talks, MedTech has seemed to be more concerned with making sure that Europe "remains fit for attracting innovation and research investments" than creating a haven of safe, high-quality medical devices.[72] While it is impossible to determine the exact sentiments of the industry regarding the MDR, it is clear that the relationship between the two is relatively adversarial, despite efforts by both parties to cooperate.

4.3 *Third-Party Influences Over Compliance*

The final question to consider is Question 4, which will help us get a closer look at third-party influences over the industry. Question 4 states:

> Do industry groups and other regulatees, customers, investors, trading partners, local communities, industry groups, non-governmental organisations (NGOs) or other stakeholders facilitate compliance?[73]

This question is particularly relevant to MedTech, a player that has been mentioned a few times already. The Nielsen–Parker holistic compliance model shows that economic, social, and normative motives to comply or not comply are "activated" through the behavior and attitudes of the many individuals, firms, and organizations that surround each business or individual. Further, these motives may not only be activated by the regulator but also by other key parties or events.[74]

In total, MedTech represents around €110 billion and over 500,000 medical devices.[75] They also engage directly with the EU's regulators and politicians to affect and shape policy within the space. Pressure from MedTech was enough for the EU to extend the initially proposed transition period.[76] Notably, the Commission acknowledged that "despite considerable progress over the past years, the overall capacity of conformity assessment ('notified') bodies remains insufficient to carry out the tasks required of them", and that "many manufacturers are not sufficiently prepared to meet the strengthened requirements of the MDR by the end of the transition period".[77]

[71] Bowers and Cohen (2018).

[72] Ibid.

[73] Parker and Nielsen (2017), p. 224.

[74] Parker and Nielsen (2017), p. 224.

[75] MedTech Flagship Brochure (2024).

[76] Proposal REGULATION OF THE EUROPEAN PARLIAMENT AND OF THE COUNCIL, amending Regulations (EU) 2017/745 and (EU) 2017/746 as regards the transitional provisions for certain medical devices and in vitro diagnostic medical devices, Brussels, 6.1.2023, COM(2023) 10 final.

[77] Proposal Regulation of the European Parliament (2023), p. 1.

The proposal seeks to extend the current transitionary period from 26 May 2024 until 31 December 2027 for most higher-risk devices (some exemptions have been given to well-established technologies) and until 31 December 2028 for medium and lower-risk devices.[78] Needless to say, the industry has welcomed this proposal and called for even more leeway during this transitionary period.[79]

MedTech, among other industry trade associations, has also had a large part to play in the Directive's design. As mentioned, the conformity assessment procedure has not changed too much from the former Directive outside of reinforcing the designation and monitoring procedures.[80] This means that the tension between the Notified Bodies and the manufacturers remains a strong issue. As demonstrated by previous studies, including one conducted by BMJ where a fake implant managed to receive approval despite explicit statements that the device was similar to three controversial implants,[81] the industry has close ties to how Notified Bodies function.[82] So much so, that in the US, only a fraction of the devices approved since 1976 have been the subject of trials. Further, very few high-risk medical devices that have been approved in the US have good quality, research-based proof of efficacy and safety.[83] This is largely because Notified Bodies are for-profit organizations. Essentially, they are contract partners to the manufacturers, which raises serious concerns over potential conflicts of interest. For example, scholars have criticized the US Food and Drug Administration's medical device division, accusing it of controlling the device manufacturers whose fees contribute one-third of the division's budget.[84] The EU regulatory system is still very much subject to this. As such, the relationships between manufacturers and Notified Bodies must be observed closely by the authorities, who should not refrain from taking corrective measures if necessary.[85] Moreover, Notified Bodies withdrawing from the market will only exacerbate this interdependence as, with more concentration, alignment between the interests of Notified Bodies and manufacturers will only become stronger.[86]

Another important point to make is that trade associations had a huge hand in devising the MDR. The Commission's initial proposals for the MDR elicited 200 responses, including: 117 submissions from manufacturers, industry trade associations, Notified Bodies, consultants, and experts; 27 from government regulators; and just 33 from healthcare workers and academics.[87] The vast majority of respondents were against involving the European Medicines Agency, but there was a clear

---

[78] Proposal Regulation of the European Parliament (2023), pp. 7–8.

[79] MedTech (2023).

[80] Shatrov and Blankart (2022), p. 1239.

[81] Cohen (2012).

[82] Shatrov and Blankart (2022), p. 1239.

[83] Dhruva et al. (2009).

[84] Lenzer and Brownlee (2019).

[85] Shatrov and Blankart (2022), p. 1239.

[86] Ibid.

[87] Bowers and Cohen (2018).

split between industry and the Notified Bodies, who firmly rejected the idea, versus doctors, academics, patients, and consumers, who were largely in favor of the proposal. MedTech warned that, should these proposals go forward, "patient care and access to new medical technology is, in our view, likely to suffer." The options under consideration were described by the lobby group as "alarming", "objectionable" or "completely unacceptable".[88] Alongside them, other bodies joined the crusade, such as the Irish Medical Devices Association, a trade association whose members include global corporations such as Medtronic, Allergan, and Abbott Laboratories. They were also against the Commission's analysis of weaknesses in the current regulatory framework. "The device industry … sees no evidence of either the alleged problems or the reasons why [the EMA] would present the appropriate solution if those problems did indeed exist".[89] A study by the International Consortium of Investigative Journalists reporting on a 2015 internal Commission memo suggests there may be more to this policy decision than a desire to avoid unnecessary public worry. According to them, the memo records the lobbyists asking EU officials for more detail on "the relationship to be established between transparency needs and [the] protection of commercially sensitive information." For MedTech Europe, the memo explained, "clarifying this adequately … is crucial to make sure that [Europe] remains fit for attracting innovation and research investments".[90] The general behavior of the industry lobby reveals exactly what was suggested by the compliance analysts: that industry players simply care too much about economic incentives. Instead of inducing compliance and tighter cooperation with the regulator, they have taken an adversarial position. Hence, while the language of industry conglomerates, such as MedTech, clearly refers to the "safety of patients" and the interests of patient health in their position statements and press releases, it is difficult to infer anything beyond a search for economic efficiency from their negotiations with the regulators.

5 Characteristics and Capacities of Members of the Target Population

5.1 Business Model

What then causes the disparity between the economic and social needs of medical device compliance? To answer this, it would be useful to hone in on some other characteristics that might shine a light on the subject. Particularly useful are the questions exploring the characteristics and capacities of the industry's members. For example:

---

[88] Ibid.

[89] Ibid.

[90] Ibid.

> Is compliance relevant to the target group's business model or is it an 'afterthought', or even irrelevant?[91]

Nielsen and Parker state:

> The 'business model' sums up the whole way an individual or business thinks about their everyday business life. It sums up what they are trying to achieve—that is, which motives or interests are most important to them and how they will try to achieve them; which stakeholders are important to them in terms of business dealings and reputation (for example, which customer segment do they target, how will they get investment into their business, who are the peers whom they want to respect them). How do they relate to their social, economic and regulatory environment?[92]

A company's business model, therefore, interacts with all other aspects of the Nielsen-Parker model, as it dictates what the trader has to do to actually make a living in their business,[93] given that regulators will generally place constraints on production and/or services. If the regulations are too strict, will businesses be encouraged to cut corners? Or will that have the opposite effect, making compliance key to a business's success? In this industry, a medical device must comply with the relevant regulations to even be allowed on the market due to the high risk involved if an unsafe device reaches consumers. If a device does not pass the relevant certification process, a business simply cannot participate in the market. As the MDR states: "A device may be placed on the market or put into service only if it complies with this Regulation when duly supplied and properly installed, maintained and used in accordance with its intended purpose."[94] Thus, complying with the MDD is an integral, unavoidable part of doing business.

5.2 *Knowledge and Capacity*

The other relevant question to consider is that of whether the manufacturers are even aware of the rules. As question 6 outlines:

> Is the target group aware of their obligations? Do they know the rules that govern the particular activity? Are the rules comprehensible or are they too complex to understand?[95]

Corporations may lack knowledge because they are not even aware that there is a rule applying to their situation. Alternatively, some organizations may simply lack the capacity to know and understand their regulatory obligations, especially if they are unnecessarily complex or uncertain. For instance, MedTech has taken a very vocal stance regarding the uncertainty and complexity of the standards provided,

[91] Parker and Nielsen (2017), p. 224.

[92] Parker and Nielsen (2017), p. 225.

[93] Ibid.

[94] Regulation 2017/745, Article 5, s 1.

[95] Parker and Nielsen (2017), p. 225.

particularly in regard to the rules surrounding the Medical Device Coordination Group and how Notified Bodies should handle their guidance documents. While MedTech agrees that such documents are important, they also argue that these rules better serve the industry as strictly guidelines because, then, they could be applied to varying degrees depending on the device or device category. As MedTech states: "appropriate flexibility is necessary as long as the overall goal is respected and against treating them as law, since they are not intended to be legally binding", and treating them as such only leads to further delays and more complex procedures.[96]

MedTech also has strong opinions on avoiding any potential delays to getting products to the market as a result of the MDR. Be it new more stringent requirements or process changes imposed by the Notified Bodies, MedTech urges that "the burden to introduce new unplanned interpretation[s] of the Regulation into the assessment should be minimised and delays to complete the conformity assessment should be avoided".[97] They take care to point out that this especially applies to any new administrative requirements, such as using certain forms or product codes. In cases where new standards are published during a conformity assessment, and the Notified Body believes the new standards need to be considered, MedTech suggests that the industry should be more involved in that process. In other words, manufacturers should not only have a say as to whether the new documents apply, but also they should be able to propose solutions and timelines for implementing a remedy. In general, MedTech is lobbying for deeper discussions between the manufacturer and the Notified Body so as to ensure that medical devices remain available to consumers.[98]

Notably, the MDR does not specify when Notified Bodies need to consider guidance documents after completing a conformity assessment. Therefore, MedTech proposes that newly published interpretations of the legislation be considered at the time of the next periodic re-assessment (at the earliest). Further, they propose that suspending or withdrawing a certificate per Article 56.4 of the MDR or Article 51.4 of the IVD Regulation should only be considered in the event considering an individual device's needs and situation does not conform to the requirements of the Regulations. This should mitigate any delays or supply issues caused by document processing delay.[99]

Of course, all this is in addition to the issues of comprehension outlined at the outset. Shatrof and Blankart recommend that, in general, future regulations should be written in plainer language with fewer cross-references between the articles and annexes to make the rules more accessible.[100] They also recommend expanding the definitions included in Article 2 of the regulation so as to make the rules easier for stakeholders to understand. Lastly, these authors echo the need for more coopera-

---

[96] MedTech (2022b), p. 8.

[97] Ibid.

[98] Ibid.

[99] MedTech (2022b), pp. 8–9.

[100] Shatrov and Blankart (2022), p. 1239.

tion between the stakeholders, the Notified Bodies, and the EU Commission throughout the whole legislative process.

This ties in to Question 7, which refers to the capacity to comply. Question 7 states:

> Does the target group have the capacity to comply with the rules? Or do they lack the money, time, education or expertise to become aware of their obligations, decide to comply and implement compliance? Do they have good enough management systems to implement compliance?[101]

This part of the model acknowledges that regulated firms have different fundamental characteristics from economic resources to technical know-how to managerial capacity and oversight. Additionally, the personal and professional backgrounds of the people who make up the firm also differ, and it is these differences that explain why some companies so readily comply with new regulations while others do not.[102] An individual's capacity to comply with the law can be greatly influenced by their general cognitive abilities, social capital, and interpersonal skills.[103] The statistics about SMEs display this extremely well, with only 6% of their devices certified for transition to the new MDR, compared to 16% of the devices produced by large companies.[104] One can also see similar problems with the MDR's sister regulation, the IVD Regulation. According to MedTech, SMEs will again suffer the greatest proportionate loss since they mostly make niche products and are less likely to be able to endure any loss of business as a result of the transition. After all, they are smaller companies with fewer resources at their disposal both in terms of manpower and money.[105] According to Medtech's survey, some 22% of in vitro devices will be unavoidably lost during the transition to the new IVD Regulation. Further, all the SMEs combined will lose 29% of their market share, almost double the 17% that large manufacturers will endure.[106] The same holds true for SMEs across the general medical devices industry. The MedTech survey also reports an estimated 17% of devices will be outright discontinued due to the cost of CE-marking under the new Regulation.

Further, MedTech reports a 28% drop in manufacturers who plan to prioritize the EU for first product launches.[107] This essentially means that the EU will see a delay in access to in vitro devices, which were first launched elsewhere in the world. Some Member States have tried to rectify this, such as Switzerland, which changed its regulatory approval process to automatically approve devices that have already received approval in other jurisdictions.[108] The survey also highlights that the "long,

---

[101] Parker and Nielsen (2017), p. 226.

[102] Parker and Nielsen (2009).

[103] Parker and Nielsen (2017), p. 226.

[104] MedTech (2022a), p. 15.

[105] MediCept, (2021), p. 6.

[106] MedTech (2022a), p. 6.

[107] Ibid.

[108] Motion 20.3211.

unpredictable, and inefficient" conformity assessment timelines pose a significant financial and resource challenge for the industry. Many respondents provided comments explaining how long and uncertain timelines contribute to "blocking or delaying their innovation activities for Europe", with an average of 18 months needed to complete the technical documentation required to put a product on the market. Many of the small startups cited financial difficulties with compliance, decrying the huge allocation of resources that need to be diverted from R&D into conformity assessments to comply with the IVD Regulation.[109]

Respondents of that survey also highlighted running performance studies in Europe as their third top concern, citing unpredictable processes, costs, and time as their primary worries. While no details on performance studies had been published as of the time of writing: "the European medical devices database EUDAMED does not yet provide a centralised point for application of performance studies – instead, a patchwork of national rules applies".[110] The long response times, coupled with the now more expensive and complex procedures explain why economic considerations are so much more prominent in the industry's complaints about complying with the MDR (and the IVD Regulation), and why SMEs are choosing to sell their products in jurisdictions other than the EU. These added economic factors are indeed taking a toll on manufacturers. Notably, these constraints are directly affecting the manufacturers' capacity to comply with the new regulations. Further, this is especially true for the smaller manufacturers, who do not have the deepest of pockets.

6 Overall Analysis

What can be taken from this brief application of the Nielsen-Parker model to the EU's medical device regulations? And what can be learned from the attitudes of the corporations towards the MDR, given the history of the industry? As Nielsen and Parker state, their model is not "a single unified model that explains compliance in every context and for every obligation". Instead, it seeks to "enlarge one's view of compliance to comprehend the complexity of regulatory policy implementation".[111]

Nielsen and Parker identify three types of businesses based on how they react to new regulations: optimizers, non-engagers, and dissenters. These types are described as follows: "Motivational types of businesses [are] primarily shown as a large cleavage between most of the businesses in our sample who agree with the substantive goals of the specific law we examined (optimizers and non-engagers), and a small group (the dissenters) who do not". Nielsen and Parker go on to note that there were significant differences in how each type of business weighs their social

[109] MedTech (2022b), p. 21.

[110] Ibid.

[111] Parker and Nielsen (2017), p. 230.

motivations.[112] Their identified groups of dissenters and non-engagers are likely the most applicable in the present case.

In their analysis of three clusters of businesses with varying combinations of motivations, Nielsen and Parker identify a distinct group of dissenters, who strongly opposed the substantive justice of their target legislation—the Trade Practices Act of 1974—but scored relatively high in terms of normative and social motivations. The non-engagers displayed lower levels of non-contingent compliance than the other clusters. While generally agreeing with the law, the non-engagers were more inclined to challenge its application in specific circumstances. The distinction between these groups raises questions about how their different motivations might affect behavior. For example, dissenters may comply with the law to a minimal degree or engage in "creative compliance" while simultaneously lobbying against it and attempting to reduce their obligations to comply. On the other hand, non-engagers are more likely to rationalize non-compliance, effectively ignoring the need to comply in particular situations.[113]

In our case, third-party organizations, a range of interest groups, and several industry trade associations hold quite a large sway over the regulator. The trade associations reflect the industry's general notions toward maximizing economic efficiencies. Yet it is important to remember that cutthroat attitudes toward prioritizing profit over patient safety are the very reason for the reforms of the MDR. Moreover, from a scholarly perspective, the sheer level of lobbying against the articles of the MDR has, unfortunately, resulted in a piece of legislation that is now compromised in terms of what it originally sought to achieve. In this sense, the industry seems to fit better into the conceptualization of a "dissenter", i.e., one who generally agrees with the regulation and aligns themselves with the idea of increased consumer safety, but simultaneously lobbies against it to maximize profit.

7 Conclusion

Overall, the tale of compliance in the medical devices industry is a complex one. This analysis shows that, based on the industry's sentiment towards the new MDR, their willingness to comply is generally low. This is largely due to very strong economic incentives to prioritize profit over patient safety. SMEs are struggling to comply with these stricter regulations because of the way their business models are set up and also because they lack resources and capacity. Moreover, some lack knowledge, either because the legislation is far too complex or because it takes too long and too much money to raise awareness in these areas. It is also noteworthy that despite the strong social demand to adopt new regulations following a series of scandals, the legislation itself did not change that significantly due to the strong

[112] Nielsen and Parker (2012), p. 18.

[113] Nielsen and Parker (2012), p. 19.

input of the trade associations. These trade associations have had far too much influence over the outcomes, which has led to significant pressure on the regulators to adopt stricter regulations, rather than increase the quality of their standards. Mapping the attitudes and perceptions of the industry around the MDR is crucial for understanding what makes these corporations decide to comply or not, and why they might react in favor of or against the changes imposed by it.

Acknowledgments The research was conducted within the framework of the PNRR project "SoBigData.it: Strengthening the Italian RI for Social Mining and Big Data Analytics" (CUP B53C22001760006).

Disclosure of Interests No competing interests.

References

Agrawal A, Soni R, Gupta D et al (2024) The role of robotics in medical science: advancements, applications, and future directions. J Autonomous Intell. 7. https://doi.org/10.32629/jai.v7i3.1008

Ayres I, Braithwaite J (2018) Responsive regulation: transcending the deregulation debate. Oxford University Press, New York

Boch-Andersen L (2018) 'Medical technologies regroup at EU level into one single representation: MedTech Europe', 2016, MedTech Press Release

Bowers S, Cohen D (2018) How lobbying blocked European safety checks for dangerous medical implants. The International Consortium of Investigative Journalists, 25 November 2018

BSI (2024) Introduction to a medical device QMS. Available at https://www.bsigroup.com/en-IN/medical-devices/our-services/iso-13485-quality-management/#:~:text=EN%20ISO%2013485%20is%20the,that%20consistently%20meet%20customer%20and

Cohen D (2012) How a fake hip showed up failings in European device regulation. BMJ 345:e7090. https://doi.org/10.1136/bmj.e7090

Committee on the Environment, Public Health and Food Safety (1993) 'PIP breast implants: "learn the lessons of this fraud", Press release, 20120423IPR43732Council Directive 93/42/EEC of 14 June 1993 concerning medical devices, Document 31993L0042, ELI: http://data.europa.eu/eli/dir/1993/42/oj

Council Directive of 20 June 1990 on the approximation of the laws of the Member States relating to active implantable medical devices (90/385/EEC), Document 01990L0385-20071011, ELI.: http://data.europa.eu/eli/dir/1990/385/2007-10-11

Dhruva SS, Bero LA, Redberg RF (2009) Strength of study evidence examined by the FDA in premarket approval of cardiovascular devices. JAMA 302(24):2679–2685

EUDAMED (2025) currently accessible at https://webgate.ec.europa.eu/eudamed/landing-page#/

Frias Z (2019) 'Update on EMA role in implementation of new legislation for medical devices (MDR) and in vitro diagnostics (IVDR)', 20 November 2019, Annual PCWP/HCPWP meeting with all eligible organisations

Gennari F (2023) What liability with the internet of things? Insights from the European case-law of the PIP affair. Glob Jurist 23(2):125–150. https://doi.org/10.1515/gj-2022-0032

Gunningham N, Kagan RA, Thornton D (2003) Shades of green: business, regulation and environment. Stanford University Press, Stanford, CA

Halpaus Y (2015) Medical Device Directive 93/42/EEC CE-Marking What Manufacturers Need to Know & Do. QNET LCC

House of Commons Health Committee (2012) 'PIP Breast implants and regulation of cosmetic interventions', Sixteenth Report of Session 2010–12, Published on 28 March 2012 by authority of the House of Commons. The Stationery Office Limited, London, p 19

Jones B (2012) Breast implant scandal: What went wrong? 27 January 2012, CNN, Available at https://edition.cnn.com/2012/01/27/world/europe/pip-breast-implant-scandal-explained/index.html

Kagan R, Scholz J (1984) The "Criminology of the corporation and regulatory enforcement strategies". In: Hawkins K, Thomas J (eds) Enforcing regulation. Kluwer Nijhoff Publishing, Boston, pp 67–96

Kirsh D (2012) PIP breast implant scandal: A story that triggered change. 13 November 2017, Mass Device, Available at https://www.massdevice.com/pip-breast-implant-scandal-story-triggered-change/

Lampert FM, Schwarz M, Grabin S, Stark GB (2012) The "PIP scandal" - complications in breast implants of inferior quality: state of knowledge, official recommendations and case report. Geburtshilfe Frauenheilkd 72(3):243–246. https://doi.org/10.1055/s-0031-1298323. PMID: 25308983; PMCID: PMC4168359, p243

Lenzer J, Brownlee S (2019) 'The FDA is still letting doctors implant untested devices into our bodies', 4 January 2019, The Washington Post

Maher L, Price N (2022) 'Ultimate Guide to IVDR for In Vitro Diagnostic Medical Device Companies', November 2022, Greenlight Guru

Martelli N, Eskenazy D, Déan C et al (2019) New European regulation for medical devices: what is changing? Cardiovasc Intervent Radiol 42(9):1272–1278. https://doi.org/10.1007/s00270-019-02247-0

Martindale V, Menache A (2013) The PIP scandal: an analysis of the process of quality control that failed to safeguard women from the health risks. J Royal Soc Med

Maxwell A (2024) EU Regulatory Round-Up: How Medtech Lobbying Altered EU Parlia-ment's Stance. 12 November 2024, Citeline, available at https://insights.citeline.com/medtech-insight/eu-regulatory-round-up-how-medtech-lobbying-altered-eu-parliaments-stance-62AFWU6TIVDNBEHKETHCORVN6Q/ 12 November 2024

MediCept (2021) Eudamed Update: Implementation is Paused, MDR Compliance is Not. 29 April 2021

MedTech (2022a) 'MedTech Europe Survey Report analysing the availability of Medical Devices in 2022 in connection to the Medical Device Regulation (MDR) implementation', 14 July 2022

MedTech (2022b) Recommendations on the use of Guidance Documents Related to the Medical Device Regulation (MDR) and In vitro Diagnostics Regulation (IVDR). 28 June 2022

MedTech (2023) MedTech Europe welcomes the adoption of amended transitional provisions of the Medical Devices Regulations and calls for continued work to address outstanding implementation challenges. 7 March 2023, MedTech Press Release

MedTech (2024) About Us. https://www.medtecheurope.org/about-us/

MedTech Europe (2019) The European Medical Technology Industry in figures; 2019

MedTech Flagship Brochure (2024). Available at https://www.medtecheurope.org/resource-library/medtech-europe-flagship-brochure/

Motion 20.3211, 'Für mehr Handlungsspielraum bei der Beschaffung von Medizinprodukten zur Versorgung der Schweizer Bevölkerung', accepted by the Swiss National Council on Monday 28 November

Nielsen VL, Parker C (2012) Mixed motives: economic, social and normative motivations in business compliance. Law Policy 34(4):428–462

Oriel STAT A MATRIX Blog (2021) Status of EU Notified Bodies Designated to EU MDR 2017/745 and IVD 2017/746. 21 April 2021

Parker C, Nielsen L (2017) Compliance: 14 Questions, pp 217–232

Parker C, Nielsen VL (2009) Corporate compliance systems: could they make any difference? Adm Soc 41(1):3–37. https://doi.org/10.1177/0095399708328869

Perez O, Amichai-Hamburger Y, Shterental T (2009) The dynamic of corporate self-regulation: ISO14001, environmental commitment, and organizational citizenship behavior. Law Soc Rev 43:593–629

Shatrov K, Blankart CR (2022) After the four-year transition period: is the European Union's Medical Device Regulation of 2017 likely to achieve its main goals? December 2022. Elsevier Health Policy 126(12):1233–1240

Sorenson C, Drummond M (2014) Improving medical device regulation: the United States and Europe in perspective. Milbank Q 92(1):114–150

Winter SC, May PJ (2001) Motivation for compliance with environmental regulations. J Pol Anal Manage 20:675–698. https://doi.org/10.1002/pam.1023

Xue L, Yen C, Boucharenc C, Choolani M (2008) The design evolution of medical devices: moving from object to user. J Design Res 7. https://doi.org/10.1504/JDR.2008.026991

The Role of Artificial Intelligence and Machine Learning in Personalizing the Control of Robotic Lower Limb Prostheses

Ilaria Fagioli, Alessandro Mazzarini, Francesca Gennari, and Simona Crea

Abstract The control of robotic lower limb prostheses is shifting from a "one-size-fits-all" paradigm to highly individualized approaches. This is because artificial intelligence, and particularly machine learning, now offer powerful tools to adapt how a prosthesis behaves to the unique needs of its user. Control algorithms capable of capturing each user's specific locomotion patterns are making the initial post-operative rehabilitation phase after having a prosthesis fitted easier, ultimately improving the quality of life and comfort of individuals with lower limb amputations. Additionally, real-time intention detection and human-in-the-loop optimization are showing a great deal of promise as data-driven methods for aligning a prosthesis's behavior with the user's intentions. However, significant challenges remain. Accuracy, real-time responsiveness, efficient tuning, and adaptability to the learning curve of users are all issues that still need to be addressed. Legal compliance is posing additional hurdles, as coordination between the Medical Devices Regulation and the recently passed AI Act remains unclear. This regulatory ambiguity could hinder innovation and market access for robotic prostheses. Hence, this chapter presents advanced control strategies for robotic lower limb prostheses, with a particular focus on machine learning approaches. We discuss the opportunities and challenges associated with developing the next generation of assistive control algorithms and present potential pathways toward addressing regulatory requirements given Europe's new legislation. Our goal is to promote both innovation and compliance in today's rapidly evolving field of prosthetic control systems.

I. Fagioli · A. Mazzarini · S. Crea (✉)
The BioRobotics Institute, Sant'Anna School of Advanced Studies, Pontedera, Pisa, Italy

Department of Excellence in Robotics and AI, Sant'Anna School of Advanced Studies, Pisa, Italy
e-mail: simona.crea@santannapisa.it

F. Gennari
LIDER-Lab, DIRPOLIS, Sant'Anna School of Advanced Studies, Pisa, Italy
e-mail: Francesca.Gennari@santannapisa.it

F. Casarosa et al. (eds.), *Enabling and Safeguarding Personalized Medicine*, Data Science, Machine Intelligence, and Law 7,
https://doi.org/10.1007/978-3-031-99709-9_12

1 Introduction

The purpose of a prosthesis is to restore the functionality of a missing limb. To this end, lower limb prostheses, such as prosthetic legs, not only compensate for an amputee's loss of mobility, they can also allow a person to reintegrate into society.[1] However, most of the commercial limb prosthetics that are currently available are passive systems; that is, they cannot generate net positive mechanical power, unlike the biological muscles of a leg. Unfortunately, using these passive systems often results in compensatory movements that lead to secondary complications such as chronic back pain and osteoporosis.[2] Alternatively, robotic or powered limbs are battery-powered mechatronic devices that can inject net positive power into the gait cycle. These systems have been designed to replace a human limb by mimicking its natural movement. Most often, they incorporate sensors, actuators, and control algorithms that inject energy at the right time in the gait cycle, giving the user dynamic adaptability to different walking conditions.[3]

Central to the functioning of a robotic prosthesis is the control framework that governs its operation. The primary aim of a controller is to manipulate the prosthesis' movement to achieve a seamless human-robot integration.[4] A key advancement in this field is the potential to personalize such control strategies according to the characteristics and preferences of the individual user as this generally makes the limbs far more effective. However, setting up these personalized control frameworks requires tuning the control parameters, which often involves long experimental procedures executed and overseen by trained personnel. Usually, the control parameters are selected manually through a heuristic approach based on trial-and-error. Moreover, the experiments often rely on pre-defined one-size-fits-all profiles. Subject-specific control strategies are, by definition, not generalizable to different users. This is why the main challenges with developing a prosthetic controller relate to its adaptability and its robustness to the variability in movements across many individuals.

Despite these hurdles, in recent years, machine learning has emerged as a promising strategy to accurately detect locomotive intentions via patient-specific physiological data. Thus, personalized, systematic parameter tuning has become possible.[5] Machine learning also offers the potential for subject-specific yet generalizable control architectures to increase the efficacy of robotic prostheses. For example, over the past few years, researchers have developed methods to automatically tune the actuators of robotic prostheses based on key performance indicators like symmetry or metabolic effort. These methods incorporate what they call "human-in-the-loop" optimization approaches. This involves acquiring performance metrics in real time

[1] Miller et al. (2019).

[2] Gailey (2008).

[3] Fagioli et al. (2024).

[4] Goldfarb et al. (2013).

[5] Gehlhar et al. (2023).

and continuously modifying the control parameters so as to optimize a defined cost function.

Technologically, these new AI techniques seemingly hold great promise for tailoring the assistance given to individual patients. Yet, from a regulatory perspective, much still needs to be determined. Starting from the very beginning, the way in which the manufacturer defines the intended purpose of an AI-driven prostheses determines which legal frameworks are even applicable. Moreover, as these highly personalized medical technologies approach commercialization, ensuring legal compliance becomes critical, particularly given the scope of the Medical Device Regulation (MDR)[6] and the newly passed Artificial Intelligence Act (AI Act).[7] For example, if the AI is framed primarily for safety, the hardware will be subject to the MDR (the physical prosthesis) while the AI Act will apply to the software (the control system). Alternatively, if the AI is intended for medical purposes, say, with the aim of alleviating a disability or compensating for an injury, both the MDR and the AI Act will apply to the whole prosthesis according to Article 2(1) of the MDR. Here, the software would be classified as "Software as a Medical Device". This scenario presents a more complex legal landscape, as the prosthetics will need to comply with both regulatory regimes.

Thus, the aim of this chapter is to present an overview of the state-of-the-art in control strategies,[8] moving from the most common control methods like machine learning approaches[9] to the newest approaches based on human-in-the loop optimization.[10] Before concluding this chapter[11] this chapter, there will be a discussion on the preliminary outcomes of introducing AI into the field of robotic prostheses.[12]

2 Control Strategies

The control framework of robotic lower limb prostheses is often implemented as a hierarchical architecture, as illustrated in Fig. 1. A high-level controller receives information from a sensory system on the prosthesis or the subject and then tries to

[6] Regulation (EU) 2017/745 of the European Parliament and of the Council of 5 April 2017 on Medical Devices, Amending Directive 2001/83/EC, Regulation (EC) No 178/2002 and Regulation (EC) No 1223/2009 and Repealing Council Directives 90/385/EEC and 93/42/EEC.

[7] Regulation (EU) 2024/1689 of the European Parliament and of the Council of 13 June 2024 Laying down Harmonised Rules on Artificial Intelligence and Amending Regulations (EC) No 300/2008, (EU) No 167/2013, (EU) No 168/2013, (EU) 2018/858, (EU) 2018/1139 and (EU) 2019/2144 and Directives 2014/90/EU, (EU) 2016/797 and (EU) 2020/1828 (Artificial Intelligence Act) (Text with EEA Relevance) PE/24/2024/REV/1 OJ L, 2024/1689, 12.7.2024.

[8] See Sect. 2.

[9] See Sect. 3.

[10] See Sect. 4.

[11] See Sect. 6.

[12] See Sect. 5.

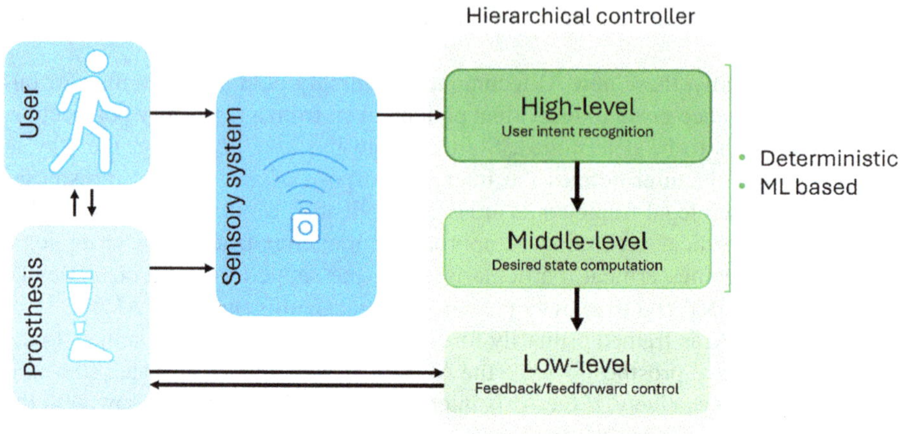

Fig. 1 Hierarchical architecture of a robotic prosthesis controller. The figure illustrates the interactions between the user, the prosthesis, the sensory system, and the controller (Adapted from Tucker et al. (2015))

identify what the user wants to do—sit, stand, walk on a flat surface, ascend some stairs, and so on.[13] Typically, controllers are designed to identify the most common locomotion tasks, which include those just mentioned, plus walking on inclined surfaces, descending stairs, kneeling down, and others. The output from the high-level controller is then passed onto a middle-level controller, which computes the desired state of the device—this being the required position or torque to feed the device at the joint level. Generally, methods for predicting the intended locomotion task and setting the desired state of the prosthesis can be manually tuned once and then used for life. Alternatively, they can be implemented through data-driven learning techniques, such as those used in machine learning.[14] Lastly, a low-level controller implements the feedback and/or feedforward control loops to shift the device into the desired state.

In the next section, we focus on the high- and middle-level controllers, describing the most common strategies and newer approaches based on machine learning and human-in-the-loop optimization.

3 High- and Middle-Level Control Strategies

A common high-level control strategy used in commercial prostheses involves direct user input. By using a remote controller, an app, or simply by performing specific movements, the user directly sets the prosthesis into the correct control

[13] Tucker et al. (2015).

[14] Gehlhar et al. (2023).

mode for the upcoming locomotion task. While these methods can be highly accurate, they do require explicit actions from the user, resulting in an unnatural and cognitively demanding experience.[15]

More seamless intention decoding algorithms infer the locomotion task from signals collected by the sensory system inside the prosthesis or through sensors placed on the user's body. These methods offer a more natural integration between the prosthesis and the user, resulting in smoother locomotion. Common approaches to high-level control are based on finite-state machines, where the switch between different finite states often involves threshold-based rules applied to one or more signals from the sensory system.[16] Finite states could represent different fundamental activities: such as standing or walking[17]; different locomotion modes, such as sit-to-stand transitions,[18] or moving up and down stairs[19]; or discretely generic phases of locomotion, such as swing and stance.[20] Another approach to estimating the user's mode of locomotion involves using kinematic models. For example, Lenzi et al. proposed a three-segment planar model of the leg to estimate walking speed,[21] while Best et al. employed a double-pendulum model of human walking for the same purpose.[22]

Further, one of two main strategies is generally used to assess the evolution of a user's gait: a discrete segmentation algorithm or continuous phase estimation. Discrete segmentation algorithms (also referred to as FSMs) divide each locomotion activity into different subphases where specific control laws are applied. However, these algorithms may contain a large number of parameters that need to be tuned, especially as the number of subphases increases.[23] To simplify the control architecture, Culver et al. implemented a unified FSM with six states, defining a different sequence of states for each task.[24] Similarly, Tran et al. segmented different tasks into the same set of states.[25] Some studies have implemented adaptability—for example, using FSMs with varying thresholds to adapt to gait characteristics,[26] using adaptive control laws to ensure compliance with different stair heights, cadences, and gait patterns,[27] or using adaptability to avoid obstacles.[28]

[15] Bhakta et al. (2020).

[16] Culver et al. (2018); Fluit et al. (2020).

[17] Flynn et al. (2018); Shultz et al. (2016).

[18] Li et al. (2018).

[19] Welker et al. (2022).

[20] Li et al. (2018).

[21] Lenzi et al. (2014).

[22] Best et al. (2021).

[23] Fluit et al. (2020).

[24] Culver et al. (2022).

[25] Tran et al. (2019).

[26] Katsumura et al. (2022).

[27] Hood et al. (2022).

[28] Gordon et al. (2019); Mendez et al. (2020).

As an alternative to discretely detecting gait events, it is possible to continuously estimate the progression of periodic tasks from 0 to 100% of the gait cycle. This approach is typically subject-independent, requires a lower number of parameters to be tuned with respect to FSMs, and has the ability to adapt to changes in walking speed.[29] A common strategy for continuous gait phase estimation involves the use of phase variables derived from the position and velocity of the residual limb's segments.[30] In this context, it is essential to define a phase variable that is monotonic and capable of capturing the volitional intent of the user during a locomotion task. As an example, Thatte et al. used the information from hip, knee, and ankle joints in an extended Kalman filter to estimate the gait phase and phase velocity.[31]

Yet another method of continuous gait phase estimation involves adaptive oscillators,[32] which are dynamic systems that adapt their parameters to learn a quasi-periodic signal.[33] Information about the mode of locomotion and gait phase estimation (whether discrete or continuous) is then translated into a desired joint state by the middle-level controller. This is typically a reference position or a reference torque. Further, the desired state can be generated through various methods, including handcrafted trajectories, lookup tables that implement bio-inspired trajectories, polynomial fitting, or model-based trajectories.

Notably, an alternative approach to prosthesis control bypasses the high-level controller, eliminating the need to explicitly detect the locomotion modes or the gait phases. This approach, referred to as "unified control", consists of applying the same control strategy regardless of the locomotion activity. Unified controllers have been developed by exploiting the idea that the quasi-stiffness of the shank remains consistent across different tasks[34] and terrains.[35] Moreover, recent studies have leveraged inertial sensors to indirectly detect the user's residual limb movement, enabling adaptation to variable speeds, inclines, and uneven terrain.[36] For example, Cowan et al. introduced a controller based on electromyography (EMG) to power a knee prosthesis that allowed the user to walk on flat surfaces and negotiate stairs without explicitly classifying the activity.[37] Similarly, Hunt et al. used EMG signals to control a prosthesis through multiple locomotion tasks using shared neural control. More specifically, by detecting activations of the flexor and extensor muscles in the subject's residual limb, the controller could predict tasks such as standing up

[29] Rezazadeh et al. (2019).

[30] Bartlett et al. (2022); Fu et al. (2021); Heins et al. (2018); Rezazadeh et al. (2019).

[31] Thatte et al. (2019).

[32] Heins et al. (2020); Mazzarini et al. (2023); Xu et al. (2020a, 2020b).

[33] Ronsse et al. (2013).

[34] Bartlett et al. (2021).

[35] Shultz and Goldfarb (2018).

[36] Sullivan et al. (2023).

[37] Cowan et al. (2023).

and sitting down, lunging, squatting, and walking, allowing seamless transitions between these tasks without any explicit classification.[38]

All this said, these pioneering approaches still typically require many thresholds and control parameters to be manually tuned by expert personnel.[39] Machine learning classifiers are generally trained on pre-collected datasets containing locomotion movements, which help to classify the mode of locomotion, whether this be in a user-dependent or user-independent manner. The common approaches use linear or quadratic discriminant analysis,[40] support vector machines,[41] and neural networks,[42] based on kinematic and kinetic information gathered from sensors onboard the prosthesis. Some classifiers even incorporate feedback from EMG sensors,[43] which generally improves classification accuracy at the expense of increased complexity.[44] Moreover, the reliability of the EMG signals strongly depends on how accurate they are and the extent to which the limb has been amputated.

User-independent classifiers usually require a large amount of data from a diverse sample population to account for intra-subject and inter-subject variability.[45] Moreover, the accuracy of subject-independent models is usually limited,[46] specifically when movement patterns have a high variability, such as is the case with amputees walking, which can be affected by different subject-specific compensatory movements like hip hiking or circumduction.[47] In fact, multiple studies have shown that user-independent classifiers have significantly lower accuracy than user-dependent approaches.[48] For example, a classifier built from linear discriminant analysis with subject-dependent geometric measurements could recognize locomotion modes with an accuracy of over 95%.[49] That said, although machine learning methods in user-dependent settings typically provide better accuracy, extensive model training tends to be required for each new user.[50]

To overcome some of the limitations of both user-dependent and user-independent decoding strategies, hybrid decoding control algorithms have been proposed as a possible solution. Hybrid algorithms not only have the advantage of providing generalizability between different users, they also typically deliver relatively high accuracy with limited training data. For example, Le et al. applied transfer learning to a

---

38 Hunt et al. (2021).

39 Fluit et al. (2020).

40 Leestma et al. (2021); Xu et al. (2018); Xu and Wang (2020).

41 Mai et al. (2017).

42 Bhakta et al. (2020, 2021); Xu and Wang (2019).

43 Hussain et al. (2020).

44 Hargrove et al. (2015).

45 Lanotte et al. (2023).

46 Hargrove et al. (2015).

47 Murray et al. (2017).

48 Bhakta et al. (2020); Hargrove et al. (2015).

49 Leestma et al. (2021).

50 Bhakta et al. (2020).

user-independent model, demonstrating improved accuracy when attempting to predict movement intentions with a group of new subjects.[51] Further, a study by Woodward et al. found that combining a user-independent classifier with real-time adaptation based on subject-dependent data produced error rates that were not significantly different from a user-dependent classifier. Thus, these authors eliminated the need for individual training sessions, while also reducing the time taken up with collecting data.[52]

Notably, machine learning algorithms can also be leveraged to detect both discrete gait events and continuous gait estimation. Additionally, machine learning techniques have also recently emerged that allow the control parameters to be tuned automatically. Moreover, neural networks,[53] fuzzy logic,[54] and online reinforcement learning[55] have all been used to iteratively tune a model's control parameters in real-time so as to reduce errors between the measured and desired profiles.

4 Human-in-the-Loop Optimization

The aforementioned machine learning approaches rely on two distinct processes: an offline data-driven training phase and an online testing phase. During the offline training phase, an available dataset, either user-specific or generic, is used to set the algorithm's hyperparameters and tune all control parameters. In the subsequent online testing phase, the algorithm is validated with the user wearing the prosthesis, allowing for fine adjustments. However, dividing the training and fine-tuning phases may be lengthy and not the most efficient approach for identifying the optimal control parameters to enhance specific aspects of human-robot interaction. In truth, learning processes are essential in human-robot interaction. For example, users tend to naturally adjust the features of their gait pattern while walking with a prosthetic. This includes their gait cadence, symmetry, and loading phases, which typically become more physiological as the users familiarize themselves with their new limb.[56] Therefore, adapting the prosthesis behavior in real-time and determining the control parameters that optimize a specific cost function during actual use could significantly improve human-robot interaction.

Approaches where training and testing are continuously performed in real-time are called human-in-the-loop optimization algorithms (see Fig. 2).[57] This control paradigm inherently takes into account how users adapt, familiarize themselves, and

[51] Le et al. (2022).

[52] Woodward et al. (2022).

[53] Li et al. (2022).

[54] Huang et al. (2016).

[55] Wen et al. (2020).

[56] Huang et al. (2021); Poggensee and Collins (2021).

[57] Ding et al. (2018); Kim et al. (2017); Zhang et al. (2017).

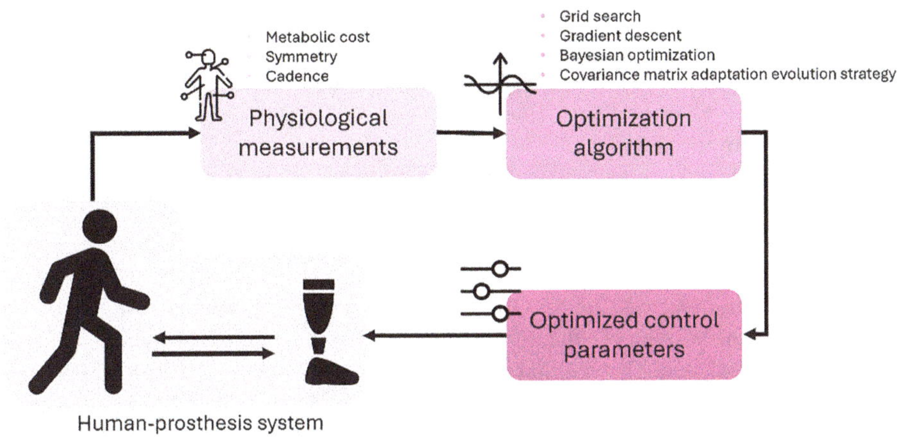

Fig. 2 A typical human-in-the-loop optimization framework. By directly observing the evolution of physiological variables of the user, an optimization algorithm iteratively produces a new set of control parameters for the prosthesis to minimize a specific cost function

learn to use a device by means of either statistical techniques or machine learning methods.[58] Recently, this kind of approach to control has gained more interest since it can embed machine learning to process human feedback and optimize how the device functions in real time. In human-in-the-loop approaches, optimizing the algorithm ends when it converges on the minimum of a defined cost function. Usually, the cost functions of human-in-the-loop algorithms consider physiological variables, such as the metabolic cost of walking for the user,[59] or some kind of kinematic measure. The most popular method of assessing the metabolic cost of walking is through indirect calorimetry, which measures oxygen inflows and carbon dioxide production. From these measurements of gas exchange, the Brockway equation can produce an estimate of the instantaneous metabolic cost of the given activity—in this case, walking.[60] However, the metabolic cost also includes slow adaptation components and history dependence. Indeed, respiratory measurements are usually meant for long testing and steady-state conditions, and they typically need at least 3 min to stabilize. Additionally, the recordings may contain high amounts of noise, and cardiopulmonary drift can occur if the tuning takes too much time.[61] Most of the time, optimizing the control parameters requires more than 15 min of continuous walking. Additionally, gas exchanges are typically measured through a face mask, which may be uncomfortable for the user. Some alternatives to indirect calorimetry for estimating user effort include EMG, which can be used to measure muscle activation and heart rates. However, although heart rates can be used to estimate the

[58] Díaz et al. (2023).

[59] Zhang et al. (2017).

[60] Brockway (1987).

[61] R Koller et al. (2016).

so-called “physiological cost index” as an approximation of metabolic expenditure, it still usually takes a lengthy testing session to obtain a steady-state reading.[62] As such, EMG signals may provide a faster response, but their use in an unstructured environment can be problematic due to the need for long setup times as skin is prepared and electrodes are placed.

In general, cost functions related to the energy cost of walking require relatively long optimization procedures as each set of control parameters should ideally be tested for a few minutes, and testing various combinations in real time may require more than 20–30 min of continuous walking. That said, other cost functions with shorter adaptation periods can be used, such as temporal or spatial symmetry[63] or cadence.[64] Then, once a cost function is defined, it can be assessed by measuring a physiological variable. The optimal set of control parameters is typically defined by an algorithm that looks for the minimum solution to the cost function. Here, different algorithms can be used depending on the cost function's complexity. The simplest solution is a grid search, which evaluates the cost function by iteratively changing the set of parameters through random sampling. The results are then interpolated to find a relationship between the control parameters and the observed measurements with the optimal parameters being the ones that correspond to the minimum value for the cost function. However, this approach can only be used in low-dimensionality problems. This is because performance can exponentially decrease as the number of parameters increases due to the curse of high dimensionality, which means the search will become more and more time-consuming and computationally expensive as the problem becomes more complex.

An alternative to the grid search is the gradient descent algorithm, which evaluates only a subset of all the possible solutions by following the gradient of the objective function. At each step, a new set of parameters is defined by following the descending gradient of the cost function. However, this algorithm requires an explicit definition of the cost function, which is not always feasible, so it may get stuck in a local minimum and not actually provide the global optimum as is the case with non-convex problems. Human-in-the-loop optimization problems typically present a non-convex, unknown cost function to be evaluated and analytically described, due to the intrinsic intersubject variability of physiological measurements. In general, one of two well-known machine learning algorithms are used to solve non-convex optimization problems: Bayesian optimization[65] and covariance matrix adaptation evolution strategies (CMA-ES).[66] Bayesian optimization is a sequential model-based approach to finding the global maximum or minimum of an unknown objective function. It relies on surrogate models like Gaussian processes. A prior probabilistic model is set first, and then sequentially refined through

[62] Brunelli et al. (2019); Chin et al. (1999); Hagberg et al. (2007).

[63] Feng et al. (2022); Li et al. (2023).

[64] Felt et al. (2015).

[65] Shahriari et al. (2016).

[66] Hansen (2006).

observations to build a posterior updated model that better reflects the objective function. A new set of candidate points (i.e., a new set of parameters) is extracted at each iteration from the updated model and tested to evaluate the system's response.

Conversely, CMA-ES is used to minimize a cost function by analyzing the covariance matrix of the prior probabilistic model set. New query points are obtained by sampling a multi-variate normal distribution. Then, a new mean and covariance matrix are estimated and updated until a stop condition is met. Moreover, different implementations of human-in-the-loop optimization have been undertaken to determine whether the metabolic cost of walking can be reduced with the majority of experiments involving ankle exoskeletons and transtibial lower limb prostheses. Here, assisting the ankle has shown promise for reducing walking effort since this is the joint generating most of the push-off power.[67] Along these lines, Zhang et al. conducted a study where four different parameters were tuned to provide subject-optimized torque profiles of the ankle.[68] Healthy subjects were able to reduce the metabolic cost of walking by an average of 24% compared to the no-torque control condition. Moreover, the walking patterns varied widely between participants; hence, the authors were able to confirm the benefits of customization, finding that this type of adaptation could also facilitate motor learning.

Feng et al. also applied human-in-the-loop optimization to control a robotic ankle-foot prosthesis while walking.[69] The algorithm was designed to minimize gait symmetry using the vertical ground reaction force recorded on both feet. The optimization was conducted using an instrumented treadmill, lasting only 9 mins on average. Unilateral amputees were able to improve their gait symmetry by 21%, while also reducing the metabolic cost of walking by 9%. This work demonstrates a correlation between gait symmetry and metabolic cost, and that by changing the cost function under analysis, the control parameters can be optimized within much shorter tuning times. These studies show promising preliminary results on how human-in-the-loop approaches can tailor control strategies to the specifics of individual users, ultimately realizing the promise of personalized rehabilitation and maximizing rehabilitative outcomes.

5 The Legal Frameworks Governing Robotic Prostheses and Their Control Algorithms: A First Look

The legal compliance associated with robotic lower limb prostheses will become increasingly complex in the near future, as multiple legal frameworks have come into force that each apply differently. The main legal frameworks include the

[67] Sawicki et al. (2009).

[68] Zhang et al. (2017).

[69] Feng et al. (2022).

GDPR[70] since active lower limb prostheses collect personal and health-related data[71] and the MDR, which governs medical devices as defined in Article 2(1). Additionally, the AI Act outlines a very broad definition of an 'AI system', which refers to any:

> machine-based system designed to operate with varying levels of autonomy and adaptiveness after deployment, which, for explicit or implicit objectives, infers from the input it receives how to generate outputs such as predictions, content, recommendations, or decisions that can influence physical or virtual environments.[72]

Hence, robotic prostheses must also comply with the AI Act. These prostheses will be categorized as high-risk AI systems because machine learning and human-in-the-loop algorithms are embedded within the devices. Several legal challenges arise from the interaction between the hardware and software components of a prosthesis, which are worth examining. These are covered next; however, data protection issues are not included in the analysis despite a growing awareness of privacy and data security matters among medical device manufacturers and AI developers. Notably, the GDPR has been in force for 6 years, and EU Member States (MS) have been applying its regulations consistently. However, the same cannot be said for the MDR, which still requires implementation in certain areas despite coming into effect in 2021. Similarly, the AI Act, which took effect on August 1, 2024, is still in the early stages of application. This raises several critical compliance challenges, especially for the designers and developers of robotic prostheses.

5.1 Hardware: How the MDR Applies to Regular and Custom-Made Medical Devices

For passive prostheses, applying the rules of the MDR is relatively straightforward. The same clarity extends to robotic prostheses, particularly in terms of their hardware components. In fact, both robotic and passive lower limb prostheses fall under the category of medical devices (MD). And, as mentioned in the previous chapter, the MDR is, in essence, an EU safety law specifically focused on medical devices. According to Article 1 of the MDR, the regulation's primary goal is to ensure that only safe and compliant medical devices are placed on the EU market and put into service.

Three key conditions must be met for the MDR to apply. First, the device must be listed within the general and extensive categories schedule outlined in Article 2(1) (including software). Second, it must serve at least one of the functions listed in that same article. For prostheses, this is reflected in the second paragraph, which

[70] Regulation (EU) 2016/679 of the European Parliament and of the Council of 27 April 2016 on the Protection of Natural Persons with Regard to the Processing of Personal Data and on the Free Movement of Such Data, and Repealing Directive 95/46/EC (General Data Protection Regulation).

[71] See Sect. 2.

[72] See Article 3(1) of the AI Act.

defines a medical purpose as the "diagnosis, monitoring, treatment, alleviation of, or compensation for, an injury or disability".[73] The third condition is that the manufacturer's intended purpose must be to create a medical device as specified in implementing rule 3 of Annex VIII. This condition is particularly relevant to the software components of the device, which will be discussed in the next few sections.

Notably, the MDR is a risk-based regulation, meaning the higher the risk to human health and safety, the more stringent the compliance requirements. Medical devices are classified into four risk categories—I, IIa, IIb, and III—all of which must undergo a clinical evaluation[74] before being marketed and all of which must receive a conformity marking[75] certifying sales for the EU market. This certification is granted by a third party known as a Notified Body.[76] To determine the appropriate classification for a device, manufacturers must follow the rules in Article 51 and Annex VIII of the MDR, which consider factors such as whether the device is implantable. Once classified, the manufacturer must then identify the correct conformity assessment procedure by applying the general rules outlined in Article 52 in conjunction with the procedures detailed in Annexes IX, X, and XI. In general, the hardware aspects of robotic prostheses are typically classified as medium-risk (i.e., IIa) as they are considered to be therapeutic devices. This, however, means they are subject to stringent and lengthy conformity procedures.

5.2 *The AI Act and Prostheses Control Algorithms: A Short Overview*

The AI Act pertains to the software associated with robotic prostheses. Starting with the simplest scenario, if the control function of a robotic prosthesis is viewed solely as a means of ensuring patient safety, the algorithms embedded in a prosthetic would be regarded as safety components within a larger medical device. In such cases, the software would only need to comply with the AI Act, which specifically governs algorithms and AI systems in this context.

The main purpose of the AI Act is to ensure the safety of AI systems from both a risk management and human rights perspective.[77] Like the MDR, the AI Act classifies AI systems based on their risk levels. This includes prohibited practices,[78] high-risk systems,[79] and systems that fall outside these categories. In terms of the latter, a mixed regulatory regime applies, combining general principles such as AI literacy

[73] Article 2(1) MDR).

[74] See Article 61–82 in combination with Annex XIV and XV MDR.

[75] See Article 20 MDR.

[76] See Chapter IV and Annex VII. Only class I devices do not require a NB to certify them.

[77] See Article 1(1) AI Act.

[78] See Article 5 AI Act.

[79] See Article 6 AI Act.

with the General Product Safety Regulation (GPSR), as inferred from Recital 166 and Article 4 of the Act. Additionally, the AI Act also addresses Large Language Models (LLMs), which are termed general purpose AI (GPAI) models.[80] These systems can pose systemic risks, defined as:

> risks specific to the high-impact capabilities of general-purpose AI models, with significant potential to affect the Union market or to have negative impacts on public health, safety, security, fundamental rights, or society as a whole, propagated at scale across the value chain.[81]

The key distinction between GPAI models that pose a systemic risk and those that do not lies in whether or not the system requires scrutiny by the newly created AI Office or any other surveillance systems put in place by the EU's MS, whose regulatory regimes generally align with the risk categories mentioned earlier. More detailed information on systemic and non-systemic GPAI is available in Articles 51-56 of the AI Act.

Regarding the control algorithms, the AI Act considers this software to be high-risk for the simple fact that it is embedded in a certified medical device.[82] Moreover, the field of application sits within a closed list of EU-regulated disciplines specified in Annex I of the AI Act. Markedly, Point 11 directly mentions the MDR, which means that the algorithms installed in robotic prostheses need to adhere to the general principles of AI literacy outlined in Article 4. AI literacy involves ensuring that those people who need to work with an AI system are aware of its potential risks, intended purposes, and proper implementation.[83] Key obligations include making transparent, well-documented choices regarding data governance,[84] ensuring human oversight,[85] and creating robust AI systems with strong cybersecurity measures.[86]

Thus, the AI Act not only protects fundamental rights but is also a product safety regulation based on risk assessment. It requires AI providers to create a quality management system, fulfill record-keeping obligations[87] and draft technical documentation,[88] which needs to be shared both with competent EU and State authorities and with those implementing or using the AI system. Moreover, as stated in the MDR, Notified Bodies must be consulted before marketing high-risk AI systems.[89]

---

[80] Article 4(63) AI Act; (Bommasani et al., 2022).

[81] Article 3(65) AI Act.

[82] Article 6(1) AI Act.

[83] See Article 4 and Article 3(56) AI Act. The complete list of fundamental principles to follow for high-risk AI systems is outlined in Sect. 2, Chapter III of the AI Act, while a more complete list of high-risk AI provider duties can be found in Sect. 3 of the same chapter.

[84] See Article 10 AI Act.

[85] See Article 14 AI Act.

[86] See Article 15 AI Act.

[87] See Article 12 AI Act.

[88] See Article 11 AI Act.

[89] See Chapter III Section IV AI Act.

5.3 *Open Questions: Will Prostheses Equipped with AI Be Considered Medical Devices?*

In Sects. 2–4 the control algorithms were considered as primarily serving a safety role without directly fulfilling a medical purpose.

However, if these algorithms have a medical purpose, they are likely to be classified as Software as a Medical Device (SaMD). When dealing with SaMD, the MDR applies the same rules to software as it does to medical devices, especially Article 2.1 MDR.[90] Additionally, Annex VIII of the MDR provides guidelines for attributing a risk class to the software. Hence, if the software is part of the device, or the software drives or influences the device's behavior, it will share the same risk class as the hardware.[91] Alternatively, if the software works independently, it will have its own class of risk.[92] Rule 11 further specifies the corresponding risk class based on the software's function, and all risk classes can apply to any SaMD. Determining whether some piece of software qualifies as an SaMD is extremely challenging. Therefore, in 2019, the Medical Devices Coordination Group (MDCG) issued a guidance to help manufacturers and regulators make this distinction.[93] This group is a cohort of experts formed under Article 103 of the MDR that acts under the supervision of the EU Commission.[94]

Since the medical purpose of robotic prostheses is the "alleviation of, or compensation for, an injury or disability" and since the software drives the device, the embedded software is likely to take on its own class of risk. Simultaneously, the AI Act would apply, as any AI system used in an MD must comply with these regulations. However, to streamline the regulation process, Article 8 of the AI Act introduces the principle of complementarity. It states that when an AI system operates within an EU-regulated field, compliance should first be based on the existing regulations, and only the AI-specific requirements should be applied. In this case, in addition to MDR compliance, AI-specific rules, such as the principle of AI literacy, must be integrated. However, the application of the complementarity principle for SaMD presents complexities. For example, one key challenge lies in aligning the MDR's requirement for a quality management system (Annex IX) with the AI Act's quality management obligations. Additionally, while Article 29 of the AI Act suggests that MDR Notified Bodies may also manage AI certification, clear guidance from the MDCG and the AI Office is essential. Also, manufacturers of SaMDs face significant legal uncertainty, making it crucial to establish precise instructions to ensure compliance with both frameworks.

---

[90] See *supra* the subsection Hardware: How the MDR applies to regular and custom-made medical devices.

[91] See Rule 3.3, Annex VIII MDR.

[92] See Rule 3.3, Annex VIII MDR, second part.

[93] Medical Device Coordination Group Document (2019).

[94] https://health.ec.europa.eu/medical-devices-dialogue-between-interested-parties/medical-device-coordination-group-working-groups_en.

Several factors can influence whether an AI provider or manufacturer classifies robotic prostheses control algorithms as a safety component or as SaMD. In two landmark rulings, *Brain Products v. Biosemi VOF and Others* (2012)[95] and *Snitem v. Philips France* (2017),[96] the Court of Justice of the EU (CJEU) clarified that, while an object may have a medical function, its classification as a MD depends on the intended purpose set by its manufacturer. Currently, there are no criteria to certify algorithms as medical devices, leaving the decision up to the manufacturers or AI providers to make. This ultimately means that their decisions tend to be based on R&D strategies and how they want to position the prosthetic in the market. Opting not to create a medical product can reduce initial investments, as clinical investigations or trials are not required, allowing faster market entry. Conversely, certifying a MD is a longer process but can offer greater market protection for the manufacturer.

In conclusion, achieving legal compliance for algorithms controlling robotic prostheses presents significant challenges, particularly in coordinating the MDR and AI Act. The specific approach taken by the manufacturer regarding how the control algorithm functions will lead to two different outcomes in terms of how the legislation applies. The first option involves applying the MDR solely to the hardware and the AI Act to the software, interpreting the term "control" as limited to ensuring patient safety. The second, more holistic but complex approach, requires applying both the MDR and the AI Act to the software, following the principle of complementarity. In this scenario, the software would be classified as SaMD, as the AI algorithms not only ensure patient safety but also compensate for injuries. This is the path fraught with the most uncertainty due to the lack of specific guidance available for manufacturers. Fortunately, some scholars are beginning to outline a framework for complementary compliance, which should help the maufacturers and developers navigate the coming days.[97]

6 Conclusions

There are numerous open technical challenges to developing lower limb prostheses. However, perhaps the most pressing is to design controllers that make interacting with the prosthetic natural and intuitive while maintaining overall safety and reliability. This step is a fundamental part of translating research achievements into solutions that can be applied in a clinical setting. As outlined, methods based on machine learning have the potential to improve rehabilitation outcomes by learning directly from the user. In this way, the prosthesis can effectively understand the

[95] *Brain Products GmbH v. BioSemi VOF and Others.* (2012).

[96] *Snitem v. Philips France v. Premier Ministre and Ministre Des Affaires Sociales et de La Santé* (2017).

[97] Gennari (2024), pp. 451–453.

specific habits of the user, adapt their control strategy in real-time, and provide a personalized experience, ultimately increasing the adoption of robotic devices in clinical practice. These methods have been key enablers of human-in-the-loop optimization strategies, which have shown promising results in tailoring the functioning of a prosthetic device to the user.

From a legal perspective, marketing robotic prostheses seems challenging because of the current uncertainty about how to apply the MDR and AI Act rules together. If the prosthesis manufacturer is also the AI provider, they face the critical decision of determining whether the control algorithms embedded in a robotic prosthesis have a medical function. In fact, the Court of Justice of the EU has ruled that the manufacturer's intended purpose is the primary criterion for deciding whether a treatment qualifies as a medical device. This applies to both SaMD and AI-based SaMD, like the control algorithms of robotic prostheses.

If the manufacturer decides that the control function is limited to patient and device safety, compliance is relatively straightforward: the hardware must comply with the MDR, while the software would follow the AI Act. However, if they determine that the algorithms serve a medical function, the software will be considered AI-based SaMD. In this case, both the MDR and relevant AI Act provisions would apply,[98] making compliance more complex. Given these challenges, it is essential that the newly created AI Office and the Medical Device Coordination Group engage with stakeholders to provide clearer guidance and ensure greater legal certainty in this area.

Acknowledgements This research was financially supported by the "Biorobotics Research and Innovation Engineering Facilities" "IR0000036" – CUP J13C22000400007 (BRIEF) project.

References

Bartlett HL, King ST, Goldfarb M et al (2021) A semi-powered ankle prosthesis and unified controller for level and sloped walking. IEEE Trans Neural Syst Rehabil Eng 29:320–329. https://doi.org/10.1109/TNSRE.2021.3049194

Bartlett HL, King ST, Goldfarb M et al (2022) Design and assist-as-needed control of a lightly powered prosthetic knee. IEEE Transact Med Robot Bionics 4(2):490–501. https://doi.org/10.1109/TMRB.2022.3161068

Best TK, Embry KR, Rouse EJ et al (2021) Phase-variable control of a powered knee-ankle prosthesis over continuously varying speeds and inclines. In: 2021 IEEE/RSJ international conference on intelligent robots and systems (IROS), presented at the 2021 IEEE/RSJ international conference on intelligent robots and systems (IROS). Prague, Czech Republic, IEEE, pp 6182–6189. https://doi.org/10.1109/IROS51168.2021.9636180

Bhakta K, Camargo J, Donovan L et al (2020) Machine learning model comparisons of user independent & dependent intent recognition systems for powered prostheses. IEEE Robot Automat Lett 5(4):5393–5400. https://doi.org/10.1109/LRA.2020.3007480

[98] See Article 8 AI Act.

Bhakta K, Camargo J, Compton W et al (2021) Evaluation of continuous walking speed determination algorithms and embedded sensors for a powered knee & ankle prosthesis. IEEE Robot Automat Lett 6(3):4820–4826. https://doi.org/10.1109/LRA.2021.3068711

Bommasani R, Hudson DA, Adeli E et al (2022) On the Opportunities and Risks of Foundation Models. Preprint at http://arxiv.org/abs/2108.07258

Brain Products GmbH v. BioSemi VOF and Others. (2012) Court of Justice of the European Union, C- 219/11, EurLex

Brockway J (1987) Derivation of formulae used to calculate energy expenditure in man. Hum Nutr Clin Nutr 41(6):463–471

Brunelli S, Sancesario A, Iosa M et al (2019) Which is the best way to perform the physiological cost index in active individuals with unilateral transtibial amputation? Can Prosthet Orthot Jurnal. https://doi.org/10.33137/cpoj.v2i1.32953

Chin T, Sawamura S, Fujita H, Nakajima S et al (1999) The efficacy of physiological cost index (PCI) measurement of a subject walking with an intelligent prosthesis. Prosthet Orthot Int 23(1):45–49. https://doi.org/10.3109/03093649909071609

Cowan M, Creveling S, Sullivan LM (2023) A unified controller for natural ambulation on stairs and level ground with a powered robotic knee prosthesis. In: *2023 IEEE/RSJ* international conference on intelligent robots and systems (IROS), presented at the 2023 IEEE/RSJ international conference on intelligent robots and systems (IROS). IEEE, Detroit, MI, pp 2146–2151. https://doi.org/10.1109/IROS55552.2023.10341691

Culver S, Bartlett H, Shultz A et al (2018) A stair ascent and descent controller for a powered ankle prosthesis. IEEE Trans Neural Syst Rehabil Eng 26(5):993–1002. https://doi.org/10.1109/TNSRE.2018.2819508

Culver SC, Vailati LG, Goldfarb M (2022) A power-capable knee prosthesis with ballistic swing-phase. IEEE Transact Med Robot Bionics 4(4):1034–1045. https://doi.org/10.1109/TMRB.2022.3216475

Díaz MA, Voß M, Dillen A et al (2023) Human-in-the-loop optimization of wearable robotic devices to improve human–robot interaction: a systematic review. IEEE Transact Cybernet 53(12):7483–7496. https://doi.org/10.1109/TCYB.2022.3224895

Ding Y, Kim M, Kuindersma S et al (2018) Human-in-the-loop optimization of hip assistance with a soft exosuit during walking. Sci Robot 3(15):eaar5438. https://doi.org/10.1126/scirobotics.aar5438

Fagioli I, Mazzarini A, Livolsi C et al (2024) Advancements and challenges in the development of robotic lower limb prostheses: a systematic review. IEEE Transact Med Robot Bionics 6(4):1409–1422. https://doi.org/10.1109/TMRB.2024.3464126

Felt W, Selinger JC, Donelan JM et al (2015) 'Body-In-The-Loop': optimizing device parameters using measures of instantaneous energetic cost. edited by Shi, Y.PLOS ONE 10(8):e0135342. https://doi.org/10.1371/journal.pone.0135342

Feng Y, Mao C, Zhang W et al (2022) Gait-symmetry-based human-in-the-loop optimization for unilateral Transtibial amputees with robotic prostheses. IEEE Transact Med Robot Bionics 4(3):744–753. https://doi.org/10.1109/TMRB.2022.3176476

Fluit R, Prinsen EC, Wang S et al (2020) A comparison of control strategies in commercial and research knee prostheses. IEEE Trans Biomed Eng 67(1):277–290. https://doi.org/10.1109/TBME.2019.2912466

Flynn L, Geeroms J, Jimenez-Fabian R et al (2018) The challenges and achievements of experimental implementation of an active Transfemoral prosthesis based on biological quasi-stiffness: the CYBERLEGs beta-prosthesis. Front Neurorobot 12:80. https://doi.org/10.3389/fnbot.2018.00080

Fu G, Zhu J, Wang Z, Mai J et al (2021) Mechatronic design of a low-noise active knee prosthesis with high backdrivability. In: 2021 IEEE international conference on robotics and automation (ICRA). IEEE, Xi'an, China, pp 7027–7032. https://doi.org/10.1109/ICRA48506.2021.9562052

Gailey R (2008) Review of secondary physical conditions associated with lower-limb amputation and long-term prosthesis use. J Rehabil Res Dev 45(1):15–30. https://doi.org/10.1682/JRRD.2006.11.0147

Gehlhar R, Tucker M, Young AJ et al (2023) A review of current state-of-the-art control methods for lower-limb powered prostheses. Annu Rev Control 55:142–164. https://doi.org/10.1016/j.arcontrol.2023.03.003

Gennari F (2024) O complementarity, where art thou? Wading through the medical device regulation and the AI act compliance: the case of software as a medical device. A primer. 3:411–453

Goldfarb M, Lawson BE, Shultz AH (2013) Realizing the promise of robotic leg prostheses. Sci Transl Med 5(210). https://doi.org/10.1126/scitranslmed.3007312

Gordon M, Thatte N, Geyer H (2019) Online learning for proactive obstacle avoidance with powered transfemoral prostheses. In: 2019 international conference on robotics and automation (ICRA). IEEE, Montreal, QC, pp 7920–7925. https://doi.org/10.1109/ICRA.2019.8794001

Hagberg K, Häggström E, Brånemark R (2007) Physiological cost index (PCI) and walking performance in individuals with transfemoral prostheses compared to healthy controls. Disabil Rehabil 29(8):643–649. https://doi.org/10.1080/09638280600902869

Hansen N (2006) The CMA evolution strategy: a comparing review. In: Lozano JA, Larrañaga P, Inza I, Bengoetxea E (eds) Towards a new evolutionary computation, vol 192. Springer, Berlin, pp 75–102. https://doi.org/10.1007/3-540-32494-1_4

Hargrove LJ, Young AJ, Simon AM et al (2015) Intuitive control of a powered prosthetic leg during ambulation: a randomized clinical trial. JAMA 313(22):2244. https://doi.org/10.1001/jama.2015.4527

Heins S, Flynn L, Geeroms J et al (2018) Torque control of an active elastic transfemoral prosthesis via quasi-static modelling. Robot Auton Syst 107:100–115. https://doi.org/10.1016/j.robot.2018.05.015

Heins S, Flynn L, Laloyaux H et al (2020) Compliant control of a Transfemoral prosthesis by combining feed-forward and feedback. In: 2020 8th IEEE RAS/EMBS international conference for biomedical robotics and biomechatronics (BioRob). IEEE, New York City, pp 452–458. https://doi.org/10.1109/BioRob49111.2020.9224434

Hood S, Gabert L, Lenzi T (2022) Powered knee and ankle prosthesis with adaptive control enables climbing stairs with different Stair Heights, cadences, and gait patterns. IEEE Trans Robot 38(3):1430–1441. https://doi.org/10.1109/TRO.2022.3152134

Huang H, Crouch DL, Liu M et al (2016) A cyber expert system for auto-tuning powered prosthesis impedance control parameters. Ann Biomed Eng 44(5):1613–1624. https://doi.org/10.1007/s10439-015-1464-7

Huang H, Si J, Brandt A, Li M (2021) Taking both sides: seeking symbiosis between intelligent prostheses and human motor control during locomotion. Curr Opin Biomed Eng 20:100314. https://doi.org/10.1016/j.cobme.2021.100314

Hunt G, Hood S, Lenzi T (2021) Stand-up, squat, lunge, and walk with a robotic knee and ankle prosthesis under shared neural control. IEEE Open J Eng Med Biol 2:267–277. https://doi.org/10.1109/OJEMB.2021.3104261

Hussain T, Iqbal N, Maqbool HF et al (2020) Intent based recognition of walking and ramp activities for amputee using sEMG based lower limb prostheses. Biocyber Biomed Eng 40(3):1110–1123. https://doi.org/10.1016/j.bbe.2020.05.010

Katsumura M, Senzaki M, Yano K et al (2022) Robotic knee prosthesis to follow changes in real-time gait patterns. In: 2022 IEEE/SICE international symposium on system integration (SII). IEEE, Narvik, Norway, pp 672–675. https://doi.org/10.1109/SII52469.2022.9708880

Kim, M., Ding, Y., Malcolm, P. et al. (2017) Human-in-the-loop Bayesian optimization of wearable device parameters, edited by Hu, X.PLOS ONE 12(9):e0184054. https://doi.org/10.1371/journal.pone.0184054

Koller JR, Gates DH, Ferris DP, et al. (2016) 'Body-in-the-Loop' Optimization of Assistive Robotic Devices: A Validation Study. Robotics: Science and Systems XII, presented at the

Robotics: Science and Systems 2016, Robotics: Science and Systems Foundation. https://doi.org/10.15607/RSS.2016.XII.007

Lanotte F, O'Brien MK, Jayaraman A (2023) AI in rehabilitation medicine: opportunities and challenges. Ann Rehabil Med 47(6):444–458. https://doi.org/10.5535/arm.23131

Le D, Cheng S, Gregg RD, Ghaffari M (2022) Deep convolutional neural network and transfer learning for locomotion intent prediction. arXiv, 25 September

Leestma JK, Fehr KH, Adamczyk PG (2021) Adapting semi-active prostheses to real-world movements: sensing and controlling the dynamic mean ankle moment arm with a variable-stiffness foot on ramps and stairs. Sensors 21(18):6009. https://doi.org/10.3390/s21186009

Lenzi T, Hargrove L, Sensinger J (2014) Speed-adaptation mechanism: robotic prostheses can actively regulate joint torque. IEEE Robot Automat Magaz 21(4):94–107. https://doi.org/10.1109/MRA.2014.2360305

Li M, Liu W, Si J, Stallrich JW et al (2023) Hierarchical optimization for control of robotic knee prostheses toward improved symmetry of propulsive impulse. IEEE Trans Biomed Eng 70(5):1634–1642. https://doi.org/10.1109/TBME.2022.3224026

Li Q, Chen S, Xu C et al (2018) Design, control and implementation of a powered prosthetic leg. In: 2018 11th international workshop on human friendly robotics (HFR). IEEE, Shenzhen, China, pp 85–90. https://doi.org/10.1109/HFR.2018.8633466

Li Q, Zhang T, Li G et al (2022) Neural-dynamics optimization and repetitive learning control for robotic leg prostheses. IEEE/ASME Transact Mechatr 27(2):811–822. https://doi.org/10.1109/TMECH.2021.3071936

Mai J, Zhang Z, Wang Q (2017) A real-time intent recognition system based on SoC-FPGA for robotic transtibial prosthesis. In: Huang Y, Wu H, Liu H, Yin Z (eds) Intelligent robotics and applications, vol 10462. Springer International Publishing, Cham, pp 280–289. https://doi.org/10.1007/978-3-319-65289-427

Mazzarini A, Fantozzi M, Papapicco V et al. (2023) A low-power ankle-foot prosthesis for push-off enhancement. In: Wearable technologies. Cambridge University Press 4: e18. https://doi.org/10.1017/wtc.2023.13

Medical Device Coordination Group Document. (2019) Guidance on Qualification and Classification of Software in Regulation (eU) 2017/745 – MDR and Regulation (EU) 2017/746

Mendez J, Hood S, Gunnel A et al (2020) Powered knee and ankle prosthesis with indirect volitional swing control enables level-ground walking and crossing over obstacles. Sci Robot 5(44):eaba6635. https://doi.org/10.1126/scirobotics.aba6635

Miller MJ, Jones J, Anderson CB et al (2019) Factors influencing participation in physical activity after dysvascular amputation: a qualitative meta-synthesis. Disabil Rehabil 41(26):3141–3150. https://doi.org/10.1080/09638288.2018.1492031

Murray AM, Gaffney BM, Davidson BS et al (2017) Biomechanical compensations of the trunk and lower extremities during stepping tasks after unilateral transtibial amputation. Clin Biomech 49:64–71. https://doi.org/10.1016/j.clinbiomech.2017.08.010

Poggensee KL, Collins SH (2021) How adaptation, training, and customization contribute to benefits from exoskeleton assistance. Sci Robot 6(58)

Rezazadeh S, Quintero D, Divekar N et al (2019) A phase variable approach for improved rhythmic and non-rhythmic control of a powered knee-ankle prosthesis. IEEE Access 7:109840–109855. https://doi.org/10.1109/ACCESS.2019.2933614

Ronsse R, De Rossi SMM, Vitiello N et al (2013) Real-time estimate of velocity and acceleration of quasi-periodic signals using adaptive oscillators. IEEE Trans Robot 29(3):783–791. https://doi.org/10.1109/TRO.2013.2240173

Sawicki GS, Lewis CL, Ferris DP (2009) It pays to have a spring in your step. Exerc Sport Sci Rev 37(3):130–138. https://doi.org/10.1097/JES.0b013e31819c2df6

Shahriari B, Swersky K, Wang Z et al (2016) Taking the human out of the loop: a review of Bayesian optimization. Proc IEEE 104(1):148–175. https://doi.org/10.1109/JPROC.2015.2494218

Shultz AH, Goldfarb M (2018) A unified controller for walking on even and uneven terrain with a powered ankle prosthesis. IEEE Trans Neural Syst Rehabil Eng 26(4):788–797. https://doi.org/10.1109/TNSRE.2018.2810165

Shultz AH, Lawson BE, Goldfarb M (2016) Variable cadence walking and ground adaptive standing with a powered ankle prosthesis. IEEE Trans Neural Syst Rehabil Eng 24(4):495–505. https://doi.org/10.1109/TNSRE.2015.2428196

Snitem v. Philips France v. Premier Ministre and Ministre Des Affaires Sociales et de La Santé (2017) Court of Justice of the European Union, C-329/16, EurLex

Sullivan, L.M., Creveling, S., Cowan, M. et al. (2023) Powered knee and ankle prosthesis control for adaptive ambulation at variable speeds, inclines, and uneven terrains. In: 2023 IEEE/RSJ international conference on intelligent robots and systems (IROS), presented at the 2023 IEEE/RSJ international conference on intelligent robots and systems (IROS). IEEE, Detroit, MI, pp. 2128–2133, doi: https://doi.org/10.1109/IROS55552.2023.10342504

Thatte N, Shah T, Geyer H (2019) Robust and adaptive lower limb prosthesis stance control via extended Kalman filter-based gait phase estimation. IEEE Robot Automat Lett 4(4):3129–3136. https://doi.org/10.1109/LRA.2019.2924841

Tran M, Gabert L, Cempini M, Lenzi T (2019) A lightweight, efficient fully powered knee prosthesis with actively variable transmission. IEEE Robot Automat Lett 4(2):1186–1193. https://doi.org/10.1109/LRA.2019.2892204

Tucker MR, Olivier J, Pagel A et al (2015) Control strategies for active lower extremity prosthetics and orthotics: a review. J Neuroeng Rehabil 12(1):1. https://doi.org/10.1186/1743-0003-12-1

Welker CG, Best TK, Gregg RD (2022) Data-driven variable impedance control of a powered knee-ankle prosthesis for sit, stand, and walk with minimal tuning. In: 2022 IEEE/RSJ international conference on intelligent robots and systems (IROS). IEEE, Kyoto, Japan, pp 9660–9667. https://doi.org/10.1109/IROS47612.2022.9982037

Wen Y, Si J, Brandt A, Gao X et al (2020) Online reinforcement learning control for the personalization of a robotic knee prosthesis. IEEE Transact Cybern 50(6):2346–2356. https://doi.org/10.1109/TCYB.2019.2890974

Woodward R, Simon A, Seyforth E et al (2022) Real-time adaptation of an artificial neural network for transfemoral amputees using a powered prosthesis. IEEE Trans Biomed Eng 69(3):1202–1211. https://doi.org/10.1109/TBME.2021.3120616

Xu D, Wang Q (2019) BP neural network based on-board training for real-time locomotion mode recognition in robotic Transtibial prostheses. In: 2019 IEEE/RSJ international conference on intelligent robots and systems (IROS). IEEE, Macau, pp 8158–8163. https://doi.org/10.1109/IROS40897.2019.8968298

Xu D, Wang Q (2020) On-board training strategy for IMU-based real-time locomotion recognition of Transtibial amputees with robotic prostheses. Front Neurorobot 14:47. https://doi.org/10.3389/fnbot.2020.00047

Xu D, Feng Y, Mai J et al (2018) Real-time on-board recognition of continuous locomotion modes for amputees with robotic Transtibial prostheses. IEEE Trans Neural Syst Rehabil Eng 26(10):2015–2025. https://doi.org/10.1109/TNSRE.2018.2870152

Xu D, Crea S, Vitiello N et al (2020a) Online estimation of continuous gait phase for robotic transtibial prostheses based on adaptive oscillators. In: 2020 IEEE/ASME international conference on advanced intelligent mechatronics (AIM). IEEE, Boston, MA, pp 1890–1895. https://doi.org/10.1109/AIM43001.2020.9158968

Xu D, Crea S, Vitiello N et al (2020b) Capacitive sensing-based continuous gait phase estimation in robotic transtibial prostheses. In: 2020 8th IEEE RAS/EMBS international conference for biomedical robotics and biomechatronics (BioRob). IEEE, New York, pp 298–303. https://doi.org/10.1109/BioRob49111.2020.9224347

Zhang J, Fiers P, Witte KA et al (2017) Human-in-the-loop optimization of exoskeleton assistance during walking. Science 356(6344):1280–1284. https://doi.org/10.1126/science.aal5054

Bridging the Gap: Overcoming the Barriers to Using Robotics in Rehabilitation

Irene Giovanna Aprile, Marco Germanotta, Maria Cristina Mauro, and Alessio Fasano

Abstract Robotics and digital technologies are increasingly emerging as promising tools in the field of rehabilitation given the benefits they offer to people with limited motor, sensory, and cognitive functions. These innovations are revolutionizing rehabilitation practices by enhancing existing services and offering patients access to advanced, personalized treatments. However, there are some significant barriers to implementing these systems in clinical settings, including resistance to adopting these technologies by practitioners, cost concerns, and ethical and legal constraints. Unfortunately, the rapid introduction of these technologies into rehabilitation settings has not been accompanied by some necessary adjustments in the organizational, educational, and regulatory aspects of healthcare systems. Therefore, to ensure today's robotic solutions remain sustainable, it is essential to develop new organizational models of treatment. Further, these models must be evaluated for their sustainability and effectiveness through pragmatic clinical trials that actively involve rehabilitation therapists with specific expertise in robotics. Additionally, we must begin to train a cohort of healthcare professionals who can effectively operate and leverage these technologies. In other words, we must begin to create a workforce capable of integrating these solutions into daily clinical practices. Lastly, it is essential that we create robust regulatory frameworks with clear reimbursement policies to ensure equitable access to all patients. The widespread and inclusive adoption of sustainable robotic solutions and treatments must be fostered on a national scale. Only through these measures will it be possible to reshape the healthcare services offered to the community in a way that promotes a true democratization of these advanced technologies. To this end, this chapter critically addresses the barriers slowing the take-up of robotic and digital therapies in rehabilitation and in healthcare more generally.

I. G. Aprile (✉) · M. Germanotta · M. C. Mauro · A. Fasano
IRCCS Fondazione Don Carlo Gnocchi ONLUS, Florence, Italy
e-mail: iaprile@dongnocchi.it

F. Casarosa et al. (eds.), *Enabling and Safeguarding Personalized Medicine*, Data Science, Machine Intelligence, and Law 7,
https://doi.org/10.1007/978-3-031-99709-9_13

1 Introduction

Robotics and digital technologies are increasingly emerging as promising tools in the field of rehabilitation because they offer significant benefits to individuals with limited motor, sensory, and/or cognitive functions. These technologies hold particular promise when incorporated into personalized rehabilitation plans, as they can be tailored to meet the specific needs of each patient, optimizing both clinical outcomes and patient satisfaction. However, despite their potential to significantly improve patient outcomes, integrating these technologies into clinical settings has not been easy. Barriers like resistance from healthcare practitioners, economic constraints, and ethical and legal concerns have all hampered the take-up of these innovations. Indeed, the rapid introduction of these technologies into rehabilitation settings has not been accompanied by some necessary adjustments in the organizational, educational, and regulatory aspects of healthcare systems. Hence, this chapter examines the potential of these state-of-the-art robotic and digital therapies, the barriers to their implementation, and possible strategies to overcome the challenges limiting their adoption in the context of rehabilitation and healthcare.

2 The Potential of Robotics and Digital Technologies

The application of robotics and digital technologies in the field of rehabilitation has evolved significantly over the past few decades[1] with a notable increase in scientific publications supporting their efficacy.[2] Recent advancements have led to the development of sophisticated systems and digital platforms that increase the intensity of movements or that allow patients to execute movements they can no longer perform on their own. Indeed, several studies have emerged that explore the use of highly advanced technologies, such as robotics and virtual reality, to meet the needs of clinicians and patients.[3]

In essence, robotic therapy has been proposed as a viable approach to both increasing the volume and intensity of a therapeutic regime as well as a way to standardize treatments.[4] It is important to note that robotic therapy can be personalized to match the specific requirements of individual patients, thus enhancing its therapeutic effects. Furthermore, the sensory feedback integrated into many robotic systems, such as visual and auditory stimuli, fosters processes of brain plasticity, improving rehabilitation outcomes.[5,6] These feedback mechanisms increase patient

[1] Van Der Loos (2016), pp. 1685–1728.

[2] Xue (2021), Article 806723.

[3] Loureiro (2011), pp. 1103–1118.

[4] Germanotta (2020), p. 1.

[5] Mauro (2024), pp. 3590–3602.

[6] Rosati (2013), pp. 1–15.

engagement during the treatment as patients receive information about their movements and interactions with the environment in real-time.[7] This individualized feedback is crucial for ensuring that patients stay motivated to follow their personal rehabilitation protocols.

Additionally, more recently, a host of technologies have been proposed for home-based treatment. These innovations have the potential to ensure a continuum of care, even during the chronic phases of a disability. Home-based rehabilitation technologies, such as portable robotic devices and telerehabilitation platforms, have revolutionized the way patients receive care. These innovations allow patients to engage in therapeutic exercises and receive real-time feedback from the comfort of their own homes, reducing the burden on healthcare facilities while ensuring they maintain a consistent rehabilitation regimen tailored to their individual needs. Plus, the ability to perform therapy at home helps to ensure long-term adherence to treatment protocols, which is crucial for sustained progress and recovery.[8]

Digital technologies, including virtual reality (VR) and augmented reality (AR), have also introduced new dimensions to rehabilitation.[9] VR environments simulate real-life scenarios, allowing patients to practice daily activities in a controlled and immersive setting. For instance, patients can use VR systems to practice ordinary tasks, such as cooking, which helps them regain confidence and independence in the activities of daily living. The immersive nature of VR contributes to increased patient engagement and motivation, which are critical factors for successful rehabilitation outcomes.[10] VR can also be customized to replicate specific environments or activities that are most relevant to a patient's personal recovery goals, making it an ideal tool for personalized rehabilitation. AR technologies, on the other hand, overlay digital information into the real world, providing real-time guidance during rehabilitation exercises. This technology can project visual cues or instructions into a patient's field of view, aiding in the execution of specific movements or tasks with greater accuracy.

The use of wearable sensors in rehabilitation is another significant advancement.[11] These sensors monitor physiological parameters like movement patterns and muscle activity, providing real-time data that can be used to personalize rehabilitation protocols. This data-driven approach allows for more precise adjustments to therapy, optimizing its effectiveness.

Indeed, the personalization of treatment is a crucial aspect of these technologies. Robotics and digital systems can be tailored to meet the specific needs of each patient, offering custom therapy plans that adapt to individual progress. The integration of AI and machine learning further enhances personalization levels.[12] Here, AI

---

[7] Mohd Zuki (2021), pp. 333–338.

[8] Argent (2018), Article e8518.

[9] Postolache (2021), pp. 155–180.

[10] Mouatt (2020), Article 564664.

[11] Patel et al. (2019), p. 21.

[12] Schork (2019), pp. 265–283.

algorithms can analyze the data collected from sensors and robotic systems to identify patterns and predict the best course of action for each patient. These insights can allow practitioners to craft highly individual therapy plans that evolve over time based on the patient's progress and changing needs. This data-driven personalization ensures that therapies are continuously adapted to the patient's evolving requirements, maximizing their rehabilitation potential.[13]

Personalized treatment through these advanced technologies not only enhances the efficacy of the therapy but also improves patients' satisfaction and adherence to the rehabilitation program. By focusing on personalized treatment, these technologies enable healthcare providers to deliver more effective and patient-centered care, leading to better rehabilitation outcomes. This personalized approach ensures that rehabilitation is not a one-size-fits-all process but rather a tailored journey that takes into account the unique needs, capabilities, and goals of each patient.

3 Barriers to Integrating Robotics and Digital Technologies

Despite the promise held in robotics and digital technologies, several barriers limit their integration into clinical settings. These barriers are complex, spanning resistance to adoption by healthcare practitioners to economic and regulatory challenges. Thus, it is worthwhile exploring each barrier and any strategies that might be used to overcome them.

3.1 Economics

From an economic point of view, deploying robots in healthcare settings is a challenging issue.[14,15] Currently, there is a great deal of uncertainty about the cost-effectiveness of robotic technology compared to traditional approaches.[16] These costs not only include the purchase price of the equipment but also expenses related to installation, maintenance, and training to guarantee they are used appropriately by clinical personnel. For many healthcare facilities, these financial demands can be a major deterrent. Additionally, the reimbursement and funding mechanisms provided by national health systems may not always adequately cover the costs of these technologies, further limiting their availability and accessibility.

Yet robotic rehabilitation has become a crucial component of patient care. As one example, robotic rehabilitation has been recognized in the 2018 revision of the

---

[13] Aziz (2024), pp. 281–308.

[14] Turchetti (2014), pp. 143–153.

[15] Banyai and Cornel (2024), Article 1720.

[16] Wagner (2011), pp. 2630–2632.

Essential Levels of Care doctrine in Italy, confirmed in 2024, which integrates these technologies into the nomenclature of specialized rehabilitative services offered by the National Health Service under code 93.11.G: "Motor re-education using high-tech robotic assistance devices" in outpatient settings.[17] In Italy, robotic rehabilitation is actually delivered almost exclusively in inpatient settings. Despite this inclusion, there is a notable absence of specific guidelines, particularly regarding economic reimbursement provided by national health systems. Rates for these services have yet to be established, resulting in a lack of recognized financial value for rehabilitation facilities employing such technologies. Consequently, there is a significant gap in the tariff structure, which means that the economic burden borne by institutions and companies in providing these advanced rehabilitation opportunities to patients is not adequately reflected.[18]

3.2 Resistance

A reluctance to take up these advanced technologies by healthcare practitioners is another significant barrier to their adoption.[19] This resistance may stem from a preference for traditional rehabilitation methods, insufficient training which results in difficulties using the new tools, or doubts about the benefits and safety of new technologies.[20] For instance, some professionals might perceive robotic devices as overly complex or unnecessary compared to traditional practices, especially if not adequately trained in how to administer each type of device. Many healthcare practitioners are deeply rooted in traditional rehabilitation practices and may be hesitant to embrace new tools due to concerns about their safety, reliability, effectiveness, and sustainability. Others may fear that technology could diminish their role in the care process. This resistance is often compounded by a lack of awareness and understanding of the benefits and capabilities of robotic and digital technologies. Many clinicians are simply unaware of the significant advantages these technologies can offer to patients in terms of improved outcomes and personalized care, as well as of the way the healthcare system as a whole can benefit from robotics and digital technologies through increased efficiency, optimized resource use, and long-term cost savings.[21] Indeed, previous studies highlight that, despite the potential benefits, many practitioners continue to rely on traditional methods due to a lack of familiarity with new technologies and uncertainty about their effectiveness.[22] Our recent

[17] Ministero della Salute (2018).

[18] Calabrò (2020), pp. 14–16.

[19] Banyai and Cornel (2024), Article 1720.

[20] Laparidou (2021), Article 181.

[21] Gower (2024), Article 1445099.

[22] Borges do Nascimento (2023), p. 161.

study showed that healthcare professionals' positive feelings towards robotics is correlated with actual usage of the technology.[23]

The lack of adequate training, among operators working in robotics-intensive centers, limits the effective implementation of robotic and digital devices in clinical practice. Many practitioners find these technologies too complicated compared to traditional rehabilitation methods, pointing to the challenges associated with wearing and operating the devices. Additionally, a lack of motivation among therapists to employ these new tools, which is often linked to insufficient knowledge and training, further hinders the adoption of these innovations. Successfully integrating robotic and digital technologies into rehabilitation regimens requires healthcare professionals to be well-versed in both the technical and practical aspects of these tools. Here, the technical elements might include how to operate the device, troubleshooting, and system configuration, while the practical aspects include incorporating the technology into treatment plans and customizing the device's operation to suit the patient's clinical needs. This gap in knowledge and motivation can significantly impede the effective implementation and use of advanced rehabilitation technologies.

3.3 Regulations

Regulatory considerations also play a critical role in the adoption of robotic and digital technologies. This is because there is a notable absence of specific guidelines or ad hoc normative standards regarding the economic reimbursements associated with robotic treatments in clinical practice.[24] Only in certain regions or settings (i.e., inpatient vs outpatient) is the use of specific robotic devices considered a minimum requirement for accreditation. For example, the recently published Essential Levels of Care in Italy includes only reimbursements for robotic systems used in an outpatient setting, and, further, this policy is not based on any specific economic analysis.

3.4 Ethics and Privacy

Further, using digital technologies and wearable sensors generally involves collecting and managing sensitive patient data, which raises significant ethical and privacy concerns. Protecting patient data from unauthorized access and ensuring the security of that data are of paramount importance. Healthcare providers must implement comprehensive data protection measures to safeguard patient information and comply with relevant data protection regulations, such as the General Data Protection

[23] Nicora (2025), Article 78.

[24] Calabrò (2020), pp. 14–16.

Regulation (GDPR) in Europe.[25] These measures include using advanced encryption techniques, conducting regular security audits, and ensuring that all personnel are trained in data privacy practices.[26] Additionally, there must be transparency with patients regarding how their data is used, stored, and shared. Patients should also be provided with clear consent forms and privacy notices. Balancing technological advancements with rigorous ethical and regulatory standards, such as data protection and patient consent requirements, is essential to fostering trust and ensuring the responsible adoption of these innovative technologies. It is for this reason that healthcare practitioners must be trained in how and when it is legal to use the data obtained from robotic systems in clinical practice or in scientific research according to the GDPR. However, overcoming these barriers and helping organizations navigate the complexities of these emerging technologies will require giving them ongoing support to build the necessary expertise, resources, and systems to comply with GDPR.

4 Strategies for Overcoming Barriers

Bridging the gap between the opportunities of robotics and technologies and their actual adoption in clinical practice is a complex process governed by a number of obstacles. Hence, overcoming these challenges will require deploying several interrelated strategies that each, in turn, address the economic constraints of using robotics, the resistance to these advanced technologies by healthcare practitioners, and the regulatory and ethical challenges associated with the digital world.

4.1 Economics

Economic assessments of innovative rehabilitation therapies are crucial for developing cost-effective and sustainable rehabilitation strategies.[27] To achieve this, it is important to develop innovative organizational models that integrate these technologies into clinical practice in a sustainable manner. By demonstrating the long-term benefits and cost-effectiveness of robotic and digital technologies through rigorous cost-utility analyses, we might better understand the value of these innovations.

With this goal in mind, Aprile et al.[28] assessed the feasibility of a new organizational model. The setting was a clinical rehabilitation center with a robot-assisted

[25] Regulation (EU) 2016/679 of the European Parliament and of the Council of 27 April 2016 on the protection of natural persons with regard to the processing of personal data and on the free movement of such data, and repealing Directive 95/46/EC (General Data Protection Regulation).

[26] Kruse (2017), pp. 1–10.

[27] Turchetti (2014), pp. 143–153.

[28] Aprile (2019), pp. 5357.

rehabilitation area equipped with four devices. Here, one physiotherapist supervises up to four patients at a time. The findings show that, despite a higher physiotherapist-to-patient ratio, the outcomes of treatment and patient satisfaction remain high. Given the demonstrated feasibility of the proposed model, the authors then conducted a pragmatic study over multiple centers[29] to compare the efficacy of using a robotic upper limb treatment with a 1:3 physiotherapist-to-patient ratio in this 4-device setting, compared to conventional therapy with a 1:1 physiotherapist-to-patient ratio. The results show no differences between the clinical effectiveness of the two approaches. Building on this study, Gower et al.[30] then investigated the sustainability of a robotic treatment based on the above organizational model as compared to a conventional model. Through a retrospective cost analysis, the authors demonstrate that a mixed rehabilitation approach, combining both conventional individual rehabilitation and robotic rehabilitation where a single physiotherapist supervises up to four patients, led to cost savings over the conventional method alone. These findings, combined with the clinical effectiveness of the robotic approach, highlight the potential of leveraging technology to optimize resource use and improve rehabilitation outcomes. Moreover, these studies provide valuable insights for healthcare decision-makers on the sustainability of robot-assisted rehabilitation models. It is therefore clear that sustainable models of treatment can be established within healthcare facilities by deploying dedicated teams that focus on robotic and digital systems. These teams can manage the implementation of new technologies, provide training and support, and ensure that technological solutions are seamlessly integrated into clinical practice. Importantly, the research also indicates that successful integration often requires a structured approach, including forming interdisciplinary teams and developing clear implementation plans.[31]

4.2 *Resistance*

Learning and training are two important factors that influence the use, disuse, or lack of take-up of a technology.[32] Investing in comprehensive training programs for healthcare professionals is, therefore, another essential strategy for overcoming resistance to technological solutions by healthcare practitioners.[33] Such programs need to cover the technical aspects, practical applications, and clinical best practices associated with the given technology. Additionally, encouraging knowledge sharing and collaboration among healthcare professionals can foster a supportive learning environment and promote the widespread adoption of these technologies. Continuous

---

[29] Aprile (2020), pp. 3–14.

[30] Gower (2024), Article 1445099.

[31] Borges do Nascimento (2023), p. 161.

[32] Andrade (2014), pp. 65–78.

[33] Laparidou (2021), Article 181.

professional development and certification programs can help maintain a high standard of care and ensure that practitioners are up-to-date with the latest advancements in the field.

Moreover, leadership within healthcare organizations plays a pivotal role in shaping cultural attitudes.[34] Leaders must champion the adoption of new technologies, highlighting success stories and evidence-based benefits to encourage take-up by the clinical team. Engaging frontline workers in the decision-making process and incorporating their feedback can also help mitigate resistance and build a sense of ownership over new tools. This approach helps reduce hesitance towards new technologies and fosters an environment where innovation is embraced rather than resisted.

4.3 Regulations

In addressing the barriers to using robotics in rehabilitation, it is crucial to establish robust regulatory frameworks. Further, it is possible to design effective regulatory frameworks based on strong evidence emanating from clinical trials of robotics in the field of rehabilitation. For example, the frameworks devised should ensure that all patients who might potentially benefit from robotics technology in their rehabilitation are not only entitled to use this technology but are also reimbursed for the cost. This could be achieved by integrating these technologies into each nation's healthcare subsidy framework with the specific reimbursement policies informed by economic data derived from clinical trials and their associated cost-effectiveness/cost-utility analyses. This approach would not only standardize access to advanced rehabilitative care but also ensure equitable distribution of resources, thus enhancing overall patient outcomes.

4.4 Ethics and Privacy

In order to overcome legal and ethical barriers, we must develop comprehensive guidelines and standards for using robotic and digital technologies. As with pharmacological trials, clinical trials involving robotic and technological systems must adhere to strict regulatory requirements regarding both data privacy and security. In this context, strong data protection measures, including robust encryption and full compliance with regulations like the GDPR, must be ensured to safeguard patient information. Moreover, unlike drugs, which typically remain stable once approved, robotic devices and digital technologies are continuously evolving. These systems frequently require updates to enhance functionality, safety, or performance.

[34] Laukka (2022), pp. 2763–80.

Therefore, it is crucial to establish a regulatory framework that addresses the dynamic nature of these technologies, ensuring that updates, upgrades, and modifications can be swiftly approved through fast-track procedures. Therefore, we must design legal and ethical frameworks that involve collaboration between regulatory bodies and healthcare institutions to accommodate the evolving nature of these systems. This will help ensure the safe, equitable, and effective use of robotic technologies, while also fostering public trust in these innovations. By aligning legal and ethical guidelines with evolving technologies, healthcare systems can create an environment that promotes innovation without compromising patient rights or safety.

5 Conclusion

Integrating robotics and digital technologies into the field of rehabilitation presents significant potential to improve patient outcomes by offering more personalized and effective treatment. These technologies enable real-time monitoring and adjustment of therapy, providing an objective measure of progress for patients with motor, sensory, and cognitive impairments. However, the widespread adoption of these innovations faces several barriers, including economic constraints, adoption resistance, and legal and ethical challenges.

To overcome economic challenges, it is essential to demonstrate the cost-effectiveness and long-term financial viability of robotic rehabilitation technologies. Studies evaluating the organizational models show that these technologies could easily be integrated into clinical practice in a cost-effective manner while maintaining high-quality treatments. A key element is to develop new reimbursement models informed by cost-benefit analyses from clinical trials as this could improve access to these technologies across different healthcare settings.

Adoption resistance from healthcare practitioners within institutions can be mitigated by comprehensive training programs that address both the technical and practical aspects of these technologies. A focus on continuous professional development and fostering a supportive environment for knowledge sharing is essential in overcoming this barrier. Furthermore, leadership within healthcare organizations plays a critical role in advocating for new technologies and reducing staff reluctance by emphasizing the benefits and evidence supporting their use.

Regulatory and ethical frameworks must be dynamic and developed through collaboration between relevant stakeholders, ensuring they can evolve alongside the rapid advancements in robotic and rehabilitation technologies. Ensuring the protection of patient data through compliance with regulations such as GDPR is essential for maintaining trust. Additionally, creating transparent processes is crucial for the safe and ethical use of these technologies in clinical practice.

In conclusion, overcoming adoption resistance and the economic, legal, and ethical barriers to integrating robotics and digital technologies into rehabilitation requires a multifaceted approach. By addressing these challenges through comprehensive research, training, regulatory engagement, and collaboration, healthcare systems can maximize the potential of these innovations to improve rehabilitation outcomes and ensure the more efficient use of resources.

Acknowledgements This work was supported by the Italian Ministry of Research, under the complementary actions to the NRRP "Fit4MedRob - Fit for Medical Robotics" Grant (# PNC0000007) and by the "Biorobotics Research and Innovation Engineering Facilities" "IR0000036" – CUP J13C22000400007 (BRIEF) project.

References

Andrade AO, Pereira AA, Walter S et al (2014) Bridging the gap between robotic technology and health care. Biomed Signal Proc Control 10:65–78

Aprile I, Pecchioli C, Loreti S et al (2019) Improving the efficiency of robot-mediated rehabilitation by using a new organizational model: an observational feasibility study in an Italian rehabilitation center. Appl Sci 9(24):5357

Aprile I, Germanotta M, Cruciani A et al (2020) Upper limb robotic rehabilitation after stroke: a multicenter, randomized clinical trial. J Neurol Phys Therapy 44(1):3–14

Argent R, Ailish D, Brian C (2018) Patient involvement with home-based exercise programs: can connected health interventions influence adherence? JMIR mHealth uHealth 6(3):e8518

Aziz R, Jawed F, Khan SA et al (2024) Wearable IoT devices in rehabilitation: enabling personalized precision medicine. Medical robotics and AI-assisted diagnostics for a high-tech healthcare industry. IGI Glob 2024:281–308

Banyai AD, Cornel B (2024) Robotics in physical rehabilitation: systematic review. Healthcare 12(17). MDPI, 2024

Borges do Nascimento IJ., Abdulazeem H., Thinagaran Vasanthan L et al. (2023) Barriers and facilitators to utilizing digital health technologies by healthcare professionals. NPJ Digit Med 6(1):161

Calabrò RS, Müller-Eising C, Diliberti ML, et al. (2020) Who will pay for robotic rehabilitation? The growing need for a cost-effectiveness analysis. Innov Clin Neurosci 17(10–12):14

Germanotta M, Gower V, Papadopoulou D, et al. (2020) Reliability, validity and discriminant ability of a robotic device for finger training in patients with subacute stroke. J Neuroeng Rehabil 17:1–10

Gower V, Aprile I, Falchini F, et al. (2024) Cost analysis of technological vs. conventional upper limb rehabilitation for patients with neurological disorders: an Italian real-world data case study. Front Public Health 12:1445099

Kruse CS, Frederick B, Jacobson T et al (2017) Cybersecurity in healthcare: a systematic review of modern threats and trends. Technol Health Care 25(1):1–10

Laparidou D, Curtis F, Akanuwe J, et al. (2021) Patient, carer, and staff perceptions of robotics in motor rehabilitation: a systematic review and qualitative meta-synthesis. J Neeuroeng Rehabil 18:1–24

Laukka E, Pölkki T, Kanste O (2022) Leadership in the context of digital health services: a concept analysis. J Nurs Manage 30(7):2763–2780

Loureiro RCV, Harwin WS, Nagai K et al (2011) Advances in upper limb stroke rehabilitation: a technology push. Med Biol Eng Comput 49:1103–1118

Mauro MC, Fasano A, Germanotta M et al (2024) Restoring of interhemispheric symmetry in patients with stroke following bilateral or unilateral robot-assisted upper-limb rehabilitation: a pilot randomized controlled trial. IEEE Transact Neural Syst Rehabil Eng

Ministero della Salute (2018) Livelli Essenziali di Assistenza (LEA) [Internet]. Available at: https://www.trovanorme.salute.gov.it/norme/renderNormsanPdf?anno=2024&codLeg=104476&parte=1%20&serie=null

Mouatt B, Smith AE, Mellow ML et al (2020) The use of virtual reality to influence motivation, affect, enjoyment, and engagement during exercise: a scoping review. Front Virtual Reality 1:564664

Nicora G, Parimbelli E, Mauro MC et al (2025) Healthcare practitioners and robotic-assisted rehabilitation: understanding needs and barriers. J Neuroeng Rehabil 22:78

Patel S, Park H, Bonato P et al (2019) A review of wearable sensors and systems with application in rehabilitation. J Neuroeng Rehabil 9(2012):1–17

Postolache O, Monge J, Alexandre R, et al. (2021) Virtual reality and augmented reality technologies for smart physical rehabilitation. Adv Syst Biomed Appl, 155–180

Rosati G, Rodà A, Avanzini F et al (2013) On the role of auditory feedback in robot-assisted movement training after stroke: review of the literature. Comput Iintell Neurosci 1:586138

Schork NJ (2019) Artificial intelligence and personalized medicine. Cancer Treat Res 178:265–283

Turchetti G, Vitiello N, Trieste L et al (2014) Why effectiveness of robot-mediated neurorehabilitation does not necessarily influence its adoption. IEEE Rev Biomed Eng 7:143–153

Van der Loos HFM, Reinkensmeyer DJ, Guglielmelli E (2016) Rehabilitation and health care robotics. Springer Handbook of Rrobotics, pp 1685–1728

Wagner TH., Lo, AC., Peduzzi P et al. (2011) An economic analysis of robot-assisted therapy for long-term upper-limb impairment after stroke. Stroke 42(9):2630–2632

Xue X, Yang X, Deng Z, Tu H, Kong D, Li N et al (2021) Global trends and hotspots in research on rehabilitation robots: a bibliometric analysis from 2010 to 2020. Front Public Health 9:806723

Zuki FSM, Sulaiman S, Awang Rambli DR, et al. (2021) Sensory feedback and interactivity: Enhancing motivation and engagement for VR stroke rehabilitation. In: 2021 International Conference on Computer & Information Sciences (ICCOINS). IEEE, 2021

Challenges of Personalized Medicine to Liability

AI-powered Medical Devices and the Development Risk Defense Under the Revised Product Liability Directive

Andrea Parziale

Abstract This chapter assesses whether and to what extent the revised Product Liability Directive (RPLD) provide the manufacturers and providers of AI-powered devices for personalized medical solutions with desirable safety incentives. To this end, the chapter outlines relevant aspects of the current safety regulatory framework including the Medical Device Regulation and the AI Act. In complement, the chapter includes an analysis on the role of the RPLD. This analysis focuses on a hypothetical scenario where an autonomous AI-powered medical device that initially seems safe continues to learn and later begins to provide flawed information resulting in patient harm. As such, the discussion centers on the potential benefits and limitations of the new legislation including the exemptions for 'later risk' and 'development risk'. I argue that the RPLD could incentivize manufacturers to react to any emerging risks that become known or knowable. However, the situation is more nuanced for the first victims of unknown risks. This is because the revised product liability regime, while limiting the opportunity for manufacturers to rely on the 'later risk' exemption, lends itself to inconsistent incentives through the 'development risk' defense. This raises the question of whether strict liability should be considered for these kinds of products. The legal systems in which fault-based, product, and strict liability regimes coexist are well placed as 'living laboratories' where one can readily test how these different liability regimes operate.

1 Introduction

In recent years, the integration of AI into medical devices has led to deep transformations in healthcare. While physicians have historically led the assessment, planning, development, delivery, and evaluation of healthcare, human deliberations in

A. Parziale (✉)
LIDER-Lab, DIRPOLIS, Sant'Anna School of Advanced Studies, Pisa, Italy

Health Science Interdisciplinary Center, Sant'Anna School of Advanced Studies, Pisa, Italy
e-mail: andrea.parziale@santannapisa.it

F. Casarosa et al. (eds.), *Enabling and Safeguarding Personalized Medicine*, Data Science, Machine Intelligence, and Law 7,
https://doi.org/10.1007/978-3-031-99709-9_14

clinical settings are increasingly being assisted by new technologies.[1] In this context, AI-powered medical devices hold the potential to significantly improve patient care, the accuracy of diagnoses, treatment outcomes, and the operational efficiency of healthcare systems worldwide.[2] This is because, among other things, AI can personalize medicine by tailoring diagnostic and therapeutic interventions to the unique genetic, biochemical, physiological, and behavioral features of each individual patient.[3] Emerging data-intensive assays, such as DNA sequencing, proteomics, imaging protocols, and wireless health monitoring devices, are playing a critical role in this personalization process.[4] Big data paradigms are aggregating massive amounts of data from different sources, harmonizing those data, and making them available for analysis to identify patterns that would not and could not otherwise be detected.[5] AI, which includes machine learning, deep learning, neural network constructs, and related techniques, has therefore become essential to both finding relevant patterns in these massive datasets and also for delivering clinically meaningful insights.[6]

Within this changing landscape, AI-powered devices for personalized medical solutions are poised to revolutionize treatment paradigms across various disease conditions.[7] These devices encompass a wide spectrum of innovations, from pharmacogenomic assays that predict medicinal responses based on genetic profiles to wearable biosensors that continuously monitor vital signs and biomarkers in real-time.[8] By harnessing the power of big data analytics and AI, such devices can seamlessly offer insights into disease risk, progression, and response to therapy, enabling clinicians to tailor interventions for optimal outcomes. For example, implantable medical devices equipped with sensors and 'autonomous' AI software can monitor cardiac function in patients with heart failure, predicting exacerbations and adjusting treatment strategies in real-time.[9] Similarly, wearable devices capable of analyzing sweat or blood biomarkers can provide early warning signs of metabolic disorders or infectious diseases, empowering people to take proactive measures to safeguard their health while also assisting in clinical decision-making processes.[10]

However, although incorporating AI into medical devices is showing great potential for personalizing and improving healthcare, it is also raising numerous ethical questions that demand careful consideration.[11] Among these, ensuring patient safety

---

[1] Amisha et al. (2019), p. 2328.

[2] Briganti and Le Moine (2020).

[3] Bommu and Jeffrey (2024).

[4] Schork (2019), p. 265.

[5] Ibid.

[6] Ibid.

[7] Ibid.

[8] Cherubini and Dinh (2023), p. 404; Donghwan and Enusun (2023), p. 658; Webster (2024).

[9] Gautam et al. (2022).

[10] Shajari et al. (2023), p. 9498; Zhang et al. (2023).

[11] Braun and Harasimiuk (2023), p. 1.

and bodily integrity is of paramount importance. To this end, Regulation (EU) 2017/745 (the Medical Device Regulation, MDR) and Regulation (EU) 2024/1689 (the Artificial Intelligence Act, AI Act) both outline an ex-ante regulatory framework that aims to ensure only safe and effective AI-powered medical devices are placed on the market (or otherwise put into service). Yet 'autonomous' AI systems may lend themselves to behaving in a way that was not anticipated from the outset. For instance, it is entirely possible that, over time, these devices can begin to communicate incorrect information or provide incorrect recommendations. In other words, in its continued learning process, an autonomous AI system may 'learn to make mistakes'. Therefore, it is important that the governing regulatory and liability frameworks incentivize the developers of AI systems to not only react to the emergence of such mistakes in a timely and effective fashion but also to minimize these mistakes from occurring in the first place—at least to the extent possible. Such safety nets are essential to fostering public trust in these crucial innovations.

Against this backdrop, the liability landscape for these and similar technologies is rapidly changing in Europe. Of particular importance will be Directive (EU) 2024/2853 (the revised Product Liability Directive, RPLD). Discussion on this Directive therefore attract the bulk of attention in this chapter. In particular, I assess how well the RPLD might go about providing desirable safety incentives to the developers of AI-powered devices for personalized medicine. As a first step, I provide some background to the regulatory frameworks already in place concerning these kinds of products, highlighting the MDR and the AI Act in particular. Next, I analyze how the RPLD would stand up in a scenario where an autonomous AI-powered medical device at first works safely but, later, starts making mistakes which cause harm to an increasing number of patients. Importantly, the insights established should be highly valuable for informing specific policy recommendations regarding the national implementation of the RPLD. Last, I build on the identified limitations of the RPLD to argue in favor of a strict form of liability for these products, coupled with a call for further research along several specific streams of investigation.

2 The Current Regulatory Framework: The MDR and the AI Act

At the outset, AI-powered devices for personalized medicine are likely to fall under both the MDR and the AI Act. The MDR defines a medical device as any instrument, apparatus, appliance, software, implant, reagent, material, or other article intended by the manufacturer to be used for medical purposes such as diagnosis, prevention, monitoring, treatment, or alleviation of disease.[12] Importantly, if

[12] Medical Devices Regulation (MDR), Regulation (EU) 2017/745 on medical devices, European Parliament and Council (2017) amending Directive 2001/83/EC, Regulation (EC) No 178/2002

software is not qualified as a medical device in itself, it may qualify as an accessory to a medical device when it is integrated into a physical device for the purposes of assisting the device to perform its intended (medical) purpose and therefore the MDR would still apply.[13]

Under the MDR, medical devices must comply with the general safety and performance requirements listed in Annex I to the Regulation. These devices must be designed and manufactured to achieve their intended performance without compromising the safety of patients or users. This involves establishing, implementing, and maintaining a risk management system that is continuously updated throughout the device's lifecycle.[14] Manufacturers are also required to document a risk management plan, identify and analyze foreseeable hazards, and implement control measures to eliminate or reduce risks.[15] Additionally, manufacturers must ensure that any residual risks are communicated to users and are acceptable when weighed against the benefits of the device.[16]

The MDR also imposes specific requirements for software, including ensuring repeatability, reliability, and performance in line with the software's intended use.[17] The software must be developed according to state-of-the-art principles that consider risk management, verification, and validation. Moreover, if the software is intended for use with mobile computing platforms, it must account for the unique features of mobile environments.

Classifying the device under Annex VIII of the MDR is crucial for determining the level of regulatory scrutiny each product will undergo and the applicable post-marketing obligations. Rule 11 of the MDR classifies software intended for decision-making in diagnosis or therapy as Class IIa, except when such decisions may cause: (i) a serious deterioration of the health status of a person or a surgical intervention (in which case, it falls into Class IIb); or (ii) death or an irreversible deterioration of the health status of a person (in which case it belongs to Class III). Software intended to monitor physiological processes falls into Class IIa, unless it is intended for monitoring vital physiological parameters, where variations in these signs could result in immediate danger to the patient (in which case, it falls into Class IIb). Any other software is allocated to Class I. Importantly, software that drives or influences a device falls under the same class as the device itself.

While there are numerous classification criteria in Annex VIII to be applied on a case-by-case basis, the MDCG 2019-11 Guidance document[18] to the MDR suggests that AI-powered devices for personalized medicine are likely to fall into the

---

and Regulation (EC) No 1223/2009 and repealing Council Directives 90/385/EEC and 93/42/EEC, Official Journal of the European Union, L 117/1. Article 2(1).

[13] MDR, Article 2(2).

[14] MDR, Annex I, Section 3.

[15] Ibid.

[16] MDR, Annex I, Section 23.1.

[17] MDR, Annex I, Section 17.

[18] MDCG (2019), Annex 3.

medium-to-high risk categories. This means that the products will likely need to be certified by a Notified Body. In addition, the device will have to comply with the obligations pertaining to Clinical Evaluation Reports, Post-market Surveillance Plans, Periodic Safety Update Reports, Post-market Clinical Follow-up Plans, Post-market Clinical Follow-up Reports, and Summaries of Safety and Clinical Performance. Clinical Evaluation Reports document clinical evaluations of the device, its results, and the clinical evidence derived from it.[19] Clinical Evaluation Reports for Class IIb and III devices, must be updated annually. The Post-market Surveillance Plan is part of the post-market surveillance system.[20] It proves compliance with the post-marketing obligations set out in Article 83 of the MDR, including the criteria and processes for the risk-benefit assessments of the device and for collecting and analyzing data, addressing complaints, and communicating data to regulatory bodies.[21] The Periodic Safety Update Reports summarize the results and conclusions of the analyses of the post-market surveillance data gathered through the Post-market Surveillance Plan, along with a description of any preventive and corrective actions taken.[22] Again, the Periodic Safety Update Reports for Class IIb and III devices must be updated annually. The Post-market Clinical Follow-up Plan aims to confirm device safety and performance, identify unknown side-effects, analyze emerging risks, maintain an acceptable risk-benefit ratio, and detect misuse.[23] The accompanying Post-market Clinical Follow-up Report documents the outcomes of the Post-market Clinical Follow-up Plan and forms part of the Clinical Evaluation Report and its technical documentation.[24] Finally, the Summary of Safety and Clinical Performance outlines evidence for the safety, performance, and clinical benefits of Class III and implantable devices, and forms part of the technical documentation.[25]

Turning now to the AI Act, an AI system is defined as a machine-based system designed to operate autonomously, capable of adaptiveness after deployment, and capable of generating outputs (such as predictions, recommendations, or decisions) that influence physical or virtual environments.[26] AI-powered devices for personalized medicine likely qualify as high-risk AI systems. This is because the AI in a device is typically considered to be one of the product's safety components, which is covered by the EU harmonization legislation listed in Annex I. This means the

[19] MDR, Article 61(12).

[20] MDR, Article 84.

[21] MDR, Annex III.

[22] MDR, Article 86.

[23] MDR, Annex XIV.

[24] Ibid.

[25] MDR, Article 32.

[26] Artificial Intelligence Act (AI Act) Regulation (EU) 2024/1689 European Parliament and Council (2024) laying down harmonized rules on artificial intelligence', Official Journal of the European Union, L 132/1. Article 3(1).

product or system must undergo a third-party conformity assessment before being placed on the market or deployed into service.[27]

Thus, an AI-powered medical device is likely to meet the qualification criteria for falling under both the MDR and the AI Act and that means that, again, the device will need to be certified by a Notified Body. The manufacturer or provider would also need to consider the product's "intended purpose as well as the generally acknowledged state of the art on AI".[28] Additionally, if a product includes an AI system that falls under both the AI Act and a piece of harmonized EU law, such as the MDR, "providers shall have a choice of integrating, as appropriate, the necessary testing and reporting processes, information and documentation they provide with regard to their product into documentation and procedures that already exist and are required under the Union harmonisation legislation listed in Section A of Annex I".[29]

In the context of high-risk AI systems, a comprehensive risk management system must be established, implemented, documented, and maintained.[30] This system should be a continuous and iterative process, planned and executed throughout the entire lifecycle of the AI system. This includes identifying and analyzing known and reasonably foreseeable risks that the AI system may pose to health, safety, or fundamental rights when used as intended. Additionally, the system must estimate and evaluate risks that could emerge from both intended use and reasonably foreseeable misuse. The risk management process must also include a process of evaluating risks based on any data gathered from post-market monitoring activities or as part of adopting targeted measures to address identified risks. The focus is on mitigating or eliminating risks that can be managed through the design, development, or provision of adequate technical information. High-risk AI systems must undergo testing to identify the most appropriate risk management measures, ensuring consistent performance and compliance with regulatory requirements. This testing may include real-world conditions and should occur at various stages of development, but always before the AI system is placed on the market. Moreover, the testing needs to be conducted against predefined metrics and probabilistic thresholds appropriate to the intended purpose of the AI system.

In addition, a single set of technical documentation must be prepared that demonstrates compliance with both the AI Act and the other relevant EU harmonized legislation.[31] Also, the design and development of high-risk AI systems must ensure sufficient transparency to allow deployers to interpret and use the system's outputs appropriately.[32] Furthermore, providers must have a quality management system to

---

[27] AI Act, Article 6(1).

[28] AI Act, Article 8(1) AI Act.

[29] AI Act, Article 8(2).

[30] AI Act, Article 9.

[31] AI Act, Article 11.

[32] AI Act, Article 13.

ensure that the AI system complies with the AI Act.[33] This includes examination, testing, and validation procedures to be carried out before, during, and after the development of the high-risk AI system, a risk management system, a post-market monitoring system, and a reporting system for serious incidents. Finally, if a high-risk AI system presents a risk, providers must investigate the causes, collaborate with deployers, inform market surveillance authorities, and take corrective actions.[34]

3 The Role of the Revised PLD

With the current regulatory framework sketched out, we will turn to the potential benefits and likely limitations presented by the RPLD. The RPLD clarifies that, for all the intents and purposes of the legislation, software is a product,[35] which may well include (autonomous) AI systems. To recover damages under the RPLD, the claimant must prove "the defectiveness of the product, the damage suffered and the causal link between that defectiveness and that damage".[36] A product is defective if "it does not provide the safety that a person is entitled to expect or that is required under Union or national law" considering all circumstances.[37]

These circumstances include, but are not limited to, the presentation and characteristics of the product, including its design and instructions; the reasonably foreseeable use of the product; the ability of the product to continue to learn or acquire new features after it is placed on the market or put into service; and the specific needs of the group of users for whose use the product is intended. The non-exhaustive list of relevant circumstances to be considered when attempting to determine whether a product is defective is longer than the existing Product Liability Directive,[38] and some additions seem particularly relevant to AI-powered products. However, others are ambiguous in terms of how they might shape safety expectations. For instance, it is not immediately clear whether the ability of the product to continue to learn (which is a clear reference to AI-powered products) should increase or decrease safety expectations.[39] After all, it is quite foreseeable that an autonomous AI system, by continuing to learn, may end up making mistakes, which would

[33] AI Act, Article 17.

[34] AI Act, Article 20.

[35] Revised Product Liability Directive (RPLD), Directive (EU) 2024/2853, European Parliament and Council on liability for defective products and repealing Council Directive 85/374/EEC, Official Journal of the European Union, L 2024/2853. Article 4(1) and Recitals 6 and 13.

[36] RPLD, Article 10(1).

[37] RPLD, Article 7(1).

[38] Product Liability Directive (PLD), Directive (EU) 2024/2853, European Parliament and Council (2024) on liability for defective products, Official Journal of the European Union, L 289/12.

[39] De Bruyne et al. (2023).

decrease safety expectations and make it harder for claimants to prove a product's defectiveness.[40] However, Recital 32 of the RPLD explicitly states that…

> …the effect on a product's safety of its ability to learn or acquire new features after it is placed on the market or put into service should also be taken into account to reflect the legitimate expectation that a product's software and underlying algorithms are designed in such a way as to prevent hazardous product behaviour.

Thus, the intention of European lawmakers seems to be that a product's ability to self-learn should be seen as something that increases safety expectations. A second issue pertains to the role of the product presentation and its instructions, particularly when the product's instructions warn that it may start giving incorrect information.[41] However, this may be an attempt by the manufacturer to shift liability risks to the users, including healthcare professionals.[42] Yet, it is hard to argue that such a vague warning could effectively shape anyone's safety expectations. Similar to the generic warnings in a medicine's leaflet that "side-effects may occur", it is unlikely that the manufacturer could dodge liability on the basis of such precautions. Since the role of AI-powered devices for personalized medicine needs to be considered, the "special needs of the users" may also have some part to play in increasing safety expectations for a product, as individual patients can reasonably expect that such a device will deliver outputs that are both safe and effective, particularly to themselves.

Finally, Article 10 of the RPLD provides several facilitations to the claimant to prove a product's defectiveness, such as if the manufacturer fails to disclose relevant evidence requested by the claimant or if the claimant demonstrates that the product fails to comply with mandatory safety requirements in the EU or under any domestic law. A causal link between damage and defect is also presumed if such a link has already been established through precedent,[43] or if the claimant faces excessive difficulties in proving such a link, especially if those difficulties are technical or scientific.[44]

Importantly, the manufacturer has the right to rebut any of these presumptions.[45] And even once the claimant succeeds in demonstrating the constituting elements of product liability, the manufacturer can still avoid liability by invoking one of the exemptions listed in Article 11. In the case of autonomous AI-powered products, the most relevant exemptions are when "it is probable that the defectiveness that caused the damage did not exist at the time the product was placed on the market, put into service or, in the case of a distributor, made available on the market, or that that defectiveness came into being after that moment",[46] known as the 'later defect' exemption. Notably, this exemption cannot be applied if the defect is

[40] Ibid.

[41] Duffourc and Gerke (2023), p. 77.

[42] Ibid.

[43] RPLD, Article 10(3).

[44] RPLD, Article 10(4).

[45] RPLD, Article 10(5).

[46] RPLD, Article 11(1)(c).

software-related.[47] Thus, if an autonomous AI system becomes defective due to its ability to continue to learn, the manufacturer will not be able to invoke this exemption.[48]

Another exemption manufacturers can use occurs when "the objective state of scientific and technical knowledge at the time the product was placed on the market or put into service or during the period in which the product was within the manufacturer's control was not such that the defectiveness could be discovered".[49] This is known as the 'development risk' or the 'unknown risk' exemption.[50] This defense can only be use if the product was always defective from the start, but the defect could not be discovered in light of "the most advanced level of objective knowledge accessible and not to the actual knowledge of the economic operator".[51] A manufacturer may, therefore, try to invoke this exemption in lieu of the 'later defect' by arguing that, while the product defectiveness manifested itself at a later stage, the defect must be due to an issue in the original programming of the AI system, which could, unfortunately, not be discovered at the time. This line of reasoning, however, would not be convincing. This is because it conflates the two concepts of (a) there being a defect and (b) the cause of that defect. Indeed, a product is deemed to be defective if it fails to meet the relevant safety expectations. This is irrespective of what the cause of the defect might be. Thus, in the scenario under consideration, the development risk defense would not apply. Further, the manufacturer would not be able to rely on the later defect exemption by virtue of Article 11(2)(b). Thus, the later defect risk seems more likely (not) to apply to autonomous AI-powered medical devices than the development risk defense. To successfully use the development risk defense, the manufacturer would need to demonstrate that the AI system was actually defective from the start. This may provide incentives that, to say the least, would be quite odd in light of the safety requirements mandated by the MDR and the AI Act.

Let us now assume the case of an autonomous AI-powered medical device intended to deliver personalized medical solutions that at first seems to be working as planned but later, by continuing to learn, starts providing flawed information and recommendations that cause harm to patients. Once this emerging risk becomes known or knowable to the manufacturer or provider, and the latter fail to take timely action, establishing liability under the RPLD does not seem to be an insurmountable task. The dense network of requirements laid down in the MDR and AI Act seem particularly helpful to claimants willing to demonstrate product defects or faults, and the disclosure obligations and causal presumptions seem to have the potential to ease the evidentiary burden on the claimants. In particular, the potential interpretive

[47] RPLD, Article 11(2)(b).

[48] Ibid.

[49] RPLD, Article 11(1)(e).

[50] De Bruyne et al. (2023).

[51] RPLD, Recital 52.

ambiguities of some of the circumstances relevant to determine product defectiveness can be solved quite easily in favor of the claimant.

That said, the situation is more nuanced when it comes to the very first victims of an autonomous AI-powered medical device, which unexpectedly starts delivering harmful output (or failure to produce output). In this case, the RPLD does offer some room for recovery to the claimant in such cases, since the later defect defense does not apply if this is due to software. However, the persisting operation of the development risk defense may provide an odd incentive to the manufacturer. The manufacturer can avoid liability by demonstrating that the AI system was defective from the outset, but such a defect could not be discovered. This does not seem to fully incentivize the manufacturer to make sure that the AI-powered product is safe from the outset. Rather, it seems to convey an incentive not to study and test the product in a way that expands the objective state of the art, in order to have room to potentially rely on the development risk defense itself.

This raises the question of whether the Member States should consider derogating from the development risk defense, as allowed by Article 18 of the RPLD. Article 18(2) and (3) impose some conditions on Member States considering amending their legal systems to this end. These conditions include that this must be limited to specific categories of products, in the public interest, and proportionate to achieve the public interest. Since Member States have quite some leeway when it comes to defining what is in the public interest, these conditions do not seem to impose an insurmountable obstacle to exclude autonomous AI-powered medical devices from the development risk defense.

4 Conclusions and Avenues for Further Research: The Role of Strict Liability

Excluding the later defect exemption for software would move the product liability regime closer to a strict liability model. Derogating from the development risk defense, which would already be quite difficult for manufacturers in this domain to use, would also be a decisive step in this same direction. Member States could also consider introducing a form of strict liability for such products on a basis other than defectiveness. Recital 11 clarifies that the RPLD does not preclude the Member States from adopting contractual or extracontractual liability regimes (including strict liability ones) with a basis different from product defectiveness. The strict liability regime for abnormally dangerous activities, along the lines of Article 5:101 of the Principles of European Tort Law[52] offers a useful reference model. The article states:

> Abnormally dangerous activities: (1) A person who carries on an abnormally dangerous activity is strictly liable for damage characteristic to the risk presented by the activity and resulting from it. (2) An activity is abnormally dangerous if (a) it creates a foreseeable and

[52] Busnelli et al. (2005).

highly significant risk of damage even when all due care is exercised in its management and (b) it is not a matter of common usage. (3) A risk of damage may be significant having regard to the seriousness or the likelihood of the damage. (4) This Article does not apply to an activity which is specifically subjected to strict liability by any other provision of these Principles or any other national law or international convention.

It has been argued in the law and economics literature that this may be particularly justified in the case of developers.[53] Since these "exert a considerable influence on accident risk and often also have 'deep pockets' [...], they should be subject to strict liability. Such a regime would generate incentives for both optimal care and optimal activity levels as well as facilitating the effective spreading of risk".[54] Against this backdrop, further empirically-oriented research of a comparative nature could help shed light on the actual socio-economic impact of different kinds of civil liability in this domain, offering insights to inform policy decision-making.

To this end, the European legal framework where fault-based liability, product liability, and outright strict liability regimes coexist seem particularly well placed to be 'living laboratories' where we could test the actual potential and limitations of each kind of liability regime with respect to AI-powered medical devices. As such, it would be highly worthwhile comparing the EU framework to other legal systems where fault-based claims and product liability exhaust claimants' avenues for recovering damages. For instance, consider the Italian legal system where a form of strict liability for dangerous activities is enshrined in Article 2050 of the Civil Code.[55] Under this law, the performer of a dangerous activity is liable unless they can prove they took all adequate measures to prevent the damage. This code could easily be applied to high-risk medical devices and AI systems, offering an ideal testbed for further legal and policy research of a comparative nature.

Acknowledgements This research was financially supported by the "Biorobotics Research and Innovation Engineering Facilities" "IR0000036" – CUP J13C22000400007 (BRIEF) project.

Disclosure of Interests The authors have no competing interests to declare that are relevant to the content of this article.

References

Amisha MP, Pathania M, Rathaur VK (2019) Overview of artificial intelligence in medicine. J Family Med Prim Care 8(7):2328–2331. https://doi.org/10.4103/jfmpc.jfmpc_440_19

Bommu R, Jeffrey B (2024) Revolutionizing healthcare with AI: advancements in medical device software. Int J Adv Eng Technol Innov 1(3)

Braun T, Harasimiuk DE (2023) AI deployment in medical devices-ethical and regulatory reflections, beyond data protection and bias – EU perspective. In: 2023 IEEE Conference on Computational Intelligence in Bioinformatics and Computational Biology (CIBCB), Eindhoven, Netherlands, pp 1–6. https://doi.org/10.1109/CIBCB56990.2023.10264892

[53] Li et al. (2022), pp. 618–634.

[54] Ibid.

[55] See Comporti (2009), p. 149; Cendon (2008), p. 801; Rossetti (2011), p. 693.

Briganti G, Le Moine O (2020) Artificial intelligence in medicine: today and tomorrow. Front Med 70(5). https://doi.org/10.3389/fmed.2020.00027
Busnelli FD et al (2005) Principles of European tort law. Text and commentary. Springer, Vienna
Cendon P (ed) (2008) Commentario al Codice Civile. Artt. 2043-2053. Fatti illeciti. Giuffrè, Milano, p 801
Cherubini A, Dinh NN (2023) A review of the technology, training, and assessment methods for the first real-time AI-enhanced medical device for endoscopy. Bioengineering 10(4):404. https://doi.org/10.3390/bioengineering10040404
Comporti M (2009) Fatti illeciti: le responsabilità oggettive. Artt. 2049-2053. In: Schlesinger F, Busnelli FD (eds) Il Codice Civile. Commentario. Giuffrè, Milano, pp 149 ff
De Bruyne J, Dheu O, Ducuing C (2023) The European Commission's approach to extra-contractual liability and AI –an evaluation of the AI liability directive and the revised product liability directive. Comput Law Secur Rev 105894. https://doi.org/10.1016/j.clsr.2023.105894
Donghwan K, Eunsun K (2023) AI-powered medical devices for practical clinicians including the diagnosis of colorectal polyps. J Korean Med Assoc 66(11):658–666
Duffourc M, Gerke S (2023) The proposed EU Directives for AI liability leave worrying gaps likely to impact medical AI. NPJ Digit Med 6:77. https://doi.org/10.1038/s41746-023-00823-w
European Parliament (2024) Legislative resolution of 12 March 2024 on the proposal for a directive of the European Parliament and of the Council on liability for defective products (COM(2022)0495 – C9-0322/2022 – 2022/0302(COD))
Gautam N et al (2022) Artificial intelligence, wearables and remote monitoring for heart failure: current and future applications. Diagnostics 12(12):2964. https://doi.org/10.3390/diagnostics12122964
Li S, Faure MG, Havu K (2022) Liability rules for AI-Related harm: law and economics lessons for a European approach. Eur J Risk Regul 13(4):618–634. https://doi.org/10.1017/err.2022.26
MDCG (2019) Guidance on Qualification and Classification of Software in Regulation (EU) 2017/745 – MDR and Regulation (EU) 2017/746 – IVDR, MDCG 11-2019
Rossetti M (2011) Art. 2050. Responsabilità per esercizio di attività pericolose. In: Carnevali U (ed) Dei fatti illeciti. Utet, pp 198 ff
Schork NJ (2019) Artificial intelligence and personalized medicine. Cancer Treat Res 178:265–283. https://doi.org/10.1007/978-3-030-16391-4_11
Shajari S, Kuruvinashetti K, Komeili A, Sundararaj U (2023) The emergence of AI-Based wearable sensors for digital health technology: a review. Sensors 23(23):9498. https://doi.org/10.3390/s23239498
Webster P (2024) How AI-powered handheld devices are boosting disease diagnostics - from cancer to dermatology. Nat Med News, 12 March 2024
Zhang Y, Hu Y, Jiang N, Yetisen AK (2023) Wearable artificial intelligence biosensor networks. Biosens Bioelectron 219. https://doi.org/10.1016/j.bios.2022.114825

The Transparency and Liability Issues Associated with AI-Based Medical Systems

Andrea Blatti and Stefano Tramacere

Abstract This chapter examines the relationship between two of the main topics discussed in relation to smart medicine: the transparency of the AI systems used and their associated liability issues. AI is increasingly being used in the healthcare sector due to its proclaimed predictive accuracy, which purportedly enhances medical performance. However, many AI systems lack transparency, leaving the recommendations and diagnoses they produce unexplained. This chapter therefore discusses the importance of the techno-normative design choices made in AI-based medical systems as a way of mitigating any risks to a patient's health. Notwithstanding this discussion, we do highlight that both traditional and AI-powered medicine are, to some extent, characterized by intrinsic opacity. Therefore, we also discuss the consequences of implementing the AI systems to standard of care.

The chapter was conceptualized and jointly developed by the authors. While Sect. 1 (Introduction) and Sect. 9 (Conclusion) are attributable to both, Sects. 2–5 are attributed to Stefano Tramacere, while Sects. 6–8 are attributed to Andrea Blatti.

A. Blatti
LIDER-Lab, DIRPOLIS, Sant'Anna School of Advanced Studies, Pisa, Italy

S. Tramacere (✉)
LIDER-Lab, DIRPOLIS, Sant'Anna School of Advanced Studies, Pisa, Italy

Department of Computer Science, University of Pisa, Pisa, Italy
e-mail: stefano.tramacere@santannapisa.it

F. Casarosa et al. (eds.), *Enabling and Safeguarding Personalized Medicine*, Data Science, Machine Intelligence, and Law 7,
https://doi.org/10.1007/978-3-031-99709-9_15

1 Introduction

Systems created on AI typically hold such significant levels of autonomy that it implies some kind of transformative potential. However, this power can have substantial implications for the liability rules that apply to their use.[1] For example, according to Article 3(1) of the Artificial Intelligence Act (AI Act),[2] an AI system[3] has the capacity to operate with varying levels of autonomy and adaptability once it has been deployed. The transformative nature of AI is particularly evident in the medical sector where clinical and therapeutic decision support systems[4] are raising substantial ethical, social, and legal concerns, particularly with reference to the protection of fundamental rights.[5]

AI-based devices analyze enormous amounts of data, which is what enables most systems to produce healthcare-related diagnoses and treatment recommendations.[6] Some literature suggests that this technology may be capable of offering the most appropriate therapeutic strategy for a specific case,[7] or that such systems can forecast potential developments in a patient's health.[8] Either way, AI is paving the way to personalized medicine.[9] Moreover, it is evident that these tools possess a remarkable novelty. They can perform an activity that, until quite recently, was the exclusive prerogative of humans. For instance, they can infer the validity of an initial clinical hypothesis from sets of data such as symptoms and a clinical history. The difference between the two is that doctors make decisions based on their expertise, while AI primarily relies on identifying statistical patterns in data based on the correlations between features. Traditional diagnostic tools typically employ methods grounded in the principles of physics or chemistry. Such tools typically allow practitioners to detect a limited number of elements (*e.g.*, symptoms) associated with a clinical hypothesis (*e.g.*, a disease); however, they do not provide the final diagnosis. Conversely, AI systems exploit their computational power to analyze extensive datasets, offering potentially persuasive and comprehensive suggestions on medical treatments.[10]

Hence, this chapter begins by addressing some of the legal issues relating to the use of AI systems in the medical sector. In Sect. 2, we emphasize the developing nature of the traditional doctor-patient relationship towards new collaborative paradigms that incorporate additional actors. Section 3 outlines the new AI Act's

---

[1] Comandé (2019), p. 178.
[2] AI Act (2024).
[3] AI Act, Art. 3 (1) (2024).
[4] Comandé (2024), p. 156.
[5] European Parliament (2022).
[6] Jones et al. (2023), pp. 501–520.
[7] Comandé (2024), p. 159.
[8] Grasso (2023), pp. 336–337.
[9] Amram (2023), p. 6.
[10] Grasso (2023), p. 336.

provisions on transparency and human oversight, while Sect. 4 discusses the significant impact of the design choices made by data scientists to ensure transparency and accountability throughout the AI pipeline. Sections 5 and 6 then reflect on how this transparency affects a physician's liability, comparing the general level of transparency accepted in medicine with that imposed by AI systems.

2 Black-Box Medicine: The Legal Risk of Technical Opacity

One of the most significant issues with AI systems is the lack of transparency in the decision-making process. This means that while one can observe the input and output, it is often challenging to understand the mechanism that transforms one into the other.[11] This often means the results of machine and deep learning systems are very difficult to explain, and therefore justify, by those who deploy them—like physicians. The lack of transparency in these models limits their traceability. It also undermines judgments of a system's reliability and makes detecting and preventing potential malfunctions very difficult. Overall, these systems generally offer very little assurance of protection for patients.[12] So, while it is not necessary for humans to understand every single stage of an AI pipeline, it is of the utmost importance that AI's deployer comprehend the logic behind a diagnosis or recommended treatment.[13] For this reason, it is essential that AI be sufficiently transparent to guarantee its deployers can properly interpret the system's output. Notably, the AI Act, Article 3 (4) states that "deployer means a natural person, public authority, agency or other body using an AI system under its authority". This definition is extremely wide. In the medical context, both healthcare facilities and the professionals that use AI systems could fall under this category.

To understand how AI systems and models relate to the requirements outlined in the AI Act, it is necessary to make a distinction between the two. More specifically, an AI model is only one component inside an AI system.[14] A model is often the output of an AI system, having been trained on some input data. In terms of the AI Act, the distinguishing feature of an AI system is its capacity to generate some output that influences the environment. This differentiates AI systems from AI models, as the latter lack this capability. While the AI Act's requirements focus on AI systems, a significant portion of the computer science literature has focused on developing techniques to make AI models more explainable. These techniques are relevant because addressing the technical complexity of AI models can help bring about both transparency and human oversight of an overall AI system, as required by the Act.

[11] Duffourc and Gerke (2023), p. 7.

[12] Maliha et al. (2021).

[13] Malgieri and Comandé (2017).

[14] Panigutti et al. (2023b), p. 1142.

Additionally, the computer science literature identifies two main approaches to enhancing the transparency of an AI model. The first is to avoid black-box AI models and, instead, focus on creating models that are transparent or explainable-by-design. Here, transparency refers to the properties of an AI model. This is the focus of the interpretable AI field that tries to incorporate explicit explainability capabilities into the design of AI models, either by integrating them directly into the model's architecture or into the learning process.[15] More importantly, the decision-making processes in these models can be directly inspected as they are specifically designed to be interpreted by humans. Most accomplish this feat by constraining the model's decision-making process in various ways.[16] For instance, one might narrow the model types used to only those that humans can follow, such as decision trees, linear models, or case-based reasoning models.[17]

The second approach, termed eXplainable AI (XAI), allows the use of black-box models but concentrates on providing explanations for the AI model's behavior in a manner that humans can understand. The benefit of this approach is that no constraints are imposed on the AI model itself.[18] XAI methodologies can be specific to a particular black-box model,[19] or they can be model agnostic.[20] Moreover, XAI methods can offer global explanations that provide an in-depth analysis of the model's overall behavior, or they can provide local explanations that explain why a model reached a decision in a specific instance. This approach is commonly known as post-hoc explainabilit. Counterfactuals and feature importance are good examples of local explanations.[21] Counterfactual methods use an interpretable classifier, such as a decision tree, that suggests the minimum modifications that need to be made to the input instance to change the model's outcome.[22] Similarly, with feature importance methods, the explainer assigns a value to each feature, denoting its significance to the AI system's prediction.[23] The more explainable the model, the more a human is able to interpret and understand both the internal processes involved in the decision and the specific content of the output generated.[24]

From a technical point of view, however, it is worth recognizing that the term explainability is often used quite broadly to include both interpretable AI and XAI approaches. This interchangeability may be misleading because it fails to acknowledge that certain AI models, such as deep learning models, can be explainable

[15] Rudin et al. (2021).

[16] Panigutti et al. (2023b), p. 1142.

[17] Bodria et al. (2023).

[18] Guidotti et al. (2019).

[19] Selvaraju, et al. (2017).; Zeiler and Fergus (2014).

[20] Guidotti et al. (2019).

[21] Bodria et al. (2023).

[22] Guidotti et al. (2019), pp. 14–23.

[23] Bodria et al. (2023).

[24] Guidotti et al. (2022), pp. 160–168.

without being interpretable.[25] In medicine, the difference between explainable and interpretable AI systems is crucial.[26] Doctors often feel uneasy about diagnostic systems that are only partially transparent, let alone entirely opaque.[27] They argue that providing patients with explanations of how a diagnosis was established is essential for maintaining trust and satisfying their responsibilities for making medical decisions.[28]

The lack of transparency in AI systems might also give rise to risks like traslational bias.[29] Traslational bias arises when a system is trained on some data with a certain statistical distribution but is then used on a population with a different distribution. This issue is explored in more detail in Sect. 4.

Another potential risk involves human perceptions of an AI system, which may be distorted because of our human connection to evaluation methods that rely on heuristics. Here, the literature suggests that, ideally, explanations of AI-driven clinical decisions should increase the physician's levels of confidence in the system as long as this level of confidence is aligned with the system's actual reliability.[30] Notably, there are several levels of confidence along the spectrum, ranging from complete distrust to overreliance on AI. Both extremes have been observed towards AI designed to deliver clinical decision support.[31] This second tendency is known as automation bias and can be particularly dangerous in critical domains such as medicine.[32]

Moreover, too little transparency might hide incorrect inferences and algorithmic discriminations that could endanger the health of patients.[33] Even though a system may have delivered highly accurate results in experimental settings, this does not mean that users will find the same accuracy rates in the real world, making systems unreliable. For example, an AI system that was meant to predict death after pneumonia cited chest pain, heart disease, and asthma as indicators of low risk, contrary to reality.[34] Of course, any doctor viewing these factors would have confirmed that these three indicators correlate to a high risk of death. Nevertheless, experimental accuracy was very high when used with the dataset on which the algorithm was trained.[35] In this particular case, the indicators were visible, so it was easy to figure out what went wrong and patients with these three symptoms were sent to a hospital to be carefully monitored. But if a deep learning system without sufficient transpar-

[25] Panigutti et al. (2023b), p. 1143.

[26] D'Elia (2023), pp. 357–360.

[27] Price (2018), pp. 295–305.

[28] Duffourc and Gerke (2023), pp. 10–11.

[29] Comandé (2019), p. 178.; Lyell et al. (2017), p. 28.

[30] Kizilcec (2016).

[31] Panigutti et al. (2023a), p. 4.

[32] AI Act, Art. 14.4(b).

[33] Bévière-Boyer (2023), pp. 278–280.

[34] Caruana et al. (2015), pp. 1721–1730.

[35] Hildebrandt (2018), pp. 102–105.

ency had made the predictions, it might have been far less obvious which of the features had caused the system to attribute a low risk to the patients. This makes reliance on such systems dangerous, as it may take time before mistakes are uncovered.

To solve these problems and ensure greater accountability, we must devise more transparent risk management systems.[36] This involves being aware of when one is interacting with an AI system and understanding how AI models are trained, which datasets they use, how they process data, and for which specific purposes.[37] Furthermore, if a system's output causes harm to patients, a lack of transparency could interfere with how civil liabilities are attributed, particularly when it comes to demonstrating causation. This form of proof is usually necessary for compensation to be awarded as, alongside causation and damage, attributing fault is one of the fundamental elements of the liability regime.[38] Hence, using black-box systems may undermine the liability of both AI providers and healthcare professionals. And, without the ability to identify a liable person or prove a causal link, injured patients could be left unprotected. Consequently, it is crucial that the providers of AI systems adhere to the legal requirements for transparency. Only with these measures in place will a system's deployers (e.g., the doctors) have a clear understanding of how the system reached its conclusions. Transparency can reduce the potential harm to the end-users, ensure informed consent to medical treatments, and reduce the risk of avoiding civil liability for professional misjudgments.[39]

3 The Strategic Role of Transparency

In high-risk contexts like medicine, a lack of information can create new forms of information asymmetry, violating the principle of free and informed consent to medical treatment. Importantly, free medical consent is recognized as a constitutional right in Article 3.2 of the EU Charter of Fundamental Rights.[40] Though there is no express reference to transparency, this is closely related to the concept of information self-determination, where transparent information is a prerequisite.[41] Nowhere better is this demonstrated than in the doctor-patient relationship, which seeks to assert greater autonomy for the person. As a case in point, see the decision of the Italian Constitutional Court, n. 438 on 23 December 2008 which affirmed: "the role [of informed consent] in combining two fundamental rights of the person:

[36] Kaminski (2020).; Kiseleva et al. (2022).

[37] Kaminski (2019).

[38] Comandé (2020), pp. 155–173.

[39] Grasso (2023).

[40] EUROPEAN UNION (2000/C 364/01).

[41] Rodotà wrote that *«consentire equivale ad essere»* (*«to consent is to be»*) in Rodotà (2012), p. 260. Read also Hildebrandt (2012).

the right to self-determination and the right to health". This argument is wholly pertinent today, especially in relation to the advent of AI-based devices. This is just one more reason for why it is essential to design and develop AI systems in a transparent and understandable way. With interpretable and explainable systems, physicians can effectively communicate the advantages of using AI to patients, while also establishing a trustful relationship. Here, the Italian *Corte di Cassazione* emphasized in its *Order n. 28358 of 2023* that algorithmic transparency is crucial to evaluating whether free and valid consent to processing has been established.

Further, it is equally essential that healthcare professionals undergo extensive training to effectively communicate with AI developers and providers. For instance, deployers should be conscious of the potential limitations of AI systems,[42] such as those relating to their use with certain persons and groups.[43] Within this framework, the AI Act's Article 4 aims to reduce possible risks by requiring providers[44] and deployers to implement measures that ensure a "sufficient level of AI literacy of their staff".[45] Considering all of this, we note that the traditional bilateral doctor-patient relationship is evolving with the advent of AI systems and that new actor(s) are being introduced into medical exchanges. The most prominent of these is the AI provider, along with their team of AI designers and developers, who are creating a new trilateral relationship in decisions about medical care. This new synergy is best understood in light of the specific design choices that upstream data scientists and software engineers are making, which develop into socio-technical artifacts that are deployed downstream by physicians for patient care.

As already highlighted, it is necessary to improve both the explainability and interpretability of AI models in the medical sector to ensure high levels of transparency. Yet, while these concepts are closely related and are often referred to interchangeably in the scientific literature, each has distinct characteristics. Our interpretation aligns with scholars who consider transparency to be a broad legal principle that includes both explainability and interpretability.[46] Transparency applies to the entire lifecycle of an AI system from its development to its subsequent use. Moreover, it encompasses various measures beyond merely enabling human actors to understand AI processes and their outcomes to impact all elements and actors involved. That said, transparency in terms of XAI techniques primarily refers to how information is communicated, while explainability specifically concerns the content of an outcome. It is something that enables the recipient of a decision to interpret the generated output. Consequently, explainability is essential for interpretability and contestability, which are context-dependent. Interestingly, from this

---

[42] AI Act, Recital 93.

[43] Béviére-Boyer (2023), p. 280.

[44] See the definition of provider in Article 3 (3) of AI Act.

[45] See AI Act, Article 4; cf. also the definition provided by Article 3 (56).

[46] Kiseleva et al. (2022).

standpoint, reaching interpretability necessitates defining who the recipient of the information is and why that information is needed.[47]

Yet, from a legal perspective, one of the main goals of an explanation is to let actors contest automated decisions. It is worth pointing out, here, that an explanation is different from a justification. In fact, understanding how an algorithm arrived at its conclusions does not imply that the conclusion follows the law.[48] Another main function of transparency is to ensure the accountability of all the actors in the value chain. Transparency is not only needed for them to justify their actions but also as oversight over their activities. In the context of AI, the strong correlation between accountability and transparency becomes especially important.[49] Opacity issues lead to limitations in interpreting the process and the outcomes of AI systems and, because of that, building an accountability architecture is one of the ways to ensure better transparency. In this sense, all the various actors in the game, i.e., the developers, the providers, the deployers, need to explain and justify their actions to ensure adequate oversight. With this onus in place, any process should become inherently more transparent; otherwise, obligations would remain an end in themselves.[50]

4 The AI Act's Obligations Toward Transparency and Human Oversight

The EU AI Act provides transparency rules for AI systems that have high potential risks to a patient's health, safety, and fundamental rights. Of course, this clearly includes AI systems used in the medical sector.[51] In fact, Article 6.1 of the Act through Annex I classified the systems used in healthcare as high-risk. Additionally, medical AI systems should comply with the requirements set forth by the Medical Device Regulation, which mandates a third-party conformity assessment.[52] Article 13.1 goes on to state that high-risk AI systems "shall be designed and developed in such a way as to ensure that their operation is sufficiently transparent to enable deployers to interpret a system's output and use it appropriately". In addition, "the instruction of use shall contain: (iv) the technical capabilities and characteristics of the system to provide information that is relevant to explain its output" (para. 3). Such obligations easily refer to the role that XAI techniques play in explaining the results of AI models, as XAI ensures that healthcare professionals are able to interpret a model's output and use it appropriately. In this way, the AI Act creates a close link between the transparency provisions outlined in Article 13 and the obligation to

[47] Ibid.

[48] Hildebrandt (2023), p. 41.

[49] Kaminski (2019), p. 213.

[50] Balkin (2017).

[51] Medical Devices (Reg. 2017/745, MDR); see also Busch et al. (2024).

[52] European Parliament (2022).; Van Kolfschooten and Van Oirschot (2024).

provide human oversight in Article 14. As Article 14 states, "high-risk systems shall be designed and developed in such a way, that can be effectively overseen by a natural person, that can correctly interpret the high-risk output".[53] Moreover, Recital 72 provides a sort of *vade mecum* to ensure transparency and accountability by addressing "concerns related to the opacity and complexity of some AI systems".[54]

From our perspective, this Recital is likely to play a central role in both the ex-ante implementation phase and the ex-post interpreting phase of design obligations. More specifically, the ex-ante phase will serve to guide developers/providers in the design choices made for these high-risk AI systems "in a transparent way, providing deployers with clear and legible information so as to assist them in using the system and supporting informed decision-making".[55] This will be what is needed to comply with (all) the legal requirements for high-risk AI systems. Indeed, the second part of the first paragraph of Article 13 suggests that transparency is the necessary fil rouge to ensure better compliance with all the provisions of high-risk AI systems. Additionally, the ex-post interpreting phase will allow national and EU courts to verify whether effective measures for ensuring the transparency of AI systems have been put in place. The main goals of this phase are to enable users to contest the decisions of high-risk AI systems and to identify the underlying causes of harmful incidents, thereby mitigating risks to a person's health.

Overall, it seems clear that the transparency measures imposed by the new EU legislation aim to not only hold system developers and providers accountable—by virtue of the design choices they have made—but also to inform the deployers of such systems, thus making them accountable as well. This approach fosters a synergistic relationship between AI developers and healthcare professionals, which is necessary to ensure a high level of protection for the patients, who are ultimately affected by the system's recommendations. This view is indeed confirmed by Art. 86.1 of the Act, which provides that any affected person (e.g., the patient) who is subject to a decision made by the deployer (e.g., the doctor) based on the output of a high-risk AI system shall have "the right to receive a clear and meaningful explanation of the AI system's role in the decision-making process and the main elements of the decision taken". This right to explanation should help empower patients, enabling them to take direct action to protect their rights and interests against accountable persons and organizations. However, the conditions for the application of this remedy are strict: they only cover the high-risk AI systems listed in Annex III, which does not apply to medical devices, and are only triggered if the AI's result had a significantly adverse impact on the health, safety, or fundamental rights of the end-user.[56] In practice, this means that, in the context of healthcare, this right can only be exercised by patients in relation to AI decisions concerning access to essential benefits and (healthcare) services, life and health insurance, emergency calls or

[53] AI Act, Article 14.4(c).

[54] AI Act, Recital 72.

[55] Idem.

[56] Van Kolfschooten and Van Oirschot (2024).

the dispatch of emergency first response services, and emergency healthcare triaging (Annex III.5).

Moreover, Article 86.1 of the AI Act seems to resemble Article 22.3 and Recital 71 of the General Data Protection Regulation (GDPR),[57] which all discuss the use of automated processing, particularly pertaining to a person's rights to express one's point of view and also to contest decisions. Even though there are considerable differences between the two regulations, at best they offer complementary protection where their competencies overlap. However, notwithstanding the significance of the GDPR, these protections would not be applicable in every scenario. First, the patient, as the data subject, would not be relying on a decision based *solely* on automated processing as any recommendations would be vetted by the doctor. Second, although the doctor is the actual recipient of the automated decision, this provision cannot apply to him/her as s/he is not the data subject. Consequently, the patient could request an explanation directly by invoking the remedy of Article 86.1 within the circumstances listed in Annex III.5. Nevertheless, we argue that, even though Article 22.3 does not apply to our case, it is beneficial to interpret Article 86.1 in a way that aligns with the provisions of the GDPR regarding the right to contest automated decisions. This interpretation could help guarantee better legal protection-by-design of the person affected.[58]

That said, given the limited application of Art. 86.1 AI Act, we argue that establishing *ex-ante* requirements specified in Articles 13 and 14 of the AI Act will enhance patients' protection, as they would apply to any high-risk medical AI systems that are otherwise exempt. Furthermore, it would improve safeguards in scenarios where this remedy is applicable, thereby alleviating the deployer's obligation from being solely accountable for managing the issue. In fact, these obligations require providers of AI systems to implement proactive measures to ensure transparency, interpretability, legibility, and oversight.

5 The Importance of Design Choices in AI Systems

Another important element is to clarify the meaning of design choices with AI systems. Initially referencing Article 11 of the Act, entitled "Technical documentation", there is a norm that creates a direct link to Annex IV and provides for the technical measures used to monitor and notify competent authorities of high-risk AI systems.[59]

Given the importance of the design choices made in AI systems, we concur with Hildebrandt, who emphasizes that, rather than focusing solely on explaining the inner workings of a machine learning system, it is much more important to

[57] European Parliament (2016).

[58] Hildebrandt (2015).

[59] AI Act, Annex IV (2)(b).

understand "the research design that defines both the inner working of ML [machine learning] systems and their output".[60] Understanding the research design requires a focused consideration of the crucial role played by data governance, proxies, and ground truths, among others. For instance, one could challenge the methodology used to select and clean the data that were used to train an algorithm. One could also challenge the features collected or created as the basis for decisions or the processes for selecting and defining labels.[61] Here, labels act as proxies for the phenomenon of interest in the real world,[62] specifically functioning as a ground truth for models, which must learn to process, classify, and discriminate between different data, features, and targets. Decisions about what constitutes a ground truth are central to machine learning models[63] and, consequently, to their output,[64] especially since analyzing these choices may reveal certain errors. In this architecture, incorrect implementation may lead to unreliable results, which, when applied to high-risk decision-making, as is the case in the medical sector, may cause harm.

Therefore, choosing the ground truth is an act rather than a given. From this viewpoint, echoing Kranzberg's First Law,[65] one could assert that AI systems are not neutral. Rather, they are shaped by intentional design choices. Data scientists and the institutions that employ them are responsible for numerous critical decisions as AI systems get developed. These decisions include selecting appropriate data sets for training the algorithms, determining the target output,[66] choosing the type of models to be used, assessing the algorithm's likelihood of producing false positives and false negatives,[67] among many other decisions.[68] These are normative technical choices that directly impact a range of users.[69] Here, technical normativity refers to the manner in which a legal norm or a specific technology enforces or excludes certain behavior. Also, the specific implementation of a technology changes the affordance of the environment of those who use it.[70]

It is essential to highlight that these techno-normative design choices are also intricately connected to the data governance requirements outlined in Article 10 of the AI Act. More specifically, paragraph 2 (f)(g) establishes that appropriate measures must be taken to prevent possible biases that are likely to have a negative impact on fundamental rights or lead to discrimination. For instance, to avoid traslational bias: (1) all real-world subgroups of interest must be sufficiently represented

[60] Hildebrandt (2023a), p. 38. Hildebrandt (2022).

[61] Lehr and Ohm (2017).

[62] Hildebrandt (2023), p. 44.; Mulvin (2021), pp. 4–12.

[63] Hildebrandt (2023b).

[64] Campagner et al. (2021).

[65] Kranzberg (1995), p. 5.

[66] Hildebrandt (2023a), p. 44.

[67] Kaminski (2020).

[68] Lehr and Ohm (2017).

[69] Hildebrandt (2008).

[70] Hildebrandt (2015), pp. 162–165.

in the training dataset without significant imbalances between them; and (2) the training data must be representative of the target population.[71] Hence, an AI system's developers need to be transparent about the statistical distribution of the feature values in their training sets. Additionally, all the different subgroups of individuals relevant to the question being addressed need to be represented in the model's training. As an example, imagine an algorithm trained to detect melanoma using a dataset of mostly elderly patients and a few non-cancerous young people. This dataset reflects a significant age bias in the design choices made about the model since, once trained in this biased way, the algorithm will tend to predict non-cancerous lesions in younger patients given the limited incidence of cancerous lesions in that population in the training data. Consequently, ensuring transparency in the various techno-normative choices throughout the AI pipeline is a better way of not only holding developers and providers accountable but also improving the actual reliability of AI systems.

Ultimately, it is crucial for physicians to have a sufficient level of AI literacy. Only knowledge can foster awareness of the opportunities and risks of AI and the possible harms these systems could cause. For this reason, we argue that AI literacy and transparency are the best tools for increasing our understanding and the contestability of the outputs generated by high-risk AI systems. This applies to both the deployer, who makes the final decision in terms of the diagnosis or treatment chosen, and the patient, who will be informed by the doctor, without either of them having specialized expertise in computer science. In this sense, if design choices are presented transparently, and if AI systems that demonstrate high predictive accuracy in real applications are made more explainable and interpretable to various users both ex-ante and ex-post, several significant outcomes could be achieved. First, it would mean that AI developers/providers could be held more accountable for their choices. Second, it would make it easier for the deployer to understand the decision-making processes underlying these models. In other words, if good synergetic relationships were established between all the actors involved, patients could ultimately be better informed about the health treatments offered to them, so enhancing their self-determination.

6 Medical Liability and Standard of Care

While the previous sections of this chapter have discussed the complexity associated with transparency in some of the most promising AI-based medical systems, the remaining sections will discuss the resulting liability issues in European member states. It is, of course, impossible to tackle all the elements of medical liability. Hence, we will focus on the hypothetical impacts AI systems might have on the standard of care.

---

[71] Sylvain and Paul (2023).

The general structure of malpractice, shared across the legal systems under analysis, can be described as follows. First, there must be a relationship between the physician and the patient that gives rise to a duty of care. Secondly, that duty must be breached, and the breach must be ascertained through the standard of care. Third, that breach of duty must have caused damage to the patient.[72]

Regardless of whether the doctor-patient relationship is framed as a contractual or non-contractual relationship,[73] the general trigger for medical liability in the case of a wrong diagnosis or therapy has historically been either fault (or negligence). Broadly speaking, a clinician's negligence can be understood as the physician's act or omission in contrast to *leges artis,*[74] which refers to the medical science and practices on which there is a consensus in the scientific community.[75] Hence, in this section, we will examine how standard of care has evolved and its current manifestation. Conversely, in Sect. 8, we will explore whether and how AI systems have impacted the standard of care.

The concept of duty of care was first introduced by the British case Donoghue v. Stevenson (1932), defined as a "general duty to take reasonable care to avoid foreseeable injury to a 'neighbour'". Subsequently, the concept migrated from general tort law to malpractice. Overall, malpractice can be understood as an obligation to exercise a specific kind of care in the treatment of a patient.[76] Today, the systems under analysis define a clinician's duty of care both in general and broad legal terms, mostly specifying it in professional medical guidelines. Notably, medical guidelines are defined as "systematically developed statements to assist practitioner decisions about appropriate health care for specific clinical circumstances",[77] which could include other rules developed by the medical community.[78] Also, within the liability assessment phase, courts may attribute major or minor persuasive evidence to these rules for identifying the standard of care content.[79] Generally, these guidelines, best practices, protocols, and similar rules[80] simply operationalize what is generally agreed-upon evidence-based practice.[81] The duty of care delineates the obligations of doctors, whereas the standard of care specifies methods and thresholds for fulfilling such obligations. And, if the standard of care is not met, the duty is breached.

The EU Member States present slightly different approaches to the standard of care they require, but, in the end, they don't differ from functional perspective (the area of medical malpractice falls under the competencies of Member States, based

[72] Koch (2011a).

[73] Oliphant (2013).

[74] Kraetschmer (2013).

[75] Mandilara et al. (2023).

[76] Hyman and Silver (2013).

[77] Field and Lohr (1990).

[78] Koch (2011a).

[79] Ibid.; Finder (2000).

[80] Miller and Kearney (2004).

[81] Mead (2000).

on Article 168 of the Treaty on the functioning of the european union). The standard of care is generally defined in broad terms, referring to "the occasion and circumstances of the treatment and the speciality or practice of the treating physician".[82] However, this is an objective threshold that often varies between rural and urban areas.[83] Moreover, the definition changes according to the resources available with only a minimum average set for the standard due.[84]

The various national legal systems of the EU each frame the standard of care differently. In some cases, physicians are required to act as an average conscientious specialist in the same circumstances, such as established by the Austrian Supreme Court.[85] In Germany, they are required to observe the medical standards generally recognized at the time of the treatment (German Civil Code, § 630a para. 2 BGB). The Dutch Civil Code requires compliance with the standard of a "prudent care provider" (Article 7:453), while in Spain, it is well-established case law that physicians must exert "utmost effort".[86] Further, only some countries require a level of care higher than the average, for instance, the Polish Supreme Court established that physician's must perform in accordance with the highest due care required from current medical knowledge.[87]

Nevertheless, when establishing the standard of care, most EU nations rely on clinical guidelines, at least to some degree. Italian law on medical liability (Law 24/2017, Article 5), for instance, explicitly requires physicians to follow guidelines and best practices unless the circumstances of the case specifically require otherwise.[88] Plus, even EU countries that do not clearly demand that certain guidelines be followed often strongly refer to them to assess a practitioner's standard of care.

The French legal system has shaped its modern medical malpractice rules based on the *Mercier* case of 1936. In this case, the *Court de Cassation* states that physicians must ensure conscientious and attentive care in conformity with the current professional medical standards, which in most cases are defined by codes of conduct and protocols.[89]

The vagueness of the expressions used, such as "prudent care providers", "reasonable standard of care", "utmost effort" etc., and the need to rely on something more than just common opinions has given rise to a phenomenon called evidence-based medicine.[90] Evidence-based medicine was first defined as "the conscientious, explicit, and judicious use of current best evidence in making decisions about the

[82] Oliphant (2013).

[83] Boerma et al. (1998).

[84] Stauch (2013).

[85] Koch (2011b).

[86] Ruda (2019).

[87] Bączyk-Rozwadowska (2013).

[88] Albano et al. (2022).

[89] Carval and Sefton-Green (2011).

[90] Birbeck et al. (2013).

care of individual patients".[91] It has emerged due to the insufficiencies of the opinion-based approach[92] with the objective of helping to make medical decision-making processes more transparent and understandable.[93] To this end, evidence-based medicine requires physicians to base their decisions on evidence generated through solid methodologies.[94] Thus, it signals an evolution in common definitions of the standard of care.

7 Evidence-based Medicine and The Standard of Care

Evidence-based medical frameworks prescribe that medical decisions be rooted in evidence obtained from established clinical research methodologies.[95] Thus, following such protocols means clinical decisions are grounded on solid scientific evidence, not on anecdotes or personal opinions.[96] A "reasonable standard of care" is therefore defined based on the practices established by evidence-based medicine. Hence, only practices with proven evidence can become the standard of care.[97]

The types of evidence that promote transparency in decision-making processes are mostly found in systematic reviews, meta-analyses, randomized controlled trials, and observational studies.[98] Hence, it is these sorts of investigations that tend to provide the input for introducing new guidelines.

Under any evidence-based medical framework, decision-making must be based on evidence. That said, not all evidence has equal value.[99] There are hierarchies. For instance, at the bottom of the pyramid, there are causal mechanisms, opinions, case reports, and case series. Next come observational studies and, at the apex, there are randomized clinical trials, systematic reviews, and meta-analyses, which represent the strongest evidence.[100] This hierarchy reflects a precise conception: clinical studies (like randomized trials), which are based on correlations and statistical analyses, are preferred over other kinds of evidence, such as expert opinions or causal mechanisms.[101] This is because clinical and statistical studies are generally designed to avoid biased outcomes. Moreover, they are thought to be better at coping with the problem of confounding, which occurs when a researcher attempts to assess the

---

[91] Sackett et al. (1996).

[92] Grosso (2020).

[93] Oliver and Pearce (2017).

[94] Zakowski et al. (2004).

[95] Masic et al. (2008).

[96] Williams (2011).

[97] Epstein (2018).

[98] Reddy (2022).

[99] Clarke et al. (2014).

[100] Palmas (2023).

[101] Worrall (2002).

impact of one factor but instead inadvertently measures the effect of another factor—namely, a confounding variable.[102] This bias can mean researchers erroneously establish a causal relationship between two or more variables, when, in reality, the cause of the influence is entirely unknown.[103]

Because they are randomized, randomized clinical trials have traditionally been considered exempt from the problems typically associated with observational studies. For example, clinical trials require minimal prior information and are run largely independent of background knowledge, which is often considered to be manipulable, biased, or otherwise suspect.[104] In terms of standard of care, medical decisions based on high-quality evidence, like randomized control trials, are more likely to be endorsed as evidence and, therefore, their outcomes align better with the standard of care. Conversely, decisions based on lesser evidence, like expert opinions, may be harder to justify in court.

8 Black-Box AI and The Standard of Care

An interesting question in the standard of care realm is whether and how such standards are affected by the high accuracy yet opacity of AI systems. Therefore, in this section, we analyze whether the traditional standards of accuracy in diagnoses should increase when AI is applied, given the high performance of most AI systems. If these systems can truly outperform physicians, should clinicians be obliged to meet the same levels of diagnostic accuracy as AI systems?

More specifically, if a certain condition is deemed to be more accurately diagnosed by a black-box model, should physicians be declared negligent for not using that model? Or for not following the AI's recommendation when harm occurs because they did not correctly diagnose that condition? Are they breaching the standard of care even though an average physician would not have been able to diagnose the condition without the help of AI?

An example is useful here. Consider a melanoma diagnosis, where the standard of care requires specific procedures whose results are proven to be effective. Let us assume that, through these procedures, it is generally possible to identify peculiar cellular features that can lead to a correct early diagnosis. Moreover, assume that classical methodologies are proven to be accurate around 89% of the time, meaning that in some cases, the practitioner will not be able to recognize a tumor, even when applying evidence-based medicine. Accordingly, based on a "reasonable standard of care", physicians are sometimes justified in not correctly diagnosing some tumors.

Let us also suppose that several physicians have published research based on their experiences with an AI system, reporting its accuracy in diagnosing specific

[102] Jager et al. (2008).

[103] Clarke et al. (2014).

[104] Deaton and Cartwright (2018).

melanoma features with an accuracy of between 95% and 99%. These physicians describe their *research design* in detail, along with the design decisions made by the AI provider. They also set out: how the system complies with the AI Act; its clinical benefits; the clinical investigations undertaken; the correctness of the data collection and pre-processing protocols; the representativeness of the dataset; the reliability of the ground truth; and other facts necessary to support the claim that the system's accuracy should hold outside of an experimental setting. More importantly, they also describe the differences in accuracy between the AI system and an average dermatologist using traditional diagnostic tools, highlighting which tumor cells the AI system is better at diagnosing than clinicians. Note, here, that we selected a 99% accuracy rate to present a compelling example., however, these levels of accuracy are not unrealistic as several studies show that AI is making significant improvements to skin cancer detection rates.[105] Given these two scenarios, which physicians are setting the higher standard of care—the ones using the AI system (diagnosing specific tumor cells with a 95% to 99% accuracy rate)? Or the average specialist relying on traditional diagnosis techniques (with an 89% accuracy rate)?

If we interpret the evidence-based framework as traditionally understood, clinicians using the AI systems are not setting an higher standard of care, since most of them are black-box models, and their decision-making process can seldom be inspected. In fact, often, only few developer's design choices can be assessed. Therefore, evaluating exactly how the model generated its output is not always possible. Thus, any diagnosis would actually be the clinician's interpretation of the results. This example shows that, according to traditional views of evidence-based medicine, there is a clear contrast between what it requires and what a black-box model produces. The former requires relying on specific and controlled methodologies, while the latter works on operating paradigms that are only partially understandable. This lack of control and explainability would prevent the AI systems from setting a new standard of care.

8.1 Black-Box Medicine

Despite the ambitious goals of evidence-based medicine and its remarkable contributions to the advancement of healthcare, actually achieving its main goals poses several challenges.[106] For example, while evidence-based medicine aims to base clinical reasoning on strong evidence, in many cases, it has been highlighted that clinicians' decisions are deeply probabilistic, relying on statistical associations rather than true causal insights.[107] It has also been reported that many explanations providing for medical interventions often resemble post-hoc rationalizations rather

[105] European Academy of Dermatology & Venereology (2023).

[106] Abujaber et al. (2022).

[107] Norman (2000).

than genuine causal justifications.[108] This highlights a significant epistemological gap between theory and practice. Clinicians frequently rely on explanations that, while persuasive, do not fully explain the underlying mechanisms of a treatment or diagnosis. Thus, clinicians' decisions can be just as opaque as AI outputs.[109]

Evidence-based medicine's reliance on randomized controlled trials as the gold standard of evidence has also faced significant criticism.[110] Several studies have shown that randomized controlled trials, while powerful tools, are not immune to methodological flaws, such as confounders and other design limitations that can distort their findings.[111] According to these accounts, the focus of trials remains largely on outcomes rather than the methods used to achieve the results, despite promises that evidence-based medicine will provide a robust, scientific basis for clinical decision-making.[112] This outcome-oriented approach often overlooks the importance of understanding the processes and mechanisms behind interventions and critically evaluating how the results were obtained, instead of simply arriving at a result. Consequently, in practice, evidence-based medicine frequently emphasizes what seems to work without fully addressing the deeper questions of why it works. In this way, it often reflects a broader tension between correlation and causality. According to its critics, evidence-based medicine does not necessarily lead to explainable clinical decisions. Some scholars even argue that requiring full explainability of AI systems would, therefore, represent an unacceptable double standard.[113] For many scholars, evidence-based medicine reliance on correlations and statistics recalled ML features, being both incapable to certainly provide causal mechanisms and medical knowledge.[114] On this basis, scholars have argued that the difference between machine learning and evidence-based medicine is superficial at best.[115] They claim that the true nature of evidence-based medicine, compared to the uncertain, probabilistic, and opaque nature of the output provided by AI systems, does not significantly differ from the evidence generated by other methodologies such as randomized controlled trials or observational studies.

Furthermore, scholars have begun to test AI-clinical decision support system (AI-CDSS) in randomized controlled trials.[116] To this end, special guidelines for AI-based randomized control trials have been developed to ensure the results produced are reliable and shareable.[117] These guidelines aim to align traditional reporting methodologies with the peculiarities of AI, essentially by requiring descriptions

---

[108] Dhaliwal (2020).

[109] Holzinger et al. (2019).

[110] Abujaber et al. (2022).

[111] Thompson (2010).

[112] London (2019).

[113] Kempt et al. (2022).

[114] Scott (2018).

[115] London (2019).

[116] Park et al. (2022).

[117] Lekadir et al. (2025); Liu et al. (2020); Vasey et al. (2022); Cruz Rivera et al. (2020).

of the AI systems design choices for both the system and the study design. For example, FUTURE-AI, CONSORT-AI and SPIRIT-AI guidelines require to report that the RCT was conducted with the aid of an AI-CDSS, and the inclusion and exclusion criteria for patients participating in the trial; the version of the algorithm;[118] the data collection processes; how poor-quality or missing data were assessed and handled; any interactions between the users and the system when handling input data; and the impact of the results on any general decision-making processes. The guidelines also recommended describing any erroneous performance and how that performance was identified and handled, along with any restrictions to the algorithm's code and its re-use. Overall, the idea behind requiring all this reporting was to render the trials more transparent so that other researchers could evaluate the studies.[119] Notably, these guidelines were only suggestions for the minimum standards to be applied to AI trials, leaving much room for further debate,[120] especially over the requirements listed in the disclosures sections of the AI Act.

Returning to our example as a way to sum up the findings of those researchers who highlight the similarities between machine learning and traditional medicine: if physicians do not provide a mere opinion but, rather, present evidence from a solid randomized controlled trial that demonstrates an AI system has a higher diagnostic accuracy than the methods currently used by physicians, that trial should be considered evidence under an evidence-based medical framework, and should therefore set a new higher standard of care.

8.2 A New Standard of Care

In this paper, we have emphasized that both traditional medicine and AI are, in distinct ways, both characterized by opacity and uncertainty. The concept of evidence-based medicine illustrates how new challenges related to transparency are compounding longstanding, unresolved issues. We have described two different views – one assuming a net divide between evidence-based medicine and machine learning, and the other remarking on their similarities. In terms of the latter perspective, if randomized controlled trials conducted according to guidelines specifically designed to evaluate AI-based methodologies show evidence of a new higher standard of care, then a new standard of care should apply. That said, the consequences in terms of liability may be harsh for clinicians. On the one hand, practitioners might feel forced to use an AI system even when they are not truly convinced of its efficacy. However, as with all AI systems, humans remain the final decision-makers, which means they can reject the results if they want to. Then, in cases of harm, clinicians will need to justify why they deviated from the output, which represent the

118 Lee and Lee (2020).

119 Shahzad et al. (2022); Genin and Grote (2021).

120 Vasey et al. (2022).

standard of care. For instance, they might highlight the specific circumstances of randomized control trials' clinical settings that render those results inapplicable. Conversely, clinicians following the AI's results will need to provide justification for why they relied on this advice, in order to avoid 'automation bias'.

9 Conclusion

In this chapter, we address some of the legal issues relating to the emerging use of AI systems in the medical sector. These systems, while often proficient in making accurate predictions, lack some transparency in terms of their operations in that they are entirely capable of producing diagnoses and recommendations, but do not always explain how they reached the conclusions that they did. In this context, we have attempted to clarify why using the predictions produced by AI might sometimes be unrealistic in the real world. The traditional doctor-patient relationship has already been firmly cast, and new collaborative paradigms involving additional actors, like AI developers and providers, are only just emerging. Many of us are yet to realize how significantly data scientists are impacting the conversations we have with our primary healthcare providers through the design choices they have made over the AI systems used to arrive at our diagnoses. And, despite the transparency requirements established for AI providers by the AI Act, greater transparency and accountability are still required to reduce the risks to patient health. Evidence-based medical frameworks dictate that standard of care should be set by evidence generated through specific methodologies, such as randomized control trials. However, in this regard, two views have emerged. One claims that, ultimately, both evidence-based medicine and machine learning are equally opaque, therefore the method with the best results should serve as the standard of care. The other holds that AI-CDSS are essentially black boxes and, therefore, we should continue to rely on traditional methods for proving efficacy, such as randomized control trials. The next decade of personalized medical care should bear the answer.

Acknowledgements This research was financially supported by the "Biorobotics Research and Innovation Engineering Facilities" "IR0000036" – CUP J13C22000400007 (BRIEF) project.

References

Abujaber AA, Nashwan AJ, Fadlalla A (2022) Harnessing machine learning to support evidence-based medicine: A pragmatic reconciliation framework. Intelligence-Based Med 6:100048. https://doi.org/10.1016/j.ibmed.2022.100048

Albano GD, Rifiorito A, Malta G et al (2022) The impact on healthcare workers of italian law n. 24/2017 'Gelli-Bianco' on patient safety and medical liability: a national survey. Int J Environ Res Public Health 19:8448. https://doi.org/10.3390/ijerph19148448

Amram D (2023) La transizione digitale delle vulnerabilità e il sistema delle responsabilità. Rivista Italiana di Medicina Legale (e del Diritto in campo sanitario)(RIML), pp 1–22

Bączyk-Rozwadowska K (2013) Medical malpractice and compensation in Poland. In: Oliphant K, Wright RW (eds) Medical malpractice and compensation in global perspective. De Gruyter, pp 327–376

Balkin JM (2017) The three laws of robotics in the age of big data. Ohio State Law J 78, Forthcoming, Yale Law School, Public Law Research Paper No. 592, Available at SSRN: https://ssrn.com/abstract=2890965

Béviére-Boyer B (2023) The French paradox of the Halftone Legislative Intervention on Artificial Intelligence in Health by the Bioethics Law of August 2, 2021. In: Artificial intelligence law – between sectoral rules and comprehensive regime comparative law. C. Castets-Renard and J. Eynard, Bruylant (edited by), pp 277–282

Birbeck GL, Wiysonge CS, Mills EJ et al (2013) Global health: the importance of evidence-based medicine. BMC Med 11:223. https://doi.org/10.1186/1741-7015-11-223

Bodria F, Giannotti F, Guidotti R et al (2023) Benchmarking and survey of explanation methods for black box models. Data Min Knowl Disc 37:1719–1778. https://doi.org/10.1007/s10618-023-00933-9

Boerma WGW, Groenewegen PP, Van Der Zee J (1998) General practice in urban and rural Europe: the range of curative services. Soc Sci Med 47:445–453. https://doi.org/10.1016/S0277-9536(98)00074-4

Busch F, Kather JN, Johner C et al (2024) Navigating the European Union artificial intelligence act for healthcare. NPJ Digit Med 7:210. https://doi.org/10.1038/s41746-024-01213-6

Campagner A, Ciucci D, Svensson C-M et al (2021) Ground truthing from multi-rater labeling with three-way decision and possibility theory. Inf Sci 545:771–790. https://doi.org/10.1016/j.ins.2020.09.049

Caruana R, Lou Y, Gehrke J et al (2015) Intelligible models for healthcare: predicting pneumonia risk and hospital 30-day readmission. In: Proceedings of the 21th ACM SIGKDD International Conference on Knowledge Discovery and Data Mining. ACM, Sydney NSW Australia, pp 1721–1730

Carval S, Sefton-Green R (2011) Medical liability in france. In: Koch BA (ed) Medical liability in Europe. De Gruyter, pp 207–232

Clarke B, Gillies D, Illari P et al (2014) Mechanisms and the evidence hierarchy. Topoi 33:339–360. https://doi.org/10.1007/s11245-013-9220-9

Comandé G (2019) Intelligenza artificiale e responsabilità tra liability e accountability. Il carattere trasformativo dell'IA e il problema della responsabilità. Analisi Giuridica dell'Economia 1:169–188

Comandé G (2020) Medical law in Italy. Wolters Kluwer

Comandé G (2024) Tecnologie e metamorfosi del danno e della responsabilità sanitaria. Danno e responsabilità.:153–160

Cruz Rivera S, Liu X, Chan A-W et al (2020) Guidelines for clinical trial protocols for interventions involving artificial intelligence: the SPIRIT-AI extension. Nat Med 26:1351–1363. https://doi.org/10.1038/s41591-020-1037-7

D'Elia C (2023) Gli strumenti di intelligenza artificiale generativa nel contesto sanitario: problemi di ottimizzazione delle risorse e questioni di spiegabilità,. Rivista Italiana di Medicina Legale (e del Diritto in campo sanitario). pp 357–360

Deaton A, Cartwright N (2018) Understanding and misunderstanding randomized controlled trials. Soc Sci Med 210:2–21. https://doi.org/10.1016/j.socscimed.2017.12.005

Dhaliwal G (2020) Clinical diagnosis—is there any other type? JAMA Int Med 180:1304. https://doi.org/10.1001/jamainternmed.2020.3048

Duffourc M, Gerke S (2023) Decoding U.S. Tort liability in Healthcare's Black-Box AI Era: Lessons from the European Union. 27:1.

Epstein NE (2018) Legal and evidenced-based definitions of standard of care: Implications for code of ethics of professional medical societies. Surg Neurol Int 9:255

Field MJ, Lohr KN (1990) Committee to Advise the Public Health Service on Clinical Practice Guidelines (1990) Clinical Practice Guidelines: Directions for a New Program. National Academies Press, Washington, DC

Finder JM (2000) The future of practice guidelines: should they constitute conclusive evidence of the standard of care? Health Matrix Clevel 10:67–117

Genin K, Grote T (2021) Randomized controlled trials in medical AI A methodological critique. pom 2. https://doi.org/10.5195/philmed.2021.27

Grasso AG (2023) Diagnosi algoritmica errata e responsabilità medica. Rivista di Diritto civile 2:334–360

Grosso S (2020) What is reasonable and what can be proved as reasonable: reflections on the role of evidence- based medicine and clinical practice guidelines in medical negligence claims. Annals of Health Law 27:74

Guidotti R, Monreale A, Ruggieri S et al (2019) A survey of methods for explaining black box models. ACM Comput Surv 51:1–42. https://doi.org/10.1145/3236009

Guidotti R, Giannotti F, Pedreschi D (2022) Explainability (30). In: Comandé G (ed) Edgar Encyclopedia of law and data science. Edward Elgar Publishing, pp 160–168

Hildebrandt M (2008) Legal and technological normativity: more (and less) than twin sisters. Techné 12:3

Hildebrandt M (2012) The dawn of a critical transparency right for the profiling era. In: Bus J et al (ed) Digital Enlightenment Yearbook 2012

Hildebrandt M (2015) Smart technologies and the end(s) of law. Novel entanglements of law and technology. Edward Elgar Publishing

Hildebrandt M (2018) Preregistration of machine learning research design. In: Bayamlioglu E, Baraliuc I, Janssens L, Hildebrandt M (eds) Against P-hacking. BEING PROFILED:COGITAS ERGO SUM, Amsterdam

Hildebrandt M (2022) The issue of proxies and choice architectures. Why EU law matters for recommender systems. Front Artif Intell 5:789076. https://doi.org/10.3389/frai.2022.789076

Hildebrandt M (2023a) Qualification and quantification in machine learning. From explanation to explication. Sociologica pp 37–49 .https://doi.org/10.6092/ISSN.1971-8853/15845

Hildebrandt M (2023b) Ground-truthing in the european health data space. In: Proceedings of the 16th International Joint Conference on Biomedical Engineering Systems and Technologies. SCITEPRESS - Science and Technology Publications, Lisbon, Portugal, pp 15–22

Holzinger A, Langs G, Denk H et al (2019) Causability and explainability of artificial intelligence in medicine. WIREs Data Min & Knowl 9:e1312. https://doi.org/10.1002/widm.1312

Hyman DA, Silver CM (2013) Medical malpractice and compensation in global perspective: how does the U.S. Do It? In: Oliphant K, Wright RW (eds) Medical malpractice and compensation in global perspective. DE GRUYTER, pp 473–512

Jager KJ, Zoccali C, MacLeod A, Dekker FW (2008) Confounding: what it is and how to deal with it. Kidney Int 73:256–260. https://doi.org/10.1038/sj.ki.5002650

Jones C, Thornton J, Wyatt JC (2023) Artificial intelligence and clinical decision support: clinicians' perspectives on trust, trustworthiness, and liability. Med Law Rev 31:501–520. https://doi.org/10.1093/medlaw/fwad013

Kaminski ME (2019) The right to explanation. Explained. https://doi.org/10.15779/Z38TD9N83H

Kaminski ME (2020) Understanding transparency in algorithmic accountability. In: Barfield W (ed) The Cambridge handbook of the law of algorithms, 1st edn. Cambridge University Press, pp 121–138

Kempt H, Heilinger J-C, Nagel SK (2022) Relative explainability and double standards in medical decision-making: should medical AI be subjected to higher standards in medical decision-making than doctors? Ethics Inf Technol 24:20. https://doi.org/10.1007/s10676-022-09646-x

Kiseleva A, Kotzinos D, De Hert P (2022) Transparency of AI in healthcare as a multilayered system of accountabilities: between legal requirements and technical limitations. Front Artif Intell 5:879603. https://doi.org/10.3389/frai.2022.879603

Kizilcec RF (2016) How much information?: Effects of transparency on trust in an algorithmic interface. In: Proceedings of the 2016 CHI Conference on Human Factors in Computing Systems. ACM, San Jose California USA, pp 2390–2395

Koch BA (2011a) Medical liability in Europe: comparative analysis. In: Koch BA (ed) Medical liability in Europe. De Gruyter, pp 611–692

Koch BA (2011b) Medical liability in Austria. In: Koch BA (ed) Medical liability in Europe. DE GRUYTER, pp 1–60

Kraetschmer K (2013) Is the Lege Artis Principle Obsolete. J Forensic Res 04. https://doi.org/10.4172/2157-7145.1000194

Kranzberg M (1995) Technology and history: Kranzberg's Laws. Bull Sci Technol Soc 15:5–13

Lee CS, Lee AY (2020) Clinical applications of continual learning machine learning. Lancet Digital Health 2:e279–e281. https://doi.org/10.1016/S2589-7500(20)30102-3

Lehr D, Ohm P (2017) Playing with the data: what legal scholars should learn about machine learning. 51:653–717

Lekadir K, Frangi AF, Porras AR, et al. (2025) FUTURE-AI: international consensus guideline for trustworthy and deployable artificial intelligence in healthcare. BMJ e081554. https://doi.org/10.1136/bmj-2024-081554

Liu X, Cruz Rivera S, Moher D et al (2020) Reporting guidelines for clinical trial reports for interventions involving artificial intelligence: the CONSORT-AI extension. Nat Med 26:1364–1374. https://doi.org/10.1038/s41591-020-1034-x

London AJ (2019) Artificial intelligence and black-box medical decisions: accuracy versus explainability. Hast Center Rep 49:15–21. https://doi.org/10.1002/hast.973

Lyell D, Magrabi F, Raban MZ et al (2017) Automation bias in electronic prescribing. BMC Med Inform Decis Mak 17:28. https://doi.org/10.1186/s12911-017-0425-5

Malgieri G, Comandé G (2017) Why a right to legibility of automated decision-making exists in the general data protection regulation. Int Data Priv Law 7:243–265. https://doi.org/10.1093/idpl/ipx019

Maliha G, Gerke S, Cohen IG, Parikh RB (2021) Artificial intelligence and liability in medicine: balancing safety and innovation. Milbank Quart 99:629–647. https://doi.org/10.1111/1468-0009.12504

Mandilara P, Galanakos SP, Bablekos G (2023) A history of medical liability: from ancient times to today. Cureus. https://doi.org/10.7759/cureus.41593

Masic I, Miokovic M, Muhamedagic B (2008) Evidence Based medicine - new approaches and challenges. Acta Inform Med 16:219. https://doi.org/10.5455/aim.2008.16.219-225

Mead P (2000) Clinical guidelines: promoting clinical effectiveness or a professional minefield? J Adv Nurs 31:110–116. https://doi.org/10.1046/j.1365-2648.2000.01254.x

Miller M, Kearney N (2004) Guidelines for clinical practice: development, dissemination and implementation. Int J Nurs Stud 41:813–821. https://doi.org/10.1016/j.ijnurstu.2003.09.005

Mulvin D (2021) Proxies: the cultural work of standing in. The MIT Press, Cambridge

Norman GR (2000) The epistemology of clinical reasoning: perspectives from philosophy, psychology, and neuroscience. Acad Med 75:S127–S133. https://doi.org/10.1097/00001888-200010001-00041

Oliphant K (2013) Medical malpractice and compensation: comparative observations. In: Oliphant K, Wright RW (eds) Medical malpractice and compensation in global perspective. De Gruyter, pp 513–562

Oliver K, Pearce W (2017) Three lessons from evidence-based medicine and policy: increase transparency, balance inputs and understand power. Palgrave Commun 3:43. https://doi.org/10.1057/s41599-017-0045-9

Palmas WR (2023) Pocket evidence based medicine: a survival guide for clinicians and students. Springer International Publishing, Cham

Panigutti C, Beretta A, Fadda D et al (2023a) Co-design of human-centered, explainable ai for clinical decision support. ACM Trans Interact Intell Syst 13:1–35. https://doi.org/10.1145/3587271

Panigutti C, Hamon R, Hupont I et al (2023b) The role of explainable AI in the context of the AI Act. In: 2023 ACM conference on fairness, accountability, and transparency. ACM, Chicago IL, pp 1139–1150
Park SH, Choi J-I, Fournier L, Vasey B (2022) Randomized clinical trials of artificial intelligence in medicine: why, when, and how? Korean J Radiol 23:1119. https://doi.org/10.3348/kjr.2022.0834
Price WN (2018) Medical malpractice and black-box medicine. In: Cohen IG, Lynch HF, Vayena E, Gasser U (eds) Big data, health law, and bioethics, 1st edn. Cambridge University Press, pp 295–306
Reddy S (2022) Explainability and artificial intelligence in medicine. Lancet Digit Health 4:e214–e215. https://doi.org/10.1016/S2589-7500(22)00029-2
Rodotà S (2012) Il diritto di avere diritti, Laterza
Ruda A (2019) Medical liability in Spanish tort law. Journal du Droit de la Santé et de l'Assurance - Maladie (JDSAM) N° 23:38–44. https://doi.org/10.3917/jdsam.192.0038
Sackett DL, Rosenberg WMC, Gray JAM et al (1996) Evidence based medicine: what it is and what it isn't. BMJ 312:71–72. https://doi.org/10.1136/bmj.312.7023.71
Scott IA (2018) Machine learning and evidence-based medicine. Ann Intern Med 169:44. https://doi.org/10.7326/M18-0115
Selvaraju, RR, Cogswell, M, Das A, et al. (2017) Grad-CAM: visual explanations from deep networks via gradient-based localization. IEEE international conference on computer vision (ICCV), Venice, Italy, pp. 618–626. 10.1109/ICCV.2017.74
Shahzad R, Ayub B, Siddiqui MAR (2022) Quality of reporting of randomised controlled trials of artificial intelligence in healthcare: a systematic review. BMJ Open 12:e061519. https://doi.org/10.1136/bmjopen-2022-061519
Stauch MS (2013) Medical malpractice and compensation in Germany. In: Oliphant K, Wright RW (eds) . Medical malpractice and compensation in global perspective, DE GRUYTER, pp 179–210
Sylvain C-B, Paul M (2023) Which artificial intelligence for augmented medicine? In: Castets-Renard C, Eynard J (eds) 2023. Artificial Intelligence Law : Between Sectoral Rules and Comprehensive Regime : Comparative Law. Bruylant, Bruxelles
Thompson RP (2010) Causality, mathematical models and statistical association: dismantling evidence-based medicine. Eval Clin Pract 16:267–275. https://doi.org/10.1111/j.1365-2753.2010.01383.x
Van Kolfschooten H, Van Oirschot J (2024) The EU Artificial Intelligence Act (2024): Implications for healthcare. Health Policy 149:105152. https://doi.org/10.1016/j.healthpol.2024.105152
Vasey B, Nagendran M, Campbell B et al (2022) Reporting guideline for the early-stage clinical evaluation of decision support systems driven by artificial intelligence: DECIDE-AI. Nat Med 28:924–933. https://doi.org/10.1038/s41591-022-01772-9
Williams CL (2011) Evidence-based medicine in the law beyond clinical practice guidelines: what effect will EBM have on the standard of care? Wash Lee Law Rev 61:479
Worrall J (2002) What evidence in evidence-based medicine? Philos Sci 69:S316–S330. https://doi.org/10.1086/341855
Zakowski L, Seibert C, VanEyck WS (2004) Evidence-based medicine: answering questions of diagnosis. Clin Med Res 2:63–69. https://doi.org/10.3121/cmr.2.1.63
Zeiler MD, Fergus R (2014) Visualizing and understanding convolutional networks. In: Fleet D, Pajdla T, Schiele B, Tuytelaars T (eds) Computer vision – ECCV 2014. Springer International Publishing, Cham, pp 818–833

(Product) Liability in the Medical Internet of Things. What Now?

Francesca Gennari

Abstract The EU Product Liability Directive has long been studied to make it fit for new technologies. However, with the advent of AI, IoT, and robotics, the European Council finally decided that a complete rework of the legislation was needed. Hence, in October 2024, they adopted a proposal for updating the Directive, and, in November 2024, that proposal was enacted into law. The main difference between the old and the new Directive is that the new rules consider software to be a product, irrespective of whether it is interconnected to some hardware. This includes AI. Hence, the research question to be discussed in this chapter is: What now? How will a general directive that still applies to traditional consumer products be adapted to more refined devices and systems, such as the Internet of Medical Things? This chapter takes the new generation of active prostheses, such as the lower-limb prosthetics described in Chapter 11, as an example. As interconnected devices that can use AI systems for security, these prostheses lie at the intersection of liability law, (regulatory) health law, and different technologies working at the same time (e.g., IoT and AI). As such, this assessment will evaluate how the new Product Liability Directive will affect the manufacturers of these devices.

1 Introduction

Until recently, EU product liability was among the fields of EU law acquis to be extensively litigated and discussed by scholars.[1] Nevertheless, scholars have argued that this kind of litigation did not consist of many judgments at the EU level.[2] Maybe

[1] Gennari (2023a), pp. 143–158.

[2] Machnikowski (2016), pp. 669–705.

F. Gennari (✉)
LIDER-Lab, DIRPOLIS, Sant'Anna School of Advanced Studies, Pisa, Italy
e-mail: Francesca.Gennari@santannapisa.it

F. Casarosa et al. (eds.), *Enabling and Safeguarding Personalized Medicine*, Data Science, Machine Intelligence, and Law 7,
https://doi.org/10.1007/978-3-031-99709-9_16

because of this happenstance, the Product Liability Directive (PLD)[3] managed to survive all the way up to 2024 with no major modifications being made to the legislation.[4] However, the fast-paced development of AI, IoT, and robotics technology has put the EU's product liability rules under strain. Over the last 6 years, there have been intense scholarly debates on what to do about the 1985 Directive.[5] Additionally, policy studies[6] have been published to evaluate if and how the old liability rules needed to be modified to make new rules fit for new technologies.[7] The outcome of this debate was twin proposals: the Product Liability Directive Update (PLDU)[8] and the AI Non-Contractual Liability Directive (AINCLD).[9] Of the two proposals, only the one concerning product liability was voted into law. This new Directive, the PLDU,[10] will become effective from 9 December 2026, and, hence, will be the focus of this chapter.

The objective of this chapter is to evaluate how complying with the PLDU will translate in practice by analyzing the application of the PLDU to a practical use case involving active prostheses. Drawing on the lessons learned about control systems in active prostheses from Chap. 11 of this book, this chapter will analyze how the PLDU will fare when applied to damage caused by an active prosthesis that relies on machine learning (ML) techniques to control the individual's gait movement.[11] The legal analysis in Chap. 11 focuses on compliance with the AI Act and the MDR. In this chapter, I will assume a legal liability perspective on these devices, focusing on how the PLDU will impact those who manufacture active prostheses. Methodologically, I will select and group the most relevant set of articles on the newly enacted PLDU and try to forecast how they will apply in practice to active prosthesis.

---

[3] Council Directive 85/374/EEC of 25 July 1985 on the approximation of the laws, regulations and administrative provisions of the Member States concerning liability for defective products OJ L 210, p. 29.

[4] Wuyts (2014), pp. 1–3.

[5] Lohsse et al. (2019); European Law Institute (2021, 2022).

[6] Expert Group on Liability of AI and new Technologies (2019); Bartolini and Episcopo (2021).

[7] European Commission (2018). Contra Colombi Ciacchi et al. (2018), pp. 185–189.

[8] Proposal for a DIRECTIVE OF THE EUROPEAN PARLIAMENT AND OF THE COUNCIL on liability for defective products COM/2022/495 final.

[9] Proposal for a DIRECTIVE OF THE EUROPEAN PARLIAMENT AND OF THE COUNCIL on adapting non-contractual civil liability rules to artificial intelligence (AI Liability Directive) COM/2022/496 final. The Commission withdrew the proposal for the AINCLD on 11th February 2025 as there was a lack of consensus on its structure and objectives, COMMUNICATION FROM THE COMMISSION TO THE EUROPEAN PARLIAMENT, THE COUNCIL, THE EUROPEAN ECONOMIC AND SOCIAL COMMITTEE AND THE COMMITTEE OF THE REGIONS Commission work programme 2025 Moving forward together: A Bolder, Simpler, Faster Union.

[10] Article 21, Directive (EU) 2024/2853 of the European Parliament and of the Council of 23 October 2024 on liability for defective products and repealing Council Directive 85/374/EEC, PE/7/2024/REV/1 OJ L, 2024/2853, 18.11.2024, ELI: http://data.europa.eu/eli/dir/2024/2853/oj (PLDU).

[11] Fagioli et al. (2025).

First, I will deal with how the compensation function underpinning the PLDU is not only the fundamental rationale for the Directive but also the key to understanding how to use the PLDU to research and develop an active prosthesis. This is crucial as it will guide the choices of manufacturers when planning their R&D and risk management activities (15.2). Then, I will focus on how the new procedural rules provided in Articles 9 and 10 of the PLDU will affect product liability adjudication, while also considering the liability exemptions listed in Article 11 (15.3). To conclude, I will synthesize and summarize the material covered, providing several overarching conclusions (15.4). The most important finding is that, even if this Directive, on paper, seems to favor consumers more than manufacturers, there are several reasons to consider that this new legislation might end up favoring the manufacturers more than the plaintiffs. These reasons include: different national implementations; different verdicts as a result of the individual judges' interpretations; the seriousness and nature of the damage; and the legal traditions of the countries considered.

2 Compensation for New-Generation Prostheses

To understand the impact of the PLDU on these medical devices, it is important to understand the basic rules under which an injured person can file a complaint under the PLDU regime. The claimant first needs to prove that the product, in this case, a prosthesis, is defective. Then they need to prove that there has been damage and, last, that there needs to be a proven causal link between the defect and the damage that accords with Articles 4, 6, 9, and 10 PLDU. The rationale behind these rules is a compensation function, which is made explicit in Article 5. However, before trying to understand how this function interacts with the software of an AI-driven prostheses, it is necessary to draft a short but essential summary concerning: (i) the meaning of compensation in the EU and the rules governing private liability laws, and (ii) how the compensation function is enacted within the PLDU. Once explained, other elements of the Directive will be explored, such as the rules on personal damage and the extent of the manufacturer's control. In fact, these are none other than different specifications of the compensation rationale. Therefore, I will make an effort to imagine how these new rules might impact cases involving active prostheses.

2.1 The Principle of Compensation. Between Collective and Individual Claims for Active Prostheses

Article 5 PLDU states in its first paragraph that "Member States shall ensure that any natural person who suffers damage caused by a defective product (the 'injured person') is entitled to compensation in accordance with this Directive." This seems like a tautological sentence, but it is not if one considers the case law involving the old PLD. Historically, there were many instances in which compensation was quite difficult to obtain for claimants, especially when a chronic illness, syndrome, or disability followed after using a defective product. Notably, such cases were generally decided before the Court of Justice of the EU (CJEU).[12] Moreover, in a specular way, the place of EU law was unclear when it came to more favorable national remedies concerning defective products. A sad example of this was the case of 'Maria Victoria González Sánchez v. Medicina Asturiana SA' when a more consumer-protective national remedy was denied to the claimant by the CJEU based on the alleged PLD maximum harmonization character. In EU legal parlance, maximum harmonization means that Member States(MSs) can neither introduce more stringent nor more lenient rules than the ones outlined in a maximum harmonization directive. Here, the solution to the González-Sánchez case was highly criticized. The case involved a person who had inadvertently been infected with the hepatitis C virus via a blood transfusion. In the end, the claimant was not able to seek a higher sum of compensation under their national law. Instead, the PLD rules were applied.[13] Then, a series of judgments made the prohibition to use the more favorable national remedy a little more nuanced.

The first example of this series was the case of 'Novo Nordisk Pharma GmBH v. S' (2013) in which it was stated that the PLD did not affect acquired rights under specific national legislation before the PLD came into effect.[14] The second example of this trend was 'Elisabeth Schmitt v TÜV Rheinland LGA products GmbH' (2015) in which the CJEU allowed the application, if present, of national liability remedies that were necessary and proportionate with EU law[15] even when not recalled explicitly by either the PLD or by the Medical Devices Regulation (MDR).[16] The last example to complete this series is the case of 'N.W. and Others v. Sanofi Pasteur MSD SNC and Others'(2015) in which national judges were allowed to use more consumer-friendly legal presumptions, but only when those presumptions were compliant with the principles of effectiveness and equivalency with EU law.[17] It is worth noting that, in this case, the evidence of a causality link between damage and defect was complicated because vaccines were also involved. However, to read this part of the article correctly, one also needs to read Article 3 of the PLDU, titled

[12] See, in particular, cases 'Declan O'Byrne v. Sanofi Pasteur MSD Ltd' (2004) Case no C-127/04. European Court Reports 2006 I-01313; or in Aventis Pasteur SA v. OB' (2008) Case no C-258/08. European Court Reports 2009 I-11305.

[13] 'Maria Victoria González Sánchez v. Medicina Asturiana SA' (2000) Case no C-183/00 European Court Reports 2002 I-03901, C- paras 29–31.

[14] 'Novo Nordisk Pharma GmBH v. S' (2013), C-163/00, paras 20–31.

[15] This case was part of the aftermath of the PIP defective breast prothesis scandal. The court was very cautious in admitting that there were cases in which national liability rules could integrate EU law. See para 56 of the Schmitt Judgment and also More in Wallerman (2018), pp. 265–278; and in Gennari (2022), pp. 132–134.

[16] Regulation (EU) 2017/745 of the European Parliament and of the Council of 5 April 2017 on medical devices, amending Directive 2001/83/EC, Regulation (EC) No 178/2002 and Regulation (EC) No 1223/2009 and repealing Council Directives 90/385/EEC and 93/42/EEC, OJ L 117,http://data.europa.eu/eli/reg/2017/745/oj.(MDR).

[17] 'N.W. and Others v. Sanofi Pasteur MSD SNC and Others'(2015), C-621/15, paras 24–43.

"Level of Harmonization". This proviso states that national laws cannot introduce more favorable remedies in the field of product liability than the ones provided by the Directive. This therefore implies that the PLDU is a maximum harmonization measure. Hence, it will become the standard for compensation mechanisms in terms of product liability claims for the EU.[18]

That said, to properly discuss the compensation rationale that underpins the Directive, I must first explain what it means in practice. Unfortunately, the concept is only ever mentioned in the PLDU, but never defined. This lack of definition is a consequence of the conferral of competencies principle set out in Article 5(1) of the Treaty of the EU (TEU). This is why liability is not per se within the legislation competencies of the EU.[19] Nonetheless, liability can still be regulated because of the principle of subsidiarity,[20] and counterbalanced by the principle of proportionality,[21] but only if this action will improve overall harmonization of within the EU's (Digital) Single Market, as explained in Article 114 of the Treaty on the Functioning of the EU (TFEU).[22] This is why EU liability law outlines concepts that are similar in words to legal concepts in other countries but does not define them. Rather, according to Article 6 of the TFEU, it falls to each Member State to adapt terms such as liability to its own legal traditions.

That is why, to make things clearer, I will give a synthetic explanation of what compensation means within the EU law systems, which are now mostly civil law tradition countries.[23]

Compensation has always been one of, if not the most important, the objectives of private law liability rules in civil law countries.[24] If damage has taken place, then the person experiencing the consequences of this damage must first prove that the damage has happened and, second, how the damage happened, according to the set of rules applying to that jurisdiction. Note that, in the EU, these sets of rules tend to vary from state to state.[25]

---

[18] This does not concern the acquired rights under national laws before the entry into force of the old PLD as it is made explicit by Article 2(4)(c) PLDU.

[19] Klamert (2019).

[20] Kellerbauer (2019).

[21] Tridimas (2018), pp. 243–246.

[22] Interestingly, it is this article that is the legal basis of this directive, not consumer protection as one might think. This implies that both the consumers' and manufacturers' interests must be balanced.

[23] The main difference between Civil law tradition countries and Common law countries is that, as for the latter ones, such as Ireland and the UK, more importance is given to the judges view and on binding legal precedents, traditionally. For a more precise framework see Gambaro et al. (2024 last ed.), pp. 33–47 and pp. 49–110.

[24] Castronovo (2018), Alpa (2018).

[25] As far as compensation for tort damages in the civil law tradition, the most widely known models are the ones of France and Germany. In the French civil code, Article 1240 (formerly Article 1382) allows the reparation of any tort damaging someone. It is widely known for its general character. In the BGB, the German Civil Code, instead, the system of torts reparation is limited to a rigid list of § 823 BGB. Only with the law on the modernization of obligations, a specific addition was done

One important variant in liability evidence rules applicability was whether a contract was or was not present when the damage took place. If a contract was present, the rules concerning contractual liability apply. If a contract was close to being drafted but the damage happened before the process could be completed, then pre-contractual liability rules apply. Finally, if there was no contract present, as in the case of a car accident, tort, also called extracontractual, or non-contractual liability rules apply. With industrialization and the advent of consumer society,[26] a new kind of liability emerged in private law: strict liability, almost always associated with product liability depending on the legal system considered.[27] The characteristic feature of this kind of liability was to ensure that the manufacturer invested properly in the safety and security of their products either: (i) by presuming (more or less rigidly) the fault of the manufacturer if damage arises and or ii) by granting the complainant an "easier" way to win the case.[28] The former PLD and actual PLDU are a mix of sub *i)* of sub *ii)*. This is shown by the fact that the complainant must not prove the producer's/manufacturer's fault but needs to provide evidence for the damage that took place, the defectiveness of the product, and the causal link between the damage and the product's defectiveness.[29] Differences existed with the rules on how to quantify damage[30] among the different sets of liability. The damage quantification was generally done by keeping in mind the principle that the amount of compensation should aim at restoring the situation before the damage took place, the so-called *status quo ante*. That is why it was stated that liability had a compensation function—this being a sum of money or an action that will repair the damage. Markedly, the function does not serve to enrich the claimant nor punish the person liable for the damage. Article 6 of the PLDU describes which kinds of damage are covered but relegates the task of quantifying compensation for those damages to national judges, as is the case in the old Directive.

Next we turn to the issue of damage types. In the EU, damage types are mainly divided between material and non-material kinds of damage. The material damages covered by the PLDU include: (i) death; (ii) injury; and (iii) property damage.[31] Unlike the old PLD, this proviso is not limited to any monetary cap, which should

to admit a particular series of duties of care, the *Schutzpflichten*. In the middle of these two systems lies the Italian Article 2043 of the civil code which is more similar to the French Article 1240 but adds the element of the injustice of the damage to allow its compensation. Gennari (2022), pp. 139–143.

[26] Reimann (2023), p. 768.

[27] The PLD was always interpreted as a form of special strict liability. Van Dam (2013), pp. 297–302.

[28] In its system of strict liability types, Van Dam indicates strict liability with (i) an extra debtor, (ii) connected to a product or (iii) liability with a limited defence. Van Dam (2013), pp. 297–302.

[29] Interestingly, this simple rule was in Article 4 PLD, whereas the same rule does not have an equivalent in the PLDU but one needs to read Article 4, 6, 7, 9, and 10 to figure out how to file a product liability complaint.

[30] For instance, in the Italian civil code, the rules for compensation of material and non-material damage are the same, except for the consideration of future tort damage in Article 1225. Bussani (2020).

[31] Respectively, Article 6 (1)(a first part) and (b), (i),(ii),(iii) PLDU.

mean consumers prefer to remediate damages under the new PLDU instead of through any national property damage laws. The non-material damages include: (i) medically recognized damage to psychological health; and (ii) the destruction or corruption of data used for personal purposes only.[32] The list of non-material damages is also applicable to defective product components. In this regard, it is interesting to think of an active prosthesis as a product made up of both hardware and software, which is relevant to paras (2) and (3) of the PLDU's Article 6. In these paragraphs, compensation for damage extends to non-material damages only insofar as they are compensated for under national law. Although one imagines that a defect in an active prosthesis will be more likely to cause material damage than non-material harm, the way this article is drafted risks creating an inconsistent legislative landscape for the prosthesis manufacturers. More specifically, it might be legal to market a certain model of prosthesis in one EU country but not in another simply because of the rules on compensation for non-material damage. Consider Italy as an example. The judicial and scholarly traditions concerning compensation for non-material (meaning non-economic) damages in tort law make it likely that judges will use those precedents in combination with the PLDU, especially if the damage to the victim is permanent or very visible. Consequently, the categories of existential damage and biological damage in tort law will likely apply.[33] However, the same might not happen as easily in Germany because of the traditionally closed and strict definition of non-material damages in the German Civil Law Code.[34]

Nevertheless, Article 5 PLDU might offer a more uniform yet indirect solution for the EU market. Article 5(2) makes it an obligation for each Member State to allow consumers who have suffered damage to claim compensation as well as any…

> (a) … person that succeeded, or was subrogated, to the right of the injured person by virtue of Union or national law or contract; or (b) a person acting on behalf of one or more injured persons by virtue of Union or national law.

If we consider a), the mention of a contract could indicate that insurance companies can not only subrogate themselves in the consumer's shoes but also in the manufacturer's. This is apparent if we combine Article 5(2) PLDU with Article 10(16) MDR. Notably, both conditions have already been heard by the CJEU. In this case, I am primarily referring to 'Keskinäinen Vakuutusyhtiö Fennia v Koninklijke Philips NV.' (2022)[35] where a home insurance company acted on behalf of a Finnish person who had sustained damage.[36] However, I also refer to 'RB v TÜV Rheinland LGA Products GmbH and Allianz IARD S.A.' (2018).[37] This latter

[32] In the first proposal this specification did not exist and was extended to damage of data for professional use, which might have been more important for manufacturers of medical devices as they need to gather data from the product itself to comply with post-marketing obligations set in the MDR in Chapter VII and Annexes III and XIV. See also Article 4(6), (c) of the PLDU proposal.

[33] Ponzanelli (2019).

[34] Gennari (2022).

[35] 'Keskinäinen Vakuutusyhtiö Fennia v Koninklijke Philips NV.' (2022), C- 264/21.

[36] See more in Gennari (2023b).

[37] 'RB v TÜV Rheinland LGA Products GmbH and Allianz IARD S.A.' (2018), C-581/18.

case might be more interesting for manufacturers as the defendant was Allianz, the insurance company of a defective breast implant manufacturer, and Allianz won the case. More specifically, the insurance company was granted the right to limit the applicability of its contract to only to one Member State (France).[38] It is worth considering here that the MDR does not oblige manufacturers to get insurance against damages: this is an issue left to the MS to decide. Thus, the insurance could not be used by patients in other, EU MSs even if they invoked the violation of the non-discrimination principle enshrined in Article 18 TEU. Knowing this in advance, medical device manufacturers might choose to invest in tailored insurance coverage for both material and non-material damage.

Transparency is another important element that might help private insurance companies set their premiums for manufacturers. These issues are outlined in Article 19 PLDU. Accordingly, each Member State needs to forward high court decisions concerning liability to the EU Commission, who will establish a searchable public database that both manufacturers and insurers will have access to. Judges might then 'take inspiration' from how other countries have dealt with these cases and decide to evaluate the non-material damage caused by the use of new technologies in a more or less uniform manner. Additionally, insurance companies can use these data to calculate their premiums in a more precise way, while manufacturers can glean intel as to where best to market their products first.

The hypothesis sub condition b) refers to forms of collective redress (e.g., class actions) that have been harmonized by the directive on representative actions for the protection of the collective interests of consumers,[39] especially in countries where non-pecuniary damages are not standardized or quantified. In the representative actions directive Annexes there is a list of EU regulations and directives for which MSs must guarantee a form of collective redress based on the indications of the above-cited directive. Also the PLD was included in its Annex I. Hence, collective redress as a remedy will be extended to the PLDU thanks to Article 21 PLDU which explains that all references to the old PLD shall be read following the translation table of the Annex in the PLDU.

2.2 *New Notions of Product and Defectiveness: What Does It Mean for Active Prostheses?*

Although the compensation principle underpins the new Directive, new notions of product and defectiveness are required for the principle to become more concrete and actionable. The definition of a product in the PLDU makes an enormous

[38] Gennari (2022), pp. 136–139.

[39] Directive (EU) 2020/1828 of the European Parliament and of the Council of 25 November 2020 on representative actions for the protection of the collective interests of consumers and repealing Directive 2009/22/EC OJ L 409, pp. 1–27, http://data.europa.eu/eli/dir/2020/1828/oj.

departure from the old PLD. Article 4(1) specifies that not only can a product include interconnections with electricity and raw materials but also with manufacturing files, like 3D printing designs and software. This means that the PLDU covers any IoT or robotic device as well as any AI systems according to Article 3(1) of the AI Act (AIA).[40] This affects active prostheses because their control techniques are typically based on either machine learning or human-in-the-loop techniques, which are considered to be high-risk AI systems, as they are part of an active medical device, because of the interplay between Article 6(1) AIA and Annex I point 11 AIA.[41] And, since these AI systems are software, hence, a product, they could be considered defective under the PLDU if they malfunction.

Moreover, because the PLDU references interconnected software, it applies to any active prostheses, whether high or low risk, and hence, excluded by the application of the AIA[42] if they cause damage. This reasoning applies to components of the product as well as refurbished/substantially modified products according to Articles 4(4) and (18)PLDU. Specifically, the notion of substantial modification consists of either: a) what is considered to be a substantial modification according to the product safety rules of the EU or member nation; or b) in case there is no such threshold, then one needs to consider whether the modification:

> (i) changes the product's original performance, purpose or type, without that change having been foreseen in the manufacturer's initial risk assessment; or (ii) changes the nature of the hazard, [which] creates a new hazard or increases the level of risk.

One important exception concerns software, in that, according to Article 2(2) PLDU, open-source software is excluded from the Directive. Given the general wording about the term software, this refers also to AI systems or generative AI models which might be released as open-source systems. This exception will impact the choice between creating software internally by the manufacturer or by third parties, which might provide ad hoc software applications or services in connection with the active prostheses.

The general definition of defectiveness in Article 7(1) PLDU is the same as that of the PLD: a product is defective when it does not provide the safety that a person is entitled to expect. However, Article 7(2) PLDU's (open-ended) list of indicators

---

[40] AI Act Article 3(1) Regulation (EU) 2024/1689of the European Parliament and of the Council of 13 June 2024 laying down harmonised rules on artificial intelligence and amending Regulations (EC) No 300/2008, (EU) No 167/2013, (EU) No 168/2013, (EU) 2018/858, (EU) 2018/1139 and (EU) 2019/2144 and Directives 2014/90/EU, (EU) 2016/797 and (EU) 2020/1828 (Artificial Intelligence Act) OJ L, 2024/1689, http://data.europa.eu/eli/reg/2024/1689/oj.

[41] AI Act Article 6(1) and Annex I point 11; Chap. 11; Gennari (2024), pp. 427–433.

[42] This is established by recital 166 it is the General Product Safety Regulation (GPSR) to apply for AI compliance as well (implicitly as it is a general principle) the AI literacy principle at Article 4. Regulation (EU) 2023/988 of the European Parliament and of the Council of 10 May 2023 on general product safety, amending Regulation (EU) No 1025/2012 of the European Parliament and of the Council and Directive (EU) 2020/1828 of the European Parliament and the Council, and repealing Directive 2001/95/EC of the European Parliament and of the Council and Council Directive 87/357/EEC, PE/79/2022/REV/1, http://data.europa.eu/eli/reg/2023/988/oj.

to prove defectiveness is longer than the previous one and takes new technologies into consideration. Several new items on this list are particularly pertinent. First, there is "the capacity to learn or to acquire new features after it is placed on the market".[43] This implies that an active prosthesis that adapts to the patient's movements and guides them in the right direction for walking could be considered defective if damage is caused by the prosthetic's gait control strategies.[44] Second, there is "the reasonably foreseeable effect on the product of other products that can be expected to be used together with the product, including by means of interconnection".[45] This element for evaluating defectiveness also pertains to active prostheses, especially if they have a monitoring function that can be checked remotely by the patient, doctor, or manufacturer as part of the post-market evaluation that is required under the MDR.[46] Third is item (e) "the moment in time when the product was placed on the market or put into service or, where the manufacturer retains control over the product after that moment, the moment in time when the product left the control of the manufacturer".[47] This item is more connected to the notion of manufacturer's control, which will be discussed in more detail in the next section. Fourth, item f) makes compliance with any relevant product safety requirements, including safety-relevant cybersecurity requirements essential for evaluating whether a product can be considered defective. This is of paramount importance for the manufacturers of active prostheses, as marketing their medical devices generally requires following a considerable number of technical and quality standards.[48] Moreover, the fact that there is no specification for cybersecurity and safety standards means that manufacturers will always need to be informed about the latest safety and cybersecurity rules applicable in this field. Nonetheless, it is important to clarify that respecting product safety and security standards does not exempt manufacturers from liability if damage arises, as set out by the CJEU in 'James Elliott Construction Limited v. Irish Asphalt Limited' (2016).[49] Further, according to item g), any recall of the product or other relevant intervention relating to product safety by a competent authority or by an economic operator could prove a product's defectiveness.[50] This clause takes on particular importance when considering how it affects an active prosthesis. Being medical devices, a recall, whether from a national market or the entire EU, means that several people might have endured serious damage or pain. Finally, item h) refers to the specific needs of the group for whom the product is intended. This makes sense as the PLDU applies to virtually all consumer

---

[43] Article 7(2)(c) PLDU.

[44] see Chapter 11.

[45] Article 7(2)(d) PLDU.

[46] Chapter 7 and Annex III MDR.

[47] Article 7(2)(e) PLDU.

[48] Gennari (2021).

[49] Compare Article 7(2)(f) PLDU and paras 48–53, 'James Elliott Construction Limited v. Irish Asphalt Limited' (2016), C-613/14.

[50] Article 7(2)(g) PLDU; Article 8 PLDU.

products, even the ones that are not interconnected. Among these objects, there might be consumer IoT devices such as robot vacuums or smart speakers. The expectations about safety and function for the cited IoTs would likely differ from the safety expectations of active prostheses users. This might mean that the safety expectations threshold will be higher for this kind of prosthesis than for a robot vacuum but might be lower compared, for instance, to a new generation of implanted pacemakers. The CJEU has already ruled that if a functioning defect is known, especially for medical devices, then it suffices that it is present *in abstracto* for the product to be considered defective without the need for actual damage to become apparent.[51]

The revised notions of product and defectiveness are tied to the compensation rationale and have been updated to keep track of the most innovative technologies such as robotics, IoT, and AI. However, this leaves the manufacturers with a great deal of work to do up to and including the prototype phase. For instance, they will need to address several compliance issues in advance due to both the MDR and the PLDU. However, by making products as safe as possible even before marketing, the manufacturer should have sufficient evidence to prove their product is safe under the new PLDU liability rules even if damage does occur.

2.3 The Notion of Manufacturer's Control and the Need to Ensure an Accountable Stakeholder in the EU

As in the old PLD, under the PLDU the manufacturer (formerly known as the producer in the PLD) is formally the preferred contact point for consumers to get compensation for defective products.[52] In the PLDU, Article 4(10) describes the manufacturer as the natural or legal person that manufactures or puts their distinctive sign on the product. However, the new notion of the manufacturer's control might be more relevant in terms of assessing product liability. This is described in Article 4(5) PLDU as the exercise of meaningful control over the connected objects, such as active prostheses. This change in the definition of a manufacturer would not likely have happened if technologies that incorporate software into objects, such as IoT devices, had not become as common as they have (think of virtual assistants on your phone or at home). The notion of control on its own is quite extensive. On the one hand, it includes the manufacturer's ability to act alone or by authorizing third parties to perform a set of actions. First, the manufacturer's control extends to the possibility of third parties to integrate, interconnect or supply a component, software updates or upgrades included. Second, the manufacturer's control includes the manufacturer's ability to substantially modify a product, either alone or through

[51] 'Boston Scientific Medizintechnik GmbH v AOK Sachsen-Anhalt—Die Gesundheitskasse and Betriebskrankenkasse RWE.' (2013) C-503/13, C-504/13, paras 36–43.

[52] Gennari (2023b).

authorized third parties. Finally, the manufacturer's control includes their ability to supply upgrades and updates either directly or through a third party.

The widespread scope of what is considered to be under a manufacturer's control should sound some alarm bells for those who produce connected devices, such as active prostheses. For example, whenever a manufacturer delegates a task to a third party, especially at the software level, they must remember that they are still presumed to have control over the product until they prove the opposite. Thus, they might be held liable for damage claims as set out in Article 7(2)(e) of the PLDU. This should also make the active prostheses' makers think carefully before making their products interoperable with commercial software or cloud providers, even if they might be quite popular. Integrating an active prosthesis with a connected environment such as a smart home is one example of how the manufacturer might end up being responsible for the faults of third parties. Further, it is also recommend to take special note of any authorization agreements between software providers and hardware manufacturers, as these might be more in favor of the third-party software provider than the manufacturer. Ultimately, the hardware manufacturer will be held liable for any defects originating in software despite the fact that they neither created that software nor have any de facto control over it.

One can argue that this extended notion of control serves the purpose of the compensation rationale, as for consumers/patients it could be difficult to bring a claim against a software company that might not even be located in the EU and the broad definition adopted follows the principle that compensation, hence a liable subject, must always be found (easily) by the consumer. Article 14 of the PLDU indeed allows the right to recourse towards the liable stakeholder. However, implementing this disposition will depend on each MS's Member State's national laws. On the one hand, this could lead to more unpredictability and fragmentation of the applicable liability rules for manufacturers. On the other hand, this proviso is an indirect incentive for manufacturers to severely limit interoperability with commercial and widely-known third parties.

Article 8 PLDU is another application of the compensation rationale. This Article lists all the possible stakeholders involved in the product and value chain of most interconnected objects, whether with or without medical functions. Called economic operators, these stakeholders can also include active prostheses manufacturers who have already successfully marketed their products. Yet a manufacturer might need to rely on many other stakeholders to put their device into the market and/or into service. One thing to note is that there is the partial similarity between Articles 8 and 16 MDR and Article 25 of the AI Act. All these articles identify who is accountable for medical devices and AI systems in the value chain. Article 8 articulates a cascade system that lines up all the different product stakeholders if the manufacturer, or the manufacturer of the defective component, is not in the EU or cannot be found. After the manufacturer, it is the turn of the importer or authorized representative, then the fulfillment service provider. Working through this chain of economic operators is only possible if the previously indicated operator is not known or not located in the EU. Liability also applies to whoever has substantially modified the product. To close this chain of possible liable subjects in lieu of the manufacturer, there are distributors and online platforms that allow consumers to enter into distance contracts. If a consumer asks the distributor (or a platform following the rules of Article 6.3 DSA) for details of their identity and how to reach the manufacturer in the case of a defective product, the distributor or platform needs to give this information in just 1 month, or else they will be considered liable. Finally, if none of the previous rules apply—for instance, if the manufacturer has become insolvent or their business has ceased to exist[53]—MSs may use "existing national sectoral compensation schemes or establish new ones under national law, preferably not funded by public revenue".[54] This long chain of potentially liable economic operators might not be of interest to a manufacturer of active prostheses at first, especially if the manufacturer is a new startup. However, if that startup becomes successful or decides to become a distributor for other kinds of connected medical devices, including prostheses, they will need to be careful about the rules concerning distributors under Article 8(3) PLDU. Just like the old Directive, the new PLDU considers the hypothesis of more than one economic operators in Article 12. In facts, national procedural laws need to take into account the possibility to consider the economic operators liable both jointly and separately.

Notably, this Article in its second paragraph also excludes the possibility of recourse if the manufacturer integrates a software component that causes damage where: (a) the manufacturer of the defective software is a micro-enterprise according to EU law; and/or (b) the manufacturer contractually agreed to waive the right of recourse with the creator of the defective software. This provision also reinforces the idea of a wide extent of the manufacturer's control notion. MSs must therefore integrate remedies (if not already present) that make it unlawful to reduce or disallow product liability when the damage is caused both by the product's defectiveness and by one party's act or omission. The only case in which the liability conferred by the PLDU is disallowed or reduced is when the injured person's behavior is faulty and causes damage alongside the product's defect. This exemption is also made for any person the claimant is responsible for. One can only presume this is an incentive for manufacturers to draft instructions of use that are not only complete but understandable to the product's audience. This might mean manufacturers need to produce video tutorials for patients alongside the mandatory instruction booklets. Such initiatives can be helpful for proving that a patient using the device incorrectly is actually the cause of the fault. That said, product liability cannot be excluded or limited by contract as established in Article 15. This is a condition that the manufacturers of active prostheses should bear in mind from the early stages of design right through to the prototype phase.

[53] This had happened with the PIP case as the manufacturer had had to file for bankruptcy. Gennari (2022).

[54] Article 8(5) PLDU.

3 Procedural Fairness as an Acknowledgment of Personal Vulnerability

This section discusses other examples of how the principle of compensation in product liability claims is being standardized across the EU's Member States through each nation's procedural laws. First, I will explain how the disclosure of evidence remedy might affect the defense of active prostheses manufacturers. Next, I will describe how the presumptions of causality and defectiveness interact for active prostheses manufacturers. Finally, I will deal with the procedural rules that are likely to matter the most to prosthesis manufacturers—these being liability exemptions.

3.1 Disclosure of Evidence

One of the things that a manufacturer has to consider is that a consumer who has suffered damage can act at any time within 10 years (a) of the date the defective product was placed on the market or, (b) in the case of a substantially modified product, from the date the modified product was put on the market.[55] There is also an exception for injuries that remained hidden for period before becoming apparent, which extends the expiry period to 25 years.[56] The rule applies unless the injured person has, in the meantime, initiated proceedings against an economic operator that can be held liable pursuant to Article 8.[57] Once the proceedings start, the claimant has 3 years to claim compensation.[58] This period starts "from the day on which the injured person became aware, or should reasonably have become aware, of all of the following: (a) the damage; (b) the defectiveness; and (c) the identity of the relevant economic operator that can be held liable for that damage under Article 8".

Article 9 allows a claimant to request access to a product's functional core to better plead their case. However, this is based on the condition that they have already presented plausible facts and evidence to reasonably infer that a product is defective and causally linked to the damage suffered. Importantly, any data supplied to the claimant to support their argument needs be provided in a format that is both understandable and that also complies with the standards established by the courts.[59] Should the request be granted in the case of an active prosthesis, the manufacturer will need to give the claimant access to the prosthetic's AI system and, if they do not comply, they can be presumed liable.[60] The issue with this Article is that it is left to

[55] Article 17 PLDU.

[56] Articles 17(1) and (2) PLDU.

[57] Ibid.

[58] Article 16 PLDU.

[59] Article 11(6) PLDU.

[60] Article 10(2)(a) PLDU.

each Member State's judicial authorities to adjudicate the balance between allowing the consumer access to necessary evidence and protecting the manufacturer's intellectual property rights such as trade secrets.[61] This may be the reason why the EU Commission will be establishing a database of court decisions—i.e., to ensure similar cases meet similar outcomes. For example, in the medium-term, judges might simply reach a consensus on how to quantify certain kinds of AI-caused damages by also reading their peers' decisions.

3.2 Presumptions of a Causal Link and Defectiveness

Presumptions are another important tool to help the consumer prove that a product is defective and that there is a causal link between the defect and the damage suffered. In simple terms, a presumption is a legal remedy used by judges to deem that a claimant has proven the defendant's liability even if they have not presented sufficient evidence of this circumstance to the court. It is in the manufacturer's best interests to be aware of these presumptions as they might help claimants to prove their claim. In most cases, the judge will make the final call as to whether to invoke any presumptions. Their decision will likely depend on the liability rules prevailing in that Member State but could also be based also on factors like the gravity and materiality of the damage and/or the understandability and explainability of the technologies that might be involved, such as AI combined with IoT objects.

In terms of defectiveness, the claimant can prove a defect with any one of these three options:

> (a) the defendant fails to disclose relevant evidence pursuant to Article 9(1); (b) the claimant demonstrates that the product does not comply with mandatory product safety requirements laid down in Union or national law that are intended to protect against the risk of the damage suffered by the injured person; or (c) the claimant demonstrates that the damage was caused by an obvious malfunction of the product during reasonably foreseeable use or under ordinary circumstances.[62]

A causal link "shall be presumed where it has been established that the product is defective and that the damage caused is of a kind typically consistent with the defect in question".[63] Both a causal link and defectiveness can be presumed when:

> (a) the claimant faces excessive difficulties, in particular due to technical or scientific complexity, in proving the defectiveness of the product or the causal link between its defectiveness and the damage, or both; and (b) the claimant demonstrates that it is likely that the product is defective or that there is a causal link between the defectiveness of the product and the damage, or both".[64]

[61] Articles 11(2) (3) (4) (5) PLDU.

[62] Article 10(2) PLDU.

[63] Article 10(3) PLDU.

[64] Article 10(4) PLDU.

Notably, it will likely prove tough for judges to determine what scientific complexity means, especially since the majority of connected objects, not just IoT objects, have very complex ways of functioning. Hence, it is unlikely that their functioning could be understood by a judge who does not have an engineering background. This means that, more than ever, the courts will need technical experts to evaluate whether or not to rely on these presumptions. Moreover, any presumption can be rebutted by the manufacturers. However, it falls on the defendant to demonstrate that any presumptions the claimant wishes to apply are unwarranted.

3.3 *Exemptions from Liability*

One of the most interesting parts of the whole PLDU for a manufacturer is liability exemptions. Thanks to these exemptions, even if it were proven that a product was defective and there was a causal link between the defect and the damage, the manufacturer would not be considered liable. Article 11 of the PLDU lists a series of exemptions, but I will focus on the ones that should most interest the manufacturers of active prostheses. First, item c) states that the manufacturer cannot be held liable if…

> … the defectiveness that caused the damage did not exist at the time the product was placed on the market, put into service or, in the case of a distributor, made available on the market, or that that defectiveness came into being after that moment.[65]

That said, Article 11(2) provides for one exception—that being if the defect occurred with a related service, new software (updates and upgrades included), or a lack of software updates/upgrades necessary to maintain safety or a substantial modification of a product- then the exemption does not apply. The notion of manufacturer's control explained in the previous section connects with this exception, its rationale being the fact that interconnected objects are quite commonplace nowadays, and not just limited to medical settings. Hence, manufacturers cannot be exempted from liability in to given that interconnected objects seldom continue to function as they did when they were first put on the market. As an example, manufacturers often continue to be aware of how their products are functioning, and even their location, through RFID and Bluetooth.[66] This is even more true for advanced medical devices such as active prostheses, especially since manufacturers need to collect data on how their products are functioning in an ongoing manner to comply with the post-marketing requirements of the MDR.

Second, item d) provides for a liability exemption when the defect has been caused by complying with a legal requirement. This item raises quite a tricky

---

[65] Article 11(1)(c) PLDU.

[66] Luzak (2020), p. 631.

situation in that technical standards are not safety rules per se.[67] Technical standards only become legal requirements when they are incorporated into law.[68] Despite this, many prosthesis manufacturers are following an increasing number of technical standards because the standard-setting organizations at the EU and international levels have such a good reputations because they represent the state of the art—take the ISO, ETSI, CEN, and CENELEC as examples.[69] Even if the manufacturer manages to prove that there is a causal link with a legally-required standard, it is highly doubtful that a judge would consider this as an exemption, especially if the suffered by the claimant is serious and visible, e.g., a physical injury or damage to property.

The last exemption to focus on is the "risk development" exemption.[70] This clause outlines that a manufacturer cannot be held liable if the damage caused by the product could not have been foreseen at the time the product was put into market as determined by an objective state of scientific and technical knowledge. Interestingly, the term 'objective' does not appear in the old Directive. I assume it was added after Advocate General Tesauro released his Opinion in the case 'Commission of the European Communities v United Kingdom of Great Britain and Northern Ireland', which influenced the CJEU in the first case ever on the PLD. More specifcally the above-mentioned case revolved around the different interpretations of the risk development defense implementation by the United Kingdom.[71] While the UK argued that 'scientific technical knowledge' meant the majority of learned opinion on a certain subject, AG Tesauro a more 'objective' approach should be used and maintained it was "the most advanced level of research that has been carried out at a given time".[72] AG Tesauro also argued that the state of knowledge must be considered to include "all data in the information circuit of the scientific community as a whole, bearing in mind, however, based on a reasonableness test the actual opportunities for the information to circulate".[73]

In theory, nowadays it takes just a few clicks to determine the state-of-the-art in a range of countries around the world. This information can then be used to establish an objective scientific threshold. But this was not the case in 1995. Nonetheless, today, the incentive for many journals is to provide quantity rather than quality, which has led to an overall decrease the worth of scientific papers.[74] What might also be more difficult today than in 1995, when the CJEU rendered its judgment, is assessing a potentially enormous amount of information on scientific and technical

[67] Gennari (2021), pp. 157–158; Delimatsis (2019), p. 9; Verbruggen (2019), p. 75; Tovo (2018), pp. 1187–1216.

[68] Basedow and Wurmnest (2005), p. 138; Lagoni (2007), p. 377; Ulfbeck and Møllmann (2019), pp. 210–229.

[69] Gennari (2021), pp. 157–158.

[70] Article 11(1)(e) PLDU.

[71] 'Commission of the European Communities v United Kingdom of Great Britain and Northern Ireland' (1995) (Judgment and Opinion), C- 300/95.

[72] Para 21 Opinon of AG Tesauro in the abovementioned case.

[73] Para 24 Opinion of AG Tesauro in the abovementioned case.

[74] Hanson et al. (2024).

topics like bioengineering as trustworthy and sound. For an active prosthesis manufacturer, the solution is to stay up-to-date through reputable scientific journals and the forums populated by technical experts.

Moreover, this exemption is subject to a certain national margin of discretion as the traditions in different Member States of the EU actually vary quite a bit. For example, the UK used to be rather liberal, embracing this exemption, while other countries, such as France, did not want to implement this exemption in their national law as demonstrated by several "failure to comply" under EU procedural law. One example of this is the case.[75] For this reason, Article 18(1) of the PLDU states that each MS has to right to enact more severe measures. Essentially, this means that even if the scientific and historical context does not reasonably lead to thinking that damage might arise from the use of a defective product, the manufacturer can still be found liable according to national law. Additionally, each Member State must notify the EU Commission that they plan to enact more stringent national laws concerning damages caused from scientific or technical development before the new Directive comes into force on 9 December 2026. The more severe change in the national laws concerning the risk development exemption implementation must follow the guidelines indicated at Article 18(2) PLDU rules. In that case, the implementation must be limited …

> … to i) specific categories of products; ii) justified public interest objectives; and iii) they must be proportionate in that they are suitable for securing the attainment of the objectives pursued and do not go beyond what is necessary to attain those objectives.

In this case, MSs must notify the EU Commission which is called to express an opinion on how the risk-development exemption was limited at a national level.

4 Conclusions

Several key points from the PLDU are important takeaways for active prostheses manufacturers. First, a compensation rationale is explicitly mentioned in the new Directive—one which entirely underpins the new legislation. Further, this rationale will be implemented through national rules that not only quantify the damage suffered but are also likely to vary greatly from one Member State to another. Knowing this in advance can help a manufacturer to choose the optimal national markets in which to launch their products first. This compensation principle will also allow manufacturers to take advantage of insurance to solve their product liability claims in future.

Second, the potential involvement of private insurance companies might be helpful for future standardization as far as quantifying damages is concerned, especially if the provisions on transparency in Article 19 PLDU are implemented. This could help manufacturers calibrate their R&D investments as well as guiding decisions on

[75] 'Commission of the European Communities v. French Republic' (2000) Case C-177/04. European Court Reports 2006 I-02461.

which kinds of risks to eliminate or mitigate over others. Moreover, because of the precedent set by the Allianz IARD case, insurance companies might also be encouraged to cover advanced devices like software-driven prosthetics since the same insurance claim for a defective product in one country cannot be invoked in another country under violation of the non-discrimination principle.

Third, new definitions for what constitutes a 'product' and what 'defectiveness' means are also tied to the principle of compensation. Further, they have been updated to account for the most innovative technologies, including robotics, IoT, and AI. However, this leaves the manufacturers with a great deal of work to do, especially during the prototype phase. They will need to address several compliance issues in advance because of the PLDU, the MDR, and the AI Act if any embedded software is deemed to be an AI system. In terms of the PLDU, manufacturers will need to think about:

(i) which elements of the product are most likely to be responsible for defects or risks even if the medical device obtains a CE marking;
(ii) which types of damage might be incurred (e.g., death, injury, psychological trauma);
(iii) drafting protocols that explain what to do in case damage is suffered for each of the countries in which product has been marketed; and
(iv) whether the insurance covering product liability claims needs to be adapted to the types of damages the prosthesis might cause.

Fourth, the new Directive seems to favor consumers more than manufacturers as far as its procedural rules are concerned. This includes disclosing evidence, allowable presumptions, the list of exemptions, and the exceptions to the exemptions. However, all these rules rest on the Member States. For example, some States may choose to implement the risk development exemption more harshly while others may opt for less severe interpretations. Similarly, it will depend on each State's judges to evaluate whether or not to grant disclosure of evidence remedies or which presumptions might apply to causal links and defectiveness.

At the time of writing, it is not possible to give a certain answer on which way the wind will blow as no publicly available judgments have yet been rendered on the PLDU. However, the historical positions of several countries on consumer protection when it comes to the damage caused by an allegedly defective prostheses, including France, Germany, Denmark, Finland, and Spain might be used as proxies to mitigate such risks in advance. These countries are named as examples due to the number of judgments found under the old Directive. If the damage is material and serious, such as a limb injury, it could be more likely that the judge will decide to accept the claimant's request for the disclosure of evidence and the use of the presumptions on defectiveness and causal liability. Conversely, the manufacturer is always allowed to refute the content of a presumption. Overall, the PLDU can be seen as more consumer-friendly under certain circumstances but, if studied intelligently by manufacturers, it enables them to not only potentially avoid many liability claims but also incentivize compliance with several regulations that active prosthesis manufacturers will need to consider such as the MDR and the AI Act.

Acknowledgments This research was financially supported by the project "Biorobotics Research and Innovation Engineering Facilities "IR0000036"—CUP J13C22000400007".

Disclosure of Interests The author has no competing interests to declare.

References

Alpa G (2018) La Responsabilità Civile. UTET, Turin

'Aventis Pasteur SA v. OB' (2008) Case no C-258/08. European Court Reports 2009 I-11305

Basedow J, Wurmnest W (2005) Third-party liability of classification societies. A comparative perspective. Springer, Berlin

Bertolini A, Episcopo F (2021) The expert group's report on liability for artificial intelligence and other emerging technologies: a critical assessment. EJRR 12(3):644–659. https://doi.org/10.1017/err.2021.30

Bussani M (2020) L'Illecito Civile. Edizioni Scientifiche Italiane, Napoli

Castronovo C, (2018) La responsabilità civile, Giuffrè, milano

Colombi Ciacchi A, Hodges C, van Leeuwen B et al (2018) Position paper on the fitness check of EU consumer law. ERPL 26(5):703–706

Delimatsis P (2019) International trade and technical standardization. In: Contreras J (ed) The Cambridge handbook of technical standardization law: further intersections of public and private law. Cambridge University Press, Cambridge, pp 7–27

Expert Group on Liability of AI and new Technologies (2019) Liability for Artificial Intelligence. Report from the Expert Group on Liability and New Technologies-New Technologies Formation. European Commission, Brussels

European Commission, (2018) Report from the commission to the European Parliament, the Council and the European Economic and Social Committee on the Application of the Council Directive on the approximation of the laws, regulations, and administrative provisions of the Member States concerning liability for defective products (85/374/EEC) COM/2018/246 final," 2, EUR-Lex, https://eur-lex.europa.eu/legal-content/en/TXT/?uri=CELEX%3A52018DC0246

European Law Institute (2021) Guiding Principles for Updating the Product Liability Directive for the Digital Age. ELI Innovation Paper Series. ELI, Vienna

European Law Institute (2022) ELI Draft for a Revised Product Liability Directive. Draft Legislative Proposal of the European Law Institute. ELI, Vienna

Fagioli I, Mazzarini A, Gennari F, Crea S (2025). The role of artificial intelligence and machine learning in personalizing the control of robotic lower limb prostheses. In: Casarosa, Gennari, Rossi. Enabling and Safeguarding Personalized Medicine, vol X. Springer, Heidelberg, p xxx

Gambaro A, Graziadei M, Sacco R (last edition 2024) Trattato di Diritto Comparato. Sistemi Giuridici Comparati. UTET, Turin

Gennari F (2021) Standard setting organisations for the IoT: how to ensure a better degree of liability? MUJLT 2:153–174. https://doi.org/10.5817/MUJLT2021-2-1

Gennari F (2022) What liability with the internet of things? Global Jurist 23: 125–150, Insights from the European Case-Law of the PIP Affair, https://doi.org/10.1515/gj-2022-0032

Gennari F (2023a) Internet of things: legal liability of IoE devices in the home. AMS Dottorato, Bologna. https://10.48676/unibo/amsdottorato/10645

Gennari F (2023b) A tale of two cities? Fennia v Philips and Article 7 of the product liability directive update. EuCML 12(6):267–274

Gennari F (2024) O complementarity, where art thou? Wading through the medical device regulation and the AI act compliance: the case of software as a medical device. A primer. BioLaw Journal – Rivista di Biodiritto 3:411–453

Hanson MA, Gómez Barreiro P, Crosetto P et al (2024) The strain on scientific publishing. Quant Sci Stud 5(4):823–843. https://doi.org/10.1162/qss_a_00327

Kellerbauer M (2019) Article 114. In: Kellerbauer M, Klamert M, Tomkin J (eds) The EU treaties and the charter of fundamental rights: a commentary. Oxford University Press, Oxford, pp 1235–1255. https://doi.org/10.1093/oso/9780198759393.003.212

Klamert M (2019) Article 5. In: Kellerbauer M, Klamert M, Tomkin J (eds) The EU treaties and the charter of fundamental rights: a commentary. Oxford University Press, Oxford, pp 372–373. https://doi.org/10.1093/oso/9780198759393.003.76

Lagoni N (2007) The liability of classification societies. Springer, Berlin

Lohsse S, Schulze R, Staudenmayer D (eds) (2019) Liability for artificial intelligence and the internet of things. Munster Colloquia on EU Law and the Digital Economy IV. NOMOS- Hart, Baden Baden

Luzak J (2020) A broken notion: impact of modern technologies on product liability. EJRR 11(3):630–649. https://doi.org/10.1017/err.2020.13

Machnikowski P (2016) Conclusions. In: Machnikowski (ed) European product liability. An analysis of the state of the art in the Era of new technologies. Intersentia, Antwerp-Cambridge-Portland, p 669

Ponzanelli G (2019) Dopo san Martino la Cassazione ci riprova a varare uno statuto della persona. Il Foro Italiano- La Tribuna

Reimann M (2023) Liability for defective products at the beginning of the twenty-first century: emergence of a worldwide standard? Am J Comp Law 51:751–838

Tridimas T (2018) The principle of proportionality. In: Schütze R, Tridimas T (eds) Principles of European Union law: the European legal order: Vol I. Oxford University Press, pp 243–246. https://doi.org/10.1093/oso/9780199533770.003.0010

Tovo C (2018) Judicial review of harmonized standards: changing the paradigms of legality and legitimacy of private rulemaking under EU law. CMLR 55:1187–1216

Ulfbeck V, Møllmann A (2019) Public function liability of classification societies. In: Rott P (ed) Certification-trust, accountability and liability, studies in European economic law and regulation, vol 16. Springer Nature, Switzerland, pp 213–229

Van Dam C (2013) European tort law. OUP, Oxford

Verbruggen (2019) Tort liability for standards development in the United States and in the European Union. In: Contrereas J (ed) Technical standardization law, part II- standardization, health, safety, liability. Cambridge University Press, pp 60–88. https://doi.org/10.1017/9781316416785.005

Wallerman A (2018) Pie in the sky when you die? Civil liability of notified bodies under the medical devices directive: Schmitt. CMLR 55:265–278

Wuyts D (2014) The product liability directive - more than two decades of defective products in Europe. J Eur Tort Law 5:1–34, https://doi.org/10.1515/jetl-2014-0001

www.ingramcontent.com/pod-product-compliance
Lightning Source LLC
Chambersburg PA
CBHW061845030925
32038CB00002B/12
9783031997082